ULTIMATE UFO

The ZETAS

History, Hybrids and Human Contacts

ZETA 1
RETICULI

ZETA 2
RETICULI

THROUGH
Robert Shapiro

Other Books by Robert Shapiro

EXPLORER RACE SERIES

1. The Explorer Race
2. ETs and the Explorer Race
3. The Explorer Race: Origins and the Next 50 Years
4. The Explorer Race: Creators and Friends
5. The Explorer Race: Particle Personalities
6. The Explorer Race and Beyond
7. The Explorer Race: The Council of Creators
8. The Explorer Race and Isis
9. The Explorer Race and Jesus
10. The Explorer Race: Earth History and Lost Civilizations
11. The Explorer Race: ET Visitors Speak Vol. 1
12. The Explorer Race: Techniques for Generating Safety
13. The Explorer Race: Animal Souls Speak
14. The Explorer Race: Astrology: Planet Personalities and Signs Speak
15. The Explorer Race: ET Visitors Speak Vol. 2
16. The Explorer Race: Plant Souls Speak
17. The Explorer Race: Time and Beyond

MATERIAL MASTERY SERIES

A. Shamanic Secrets for Material Mastery
B. Shamanic Secrets for Physical Mastery
C. Shamanic Secrets for Spiritual Mastery

SHINING THE LIGHT SERIES

Shining the Light: The Battle Begins!
Shining the Light II: The Battle Continues
Shining the Light III: Humanity Gets a Second Chance
Shining the Light IV: Humanity's Greatest Challenge
Shining the Light V: Humanity Is Going to Make It!
Shining the Light VI: The End of What Was
Shining the Light VII: The First Alignment—World Peace

ULTIMATE UFO SERIES

Andromeda: UFO Contact from Andromeda
Zetas, Hybrids and Human Contacts

SECRETS OF FEMININE SCIENCE SERIES

Book 1: Benevolent Magic & Living Prayer
Book 2: Disentanglement & Deep Disentanglement
Book 3: Disengagement, Engagement & Connections

SHIRT POCKET BOOKS SERIES

Touching Sedona
Feeling Sedona's ET Energies

ULTIMATE UFO SERIES

The ZETAS

History, Hybrids and Human Contacts

THROUGH
Robert Shapiro

3ↄ LIGHT
Technology
PUBLISHING

*   *   *

ISBN-13: 978-1891824-36-8

Light Technology Publishing, LLC
Phone: 800-450-0985
Fax: 928-714-1132
PO Box 3540
Flagstaff, AZ 86003
www.lighttechnology.com

Dedication

A Note from Zoosh

Any time we are referring to people who are alive, since they are not asking, I want to note that none of the contactees actually asked us about their experiences. We explored these ET/UFO contact cases on our own, for the benefit of all people, and hope that it is also of interest to the contactees themselves. We acknowledge these people who had these encounters and appreciate their courage in making the public aware of their experiences.

By exploring these experiences from the view of those who contacted the humans, we want to remind people that these contacts are real. Just because contacts between Earth humans and extraterrestrials are often fantastic—not necessarily wonderful, but strange and out of the ordinary—does not make them any less true. It is our intention to make this information available to all who are interested, and it is not our intent to cause offense.

Special Thanks to these Contactees:

Betty Andreasson

William Herrmann

Travis Walton

Billy Meier

Woodrow Wilson

Benjamin Franklin

Johann Sebastian Bach

Jean Hingley

R. L. Johannis

Lyndia Morel

Pat Roach and her daughters Bonnie and Debbie

Tom Dongo and Linda Bradshaw

Lori Briggs and Joe Maine

Joao Valerio da Silva

Charles Hickson and Calvin Parker

Table of Contents

Introduction xv

1. **The Zeta Contacts** 1
   Zoosh: October 31, 1998
   Betty and Barney Hill 1
   Hybrids for the Preservation of the Species 4
   Contacts Were Benign 5
   The Magic Book of Light 6
   The Final Regular Contacts 9
   The Power of Human Emotion 10
   Children of the Zetas 12
   Timelines and the Limits of Linear Memory 13

2. **Betty Andreasson and the Ceremony of Renewal** 17
   Joopah: November 2, 1998
   The Corridor to the Creator 18
   The Experience Behind the Door 20
   A History of Humanity on Display 21
   The Hybrids on the Ship 23
   Sampling and Marking Candidates on Earth 24
   The Ceremony of the Phoenix 25
   Heightened Sensibility after UFO Experiences 26
   Betty and Barney Hill onboard a Ship 27
   The Book of Light Mentioned by Zoosh 28
   Update on Joopah and Other Zetas 30
   The Gift of Jumps to Higher Dimensions 31

3. **Children of Isis: Path of the Zeta** 35
   Yo or Jo Seeka: November 3, 1998
   Giving Up on Governments and Working with People 36
   The Teachers Are Made of Compressed Energy 37
   The Bible and Zeta Scientific Communication 39
   Zetas and Religion 39
   The Human-Earth Body Connection 40
   The Remaining Zetas on Earth 41
   Crashes: Rescued Zetas and Imprisoned Zetas 43
   The Book and the Keys 44
   The William Herrmann Contact 45

The Zeta Network 46

The Ceremony of Renewal 49

Organization and Development among the Zetas 50

Zetas and Humans Are Naturally Complementary 51

4. **Diplomacy and ET Contacts** **55**
    Sha Don: November 4, 1998

    The Experience of William Herrmann 56

    The Purpose of Contact with Herrmann 57

    The Overall Purpose of Contact 58

    Nuclear Risk Reduced 59

    Assessing the Spiritual Awakening of Humanity 60

    The Zeta History with Earth 61

    Other Races Visit Earth with the Zetas 62

    The Tableau 63

    Transcending Language 64

    Reasons for Involvement: Cold War 64

    The Offer of Peace Refused 66

    The Explorer Race and the Yellow Book 67

    Sinister Secret Government Intervention 68

    Zeta-Human Soul Lines and the Communicator 70

    The Hybrid Program and "Abductions" 72

    Roswell and Other Crashes 74

    Universal Implants 75

    Freedom or Bondage? 78

5. **Describing the Zetas** **79**
    Sha Don: November 5, 1998

    Crash and Rescue in South America 81

    Population and Life on Zeta Reticuli 83

    Zeta Learning, Knowledge and Form 86

    Raising Human Awareness 87

    Artistic Hybrids 88

    Culture, Crime, Architecture and Art on Zeta Reticuli 90

    Prospects for Mass Contact 91

    The Responsibility of Hierarchy in Cat Beings 92

6. **The Zetas in Human History** **95**
    Sha Don: November 6, 1998

    Woodrow Wilson's Contact Experience 95

    Benjamin Franklin Meets a Pleiadian 97

    Johann Sebastian Bach and Celestial Music 99

7. **The Truth of Travis Walton's Case, among Others,**
    And the Planet of Cats **101**
    Sha Don and Zoosh: November 7, 1998
    The Travis Walton Case 101
    HAARP and Its Interference 107
    The Reasons for Taking Humans Onboard 108
    An Unselfish Mother of Twins Seeking to Serve Humankind 109
    A Visit to Kaath, the Planet of Cats 110
    The Wisdom of the Cat People 112
    Handling Electronic Interference 113

8. **Gifted Spacecraft, Crashed Spacecraft and the Test of Technology** .. **115**
    Sha Don: November 9, 1998
    Roswell and Aztec 116
    Gifts of Ships 118
    How Earth Is Tested 120
    Crashes in the North 121
    Why Life Is Hard on Earth 122
    Misperceptions of ETs 124
    Sources of Modern Technology: Guided rather than Given 126
    ET Captives and the Secret Government 129
    Cross-Species Communication 129
    Transcendent Tribal Wisdom 131
    ET Humor 133
    Natures of the Dimensions 133
    The Travels of Sha Don 135

9. **The Zetas Interact Emotionally** **139**
    Sha Don: November 10, 1998
    Spontaneous Transitions to Golden Lightbodies 140
    The Time Is Coming when Humans and Hybrids Will Meet 141
    The Formation of the Tableau 143
    Contacting the Tableau through Meditation 145
    Selection and Management of Contacts 146
    Underwater and Underground 150
    The Unconscious and the Subconscious 151
    Never Underestimate Human Consciousness 152

10. **Roswell and the Case of Billy Meier** **155**
    Zoosh: November 15, 1998
    Overcoming the Cruelty Factor 155
    Resisting Expansion and Resisting those Resisters 156

The Expansion of the Universe Is the Expansion of Consciousness 157
The Expansion Is Always and Infinite 160
Theft and Imprisonment by the Secret Government 162
The Gift of Technology 164
The Case of Billy Meier 165

11. The Effects of Time Travel **167**
Zoosh: November 30, 1998
Bloodlines 167
Early Zeta Contacts: Misunderstanding on Both Sides 169
Learning the Value of Emotions 171
Back in Time, Modifying Contacts 173
Alternate Means of Contact 173
The Variability of Sophistication across Time and Dimensions 175
The Mathematics of Compression 178
Protection against the Effects of Compression and Decompression 179
Botched Experiments in Time Travel 181
Hybrids and Clones 182
The Value of Pain 184

12. Zeta Diplomacy and Ancient Contacts on Earth **187**
Zwo Ti: November 30, 1998
Diplomat to the Zetas from their Parent Race 187
The Chinese Connection 188
The Life of a Diplomat 191
Destined for Diplomacy 193
The Appearance of the Parent Race 195
Hybridization, Implants and Experiments in Zeta Sexuality 198
Technological Development among the Zetas 200
The Golden-Bodied Zetas 202
At Home away from Zeta Reticuli.. 204
From Diplomacy to the Teaching of Diplomacy 206

13. Parent Race of the Zetas **209**
Tlingt Cha: December 2, 1998
Beyond this Universe 209
The Limits on Emotion 210
Love's Creations 211
The Origin of the Parent Race 212
Participation in the Formation of the Explorer Race 213
The Synthesis of the Earth 215
Assisting Other Races 216

Being of Parts and of the Whole 217
The Connection to the Zetas 218
Unifying the Parts (Races) into the Whole (Humanity) 219
The Zetas as Future Humans 221
ET Inspirations of the Egyptians 222

14. **Creation of the Zetas** 227
Zoosh and Tlingt Cha: December 3, 1998
Tlingt Cha Speaks of Zeta Creation 230
Zeta Influence in the Development of Primitive Humans 233
Incarnation into Zeta Bodies 236
You Are Changing Future Incarnations 238
Personal Perspectives on the Resolution of Mysteries 240
Spiritual Advances in Future Human Technology 241
The Future of the Diplomatic Liason 242

15. **Contacts from Faces of the Visitors** 245
Zoosh: December 4, 1998
Sinister Reach from the Past: Contact in France 245
Contact in Italy 248
Long-Range Galactic Exploration 250
Contact in Kentucky 251
Contact in New Mexico 255
Contact in New Hampshire 259
Contact on the Franco-Belgian Border 261
Contact in England 264

16. **Visitor's Book and Sirian Mapper** 269
Zoosh and Etcheta: December 5, 1998
Contact in Utah 269
Copying Memories on the Cellular Level 273
Each Atom Is a Unit of Memory 275
ET DNA in the Mormons 276
The Andromedan Who Assumes the Form of a Human 278
The Vast Scope of the Grand Experiment 279
The Sedona Sightings 280
Soul Memories Stored in Cells 283
The Perfect Disguise 284
Mapping Endangered Races 285
Etcheta Speaks of Sirian Contacts 287
The Life of a Sirian Mapper 288
The Technology of Mapping 289

Projects in Our Solar System 291
Saving Lost Beings for Possible Re-Creation 292
Recreation and Family Life on the Home Planet 293
The Use of Mapping Technology 295

17. Bears and Mediation Beings **297**
Zoosh: December 7, 1998
The Little Bears 297
Animal Mediators 299
Watchers from the Fifth Dimension 302
Gentle Encounters 304
Scanning for Anomalies 305
Reasons for Diplomatic Languages.. 307
The Profound Benevolence of the Sirian Version of Earth 307
A Message of Warning and Hope 309
A Celebration of Difference 310

18. Untold Stories: Contact with Criminals and Microbes **313**
Zoosh and Ktook: December 8, 1998
Ktook Speaks of the Transformation of His People 313
A Calling to a Special Project 315
Communing with Criminals 316
The Escaped Prisoner 317
A Beautiful Transformation 318
Worldwide Healing of the Heart 319
The Criminal Colony Redeemed 320
Life on the Colony Island 322
First Encounters with the Universe 324
Contact with Earth Animal Beings 325
The Powerful Effect of Songs and Stories 327
Zoosh Speaks of the Visitors to Criminals 328
Visits from Microbes 329

19. Creatures Great and Small **333**
Zoosh and Bear Representative: December 9, 1998
Union and Individuality in Microbes 335
The Home Space of Microbes 336
Microbial Communication 337
The Bears Speak 339
Liaisons for Earth 342
Expression through the Bear Form 343

The Bear Community 345
The Goals of Planet Earth 346
In Communication with the Earth 347
Revitalizing the Planet 349

20. Earth's Work with Quantum Mastery and the Loop of Time 351
Bear Represntative: December 11, 1998
A Mission of Diplomacy 353
Finding Qualities of True Diplomacy 354
Beings of Vast Projection 356
Dangers of Interacting with the Past 357
Allowing the Explorer Race to Experience Consequences 358
Avoiding Time Complications 359
Unraveling Accidental Time Tangles 360
Several Planets Are Working on Quantum Mastery 363
Quantum Teachers 364
Earth's Soul in Our Bodies 365
Understanding the Subconscious 367
The Role of Earth's Soul 368
Communicating with the Earth 369
Accessing the Subconscious through Dance 371

21. Joao and the Andromedans 373
Zoosh: January 24, 1999
Contact in Botucatu 373
Rescue of a Trapped Being 375
Universal Symbols of Greeting 376
Massive Amounts of Contact in Brazil 377
The Creation of a Special Child 379
Other Beings on the Ship 381
Preparation to Help Others 382
The Andromedan Lifestyle 384
Family Appearances 385
Lifespan and Governmental Structure 387
Language and Symbols 391
The True Nature of Healing Crystals 392
Joao's Son 394

22. The Pascagoula Affair 395
Zoosh and Guardian Number Ten: January 26 and 27, 1999
Inexperienced Beings on a Maiden Voyage 396

The Purpose of the Visit 399
A Missed Connection 401
Consequences of a Rash Decision 402
Protected by the Mediators 404
Zoosh on the Guardians 406
Without Their Souls' Permission 408
Beings Not Dissimilar to Humans 410
Later Contacts with Charles Hickson 412
Guardian Number Ten Speaks.. 413
A Culture Bringing Peace and Harmony 415
Telepathic Communications with Charles Hickson 416
A Message for Earth: Remain Focused in Your Heart 417
The Original Plan for Contact 418
Zoosh on the Guardian 419

23. The Minister **421**
Zoosh: January 28, 1999
A Visit to the Andromeda Galaxy 422
A Student of Spirituality 423
The Return to Earth with Wisdom to Share 424
A Final Home in Andromeda 424
Learning of Heart Connections 425

Afterword **431**
Zoosh: April 8, 1999

Reference List **432**
Image Sources **433**

Introduction

Greetings, fellow beings of the universe. You are space travelers, though you do not know it. We—our people, the Zeta Reticulans—live in a world that encompasses the past, the present and the future. You as individuals are aware of your past and hoping for a benevolent future, individually and perhaps on a community level as well. And you live in the present. On some worlds like my own, such a familiarity and continuity with the past, present and future would be considered a thread of connection. This is why I'm referring to you as space travelers. When one or more have travelled in space, as several of your peoples have done—albeit short distances by comparison—all of you inherit that quality. If it can be done by a few, it can be done by many.

Many of you will look to other places, other times and distant areas to somehow be an inspiration for you to live better or even differently, but it will be the other way. You will inspire more than you are inspired, and as travelers, when you return to your home planet, you will marvel at the diversity. Even though you will find variety in your travels, you will never find on any given planet the diversity you have on your own. So when you return home, as space travelers, you will always marvel at what your planet has to offer.

If you can do nothing else when you read this book, look around on your planet. Look at all the different forms of life and know that from the smallest to the largest, they all have cousins on other planets. And while they might not look exactly the same on other planets, there are similarities that you would notice, not unlike how you notice similarities from one family member to another. They do not look identical, but there are similarities. When you travel, you will note that, but when you return, you will always be happy to be home.

Welcome to the universe.

—Joopah through Robert Shapiro

The Zeta Contacts

Zoosh
October 31, 1998

Many of you have read with great interest the experiences of various contactees with UFOs and sometimes with those who ride in UFOs. There are a few of you reading this who have not had exposure to such material. Either way, it is the intent of this book to reveal to you more about the occupants of those ships, perhaps even commenting on things that the contactees themselves either do not remember or were not exposed to at the time of their contacts. There will be some attempt to explain the civilizations and their motivations, what prompted them to come to Earth to contact the citizens of Earth and what, in general, this all has got to do with you now.

Betty and Barney Hill

Starting with Betty and Barney Hill is a fine beginning. These people, after all, took a great deal of flak from fellow human beings because of this experience. But on the other hand, they were very—how can we say?—influential with the average reader since the story appeared in well-circulated magazines of the time, thus exposing the entire UFO phenomena to a broader audience and offering some significant insights into the potential truth of the experience because of Betty's memory of the map.

The Hills were contacted by Zeta Reticuli beings who were quite active

1

Figure 1.1: Betty and Barney Hill, after their famous 1961 experience.

at that time. These true contactees were not recognized for their full experience, but this was partially due to the fact that neither one of them wanted to broadcast it. But after a time they felt that they needed to understand the experience and were open to a certain amount of exposure so long as it was not harmful.

I want to say this right off the top: Barney's passing was not related to the experience. I want to say that for his family. It might seem that way to some because of the extra stress. However, at the time of the experience, it was noted by those who took Barney into the ship that he had certain conditions, and there was some therapy given to Barney. This was considered to be a reasonable thing to do. The two were picked up because they were available and because they both had had previous lives on Zeta Reticuli.

The Zetas are unique in this aspect. Other ETs do not exclusively contact people (human beings) who have had previous lives or might have future lives on Zeta Reticuli. Other ETs contact people with whom they have not had any acquaintance, but the Zetas will only contact people on Earth who have either had past lives or will have future lives on Zeta Reticuli.

Since Betty and Barney had both had previous lives on Zeta Reticuli, the Zetas felt that there was acquiescence, a permission that came from the past soul experience. When they were taken aboard, Betty and Barney were both taken to separate chambers in the ship. They would refer or relate to them more as chambers than rooms, and it was quickly noted by the ETs that Barney had certain medical conditions. This is not unusual to ETs, especially Zeta beings. If they know that a human has certain medical conditions, they will first check with their guides to see if any interference that they might be causing would bring harm or if it would be possible to perform some action or activity that would be acceptable and might help the person, in this case Barney.

Receiving permission that it would be all right to do some therapy since being picked up might in fact have caused Barney some stress, the Zetas felt that they were obligated to do something. So they actually did compensate for the stress by making some slight alterations to Barney's endocrine system, which from that day forward, to give you one small example, changed the makeup of Barney's sweat.

This allowed him to sweat off a little more of the toxicity in his body associated with his medical conditions and allowed him to live his life out to the end of its natural cycle. In fact, Barney lived a couple of years past what would have originally been the end of his natural cycle, because the Zetas felt obligated to assist him, since they did not wish to harm him in any way. I want this passed on to the families so they know that the overall experience was benevolent.

Neither one of the Hills remember this, but there was some time lost. The Zetas remember that. The vehicle actually did not remain on the ground; the Zetas realized that they could not park a ship on the ground, even in a remote area, without drawing some attention. So the examination as well as other experiences took place well beyond Earth's atmosphere. They did not go to their planet, but there was some cruising about. They showed both Betty and Barney Earth from a distance and a little bit of the control room of the ship.

Did they pick up the car too?

No, the car remained there. They thought that was all right, since a car parked in the woods would not be considered suspicious. The flight and the examination took a couple of hours. The Zetas made a request to the spirit guides of both of the Hills that the Hills not remember much of the flight for a time, although it is possible that they did dream about it later. I'm pretty sure that Barney did. I mention this because Barney did speak of things and write some things down. Some family members who are still around today might remember it, and I want you to know that what he remembered is true.

Hybrids for the Preservation of the Species

This is the early 1960s. What was the Zetas' main motive? Why did they pick the Hills up?

At that time, the Zetas were finishing up their contacts with people on Earth because they knew that very shortly the U.S. and the Soviet Union would be developing radar systems so powerful that they would unintentionally be interfering with navigation systems associated with physical travel (as compared to time travel), and the Zetas knew they would not be able to come to the planet much longer. So they were still checking Earth people. At that time, Zeta Reticulans believed that their civilization was dying out. As a result, they were still gathering genetic material in the hopes of perpetuating their species, and they were trying to gather it exclusively from beings—souls, you might say—who had some connection with them, so at the soul level there would be a desire to preserve the species. That would be from the Zetas' point of view.

Occasionally, people they would contact would be with other people who would also come onboard—for instance, the children of the people they would contact and so on. The people donating genetic material, in this case the adults (I'm talking about an example here, not the Hills), would always be those with a connection to the Zetas. But even if the children did not have a connection to the Zetas, they would still be taken onboard, and a crew member would be assigned to play with them.

At that time, the Zetas were still concerned about this. Years later they discovered, as is explained in the first and second *Explorer Race* books, that their civilization was changing dimensions and therefore the need to perpetuate their species with various types of hybrid races was not necessary. As a result of their hybridizing their race, the Zetas would now have the responsibility to look after those hybrid races and see that they be raised properly, and that caused the Zetas to make a few extra contacts, especially with mothers with children, to make certain that the Zetas would be able to give the children of hybrid races that had been fostered by the Zetas the proper attention when they (the parent race, from their perspective) visited, although the hybrid races themselves would, of course, have natural love for their children.

Do you think they picked up mothers and children in order to learn how the mothers mothered their children?

Yes, because for thousands of years their race had been cloned, and mothering was something they did not know. However, since they had created hybrid races and had brought them along as best they could and the hybrid races all had children the way you have children, the hybrid races had a greater knowledge of how to mother children than the parent race did. The parent race wanted to know how to mother children when they visited them, so they would have to get advice from beings they thought would be experts on mothering. And so, of course, they came to Earth.

Contacts Were Benign

So does that hold as a principle, then? So many of these people who have recorded these experiences have called them abductions, but all they were really trying to do . . .

I'm going to tell you something now. Abduction is a currently popular word that has been placed upon these experiences. Very few contactees have ever called these experiences abductions. Only in recent years have other people called them abductions. Now, some contactees will call them abductions, but they were not abductions, because, granted, they were taken from their lives for a few hours, but it was not done for any malevolent purpose. If you go back and read the material from the 1950s and 1960s, you will not once see the word "abduction" appear in any of that material—not once. It's only a current buzzword.

Okay, so the Hills were picked up and genetic material was taken. This was not always sexual; it could be just DNA, right?

It was rarely sexual. Usually it would be some thin scraping of the skin's surface to pick up some dead skin cells in order to get the idea if this DNA would be useful to them and whether it would be worth going any further. And if it would be worth going any further, then there might be other samples taken.

Sperm was not so common, but sometimes sperm and eggs were extracted if—and this all depended on a big *if*—the Zetas felt in that moment, with those people, a great concern that their race was dying out. So it wasn't always done. It also had to be when they scanned the material, the initial collection from the surface of the skin, that they felt, "Oh, this is really powerful DNA, and it will combine with ours well."

There were usually some deep-set memories placed at the subconscious or unconscious level, inside the innermost consciousness of the participants—as the Zetas would call them, the Earth people, the contactees—about why this was going on. And the Zetas, being an unusual race of beings, would not explain why, because they would insert a memory, as you might insert memory into a computer, that was intended to flower at a later date, usually in the form of a dream as to what this was all about.

It was their belief at that time, in the 1950s and 1960s, that the rest of the population, the Earth population, could not handle too much knowledge about extraterrestrials, and so they tried to make the contacts with the contactees as discreet as possible—not because they were trying to hide out or protect themselves, but because they wanted the contactees to remember as little as possible so that their lives would not be disrupted. It was a kind gesture, even though it did not always work out.

That's why when people would ask, "How come you're doing this? Why are you doing this?" they wouldn't answer, because they didn't want to talk to the conscious mind about this knowing; the unconscious or subconscious would reveal it later.

What percentage of people actually remembered? Many people never did, right?

Most people remembered at some point in their lives, some of them very quickly after the experience, such as Betty and Barney. Others took twenty, thirty, forty, fifty years, but all would remember at some time before the end of their natural cycle.

Some people obviously never talked about it then?

Of course.

The Magic Book of Light

How many people would you say the Zetas contacted, beginning in the 1940s?

Beginning in the late forties, I'd say they contacted no more than thirty-eight hundred. And I'm not counting contacts where children were with their mothers, because while this was a contact, there were no scientific experiments going on and the children would just be entertained. The Zetas love children.

But these thirty-eight hundred . . . Were some of those multiple contacts?

Yes, some people were contacted numerous times, because either they had something to offer to the Zetas, or some kind of conversation or interaction occurred between the Zetas and the contactees that prompted the Zetas to feel that working with these people—even just communicating with them—or, as in the case of certain contactees, that giving them the book (as I will talk a little bit more about in a moment) would encourage them to develop their spiritual lives more profoundly while they were on Earth and hopefully help the civilization on Earth in some benevolent way.

So some of the contactees, though not many, were temporarily loaned the book—or, as in Betty's case, they were allowed to see the book, to examine it and, most importantly, to touch its pages. The book had different guises. In one guise, it looked exactly like a book, with what appeared to be foreign lettering on the outside and a little bit of lettering on the spine—on the cover and on the spine, you understand. If one opened the pages, there would be something like paper, and there would be more letters in a foreign language, a Zeta symbolic language.

But that is not the only guise in which the book appeared. The book could also take on a different form. The same book, the book of light, is described in significant and exact detail in a story that Robert was inspired to write, a fictionalized account of his own contact with the Zetas called *Jamie and the Magic Book*. It was fictionalized, but in fact many of the things described—not all—were actual, specific recollections of the contact.

Is this something to promote or put out?

You might, but I think it would be better to put it out as an actual contact experience rather than as a fictionalized story. It wouldn't be difficult for him now to go through it, describe or just cull the parts that are actually associated with his own personal contact and talk more about that, and I can fill in details too. The story is nice, but I think it is meant to be reported as a contact experience. He has discussed it numerous times at UFO conventions and so on.

In any event, the Zeta book in its other guise is a book of light. It would have covers like an ordinary book, but when closed it would have light coming out of it, light of many different colors. When opened, the pages would not be possible to grasp as one might grasp an ordinary book page, but . . . Do you have your camera? I'll tell you when to take the picture.

You couldn't grasp the pages. You'd have to turn the pages over like this. You put the flat of your hand under each page, like this, and you would simply turn them over. So the pages, in other words, would have to be nudged over, and then as one page was turned over, another one would pop up enough so you could get your hands under it and turn that page over. The pages had nothing printed on them but were color, like a rainbow of color, and the colors would dance about and were quite astonishing. Touching the pages in this way, you would get your hands on the pages and feel a great deal of energy running up and down you, and the energy itself would greatly enhance your spiritual capabilities within that life.

At most, people would be given a loan of the book for ten days. In Betty's case, although several of the people on the crew wanted to loan her the book for ten days as was their custom, there were others on the ship who felt that it would not be safe, because—and this is why, in case

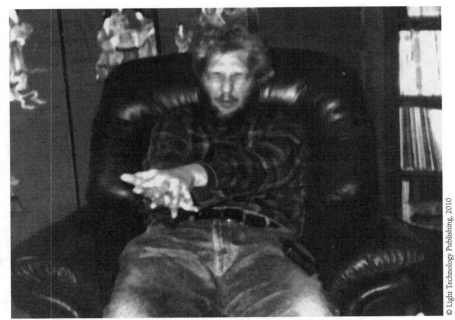

Figure 1.2: Zoosh through Robert Shapiro, demonstrating how one holds the book of light.

there is any lingering doubt—they were not sure they could come back to where Betty and Barney lived to pick up the book. This was because there was a military installation close to where the Hills resided, with radar powerful enough that it might not be safe for them to come. That is the exact reason why the book was not given to Betty, even though some of the beings—some of the Zetas—told Betty they would loan her the book. She was disappointed when they did not, but that's why. In any event, those who did have the book would not necessarily remember it. In Robert's case, he didn't remember for thirty years that he had the book, but that memory came back to him. It just took him about thirty years to remember it.

So some of the multiple contacts would simply be to get the book back?
Yes, but oftentimes the people who had the book were given it because the Zetas felt they could make some kind of spiritual contribution to the Earth people—of the Earth people's choosing in some way, in a large or small context—that would perhaps be benevolent for the people of Earth. As a result, if it was safe, the Zetas would come and see these Earth contactees once a day. In Robert's case, they came once a night, for ten nights. And

on the tenth night, they showed him what the book was about. We'll put out Robert's full contact experience here at some point.

Robert just thought it was a book of light. He didn't quite remember what it was about, but one of the Zetas waved a hand over the book, and by utilizing a small circuit within his hand (it wasn't magic), the book changed from a book of light into a book with physical pages—the same book, with print on the outside. Robert said, "What does that print mean?" The print read, *How to Be a Good Ambassador*. That's what they told him.

Their idea was that Robert had the potential to help prepare the human race for contact with extraterrestrials. Of course, he is not alone in this; there are many people who are helping, but they believed he might make a contribution, and so they invested their time and energy in his education.

The Final Regular Contacts

When was the last contact with them, then?

The last regular contact was right around 1961. They've been able to sneak back in briefly a few times between radar waves, but they've done so reluctantly, partly because they try not to upset you. After all, with the sophisticated air defense warning systems that many of your countries have now, it would be very easy for France, England, the United States, the former Soviet Union or Russia and other countries to see something streaking across the sky, think it was a ballistic missile and respond by starting a war. The Zetas' whole point is that they wanted to be discreet. However, at times they were able to make appearances, and they continue to make some appearances with the ships, without directly contacting human beings on the Earth—with a few exceptions.

You said the last time they contacted humans was in 1961, and then you said they continued.

They continued revealing their presence, meaning that their ships would show up.

For how many years?

Oh, they still do it.

They still do it, and they started before the late 1940s. They were here in the late 1930s, weren't they?

Not contacting human beings directly.

They weren't?

They weren't picking people up and taking them on the ships.

How many Zetas were there? How many crews and ships? Did they have ten, a hundred, a thousand? How many books of light did they have? How did all that work?

At any given time they had no more than three ships that would be around on the Earth. Occasionally they would have five, but that would be it. And each ship had a book. That's all. It wasn't very complicated.

How many beings were there on a ship?

Oh, from three to nine, tops. They weren't always Zetas. Sometimes there would be a Pleiadian or two. The Zetas had a good working relationship with the Pleiadians. Occasionally they would ride on Pleiadian ships if there was considered to be a value or purpose to it.

When the Zetas talked to Barney and Betty and showed them the map and the book, how did they communicate? Telepathically?

Yes. They would communicate telepathically, because the physical makeup of their bodies did not allow them to make the elaborate sounds that human beings make. They did not have the physical apparatus and so on. Telepathic communication was the natural way of doing it. Their natural way of communicating telepathically between each other isn't with words, but they utilize that system to communicate with humans.

The Power of Human Emotion

Did they put some sort of force field around themselves so that they didn't feel the humans' field?

They had a mechanism that they used so that they were not impacted by the emotions of human beings, because emotions are significantly more powerful than even you on Earth realize. Sometimes one human being's emotions can greatly affect another human being's emotions even if they don't come into any contact with each other. The Zetas have basically one expressed emotion, which is sort of a mixture of calm and peace and love or gentleness (love from them would be felt by a human being as gentleness), and your full human array of emotions, including fear or anger, would cause them to become physically ill and would probably kill them. So they needed to protect themselves.

How were the first few contacts with humans when the Zetas decided they needed DNA? Were there Zeta casualties? Did they protect themselves before they ever started?

The Zeta beings lost about eight or nine people before they realized the full impact. At first they thought they were picking up a germ organism from human beings and they became very sanitary, not unlike what one would find in a surgical operating theater. But that didn't seem to prevent it. It takes Zetas a while to understand things. Even though they have amassed a great amount of knowledge, it's working knowledge, and to acquire new knowledge that is not within their species or their culture is difficult, not unlike how it is for you. It is difficult for you, for instance, to go to another completely different culture and amass a great deal of understanding about that culture immediately. You need time. The Zetas are the same.

The learning curve.

Yes, it took them a while to grasp that they were being impacted by your feelings, and they got most of this guidance from their guides, but they couldn't believe it at first. It wasn't that they disbelieved their guides. They just couldn't believe that they could be impacted by feelings to the point of death. After a while they had to admit it, and that's when they reluctantly started using this device that electronically creates a thin barrier around the individual wearer to keep the wearer from feeling the feelings of others.

This was something they did very reluctantly, because they were fully aware that it would greatly complicate communication between the different species; that's one of the reasons why they were so reluctant to use this mechanism. Finally they did it and then continued communications with Earth people in the blundering style often reported by contactees.

It sounds callous and distant, and the human being wants to know, "How come you don't understand I'm in pain?" Of course the Zetas can't understand pain, because the experience would kill them. Those Zetas who were allowed to contact human beings, you understand, were also specially trained to never get agitated, because there are circumstances on Zeta Reticuli in which Zetas do get excited or intensely involved in experiences of their own. But they were trained to remain as calm as possible, because it was believed that this would help the human beings to be calm, and to some extent that's true. Even today, one finds that medical professionals are trained to remain calm even if they are upset on the inside.

So the common denominator of all the Zeta interactions during those years was to procure DNA samples or specimens?

Let's not call it the common denominator. Let's say it was the basic motivation, but it wasn't always the common denominator because there were some people whose genetic samples weren't . . . They were looked at, and the Zetas said, "Oh well, these won't do us any good." The only reason they would continue contacting those people is because there was some feeling that these individuals could make some spiritual contribution.

This is not to say that other contactees—those who didn't have the lengthy ten-day contact, for instance—were not making spiritual contributions in their lives. Everybody who had this contact would have his or her spiritual body invigorated. But it was more so for the people in whom they invested a ten-day contact. That was more like a ten-day apprenticeship.

How many of the thirty-eight hundred did they do that to?

They only did that with, depending on how you count it, about eighty-nine to one hundred fifteen, and the reason I say "depending upon how you count it" is that sometimes, although they had mothers and children on the ship, they would be working with the children, but this wasn't their primary . . . In any event, I don't have to go into those details. They did it with eighty-nine to one hundred fifteen.

Children of the Zetas

I see. If they saw that the children would make a contribution, they would work with them.

Yes, and they would do things besides play. They would turn the play into something educational.

There are books about many, many children gathered together on what they are saying are Zeta ships where they are being educated. Are these Zetas? Is that true?

Yes, that was done in the hope that these children would somehow blaze the trail and get your society, your global society—the Zetas never recognized political boundaries—prepared to meet them and others. Although when you have a public contact—meaning everybody knows about it—the first one is most likely not going to be with the Zetas. It's going to be with someone who looks like you. Nevertheless, they would work with the children, because the children could interact with the Zetas without fear. With no fear, the Zetas can release the mechanism that protects them and have much better communication with the children, and the children with them. That's why the Zetas tend to trust children more than they trust adults, because they are not concerned about the children exhibiting fear. Little children see an ET, and if that ET looks different to them, it's nothing. For a child to see a dog or a cat is no more or less of an ET experience than it is with an actual ET like a Zeta.

The Zetas didn't have large groups of twenty or thirty children coming up regularly, then?

Not on these ships, but some Zeta beings did. That was on a larger ship, which wasn't always a Zeta ship. But the Zetas might be present because of their special affinity for working with children. Pleiadians also have this affinity, but after a while it came to be that the Pleiadian ships couldn't come as regularly as the Zetas, because the Pleiadians—being much closer in alignment with the biological makeup of human beings—would be even more susceptible to feelings radiated by human beings or pollutants in the air, to electrochemical pollution and so on. The Zetas could still show up, in their ships at least, after the Pleiadians couldn't anymore. The Pleiadians are a little more susceptible.

So these children who were trained on these other ships—without naming any of them—was that energy put into them? Did it flower? Did they make a contribution to the planet?

They didn't have memory capsules put into them. They showed the children the past history of the Earth. Of course, the Zetas and Pleiadians didn't show everything, but they showed some of the drama without making it traumatic for the youngsters. They didn't want to scare them. They were shown the past history of the Earth as it has been, as well as the present and the future—what would result if you stayed on that same timeline.

Then they showed them the desired past, the desired present and the desired future, which are all very benevolent. That's it. The children, while they might be young, are not stupid; they understand what's better and what isn't. The whole point was to say, let's work to bring about that benevolent past, present and future.

And the children did that?

They're working on it, obviously. They're not there yet.

Timelines and the Limits of Linear Memory

But you said we did leave the old timeline.

We left the old timeline, but looking around it is obvious even to the most casual eye that you do not have a benevolent present, is it not? You're not there yet.

So is this like an intermediate timeline?

Certainly. When you get to the point where your body consciousness can recall and experience only a benevolent past, a benevolent present and a benevolent future, then you'll be in a better space and on different timelines. The timeline continually changes. This is, of course, another reason why people are having more difficulty remembering things;

Never Forget That

WITH TIMELINE CHANGES, YOU CANNOT UTILIZE A LINEAR MEMORY IN A NONLINEAR CONTEXT.

If we search out cases then, and they are related to the Zeta, they're basically going to be all pretty much the same.

There will be a lot of similarity. One of the more famous Zeta cases, where fortunately the contactee was a pretty good artist and has given the world a wealth of sketches and drawings and recollections and so on, is the now well-known (and in this field of discussion, well-established) case of Betty Andreasson. I urge you all to read books about Betty's contacts, and you will learn a great deal about Zetas. They singled her out. They wanted her to know lots and lots about them; they took her to their planet and they honored her. They did many things.

I was going to ask about that one.

Occasionally they would honor someone. They would feel something special from someone and they would take that person to the planet, and in Betty Andreasson's case they gave her a great honor. They had an assembly wherein they did a renewal. This is part of their spiritual existence in which they have an experience that they create both on the feeling level, with all the Zetas present, and on the mental level. It is very much like an image of a renewal with a phoenix experience. [See Chapter 2 for a more detailed discussion of the Ceremony of the Phoenix.]

I didn't realize that was Zeta. Did she use the word Zeta in the book?

You'll have to check the books, but she made it very clear. Take one look at any sketch of the ETs that she was in contact with and you'll say, "Oh, well, those are Zeta beings. I think they're recognizable." It is a great blessing, you understand, that she is as good an artist as she is, because very few contactees are good artists. There's another one who I think sent you some slides of his once where he showed pictures of Zetas jumping around in a field. He grew up on a farm. His name does not come immediately, but he has a wonderful painting of Zetas as he remembered them, jumping around in the flowers in the way they would to entertain a young boy.

The goal of our present-day opening to our potential is eventually not to remember any of these at all, then?

It is like steps. Think back on your own progress. There are many things you now know absolutely—not just on the spiritual or intellectual level, but also simple things. For instance, you might not remember all of the steps from when you first learned how to drive or when you first learned how to type, but you have the knowledge that you have today, and it is now first or second nature—you drive and you type, and you don't even think about it. You might say that it is similar in the sense that one learns things in stages, and as one becomes an expert, at an advanced stage, one tends to forget the earlier stages.

That's a good way to look at it.

Tomorrow night we'll probably hear from Joopah and get more on this, because Joopah is the person who contacted Robert, and he has been contacting and has contacted others on the Earth, and he will talk about that. So we'll continue with this Zeta business on Monday.

Betty Andreasson and the Ceremony of Renewal

Joopah
November 2, 1998

It has been some time. Question?

Are you familiar with Betty Andreasson, the times that she was picked up?
With some of them, not all. You will have to ask specifically.

Were you on the ship when she was picked up?
No, but I can consult the records. We keep extensive records on all the people we invite aboard, whether they are from Earth or elsewhere.

Can you tell me why she was invited?
She was invited because it was understood that she was going to evolve in her life toward being particularly spiritual, and before this life she had asked us (since we are her friends and companions at other times in other lives) if we could get together in some way; she said that it would be nice to be steered toward something by which she could reveal the connections between our two peoples. She had a purpose here. The purpose was to help create affection in both races toward each other.

She understood before this life that tolerance is not enough. Tolerance is grudgingly given, but affection is open and can take years off the building of a relationship between peoples. As you understand one another on a personal level, so it is on a diplomatic level as well. This is why she and others with whom we invited close contact were awakened a little earlier than the expected time in order to accelerate their given spiritual identity.

The Corridor to the Creator

Can you discuss the trip you took her on when she was twelve or thirteen and went to see what she called the One-Behind-the-Glass-Door?

What did she say about that?

She said that she couldn't talk about it, that she was in a great state of . . . that she felt more loving afterward. They took a picture of her in a hypnotic trance and there was a beatific smile on her face. They told her she could not talk about it.

This can be revealed now without creating a problem. It was felt at the time that your people would be threatened by our people revealing the corridor to Creator. This door, as it were, was designed to keep her from going into this energy. The energy is so loving, so benevolent and so benign that it is not possible to resist it. You want to get closer. If someone said you could be kissed and hugged by Creator, wild horses, as you say, could not keep you from it.

She went in, though. She went in and experienced it but she was told she could not say anything about it.

This is not unlike people who have had what you call after-death experiences. In these experiences one often feels some connection to whatever version of Creator one holds dear, and one is overwhelmed by this love and so on. I believe that she was asked not to reveal it because some religions on Earth might have felt threatened, or she might have been deified and it might have created a complication for her life. So she might have been asked not to talk about it to protect her. There is not so much to reveal.

Courtesy of UFO Casebook

Figure 2.1: Betty Andreasson's experience is described in great detail in Raymond Fowler's 1979 book The Andreasson Affair.

What is her version of the Creator? Does each person after life see what he or she expects to see?

If you go after life, at the end of your natural cycle, you might see Jesus if you are Christian. You understand? If you are some other religion, you might see some spirit . . . Yes, you might see something like that. In this case, she saw and felt a living, moving light. It's not so much what you see, it's what you feel, because you feel it with 100 percent of your being, and you never forget it.

Through that door there is some corridor directly to the Creator. Is that what you're saying?

The corridor—and I'm referring to it that way—is invited; it is not permanently there.

Like a portal?

Yes, it is invited through the actions of certain spiritual beings.

There were some very tall beings with white hair and white gowns outside the door. Who were they?

These are the beings who invite the energy. My people have been the beneficiaries of this energy before, but we are not so spiritually advanced that we are able to invite it yet. These beings who were there are healers. They are special teachers, but it is not in their natural way to speak. They teach by showing or doing.

And where are they from?

They are from a much higher dimension. I'm not certain that they have a location physically, but I have been told that they are from the eleventh dimension.

They don't live on your planet, and they come when you ask for a ceremony?

Or they come if they feel it is time for us to be doing something that we are not doing—or on occasion, for a special guest like this person, they will come to provide the service that we ourselves cannot provide.

Were there also a number of your beings behind the door? Since the beings came to provide this experience, was it just for her, or were any of your people there, too?

It was for her.

How often do your people go there?

Well, you understand, you want to make it a place, but such energy can be brought anyplace, invited anyplace. Instead of "going there," let's change that to how often we experience it. Usually every one of the people experiences it at least once in his or her lifetime, but usually not more than that. My people have what I would call a 100 percent experiential memory. This means that anything we have ever felt or learned is 100 percent available all the time should we desire to feel it or have that moment of discovery again, whereas, you know, when you have a memory, much of the original experience is lost, and one recalls the experience but one does not reexperience it. For us, we have a 100 percent memory that allows us to reexperience it, so once is enough.

So then it is usually when you are young that you experience it, so you can reexperience it many times?

Young is relative. We do not have young or old like you. We are created at full maturity, but in terms of length of lifetime, it usually happens earlier rather than later.

So that you can reexperience it?

It happens earlier so that the being understands the nature of existence. When one feels this energy, there is never any doubt from that moment forward what life in all forms is about. It's about love first, and it's about variety second. In my experience, there is never any doubt about that for anyone after this experience.

The Experience Behind the Door

That's very beautiful. She said that when she came into the planet, she went through water and down into a tunnel. Is that true?

She went through liquid. I don't know that it would have been H_2O, but she probably went through liquid, yes.

Liquid what?

We don't think of it as water. We don't consume it. It is something that creates our atmosphere. You might take water and create at least a partial atmosphere for you. So this liquid creates our atmosphere.

She said that when she landed, she was in a tunnel. Was that just her perception? She said it was very misty and foggy.

I think it was done in order to—how can we say—create, to allow her to feel . . . not overwhelmed with the experience. It would be as if you were in a crowded room with many people, but the people who are leading you through the room do not wish you to become distracted or overwhelmed. They might create a screen of some sort for you so that you are not overwhelmed by your surroundings, which are already unusual and strange for you. To overwhelm you with more of the unexpected could be working against the purpose—the purpose, of course, being communication, and communication happens best when all parties feel safe. So that is the main reason she was given this experience.

She was encouraged to have this experience so that she would know that the people she was with wanted the best for her. It's one thing for us to say, "Oh, we've known you before." But you know, she was coming from a planet where she'd been cut off from her full knowledge. So when one demonstrated one's benign intent, then after that she would know, "Well, these people must be all right."

It was like a smokescreen then? Something like that?

No, no, I'm talking about the experience behind the so-called door.

A History of Humanity on Display

I understand that. So, on the way, she said that when she landed, she saw humans from all different eras of the planet Earth, from a thousand years ago, white and black and Indian, looking like they were encased in ice. Are these humans who were mummified?

Not mummified. What she saw would have been lifelike. But these were people who had come to the end of their natural cycle and acquiesced to being preserved in this fashion, meaning that we asked them their permission to be on display like this, but they're not on display as in a museum for us. It was to show her that we had had former contact with human beings and that we had a high regard for them. I grant that you might not have done that. I think in hindsight that it probably would not have been so comfortable for her. But you know, we did not know so much about the social aspect of interacting with the human race, which is much, much more complicated than our race, socially and genetically.

So have you had that display there for many, many years, or did you put it there just for her?

We went back in time and contacted these different races of people. Some of them wished to come to our planet, and since they had no relatives or friends who would miss them, they were granted that privilege. When they came toward the end of their natural cycle, we asked them if they would like to be preserved—have their bodies preserved, of course; their souls would go on—and they said yes. If they had not said yes, it would have been all right also; it was not expected of them.

So you brought various beings there, and they lived out their lives?

Usually they would only leave Earth if they felt no lasting attachment to the planet, so this would be people who would not be missed very much for whatever reason and who might have the kind of lives they would enjoy where we were. Some of them also—if they wanted to do other things—would sometimes have visitors from other planets. Pleiadians have been very cooperative with us over the years, and we have been cooperative with them, and they would sometimes come and communicate with these individuals. Often they would be asked if they wanted to go back; if they said yes, somebody would take them back.

So can humans live on your planet, or do you have to create a special habitat for them?

No, we have to create a special area for them, just like we did for this honored being you are asking about.

And you put oxygen in and do all the things that would make . . .

Provide for their needs.

Courtesy of Near-Death Experiences and the Afterlife

Figure 2.2: The hybrid beings described by Betty Andreasson were over five feet tall, with wrap-around eyes and silver faces.

The Hybrids on the Ship

She says the beings on the ship were over five feet tall. So who were these beings?

If she was speaking of beings over five feet tall, they were probably hybrids.

Ah yes, because she described the wraparound eyes and the silver faces. So hybrids were working with you even . . . Well, let me see. The first time, she was twelve, so even in the 1950s?

We have had hybrid races of beings—hybridized between ourselves and other beings—for over four hundred thousand years. Hybrids are not new.

I didn't know that.

Yes, we have been experimenting for a long time.

That's never been talked about. How far back do the human hybrids go?

Human hybrids do not go back much further than five thousand years, but there was always a desire by my people to create the optimum hybrid who would have all of the qualities we hold dear as well as the qualities we came to discover over time, qualities humans have that we felt would be compatible. It took us a while to discover these qualities because of the electronic barriers that were necessary.

It took us almost thirty-five hundred years to discover the qualities of the human being that we felt would be essential in order to create the best possible hybrid race—one that would not only be happy to be in existence but that would also pursue the higher ideals that we hold dear while having enough of the, you would say "humanity," to be inspired in more broad directions. However, the beings she saw were not the human-Zeta hybrids. They were hybrids from a different source.

What source?

They were more Zeta than anything. That's why height is not something that is typical for us. There are some of us who are a little taller, but I think that height is not so typical.

What qualities did you finally settle on that you wanted from the humans?

The qualities that we decided were the most essential were the will to live . . .

Yes, because you feared your race was dying out.

Well, we had reason to believe—not fear—that it might.

So that lust for life would have been really . . .

It would have been essential. I saw that when wounded, the body would have the capacity to heal itself to some extent, which is a capacity you have now. We do not heal from wounds as well as you do. Just on our own, with the electronic barrier, we do not get wounded. Another quality was friendliness, which is something we have, but we do not express it in the same cheerful way you can. We felt this was important because we wanted our hybrid race to be social, to contact others and to be open to contact. We also felt that courage was important, since sometimes the survival of a race might depend on one or two individuals' acts of heroism. Such a threat has not happened to my people, and we believed we would be heroic like this, but we didn't know for a fact. So we had to encourage that: we had to look for that in the human beings, who are heroic very often, nearly all the time, just by having to deal with life as you experience it. And of course, there had to be respect and appreciation for love. These are the most important qualities as we see it.

Sampling and Marking Candidates on Earth

Did you look for these qualities in specific humans? Of course, a few hundred years ago there weren't so many people, but how do you look through this vast population and find the ones that you want as DNA carriers?

This is very easy. We have the capacity to sample your essential personality makeup from a distance. We can know you from a distance, and of course it took us time to know what we were knowing [chuckles]. At first, our machines and so on would understand you much better than we could understand you, because we could not comprehend you yet. It took us quite a while to be able to comprehend you—it takes us a while to learn—but once we could, then we could isolate certain strains or bloodlines, as you say, ancestry lines, or we could simply go back in time and speak to individuals and ask them if they would like to participate, or we could invite them on board and ask them if they would be interested in being involved in this way. We'd tell them what their involvment would be about. If we felt their society would give them some difficulty about it, we would encourage them to forget about the experience, except that it would be all right to remember it in dreams, because most societies on your planet will accept dreams, no matter how unusual, but they are less tolerant of an experience stated to be a fact.

When you come to a planet then, you could go not only anywhere but also to any time?

Any time, and we could also be off at quite a distance, focus our array on the planet and be able to locate individuals who would be the most likely candidates. Then, using something not unlike what your computers use to mark something, we would be able to put a mark on the individuals without harming them or causing any contact whatsoever and then find them again. This is no different than your computer registering data for a file. It is very similar to that technology, only this works with people and without inflicting any interference in their lives.

Did you ever go to heroes, to people we're familiar with?

But you see, those people would all be needed by your society; they would all be wanted. So no, we did not go to . . . Well, there was one exception.

Fascinating. So what you basically did was put a mental block . . . I don't think she could have talked about the experience of going through the glass door even if she'd wanted to. Did you somehow place a posthypnotic suggestion or a block?

It is not a mental block. It was something that was actually more of a physical thing. When you develop a more sensitive magnetic resonance machine . . . What do you call it—an MRI? When you develop something more sensitive, you might actually be able to find it. It is a physical thing that does not harm you but creates a specific memory . . .

. . . block?

But only to the conscious mind. It does not represent a block to the subconscious or the unconscious, which allows for dreaming—very soon thereafter with some people and later with others. We feel that this way the experience can be revealed in a more palatable way for the average person.

They tried every way you could imagine to find out what was on the other side of that door. But even under hypnosis, she couldn't or wouldn't reveal it.

This was because she gave her word and she is honorable.

So even in her subconscious, then . . .

You understand, hypnotists will tell you that even if you hypnotize a person, you cannot get that person to do something that is against his or her will. This is something about which she gave her word and that was that. She is an honorable person.

The Ceremony of the Phoenix

I see. What about Betty Andreasson's other experience? She was taken, I think, to the same place and shown the Ceremony of Renewal—the Ceremony of the Phoenix.

Yes, she was given this experience because she was, as I say, a particularly honored member of the human race, and we wanted her to have the sense of our philosophy, our way of life; we wanted her to see that, while we weren't simply all alike, there were some similarities between our peoples. Your people might go to church on Sunday for renewal. In the same way, we go to a ceremony like this for renewal—only we fuel it on the energetic level within our physical selves, and it is a purifying mental experience. I think some of your people who go to church might have the same energetic experience as well as a mental clarification. She was exposed to this so she could understand our similarities.

I don't know much about it, but doesn't it take a lot of you to produce this hologram, this phenomenon? What would you call it?

It is physical. We focus the energy, and our tall friends are nearby. They have taught us a little bit over the years about how to focus the energy by our need for a contact with Creator as we experience Creator to be. We do not experience Creator as a bird, or as a worm that crawls out of the pile of ashes like the phoenix, but we experience the energy and we focus and then they—our tall friends—focus. It is sometimes different than the phoenix, but I believe the phoenix was chosen because it has an Earth identity as well as an identity to us. Sometimes it would be quite different and there would not be any symbolic connection to Earth, so our teachers, the tall people, would have chosen this particular symbol for her sake. Even though she was younger, it would not take her very long to find out—if she did not already know—about such symbolism on Earth.

But in this case, even though you—the group that manifested this event—did it for her, you were also hopeful or knew that this would get publicized at some time and that many, many people would know about it at some point, right?

Yes.

What I'm trying to connect to is that although going through the door was just for her, the renewal ceremony was good for everybody involved, including her, yes?

Yes, it was our ceremony and it was for us, but at that time we had the ceremony to honor her. It might also have been at some other time that we would have had it, but because she was there, we had it in her honor.

But the people who were there were renewed?

Yes.

Heightened Sensibility after UFO Experiences

There's another aspect of this. It seems that when humans are taken aboard a ship and then brought back, their spirituality, their sensitivity, their ability to see beyond the veil—all that seems to be heightened. Can you talk about that?

Yes. This is because when you have contact like this, even going inside a ship that is on the Earth, the whole atmosphere, the whole experience of Earth stays outside the ship. So during your time on the ship, although you might not remember who you are—some people do, but you might not—what you experience fully is the natural state that you experience in those other places where you have your full capacity to learn. Think of the example of a child born on the Pleiades (since they are our allies and friends): After a reasonable amount of time of growing up, that child will be trained and given education, as any child would, yes? When you go aboard one of our ships, whether it leaves the Earth's atmosphere or not, you are in a state of being in which you are like that child on the Pleiades. So your psychic powers, as you call them, which are really your heart energies, expand and grow forward from that point. Even if you were on that ship for just two hours, your heart would grow forward quite a bit, and some who have had good amounts of time in contact go forward a great deal more. This is one of the reasons people who have had contact on various ships are very vulnerable afterward—because their hearts are very open. If they are traumatized by Earth people afterward, even by people yelling questions at them, it can harm them.

This is why, in general, people are let off the ships at some remote place, so they won't immediately be set upon by curious human beings while their hearts are wide open. This is always done to protect the individual. Granted, it does not make up for some circumstances with various ETs over the years, which were not the best, but that is the reason that's done. It's not done so the ETs can make a getaway. [Chuckles.] I laugh now. . . . See, I can laugh now.

Betty and Barney Hill onboard a Ship

The other case we talked about was Betty and Barney Hill. Can you talk a little bit about why they were chosen and the results of their being onboard a ship?

Those people were considered special. Of course, we consider most of the people we invite onboard special, but we thought these people were very special. Both of them are destined to have future lives on Zeta. We felt their souls' permission to invite them onboard. They both, when they were onboard, said they would be willing to continue to help with our attempts to hybridize a more sturdy type of human Zeta. I don't know whether they remembered saying that, but they did.

I don't think anyone thought to ask them that under hypnosis. They didn't know to ask.

Unfortunately, the beings who had them onboard, my people, had not done many of these encounters, and the woman experienced some discomfort. This is regretted. I believe that my people, those who made this contact, were simply not sufficiently experienced to give her the protection that she needed, and this might have been why she was shown around the ship afterward and my people discussed things with her and showed her the book. Some of the people wanted her to be able to take the book, but others felt differently. This all took place while her husband Barney was asleep. Barney fell into a deep sleep at the beginning of the contact and maintained that sleep throughout most of it, although at one point he was awake and talked to the technicians.

Did his soul protect him by doing that?

Yes, his soul had to protect him; he had fears when he was a youngster, because some people were cruel to him. So his soul said, "We will let him sleep," and he slept during most of it. But he did talk to the technician, who put her hands on his forehead, and he asked her some things, and she told him some things, and he remembered this later on in dreams.

What about the fact that they showed Betty Hill the map, the famous map?

This was a gift. I think they did it because they felt badly that she had suffered some pain and they wanted to give her something. Also it is unusual that a person be as alert and conscious as she was. Most people are a little bit more subdued, but she was, as you say, as vivacious on the ship as she probably was in her day-to-day life. As a result, my people on the ship were intrigued and enjoyed talking things over with her, and if things had been different, they might have wanted to take her to the planet for a visit, but it was understood that Betty and Barney would be missed. So this contact was the only one they had.

The Book of Light Mentioned by Zoosh

If you'd be so kind, Zoosh mentioned a book, a book of light. Can you talk more about that? How did it start?

The purpose of the book of light is to amplify a person's natural spirituality. We do not induce an agenda of our own into anyone's spirituality, but we were granted permission to expose certain people who we were informed would become spiritual anyway, to accelerate their spiritual growth—especially if our teachers advised us that they would make some kind of contribution toward the benevolent and beneficial interaction between our two species, and perhaps between your race and other extraterrestrials as well.

So, because of this potential for diplomatic spirituality, a few of these individuals had the book for a time. The book could be seen as a typical hardcover—you say "book"—with regular pages and print, but the print would be in our language. Here is a demonstration [draws] of a few letters, just a few letters [see Figure 2.3].

Can you tell me what they mean? . . .

"God." It is not dissimilar from the scripting style one sees in some languages on this planet.

Which means that you . . . ?

We may have had some small influence, but certainly others did too. Now, what were we talking about?

The book of light.

In order for the book to have its best impact, the pages would be of light. You understand, we often contacted people when they were young. We like working with the young because they are more open; they have not yet been made callous by the struggles that life on Earth forces upon many people. We would sometimes loan the book to people for no more than ten days, during which we would often have contact with them, either every day or at the least every other day. We would discuss different things, talk about things, maybe go up in the ship and do different things, all of which encouraged them to grow spiritually. So the talk would be for the mind, and the appearance of ourselves would also be for the soul, for the faith—not because we are so inspiring, but because one needs to have faith when one is dealing with something that is entirely unknown.

With the book it is easier to have faith, because it feels good. You touch it and it feels wonderful. By touching the pages of light, you absorb the meaning written down in the book. There are different variations of the book. Robert, for instance, had the book titled *How to Be a Good Diplomat*, which has, I think, served him well. Others would have the book that might have a title more akin to *Creation*, meaning, generally speaking, how the universe was created and what

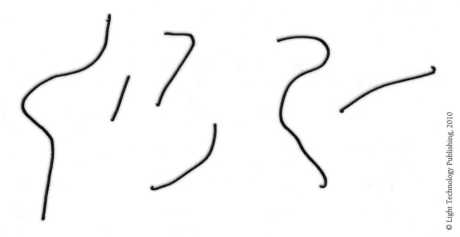

Figure 2.3: Joopah's demonstration of how letters from the book of light would be seen.

the unifying principle is—that being love, of course, unconditional love. So there might be different variations of the book's text, but the format is the same.

Where did this book come from? Have you always had it?

We were given . . . We could create the script, but two different friends gave us the structure of the book, with the light and so on. One of our friends was from the eleventh dimension, and some of the light technology was from our friends from the Pleiades. The Pleiadians, especially higher-dimensional Pleiadians, have worked extensively with liquid light.

So was this originally given to you for your own soul growth?

Yes.

And then you shared it with others?

We believed it would be acceptable to share it with certain humans, and some were given it as a loan, meaning to have it for a time.

Do you still do that now? You don't visit much anymore, do you?

We do not visit so much these days, because your technology—satellite, radar, sonar and, generally speaking, your electronics—sometimes unintentionally makes our presence known.

You were still visiting people in the early 1980s?

We visited a few people then, yes.

Not many, though. Was that the end of your visits?

That was coming to the end of our more frequent contacts. And we had really slowed down quite a bit by then, but William Herrmann, contacted in 1978, was an exception.

Update on Joopah and Other Zetas

Well, let's take a little time now to talk about an update on your life. What's happening with you and the other Zetas now?

There is not so much to say, because it has not been that long since the last update. The only big change is that there are now other gold-light versions of Zeta beings: I am not alone. There are a few more. And other than that, I can't think of any great changes.

But the big change is that all Zetas know that the gold plasma body is in their future, right?

It is known, yes, so there is no longer any concern about us continuing. Of course, this has created a responsibility for us to not only look after the hybrid species we encouraged to start their own civilizations, but also to encourage them to become autonomous, which we have done, giving them more encouragement to develop their own culture and their own purpose for being.

Wonderful. So you've created a lot of stage settings for souls to inhabit, right?
Perhaps.

So what is your reality? What do you do now? You're not out in the spacecraft anymore, are you?
No. I'm on our various planets where our people live, walking amongst the people and communicating in the way we do about our next level of existence. That's all.

You're like a golden-light ambassador?
Yes, that's a nice way to put it.

And they can see you?
Certainly. [Tiger the cat comes into the room.] We do not have cat people on our planets, and it a great privilege to have one so close. They have their own place where they are from, but they have the capacity on their own to seed themselves on planets where they are needed. It is true that some of their people have been brought here by various civilizations, but it is . . . [Addresses the cat.] Is it all right to reveal this? He says, "Acceptable." They do have the capacity in their higher-dimensional selves to immigrate to where they are needed and become physical in time should their presence be beneficial to populations.

We have learned so much through the cats, because they jump on the channel's lap when a few beings—not many—speak through Robert.

The Gift of Jumps to Higher Dimensions

You are, of course, aware of the whole Explorer Race experiment. What's going to happen with the Zetas within the expansion? Is that something that you're talking about, something that concerns you?
No. While our main concern is what is going to happen to us all, we have not even begun to consider alterations beyond those we are experiencing at the moment.

Well, what you are experiencing is pretty dramatic. It's like skipping two grades of school, going right from the sixth to the ninth dimension, isn't it? That's awesome.
It's quite a sudden jump.

Do you know why that is happening?
It has not been revealed to us, but I don't think any of us is interested

in why. We are just happy to know that this is happening rather than seeing our people come to an end.

On your planet you had such a thing happen before, too. A people with a peaceful culture were living in what is now North America. The people of your time call them the Old Ones. Some—not all—of these people also made a jump to a higher dimension. The ones who did not emigrated northward, joined other tribes and shared their knowledge and wisdom as people were open to it. But at least half of the Old Ones jumped dimensions and departed for their homeland.

When was that?

Many hundreds of years ago.

Within the past thousand years?

Yes.

How far did they jump?

They jumped several dimensions, to about the sixth.

And how did they achieve that?

They did not achieve it. It was given to them the same way it was given to us. It happened. Those left behind chose to immigrate to other tribes so that their culture would not die out, to spread the valuable and adaptable parts of their culture and help other peoples if those peoples wished such help.

Maybe we'll ask someone about that. That's pretty interesting. How many beings left—two, a hundred, a thousand?

I could not say.

Okay, we'll ask somebody else about that later. Do you follow the careers of those you took onboard, especially the ones you gave the book to, as they go forward in time?

Yes, we are allowed to do this. All the people who had the book—we do not monitor them as if they were test subjects, but others tell us how these people are developing.

And mostly, there has been a real acceleration as a result of your attention, right? Most of them are doing something that helps the rest of humanity?

Yes.

So that's a wonderful thing you did. The book was something very precious to you; it was your spiritual teaching, right? Whose idea was it to give it to humans?

It was our teachers, the tall people, who felt that under certain select conditions, some people could have the book for a time—not permanently.

Okay. Do any of those teachers want to talk? Can they communicate through others?
    Maybe one.

Okay.

Children of Isis: Path of the Zeta

Yo or Jo Seeka
November 3, 1998

This is Yo or Jo Seeka. I am a guide for the Zeta beings, but not those guides you requested. My wisdom lies in the area of encouraging them to move beyond their mind into their feeling bodies with greater experimentation. I am not going to speak too long, but I want you to understand their path.

Their path now is gently coming into the exploration of the feeling self as Joopah and others have had to do in order to embrace their gold lightbodies. Joopah's channeling through Robert allowed Joopah to experience a greater range of feelings than he would have otherwise. This prepared him to make the jump sooner than the others.

This is the Zetas' path, and one of the advantages for them in interspecies communication with your race is that you are such feeling people. You sometimes discipline yourselves to be of thought, but it is your nature to be of feeling. You don't have to discipline yourselves to be of feeling. That's your nature, and so the contacts were arranged, not only on your behalf, but also on behalf of the Zetas so they could be accelerated onto their path simply by contact with you.

There are always at least two sides to such things, and I thought you might be interested to know the motivation, even the sense of urgency. The Zetas were told through me and others that their means to survival depended upon establishing benevolent relations with the human race.

They were not told how to do that, because that would interfere with their growth.

Giving Up on Governments and Working with People

So their initial interaction in recent times—your recent history—was to approach governments. When that did not work, they went back in time to your race on Earth and approached heads of tribes or clans and worked with people from the past as you would see it. They had much greater success there, and that's what started them with making contacts in your more recent history with people who would live in more remote places. They believed that it was more likely that these people would be independent thinkers and would not necessarily follow the dictates or the preferences of government officials.

So they contacted people in remote places not only to avoid being seen, but because of their belief that the freethinker, the independent person, might be found someplace away from the big city. Of course, the Zetas still contacted some people in bigger cities, but not as many. I am not saying this is absolutely true. What I am saying is this is what they believed, and that is why they acted on this belief.

The Zetas were encouraged all along to maintain contact with you as a race, even if things became difficult for them, and this is why they have stayed in connection. As you know, they have also recently come to discover your key involvement in their lineage, and now that they understand that, they have an easier time grasping how to interact with you.

Once the Zetas understood that there was a lineage involved on the soul line, since they had access to soul lines, they promptly started to conduct soul-line research, finding people of their own kind and hence finding past lives of their own kind back in your time on Earth. They decided that these people would also be good to contact (I reiterate this for the sake of the reader who may not have read the discussions of soul lines in the earlier volumes of *The Explorer Race* series).

So much of the intention of my guidance has come out as a result of knowing these people for so long, and some has come as a result of my interactions with Zoosh and Isis and a few others. There are others who are associated with the refined state of mental being of the Zeta people. I work with them too. Most of what I say has to do with consultation with these beings, but there is also a large portion that has to do with my focus in the heart center. This heart-center focus allows me to radiate a certain energy that my people (if I can call them that) can feel, and when they feel that energy, I say to them that this energy will protect them, nurture them and help them to feel welcome wherever they go.

My people know this energy because it is love, and it is even more than that. It is love, it is safety—which is also an energy—and it is welcoming. The energy of welcoming causes them to feel comfortable, and also as they assimilate that energy and learn to radiate, it allows others (especially the human race) to feel a little more at ease with them, because my people look different than you—not terribly different but enough so that a first interaction with them from a human point of view can be startling.

But once you accept the fact that my people are not human and that they are trying to communicate with you, it then just becomes a matter of finding the common ground for communication. This is always a bit amusing and sometimes frustrating, but it can be done. As my people learn more about love and feelings, it will be easier for them to communicate with you, the passionate people. As your people learn more about the mental body and thought, so will you be able to understand the desire for pure perfection of thought that my people have attempted to achieve.

It is not possible to achieve pure perfection of thought, however, without having this special feeling that I mentioned, and the more they experience that feeling, the easier it will be for them to achieve the clear thought they desire so much.

The Teachers Are Made of Compressed Energy

Have you always been a guide or have you incarnated?

I have always been one of their guides.

So how can we understand your origin?

Is this important?

Well, I just like to know where everyone is from.

You want to know my bloodline? Who were my mother and father, eh? [Chuckles.]

I don't know how it works with a guide.

I am one of the children of Isis. I came from Isis. We think of ourselves as the children of Isis, because we emerged from her.

We? Who is we?

There are others.

Who are guides like you?

Wherever they are, they are doing what they are doing. I do not know the specifics, but I know there are more than me.

So how long have you been aware? Can you place it in time?

I cannot give you a time in years, but it was before your universe was created.

And did you have other "jobs" before guiding the Zetas?

No, I have always been a guide. I came from Isis straight to the Zeta beings. They are my loves, my pets, my favorites.

Okay, then tell me who these teachers are, these tall white-haired beings with the gowns. Can you say a little bit about them?

They are made of compressed . . . as you would feel it if you were to stand near them—you could have a little joke—you could hold a light bulb near them, and it would light. They are made of an energy that is very much like compressed electricity, and that's why Robert could not channel them.

I see, I see.

Therefore, they are able to traverse the dimensions within the narrow corridor. It is narrow in some dimensions where electricity is welcome and comfortable. As one goes higher in the dimensions, one finds that magnetism is more the accepted energy and the corridor of acceptance for the pure electrical being gets smaller and smaller.

They are able to interact comfortably between the first and the nineteenth dimensions, but past that they are not able to go comfortably. Their job is to help the different dimensions—and Creator beings in some cases—to connect on a personal level with various civilizations from place to place, meaning, of course, that they are not always with the Zetas. Sometimes they travel to other places, but when interacting with civilizations, such as humanoids like Zetas, they will always bring some kind of portal that reveals a kind of energy of beauty and grace on the feeling level with my people. It is true grace.

So they brought that portal that was behind the door that Betty Andreasson . . .

Yes, but if you were to experience it, it wouldn't feel like a portal in the sense of a transit portal. It would feel more like a place—an experience of *being* somewhere, rather than *going* somewhere.

I think that Joopah said that each of the Zeta beings have that experience at least once in their lifetimes.

Yes, and most likely they will begin to have it a little more often. It will help them to make the jump to their lightbodies and the gold color, but in time the energy will have to be more magnetic. The magnetic energy is also necessary to prepare one to make the leap into the gold lightbody. Gold light can access electricity easily, but its natural source is magnetic.

You're magnetic and gold because I can feel it . . . I can see the gold light coming out through Robert.

Yes.

The Bible and Zeta Scientific Communication

Was it sort of a ruse, then, to tell the Zetas that their civilization was going to come to an end to force them to become more feeling?

No. Think about it. They weren't told that their civilization was going to come to an end. They were told the same thing that your civilization was told, and they made the same interpretation that your civilization has made, and that is that life as they know it would come to an end.

That is the purpose of the book of Revelations in the Christian Bible. That can be summed up as, "Life as you know it is going to come to an end." This does not mean that life is going to come to an end, just life as you have known it. The Zetas jumped to the same conclusion that your people did, that life was going to come to an end. You're going to change the way you do things, feel things and experience things. As a result, the way you "be" will change. I mean the way you are, you understand, but "be" is the more appropriate word.

So when the Zetas move to the ninth dimension, will they still be the technological types, the scientific types of the galaxy?

No.

What will their lives be like then?

Some of the hybrids they have created will take over this task. The Zetas will become able to experience the purpose for their being, which is to experience pure thought in grace. Once they have that, they will be satisfied for quite a while. Only later, after experiencing this for a time, will they find another way to serve, but that is not immediate, not imminent.

Zetas and Religion

Oh, that's wonderful. All right. I would like to ask some more questions. In the Fowler book and in many references, what is the connection between Zeta and religion? One being came to Betty Andreasson and talked like someone out of the Bible.

Is this a result of a hypnotic session with Betty, or from her talking? *No, it was a being who brought her back. She was drawn to go through the woods and then up to meet this being, and he was a tall . . . I don't think he was one of the really tall beings, but he was like a lightbeing, and he sounded like some of the quotes from the Bible. Now Betty is very Christian and it could be that it was filtered through her belief system, so that's kind of the question: Did they bring this way of speaking with them, or do they talk to people according to their belief system?*

I think that, as you say, since Betty is believing in the loving aspect of this religion, it was easier to communicate with her in this manner.

As if you were an angel talking like someone in the Bible.

Yes, because that way she could hear it in the manner that was most pleasant and benevolent for her. It is better that way, and she found comfort in it. With other dimensional beings, extraterrestrials and, for that matter, sometimes people on Earth, it is going to be the intention to always talk to one another in the way that is most easily understood.

The Human-Earth Body Connection

Now Zetas are scientists. In the past, we've been told that Earth scientists went to Zeta, and Zeta scientists were here. What is the status of that now, since the ships won't land very often?

The Earth scientists are no longer on Zeta. Some had the privilege of going there for a time, but it is not the case now because of exactly what you said—that the transit mechanism is no longer reliable. However, Zeta scientists can be on Earth, because they can, if necessary, go into bases where they are safe and protected. But it is not the same for Earth people. Earth people cannot exist indefinitely on Zeta, because it does not have the Earth energy. Your bodies are made of Mother Earth, yes? They require interaction with Mother Earth's body.

You can stay away for a time. You can stay away, and when I mean away, I mean well away from the planet. For example, you could go to Mars for a while and feel fine because that's not that far away, but if you were to go outside of the solar system, you would feel increasingly uncomfortable on the feeling/physical level. That discomfort is because Earth's body is essentially what you are on the physical level; her water, her soil is what you are made of, and she is uncomfortable having parts of herself taken elsewhere. And if she is uncomfortable, since your bodies are part of her (not just euphemistically but actually), you will feel that discomfort as your own. This is intended so that you will not stray too far away. That's why, in the future, it will be necessary to develop a means of transit that can get you to where you need to go quickly so that you can return.

Astronauts who stay well away from the Earth—not on the Moon or Mars but out of the solar system—for up to three years might be harmed without Earth contact. There would need to be a significant amount of Earth energy present to protect them from harm. How much? It might take, for instance, a minimum of four hundred cubic yards of Earth soil and several half- or two- or three-ton rocks that a person could lie on. It might require raising grass or vegetables. You'd have to dig in the dirt and lie on it and smell it and feel it. This would comfort the physical body and allow you to remain in space longer, but not indefinitely.

This is in contrast to the Zetas who, because they are made of compressed light, or compressed plasma, can go anywhere?

Yes, because this plasma is a universal. This is intentional, you understand, because your growth here is on Earth. Only in time, when you become the Explorer Race in ships, will your growth continue at a lesser rate by contacting ETs. But their growth will then accelerate, and you will be bringing something to them, and so you will be in service. So, these kinds of voyages will require a lot of rotation of personnel so that the Earth body does not decompose. If the Earth body becomes too lonely for the planet Earth, it will begin to decompose.

The Remaining Zetas on Earth

What about the Zeta scientists on Earth? How many of them are here now?

Not many. No more than five. They are all sheltered.

They are not working with governments?

No.

They are in your bases?

They are in bases that are not ours.

Whose, then?

Other extraterrestrial bases.

But not connected to humans in any place? I see.

No. This came to be necessary when they discovered that even with the best of promises from the heart, promises that were sincerely meant, people higher up in the chain of command would countermand these commitments—work that was being done together was being corrupted. Therefore, the scientists were sequestered.

Say more about that. Why? The secret government was corrupting it? Our government officials? Who? How?

Well, if someone presents to you something about the size of a one-inch cube and says that all the energy you might ever need can be extracted from this cube, it is very hard for even the casual citizen to not be overwhelmed by that. Although this is not unusual in other places away from Earth, it is unusual where you are. Let's just say that it wasn't necessary for the sinister secret government to meddle and that many people became overwhelmed with such potential.

They wanted it for themselves, or they wanted to make money with it?

Or they wanted to use it for military purposes. The idea of, for example, your average fighter jet . . . Think now of how much smaller they could be if they had an infinite amount of energy that would only take up a one-inch cube of space and that weighed almost nothing.

So did the Zetas get all their one-inch cubes back?

In order for the one-inch cubes to work, they have to be activated, and if they are not activated, they basically look like lumps of lead. [Chuckles.]

And needless to say, they are not activated.

No, they are not activated, but, as I say, if they are just sitting there, they look very innocuous.

But they were working side by side with Earth scientists like at Area 51 and some of these places, weren't they?

Only for a short time. It was believed for a time that the base you mentioned, this . . . Well, I think it is actually different digits, but it is in fact a place where some ships are in storage, and there was some cooperation for a time, but it wasn't too long before my people understood that the intention was military rather than transportation for diplomatic and peaceful purposes.

There was a report on television that had an old man, an engineer, who said that he had worked side by side with off-planet beings. I don't know if you can reference that through such a limited description or not, but was that true?

I have heard that this was true, but I do not think that they were my people. Sometimes people can be from other planets and look very much like you and pass a casual inspection easily and yet can make it crystal clear to another person that they are not from Earth.

So are there other beings who look like Zetas but aren't?

Many of the hybrids look like Zetas because they have Zeta parentage, at least going back in ancestry, but you might say they had evolved past a strict lineage.

But they're usually a lot taller, aren't they?

Not a lot. They are sometimes taller. Three and one-half feet to five feet two or five feet four inches tall. Usually not much taller than that.

But five feet instead of three. That's a big difference.

Yes.

So there have been hybrids working on the planet, on Earth?

Only occasionally. It has to be done very carefully.

Because?

Well, as a modern person with your knowledge of modern things, if you were to go back in time to be with warring nations, I do not have to tell you that the overwhelming desire on either side would be to find some weapon they could use to finally put an end to the other side's offenses. They would continue to pick your brain about whatever you could think of, whether you wanted to talk about it or not. You'd never hear the end of it.

Crashes: Rescued Zetas and Imprisoned Zetas

Early on, several ships that crashed were Zeta craft, right? Roswell, Aztec—several of them, right?

There were two.

Only two. Which ones?

I cannot be exact, but one was in New Mexico. The other one was in South America. It was a blessing for the ship in South America, because the local people took them in, hid them and protected them for three days. They could not feed them or give them what they needed, because the Zeta people do not eat what you eat, but the local people took them in and sheltered them. After three days, it was possible to effect a rescue, whereas the ship that crashed in New Mexico . . .

Was that the one we call Roswell?

I cannot say, and I will not. It was almost immediately surrounded by military troops who, under orders from their superiors, essentially imprisoned my people, and—regardless of repeated requests from various extraterrestrials—refused to let them go for exactly the same reason that I mentioned to you if you were to go back in time.

It was not because the military authorities thought you were being invaded. It was because after two weeks or so they thought, "Well, we have these fabulously sophisticated technological people here. What can we get out of them?"

Were some of our military telepaths able to communicate with the Zetas who were in prison?

They were able to send messages, but because of the circumstances . . .

Your people didn't answer.

No, my people answered, but the translators for your people were not able to present the message to their superiors in a way that the superiors accepted. When my people gave messages of love and friendship and said, "Please let us go home," these messages were received with deaf ears, as you say. When the guards, the humans who held my people, demanded to know how the technology worked, the weapons systems and defense systems, my people said only what they had said before.

How many were held for how long? Did any of them get away?

They got away through death.

How many?

Three or four.

So the other ships were not Zeta ships, then? Who were they, the other crashes?

They were not from Zeta, but I do not know where they were from. I do not know everything. I know my people.

The Book and the Keys

When the Zetas gave the book to a person, what was the difference in qualification between giving the book or giving the keys? What was it that they were looking for? What qualities?

Now, you are going to put some of this information in the book that has been given previously, and so I do not have to reiterate—with one exception. Then, I'd say that it was deemed to be of value to have very few people who are keys or who have keys, because one key can unlock many locks, whereas one book can be read or felt by only one at a time. But the key can unlock all the doors, and so fewer keys are better. With the book, the qualification was that the person could be traced directly on a linear soul line, either from the future to the past or the past to the present, your present, as having had Zeta lineage somewhere.

Instead of or sometimes in addition to this, the person had to be seen to have a very vast potential on the spiritual level that he or she would not be able to accomplish in one life, but might be able to with exposure to the book. It was felt that it would be acceptable to loan such a person the book for a few days, as long as it was not left there.

In the book I'm reading, Contact from Reticulum *by Wendelle Stevens, he says that in one of the crashes there was a book. Was one of the books in one of the craft in one of these crashes? It would have to have been the one in New Mexico, if that was the only one we know about that was Zeta.*

That was the one discovered with the symbols?

I think it was in Aztec.

That was not the book we were talking about.

Do you know the origin of the Zetas? Because we talked to one Zeta a couple of nights ago who was from a past lineage of the Zetas. He was here working on the birth cord, learning to love babies [see ET Visitors, *Chapter 11].*

Zetas were originally created as an idea not unlike a drawing board, a thought. They were created by beings you would identify as individuals, and the type of beings who were created were not unlike typical hybrids. The desire was to create a being who would be universal, who could fit in anywhere and who could serve in a multitude of different capacities and still have a sense of individuality, even while being very cooperative—not as a slave, but one who was born to service.

The hybridization process was physical in the beginning, but because of the intention for the race, it was a natural evolution that the early Zetas would eventually desire to clone themselves when they achieved

Courtesy of UFO Evidence

Figure 3.1: Wendelle Stevens, a retired USAF fighter pilot who has devoted more than 50 years of his life to UFO investigation and research. He has written and co-written numerous books on the subject, including UFO: Contact from Reticulum.

a level of perfection that they themselves felt good about. That's when the change in the method of reproduction took place.

The beings who were involved in the creation of this race were, for lack of a better term, various ETs. They were from another universe. I am not aware of the names of these beings, but their primary interest in life was to create species who would be of service, and so it was with that intent that they generated the Zeta Reticulan culture. Perhaps their devotion to service is how the Zeta beings themselves came to be so easily devoted to this cause.

Were they created in the other universe, or did the other universal beings come here?

They were created in this universe. My understanding is that they came here and that they are now in another universe doing something similar, although the beings they are creating there will not look like my friends here.

The William Herrmann Contact

We didn't know that before. We had asked about particular contact cases last night. They also had contact with a William Herrmann. They saw him at great length. They took him on the ship, and they transmitted information to him. He took pictures, color pictures, all kinds of pictures. They called him Andvhati. [Spells the word out.] What is that?

They called him that?

They gave him that status, they said.

How do you pronounce that?

I don't know. I never heard of it before. It was part of his transmissions—where they sent information to him through automatic writing.

I think maybe this didn't come out quite correctly.

What should it be?

I think there is a *c* sound at the end: "Ahn-bah-teek." I think it has to do with a wave, as in an electronic wave—a wave signature. That's how he registered to them, as that particular wave signature, which is one of the ways my people know how to entrust greater information or less information to the individuals—by reading the wave signature.

All right. I see. I think that was misunderstood. They also talk about putting information into the lexicon. Is that the Zetas' body of knowledge or something?

Yes, a lexicon is another word for such a thing.

The Zeta Network

This is one of the pictures he took, this color picture of the ship.

Yes.

So they were evidently very eager to show themselves to him.

They knew that he would have the courage to present their existence to others, and again I believe he lived in a remote place. They believed, especially then, that people who lived out in more remote places would be more independent. If they wanted to keep contact private without ever becoming public, then they would usually contact someone who they were certain would never speak of it for various reasons. But if they wanted some of the information to become public, then they would contact someone who they were sure had the courage and independence to reveal the contact.

Okay, here it says, "Data injected into lexicon." They then say, "Direct observance subject," (which would be Herrmann) "given Andbahti status," and then they talk about "the network" (Herrmann and Stevens, Contact from Reticulum, 393). Is this an organization the Zetas belong to?

It probably refers to the network of various Zeta-type cultures rather than a broader network, so the statements that sound kind of dry are really no different than statements, observations your own scientists would make. It is what you call "tech talk." It is not because they have no feelings. It is because they are trying to be precise, not unlike your own scientific people.

So whenever they talk about the network in here, then, there is an organization of just Zeta cultures that is called the network?

It is not called "the network" per se, but it might be referred to as the network because it would include not only Zeta Reticulum planets where

Courtesy of Wendelle C. Stevens

Figure 3.2: Mr. Herrmann described the ship as a shiny, silvery craft that was forty feet in diameter and shaped like a disc. According to Mr. Herrmann, it emitted a distinct buzzing sound (Contact from Reticulum, *Plate I*).

the culture itself resides, but would, at least to some degree, include other cultures that have profound Zeta connections, which would not exclude your own race. The information would be available to your own race on the deep levels of either the subconscious or the unconscious levels that can be tapped, such as through channeling. In this way you are a portion of the Zeta network.

But not consciously?

Not consciously, but within their context, not only the way they see it but the way it actually functions for them. The network, to them, is not something that is set up as one programs a computer but is an acknowledgment of connected beings, meaning that since you are connected to the past lives on the soul level of Zeta Reticuli, then you are a portion of the network. It might be useful to speak to one of the people who were on the ship—an eyewitness, as you say.

About each case?

Sometimes the same people were involved on more than one occasion, but not always. We will try to arrange that for you.

Excellent, excellent. But you have given us an overview that we didn't have before, and that's just wonderful.

Good. It is my intention to help you understand my people so that you will know that they bear you no harm. Even though their level of social sophistication has not yet reached your level, they are learning and they are open to learning, but they take a while to learn. Your people understand certain dos and don'ts—social niceties, as you say—but my people do not understand that on an interspecies level. For example, when Pleiadians come to interact with my people, the Pleiadians adapt to the style of communication of my people. My people do not adapt to them, because they are not there yet. So their evolution on the mental level is profound, but on the social level . . . Well, there's a way to go yet.

That is also why my people have been so easily duped in the past by people who have said, "Oh yes," as in these exchange scientists' programs. "Oh yes, we will work with you exactly as you wish," and my people, being trusting and not understanding a lie, would not be sophisticated enough to look past the spoken word. So this, you see, is an element of caution that they are learning.

But everyone who interacted with them had their spiritual development accelerated, right?

Yes, because one can be spiritually advanced and even mentally advanced and not necessarily be hip—is that what you say?

[Laughs.] It sounds like Zoosh helped you on that one.

Zoosh is giving me some help in the areas of the "lexicon." [Chuckles.]

Okay. A couple more things. What dimensions do you interact in? Do you have a lightbody form?

One question at a time please. I can go anyplace from two and a half up.

Have you been out of this universe?

Yes. Coming from Isis.

Coming in from Isis, but not since you got here?

No.

Who do you talk to when you need information? To Isis?

I can talk to Isis at any time. Sometimes I'll talk to one of the others: friends, Zoosh . . . and there is another one.

Can you say who?

He is shy.

All right. I just get more curious, you see. [Chuckles.]
It is your nature.

Okay, so do you have something you look forward to?
I am doing what I look forward to.

All right. Do you have peers?
My peers, I would gather, would be the other children of Isis, although I have no idea where they are or what they are doing.

Maybe we could ask Isis sometime. That would be an interesting question.
I do not feel the need to know, but you can ask her anything you wish.

The Ceremony of Renewal

Do you work individually with Zetas? Do you work with them in groups? Do you talk to them? Do you transmit feelings? How do you work with the Zetas?
Yes, all the things you said, and I also work with them through ceremony so that they can feel united—not only in the mind and in the heart, of course, through love, but also so that they can feel union through symbolic methods. This is most helpful in their education as they interact with other species who have symbolic ceremonies they hold dear. It was my suggestion that prompted the phoenix meditation. Because this symbol is understood by many races all over this universe, I felt that it would be a celebration, a ceremony they could share with other races who would be able to identify with some aspect of it and feel that the Zetas had some common ground with them. So this is sort of a philosophical education.

So that is called their Ceremony of Renewal. Do they do it frequently?
From time to time it is done. It is also celebrated on special occasions, such as when Betty Andreasson was there, to honor her and show her that there are similarities between the races, that the goals and ideals are symbolically similar.

How do the Zetas perceive you? Do they see you?
They see me and they can feel me, and so it is a necessity since their mind is refined. They require, for the sake of their own relaxation and, you would say, peace of mind, to have some physical evidence—seeing me, feeling me gives them that physical reassurance that what they are experiencing is an actual physical fact as compared to a meditation.

How do they see you? What is your form?
They see me as a fairly tall lightbeing—a white light with a little amber

mixed in. I cannot describe a face so much, because they do not see one. But they can tell it is a feminine energy.

Oh, your energy is feminine! I'm slow. I didn't get that.

You're not slow. You do not have enough facts to base your observation on.

The reason I asked is because frequently spiritual teachers will appear to the particular race of beings in their own shape so they feel comfortable. That's why I asked.

I have not done that and the Zetas do not require that. They are perfectly comfortable accepting spiritual beings in whatever manner those beings choose to appear.

Organization and Development among the Zetas

What is the organization of the Zetas? There is this unity, but are there elders? Are there decision makers? Is there a council?

No, they are a completely democratic society. They have a union in feelings and they are educated en masse, so there is no hierarchy. There are at times individuals who are meant to be in temporary authority, such as a captain of a ship or a manager of business as you would need to have. These beings will be demonstrably different by having some physical difference, usually in the form of being taller, which is a universal symbol for being different—not necessarily for being better, but being different. It is a way to catch the eye, as it were. But there is not a hierarchical system per se.

Zetas are born fully grown. Are they inculcated or do they have a university system? Do they just tap into the common mind and then they know everything?

They are inculcated. They are given the necessary body of knowledge in order to function as a member of society up to the point that the society has evolved when they come into being, but not past that point, nor do they have to come up at a graduated level. They come up to that point as all other beings do. In this way, they can communicate freely and immediately with understanding.

It sure beats learning to walk and crawl and learning how to be emerged, doesn't it?

It seems that way to you because your life seems slow. But on the other hand, they miss a great deal of education because they are not required to learn it.

What about specialization? If they are particularly interested in a topic, is that available to them, to specialize in a particular discipline or subject?

They can do so if they choose, oftentimes. The capacity of each individual is equal to the capacity of others, so an individual will feel comfortable with the assigned task. It is not slavery or mindlessness. It is more of a "capacity." If you could do anything in your society comfortably, without any strain, you as an individual might have a desire to do one thing over another. And yet if there were no opening for that thing you desired to do, then you would do what was needed to be done until an opening became available, and then you would be doing the thing you want to do.

Do they have a workday and then time for their own interests and hobbies and pursuits ?

No, it is not like that. Their day-to-day life is their hobby, their work, their pursuit. They don't go down to the dance hall and listen to rock-and-roll, but they know how to have fun. They tend to have fun in innocent, childlike ways. This is another reason why they like children, because the way children play is the way they like to play. They like to be silly. They like to do silly, funny things, and they love to entertain children in this way, and so that is their pleasure. One of the reasons they created one or two of the hybrid societies was to have children available, because they cannot access human children so much anymore. They thought, "Perhaps it would be fun if we had some of our own, and then we can have fun and see how that works."

But Joopah said they've been hybridizing for 400,000 years.

But you have to remember what they means. It means they have gone back 400,000 years from your present.

I didn't understand that.

Why would you? But that is the way they talk. It doesn't mean that they have been working on this for 400,000 of their years. It means they would go back 400,000 years, say, from your point in time to involve different races, hybridizing if they chose to, and they have not gone back in time further than that.

Okay, I'm glad you cleared that up. So when I asked how long they have been doing this in the United States, and they said five thousand years, that means they went back five thousand years in time?

Yes, they went back.

Zetas and Humans Are Naturally Complementary

I have a question before you go, but what would you like to say about the Zetas, rather than just responding to my questions?

My people and your people are much more complementary than you realize. We have some things that are similar, such as the way your scientists talk and our scientists talk and such as the way my people like to play and your children like to play. We have plenty of common ground, and even better, we have things we do that you would like to be able to do. In this way, we can complement you, and you have things that you do that my people have not yet learned how to do. Also complementary. It is easier to do the work with someone who can do something you can't do, but you need to have it done.

You will find in time that the relationship between these different species, you and the Zeta people, will come to be affectionate and sincere, although in the beginning it will seem austere and diplomatic. You will get past that as soon as you realize that the way to my people's hearts is through fun in a childlike, loving and pleasant sense—not in a cruel sense, the way children learn how to be from adults who don't understand that all children really want is love and happiness. When you understand this about my people, you will be able to immediately break down social barriers and communication will get better. I think that's not so different from the way on your planet.

Well, when humans go out to travel to other planets, will Zetas have all gone to the ninth dimension yet? I don't know how fast they're going to be moving. Will they still be out there, and will we meet them?

They'll still be out there. It will take them a while. Plus, once you begin to establish interspecies diplomacy on a heartfelt level, you will get more cooperation, and you will have opportunities to travel on very high-speed ships that you do not have now, and your cosmonauts and astronauts will be able to go to the Pleiades in a day and a half and have a year or two there. They will be able to come back in a day and a half and be dropped off at your space station, for instance.

You are building a space station. I support that. I think it would be good for you to build several space stations, because they would be like way stations, and I think you will find that this will be most satisfactory once extraterrestrials believe you are established in a heart-centered diplomatic arena.

That's wonderful. We only have to open our hearts. We don't have to understand all the technology of interplanetary travel before we can do it.

That's correct, and that is often the case for civilizations that are ultimately embraced. You will take 1,000 or 1,500 years to develop some of this time traveling, travel that is done benevolently and benignly, with no discomforting effects for anyone. You won't have to, because others will provide it for you.

Wonderful.

This is a rule. As you serve, so shall you be served. This is what you might call my people's golden word.

I can't wait until we communicate. Okay, so we'll talk again as soon as I have more questions.

Certainly, or one of the other representatives might be available.

Thank you. Have a wonderful life.

Good night.

Diplomacy and ET Contacts

Sha Don
November 4, 1998

My name is Sha Don. I was in charge of coordination on several of the flights that picked people up in the U.S. and other places. I have been present for several of these experiences. We do not have what you call a captain of a vehicle; rather, a "coordinator" is what we say.

Welcome, welcome. Which people did you interact with?

If you can ask their names, then I can consult my memory tableau; I do not identify them by name but rather by appearance.

Okay. Betty and Barney Hill?

No.

Betty Andreasson?

Yes. I was not in charge then, but I was assisting the individual who was in charge.

William Herrmann?

Yes, I was present. I was the coordinator on the flight that interacted with this person.

Someone named Moody?

No.

Colborne?

No.

Charmer?
No.

Travis Walton?
No.

The Experience of William Herrmann

Perhaps these two are enough to start with. I would speak of the man, Herrmann. Do you have questions?

Absolutely. He was taken aboard and he learned incredible amounts of information that you inculcated into him. He was given information on propulsion, and then on his last visit he said, "Now I understand everything." But then he refused to talk about it anymore. His wife threatened to leave him. His church excommunicated him. His house was burned down and everyone said he was consorting with the devil because of the nature of his church. We lost track of him in 1983, I think, right after this last meeting. Can you tell me what you were attempting to do with him? What was the aim of the information you gave him? Describe your purpose in talking to him.

Which question do you wish to ask? One at a time, please.

What was your purpose in contacting him?

This person has had more than one life on our planets and other places where we are influential. He let it be known through his soul that we would be welcome and that he would welcome us, which he always did.

This knowledge was placed in him, and then you would send further knowledge via a beam while he did automatic writing of symbols. Correct?

Close enough.

Would you describe it?

It is similar to a beam, and this description might have been given because it is understandable. It is a series of bursts of information that, if concentrated, would look like a beam. But if you could examine it closely, it would look more like blocks of information with gaps in between. The gaps have to do with changes of subject.

And that causes his hand to spontaneously write shorthand symbols?

Not exactly spontaneously. By the time he was doing this writing, he was allowing himself to move. Totally spontaneous motion usually results in a messy piece of paper, but allowance with discernment creates a readable—or at least understandable—text, something with some kind of clarity.

So if someone could read the language, he or she could read these pages of symbols that he wrote.

Yes, and a sensitive could touch the symbols, although they would also pick up the energy of the paper. They would be able to get the general meaning on the basis of touching the symbols but, as you say, someone familiar with the language, or at least its root, could discern it.

Is this the Zeta language? Is this the way you would write your language?

We do not write anything. We will use symbols at times for clarity when beings, people other than ourselves, are aboard the ship. These are not unlike your universal symbols, those that you see these days, but we do not have text. We retain information in our minds or, if necessary, in a tableau (as we call it), which is similar to computer memory but is entirely sequential rather than in separate bits. Yet if we were to have this language in writing, it would appear like that. That writing is more associated with the past on our planets, where the thoughts and philosophies of our people were put into such symbols for dissemination to peoples other than our own, should they desire to understand us better.

And would the writing look like that on the book of light?

Yes, yes.

Sometimes you would send information to Herrmann and he would type it, one letter at a time, on a typewriter.

Obviously he did not do this very much, because it was so slow, but . . .

The Purpose of Contact with Herrmann

Was your purpose in giving some of the information to him—like your propulsion system and scientific information—that it be disseminated all over the United States?

No, our purpose in giving it to him was that if he chose, he could disseminate the information to whomever he chose or felt could use it in the most benevolent and beneficial way. It was not intended exclusively for the use of any nationalistic state, but rather for Earth people at large. Toward the end of our contacts, it was understood by this man that he would soon understand all that we were about and have a greater grasp of the future development of national and international destiny. I believe this occurred for him at the right time in his personal life, because when those around you have mistaken your purpose, it is some comfort when you are equipped with such truths.

They certainly did mistake his purpose. Were you aware that everything he wrote to Wendelle Stevens was intercepted by someone, some governmental agency? Were you aware of that?

Stevens's mail has been intercepted for a very long time, and so it does not surprise me.

But that didn't bother you?

We do not feel that it created harm. The harm that came to this man's life had nothing to do with those who read that communication.

I only have information about Bill Herrmann in this book (Wendelle Stevens' Contact from Reticulum Update) up until 1983. Did you contact him after that?

Yes, occasionally. Once the telepathic link is established, then further contact is inevitable.

Is he okay now? Is he alive and well? His last communication said, "I understand everything now." What did he understand? Can you share that with us?

He understood his purpose, his reason for being. He understood why your communities and standards and ethics were the way they were. He understood what would come. He understood why, and perhaps most importantly, he understood the purpose of our visits and the ultimate expression of your societies as a whole.

Is that something you can talk about here, or was that for just his information?

It was given to him and a few other contactees so that they might be, for the most part, influential behind the scenes and occasionally influential in the public eye. We did not want to involve ourselves overly in your society. Rather, we wished to provide your society with the wisdom and insight it needs to make informed decisions.

Well, can you talk to our leaders about some of this information?

Perhaps.

The Overall Purpose of Contact

Would you like to discuss your purpose on the planet? I think we're somewhat aware, but can you talk about your overall purpose?

Our overall purpose is to understand our soul past and make some greater leap of faith in our present in order to be able to most easily establish our society for its true value. For us, the past—our own and that of others, if they relate to us—is vitally important. Since we have discovered that you have a profound connection to us on the soul line, we have reinterpreted a great deal of the information we have gathered from interacting with your human race over these many years. Now, are you asking about our purpose here on Earth?

Yes.

Our purpose is also to provide this knowledge and wisdom to your people internationally, to individuals who can and would speak of it, either couched in philosophical terms, or—in certain conditions— spoken of as a fact of reporting.

So when Bill Herrmann understood his purpose, was it different from that of any other humans on the planet?

Generally speaking, everybody's purpose on the level of human beings is similar: to inform and to provide insightful wisdom on the basis of future events as they may unfold, and especially to encourage the transformation of your peoples away from the glamour and glitter of technology for its own sake and toward technology for the sake of the human heart. The latter would (and perhaps will) provide benevolent living conditions for all humans on Earth, and we believe in the utmost in this course.

So are you still in this area, or are you speaking from a long way away?

The latter. I speak to you now from my home planet.

But can you see what's going on here, or do you just know?

See you?

No, the planet and the state of humanity at this moment.

I see what is on the tableau. I do not visually see the planet and its people.

But there have been ships here recently enough that you have up-to-date information?

Maybe not up-to-date, but recent. The tableau is fed not only by our own peoples, but by all extraterrestrial races with whom we are in benevolent connection—and to some extent by the projected messages from some individuals on Earth.

Nuclear Risk Reduced

The reason for my question is that when you first talked to Bill Herrmann, you were warning the world through him of potential nuclear destruction. What is your opinion of where we are at this moment?

The chances of nuclear bombs being fired from one country at another have now been greatly lessened. However, they still exist—partly because the technology that is required to make a bomb is more easily obtained these days, even by an individual with the motivation and the medium of exchange. As such, the risk in terms of, say, a terrorist act is much greater than an exchange of missiles between major countries of influence. An exchange of missiles between major nations is almost negligible, but there is still risk of it between smaller countries that have certain strategic materials and geographic importance. So there is still a risk, though I must say that the risk has been reduced.

Assessing the Spiritual Awakening of Humanity

What is your perception of the level of spiritual awakening of humanity? Did you see a change from the time you first came until now?

There has been some change. There has been a greater understanding of what is "not so," which is often the precursor to what "is so," meaning the universal truths that unite us all. There has been some progress, especially in the Northern Hemisphere where progress was most needed. In the Southern Hemisphere, there has been less progress, but they were further along than the Northern Hemisphere, and so that does not represent a problem.

Do you mean as far as an open heart and a loving understanding?

Yes, as far as having greater compassion and acceptance, generally speaking. So there has been progress, but there is still much to do. As long as people focus more on what they disagree on or the differences in general and overlook their similarities—which are always greater—there will be problems.

But there's a lot more hope now?

There is more hope. A moment. [Being blows the channel's nose.] A curious sensation . . .

How does it feel to have a body with fingers, toes and ears . . . and hair?

Again, a curious sensation. We are humanoids like you, but you are different from us.

Have you ever done anything like this before?

Yes.

You have channeled through beings before?

Yes, but not on this planet.

Through other humanoid-type beings?

Through water beings on Sirius. They wished to know about us before they came to Earth, since they seemed to know things we did not know. I am not that old. They can do this through time. We cannot. But they have great spiritual advancement. Some of those beings contacted myself and others and wanted to know about us in general. Looking back on it now, I realize that they knew about our connection to the Explorer Race who would be coming to Earth, but we did not know at that time. Nevertheless, it is our intention to be open about our culture and peoples to those who inquire.

Wow, that must have been a different feeling. A water being.

It was unique.

The Zeta History with Earth

Okay, I'd like a little history from your perspective. When did you first come to this planet? You've been coming here forever, haven't you?

Oh, you are speaking about our people?

I'm sorry. The Zetas have always been coming to this planet, right?

You measure time differently than we do. If I say we have always come to the planet, it would be true, and yet you might say that we have been coming in a narrow window from a certain recent date forward. But since we can travel in time, we can come through that time window and then go into the past. In this way, I can state that we have always come to the planet. It has been in this space, however.

I understand that.

Both statements would be true, say from the late 1940s onward, plus always. It appears to be paradoxical unless you understand the time travel aspect.

Okay, I'm glad you cleared that up. So from our point of view, let's say you came in the 1940s. Did you make any agreements with any governments? Were you involved in the meeting at Edwards Air Force Base with Eisenhower?

I was not present, but some of my people were, plus other extraterrestrials were present in meetings that took place between extraterrestrials and those on Earth who possessed weapons of mass destruction or the capacity to produce them, such as the Soviet Union and a few others. Our people then made some connection with the Soviet Union and the people of the United States, yes. The intention at that time was to allay the great risk of a nuclear exchange in the early 1950s between the Soviet Union and the United States, which would have . . .

Obliterated life on Earth.

No, the reason it wouldn't have is because there weren't that many bombs then. The U.S. had a few by that time and the Soviet Union would have had a couple. The Soviet Union would not have used a missile system to release the bombs in the U.S. but would have used couriers (you say spies) or possibly a ship, a water-going ship. And so the intention was to allay the potential for catastrophic loss of life and certain delay in your spiritual and feeling progress. This is why the governments mentioned were contacted, because they had such weapons.

It was hoped that the governments who had these weapons would be open to establishing a public contact with ETs. We were given permission to invite the Earth people into an outer-perimeter, loose-knit organization of extraterrestrial compadres, mostly involved in trade as compared to diplomatic inner circles, but the suspicious nature of the Earth people at that time prevented such parties from choosing to go public, and so the gifts we gave and those that were returned to us remained unknown by the mass of the people.

Other Races Visit Earth with the Zetas

Specifically, what other races were there with the Zetas?

There was a Pleiadian. The governments of the United States and the Soviet Union were shocked. The people were shocked to see an extraterrestrial who looked exactly like a human being. They were perhaps stunned. They seemed to be more accepting of those of us who looked different. I think hindsight would suggest that, if we had to do it over, the Pleiadian might not have come along: These representatives of the government felt more threatened by such benevolent peoples as Pleiadians because they looked like Earth people and could, in the minds of these individuals, perhaps walk about on the Earth unnoticed. This greatly frightened these military people, even though they felt that the Pleiadians were beautiful, gentle people. Looking past that, they felt that their gravest threat was from these look-alikes, as they would call them.

Obviously, those others of us could not walk around in public without being identified as non-Earthborn citizens. There was someone from Andromeda who did not look exactly human, but with a disguise might pass a casual inspection. There was someone from Sirius who did not look human.

What did he look like?

You would look at him and you would say, "This is a man-fish." His being had been adapted by the people of Sirius to be able to breathe air for a while, but in his natural habitat he would use his gills. He had arms and legs and a body, but his face clearly suggested an aquatic being.

Okay, and what did the Andromedan look like?

Not too much different from your people, but the head, the hemisphere for the brain, was larger—just large enough to look not quite human.

But as tall? Five feet six or six feet or something?

Taller.

Seven feet?

Closer to that.

Who represented the Zeta?

Individuals from our planets.

How were they chosen?

The mission was needed and they were available. It is not something we try to do or want to do or are told to do. They were available.

They were considered diplomats? Were all of them considered diplomats?

My people are not so very diplomatic, and so they had no formal training like the Pleiadians and Sirians and Andromedans, who all had formal training. My people were not talking so much to the Earth people, and that's why the Earth people got the idea that we were automatons or some kind of a slave race. [Laughs.] But in fact, since everyone was in agreement that my people had no training to communicate with species totally unlike us or ones that had no consciousness of extraterrestrials, we stayed out of conversation. Therefore, we were perhaps misunderstood, but we felt that would be an acceptable risk.

I see. I think at some point, someone said—I don't remember who—that there was a hybrid there. Was that true?

It depends on how you think about it. The being was not interacting with anyone in the United States but was present on the vehicle.

The Tableau

You all belonged to an association of some kind, right?

It is not a club. It is similar to when people on your planet are like trading partners as well as people who see each other for pleasure, but often it has to do with some commercial aspect too, such as trading. It is like that. It is also a loose-knit organization designed to create and sustain compatibility among all peoples so that misunderstandings do not take place. You can see how misunderstandings might take place between completely different cultures that have mannerisms and symbols and so on that might contradict other cultures. So there need to be organizations to smooth things over and maintain clear communication. It is more like that rather than an actual organization of states like you have in the United Nations.

What do you call it? What do you refer to it as? Is that what the network is?

It is called many things. Some beings refer to it as a network, because it is truly a network, but it has many names depending upon the culture asked.

Well, what do you call it?

I don't even have a word for it. I just know it exists, but our people do not have that many words. If you broke our communication down into numbers of words, ours would have fewer words than the Spanish language.

Transcending Language

Is what Herrmann called the "lexicon" your computer translator?

It might be closer to what I would call the tableau.

How can you describe it? Is this where you store your knowledge or your data stream or something?

I cannot say we store it there, because that suggests that it was put in by someone. I would rather say that . . . Did I not say this already? I would rather say that . . .

I see. It's fed in by everybody. But how?

It is available to us.

Okay, but you do have some kind of a translator, because the words in English that came to Herrmann were sort of stiff and not always related to the meaning as he thought it was?

Yes. We have a translation system, a mechanical device that can provide elaborate and specific answers given the device's interpretation of either the question or the need for information.

Did it take you a long time to gather all the Earth words and put them into it? How did you . . .

We didn't. We have no Earth words in it.

How does it translate to English, then?

It is like this. If you took a Beethoven symphony and played it and then played a country music tune, they would not be compatible, but they use the same notes. It is not that the machine, if we can call it that, has any language in it. It utilizes and synthesizes the sounds of one language into the sounds of another language without needing to know or have any dictionary of language at all.

That's amazing. Is that how you talk to people when you take them aboard a craft, or do you do it telepathically? They report that they hear it like surround sound.

Sometimes we use the device. Other times we are able to perform the same function without the device, but the "technology" is identical.

Reasons for Involvement: Cold War

Okay. That was a detour. How did the decision to come to the Earth and talk to these governments that have weapons of mass destruction come about among this loose association?

We were informed—initially by the Pleiadians, who feel a great sense of kinship with you—that the situation of an emergency existed. If enough individual planetary bodies approved of contact, then they would appreciate it if we could attend to this matter at once, since they felt that an atomic exchange was imminent. Under the circumstances, we acquiesced, although it had been originally intended that contact would not take place until 1952.

What year were you notified?

The request and contact took place in 1947.

And why did they want to wait five years?

I do not understand. It wasn't a matter of waiting five years. The intention was to contact you in 1952. Your question would be the opposite and has been answered, meaning that the plan was to contact you in 1952. We contacted you five years earlier, not because we wanted to wait until 1952. Understand?

The contact was in 1952, wasn't it?

The contact was in 1947, five years before the intended contact date.

So our information is wrong, then.

The contact was in 1947, not too long after the end of the Second World War.

So you met with our President Truman, then?

My people met with this person's representative. The President's people considered it a security risk for a president to be there, and so it was his trusted representatives who met us. It was the same for the Soviet Union; we did not meet with the head of their government there, either.

I see. The instance we know about is completely different, then, because that was in 1952 or 1953 with Eisenhower. So where did you meet in the United States? Do you know where? Do you know what state or what part of the country?

It was at a major military base that is still in operation in the continental United States. I can say no more specifically than that.

Fifty years later? Somebody is telling you not to say it?

The request has been given to me and I must honor it.

Who is requesting it? Zoosh told us that there was a fifty-year secrecy commitment. Is that true, that there was a fifty-year commitment to secrecy? But that's over.

Not for those who are concerned.

Who were the representatives of the president?

I must be vague, but I will say that one person in one of the men's families is still active politically, and he came to be known later for his international political agreements. Those who met my people (meaning I was not there) were influential people in the government of the United States or associated with the government.

Okay. Who was the spokesman? The Pleiadian?

The Pleiadian was the initial spokesman. It was thought that someone who looks like you would be considered less threatening, but that was not the case, as it turned out. The Andromedan was the chief communicator. The Pleiadian first gave greetings and pleasantries, and then the Andromedan spoke in detail.

The Offer of Peace Refused

Okay, so can you briefly summarize their message, request or communication?

The message, summarized, was: "If you as a country will make a commitment not to use nuclear weapons unless they have been used on you first . . ." That's as good as we could get, and it wasn't our initial negotiating point, but that was the ultimate agreement. Would you want it like that, or would you want what they originally said?

Any information you give us will help.

What they originally said is, "If you will give up your pursuit of nuclear weapons and weapons of mass destruction, we will provide you with an unlimited source of energy that will last your people forever."

Oh my God. And they wouldn't do it?

Think of the political climate of the time. You were just over this huge war and another one was coming right down the road soon for the United States and other places, so the military people won the day, although the nonmilitary people were in favor of it. The demand or negotiating point from the government representatives was, "How can we be safe in a dangerous world?" Our people said, "We will extract the same pledge from all others who represent or may come to represent a threat with such weapons, and we will provide you with a means to detect such technology being produced or deployed. Or, if you prefer, we would provide you with an authority source to stop such production and deployment," meaning volunteer ETs would have the authority to eliminate such weaponry.

You offered to provide something like a monitor, but then it ended up that they made an agreement not to shoot first. Is that basically what you got?

Yes, ultimately it was agreed upon by all sides that no one would shoot first. It wasn't the best outcome, but it was better than what some felt could be accomplished. There were people even on the ship who felt that your people would be obliterated by 1959, but I am happy to say they were wrong.

I think we've got a lot of angels.

. . . also some very brave people in a position to not only lose their jobs because of their decisions, but in some cases to lose their lives. Decisions were made by courageous human beings to not attack or to not defend with total destruction when an unintentional or a minor attack took place. The next point of serious danger took place in the Korean War when there was almost a nuclear confrontation. We did not intercede, but that is why there were those onboard the ship who thought you would never get past the 1950s.

Did those same courageous humans make the tough decisions not to do it?

Yes, certain leaders of certain countries—some of whom were executed, and others who were shamed and stripped of their former glories and respect—made decisions either not to shoot back or to wait and see what the actual intention was. Enough of these incidents took place so that by the time the United States had its confrontation with the Soviet Union over the Cuban circumstance, there was the knowledge by both sides that it was possible to not constantly push for confrontation but to accept some lesser position gracefully. It took great courage on Chairman Khrushchev's part to withdraw the missiles, and then he was . . .

Retired.

Yes. So, because of decisions like that and others in other countries, your people made it past the 1950s and more. So my people and others, other extraterrestrials, breathed a sigh of relief or said, "You have managed it somehow." Some of the people were too sensitive to stay too close because of the anxiety of the situation.

Some of your people?

Some of the extraterrestrials. My people were not affected by such feelings. We are protected from such external feelings, and so we were able to be closer and just allow it if your people did destroy each other. Of course, your souls would not be destroyed, and so we were able to accept whatever the outcome would be, although we are happy that you were able to maintain your civilizations.

The Explorer Race and the Yellow Book

But you're aware of the incredible importance of the Explorer Race, right?

Yes.

So it was much more than one little group of happy shooters on a faraway planet.

But we did not know that then.

When did you learn about it?

We did not know about the ramifications of the Explorer Race until recently. We did not always know, even though we could travel in time. We were screened from this information until recently.

Then how did you learn it?

We were told by our advisers. They explained to us that we had not been told before because the advisers felt that we might become overly attached to your survival and unable to work with you objectively.

I see. So then you don't necessarily know the future. What was that famous yellow book that talked about the future, then?

It was not our book.

I didn't know that. Whose book was it?

It was a book from another civilization that was intended to be a gift to one of the governments of your world, but as it turned out, a different government obtained it.

What civilization gave Earth the yellow book?

All I know is that it came through Andromeda. I am not sure where it originated in idea or where it was constructed, but the Andromedans presented it originally. I cannot state for a fact that they created it.

Well, you're certainly clearing up a lot of misconceptions, here. All right, so I assume the good old United States ended up with it.

Yes.

Okay, and it went off into the future.

It reported the potential future events on the basis of the present and the past, meaning a certain timeline. It would, of course, become less accurate should the timeline become future oriented or more benevolent, but if it remained tied to the past and old disagreements and angers, then the predictions would be of a very high potential in terms of accuracy. Of course, now you are beginning to move onto a slightly more spiritual path, and so some of the predictions will gradually become less accurate.

Sinister Secret Government Intervention

I know that you are familiar with what we call the secret government.

Yes, the sinister secret government is a good term for them because they are so very shortsighted.

So they were using that information in their plans and predictions?

Yes.

Supposedly there was a meeting at Edwards Air Force Base in 1952 or 1953 with Eisenhower and a similar group as you discussed with Zetas and Pleiadians and others. Is that not true? Is that disinformation about the 1947 meeting?

I think it is possible that President Eisenhower was at a meeting where extraterrestrials were present, but I do not think my people were attending that meeting, which would make sense, since at the time it was considered more advantageous to have meetings with beings who looked like you and caused you to feel reasonably comfortable. My people sometimes unnerve you because of our inner eyelid that gives us the appearance of having a huge black eye. This eyelid is like a screen—not dissimilar to you wearing dark glasses. Our eyes are light sensitive, and so we must use this inner eyelid when there are lights brighter than we are comfortable with.

I didn't know that. So your eye is not that large under the black eyelid.

No, the actual eye is smaller.

There's so much we don't know. That's why we want to put these books out, because eventually, hopefully soon, we'll all be meeting, and we'd like to know as much as possible about all of you.

I can assure you that before the meeting takes place there will be attempts to communicate, not only with governments, but also with those who disseminate information, meaning that there will be communications to news services, to the media, perhaps even to casual communicators such as radio operators, who are private, perhaps even some well-known and influential people.

Is this in the planning stages now?

No, the plan is already fixed.

It's fixed?

And will only be altered should there be a radical change here, but none is foreseen.

Can I ask what date? All you can say is that you can't tell me.

You can ask. [Chuckles.] That's a joke.

[Laughs.] That's a joke. Okay. This time travel thing—if I were able to get to Zeta at this moment in this time, would I see you there or would I just see your past?

If you were able at this moment . . .

To travel as fast as you can to your planet, would I see you sitting there right now?

No. In terms of your time, I am utilizing the curvature of space. It is not clear to you. It is the same thing as saying that I am a million years in your future, but if you traveled instantaneously from where you are now to where my planet is, you would not be able to find me.

What would I find?
Others like me but not me. I would not have been born yet.

But in my time now—this time that you are talking to me from my end—would you, the Zetas, already be cloned? Would you already have a communal ability to interact mentally in a communal way, similar to what you are?
Similar, but not quite as advanced. Advanced from our point of view.

What dimension are they in?
Five.

And you're still in six. You haven't made the jump?
I am in seven.

When you say that it's like a million years in my future, then . . .
To give you the feeling, it is easier to use such terminology, but it isn't factually a million years.

But there's no other way to explain it to me?
That is the best analogy available.

All right.
If you can completely understand $E=MC^2$, then you will have some greater understanding of my analogy.

All right. We'll stick with the million years.
Well, it is a useful euphemism.

Zeta-Human Soul Lines and the Communicator

I've never understood from what I've heard or read about our souls being in your past. Last night, the daughter of Isis, one of your guides, talked about your creation, and then according to Zoosh there were these wild emotional and sexual orgies that caused you to seek something like being calm. Where does the human soul fit in? At what point? Were we the wild emotional ones?
That's an interesting question, although not true, but I like the way you are thinking. We as a people do not see any difference in the soul of a cat or the soul of a human or the soul of a Zeta. Souls manifest as different types of beings according to their personal agendas, and so the idea that many of our people—not all, but many—were once your people is reasonable and easily understood by us.

Oh, it's the other way around. Many Zeta souls once inhabited bodies of humans.
Yes.

Oh, I had it backward. I see. Have you been able to trace on the soul line? Were you able to find someone on Earth who was your past life?
Yes. A person in the countryside of France in the year 1407 A.D.

Fascinating.
A woman.

A woman. All right. I understand it now. I didn't before.
Good.

Let's go back to the Herrmann thing again, because that's as far as I've read. He said that in the last encounter listed in this book, which was 1982 or 1983, there was an elder onboard the ship—Shaugel, the elder. Is that someone you're familiar with?

I am not, but I believe what this man says. It is certainly possible. After all, he was being entrusted with not only more wisdom but the insight to grasp its significance. That an elder should be aboard to communicate in some way that should be more accessible by this man makes complete sense.

Okay, can you expand on that a little? You've always said that you're all equal and the same, except maybe like the coordinator on the ship. Do you have a group of elders on your planet, or do you have a council, or do you have . . .

The term elder would have been given to this man so that he would understand that he was being honored and that the communicator had capacities beyond the normal levels of communication of my people. But elder or not, he would have been an equal.

So there isn't any differentiation?

There is no council of elders who advise us, no. But such a presentation to other species like yourself would be more palatable to you. You honor your elders, yes?

Yes, absolutely.

So this way of referring to this person who communicated to that man would be easily understood and received with honor.

I see. I understand. In 1947, when your offer was refused, had you started the interaction with humans to do the hybridizing?

We had not by then, but by the time the early 1950s came around we were beginning to suspect that we were dying out, and we requested permission from all beings we were in contact with to begin hybrid programs. Everyone said yes, and our people received a yes from Earth as well. Some governments wanted a trade, and we provided a small communications device as a trade. The device would not allow the communicator to have a conversation. In a narrow band, it might allow the communicator to see things on other nearby planets—Mars, the Moon—but you would not be able to talk to people. This was considered a satisfactory exchange. Not all parties demanded that on your world, but one in particular insisted and another said that it would be nice, and so it was granted in both cases.

Okay. So who has those now? The secret government?

The sinister secret government has one. One other is in private hands, meaning an individual. The one in the Soviet Union is in private hands at this time.

The Hybrid Program and "Abductions"

All right. I'll leave that one alone. Okay, so in the early 1950s until when? How long did this hybrid program go on? How many years?

It went on until the early 1960s. There was also traveling into the past by our people and occasionally into the short-range future, but the program itself, as far as the participation of Earth people, was terminated in its more frequent encounter level in about 1962 or 1963.

So, ten or eleven years? And this was in every country on the planet?

Yes, but in most countries people were more openly volunteering. We would then contact different races, of course. It is unusual for a planet to have so many variations in race within this same type of being on this same planet, and so we went to different races, and some of them were very cooperative and others were less so.

So it was only in the United States, then, that we have what are called the "abductions?"

These were never abductions. They were invitations, and they happened globally.

I know, but from the human end . . .

No, not from the human end.

They are called abductions.

No, they are not, and I do not wish to be stubborn, but this term abductions is a recent term and was not used by the participants. So I cannot agree that they are called that. They have been called that by people who were not invited on the ship and so these were not participants. They were called abductions in order to make it more frightening.

For what purpose?

Perhaps to instill a sense of urgency in the reader, or in the case of investigators also.

All right.

That is my perception.

I think somebody last night said that also. It is a very useful thing to know. So many of the cases that I have in my library that are with Zetas . . . some of them talk about sexual contacts. But that was mostly rare, the taking of egg and sperm, yes?

That was very short lived. Mostly it was a gentle scraping of surface cells—from an arm usually—but the sperm and egg happened for a short time during which some of our technicians felt that this particular type of matter might be developed faster into beings. But as it turned out, it represented no advantage and was dropped from the program.

So you used your normal cloning method, but with DNA from humans?
Yes.

Something just went through my head. There has been so much, if you pardon the expression, bullshit about the Grays. Who are they? What is that? They're not talking about the Zetas, are they? What are they talking about?
They are talking about one of the hybrids that we have been involved in, and sometimes it is more than one different hybrid race. A massive amount of disinformation has been put out about these beings. I will give you the basic energy of these beings, comparatively speaking, toward the average Earth person, and that is that these beings are naïve and therefore can be slightly foolish at times, but they are not malevolent or lethal. This is a massive disinformation campaign to encourage distrust of extraterrestrials, which I have to say has largely not influenced the general public. The average citizen believes that extraterrestrials exist, and fully two thirds of them believe that extraterrestrials are benevolent. The other third isn't sure. That's all. Not many people believe that there are such things as malevolent extraterrestrials. Maybe they believe it for a moment at a moving picture but they get over it.

Well, there's a joke that more people believe in extraterrestrials than in Social Security.
Well, I can assure you that Social Security will have a good life.

All right [chuckles]. But say more. I'm confused about it, too. Who are the people using some of these hybrids as dupes?
No, no. Not using them as dupes. The information is false.

Oh, you said that they were very naïve and so I thought that someone was using them for some . . .
No, I am saying that they can sometimes be foolish, meaning that they can act in a manner that can be considered silly, but they are not being manipulated.

They're not being manipulated by anybody. Then what are they doing here?
This whole thing about the so-called Grays . . . Let me say this: 93 percent of what you have heard or read is not true. There is only about 7 percent of the information that is true, and that is because these races are not encouraged to interact with species who are more socially evolved than they are. You as a race are more socially sophisticated than these people. They were allowed to interact with you a little bit, but that's all, and often the interaction

bordered on the childlike—if not actually juvenile. Sometimes people would describe the interaction as almost teasing, which is like a child.

Okay, help me understand, then. They did come to this planet from wherever and interact with humans, then?

Yes.

What was their purpose?

To learn and understand. And, of course, because we were coming here, they wanted to know why. What was the attraction? We had to give them some autonomy to find their way since we were involved in their creation, but after a time we discouraged them from connecting with you. However, there were a few members who were captured by malevolent forces such as the sinister secret government who managed to clone them and create a race of beings in the image of the sinister secret government.

Okay. So that's how it happened. [Cat meows.] Do you have cats on Zeta Reticuli?

We do not. We are very intrigued by them. They are a very advanced race. You are most fortunate to have them with you.

I dearly love both of them.

They have profound capacities.

Roswell and Other Crashes

All right, so did they crash at Roswell?

I and my compadres are saying little about the Roswell crash, because it is still a bone of contention between various extraterrestrial civilizations and the government of the United States, and so it would be better for us at this time to say no more about this. Perhaps at a later time we can be more specific.

All right. I'll certainly honor that. Can you talk about a crash that we have heard about that we probably thought were Zetas but that were in fact the hybrids the secret government were able to clone?

The crash where they were captured by the sinister secret government took place near the Arctic Circle, and you probably would not have heard of it. There may have been a story that filtered out.

No, I never heard anything. What year was that?

In the 1950s.

So they cloned them. And what is the situation now, today? Do they still exist?

They still exist. This is a further challenge to the peoples of my planets and the sinister secret government. We do not hold the government of the United States and other world governments responsible in any way, but we will ultimately resolve this matter.

Well, I think that you're being very forbearing. Herrmann talks about a planet called 50 Zone 754DA where they captured one of your ships and you brought in a lab ship. Is that like a mothership or is that a scientific ship?
     And what else did he say?

How did you do it?
     The first ship that came couldn't really do very much all by itself, but when the lab ship came and the other ship was trying to work with the orbiters, they were called, and it accidentally ran into one of them and most of them were killed. The lab ship let out eighteen little ships and went down and rescued the ship and took it back up. Sometimes my people have been assertive to regain our citizens, but we are more gentle with the people of Earth because of your influential potential.

I mean, you're perfectly capable of coming to get them?
     I am authorized to say that we have the capacity to do whatever is necessary to retrieve our citizens, but we do not exercise that capacity because of the importance of the citizens of Earth. It is our intention at all times to be diplomatic with you of Earth. Should this have occurred on another planet where diplomacy was not such an urgent factor, the incident would have been resolved within a minute or two.

Universal Implants

Tell me about implants—little BB-like things put in people's noses and eyes. What was that for?
     This was done massively in the beginning, having to do with the desire by some of my people to see if it would be possible to accelerate your interest in the universal community. The device would support certain benevolent urges within you and attempt to create an artificial (as we understand it now) balance for you, but even at that time we did not understand the complexity of the human being. In those early days when the devices were installed, the understanding of the human being was more of a biological basis with my people, but as time went on, we understood the subtler and more pervasive impact of the spiritual, of the feeling, of the instincts, all of that, and once that was understood, we realized the devices could serve no useful purpose, and they were retrieved. In cases where they could not be retrieved gently, they were necessarily and unfortunately retrieved surgically.
     It was believed to be necessary to retrieve the devices so they could not be misused by your governments should one or more of the devices

accidentally, as you say, or by chance, as we might say, exit the physical body and be discovered, because once exiting the physical body in a physical world, such as the one in which you live, the device would then be seen and touched and so on—physical. But when inside the body, it would be able to maintain its higher dimensional function and therefore would not interfere in the physical processes of the body, even as it maintained a small area of influence of higher dimension. It was believed that higher-dimensional influence might encourage you to desire such a goal. It is perhaps also a bit of interference, but no one told us not to do it, and so we tried it.

So as it turned out, it did not work, but at least we got the devices back. These devices are so complex that when they are viewed in their physical form, they might have encouraged you in different directions technologically, and that could have been very influential on your weapons manufacturers, who would have been the first ones to be able to access such materials.

Could they have used it for mind control or something?
No.

But it actually had applications as a weapon if they'd understood it?
No, but the technology (if it had been applied to weapons designs, though it was not meant for that) might have prompted your civilization in a direction—technologically speaking—that could have caused the destruction or worse of your peoples.

Worse? Okay. How many people did you put the device into?
Everyone.

Five billion people?
There weren't that many then. Most of it was done when the people were asleep, and it was done gently.

Everyone on the planet?
Yes. Most of them were taken out when you were asleep, gently. A few of them had to be taken out more directly using a surgical procedure, unfortunately.

Why?
Some people who had been affected by the device and who were higher than the third dimension but still physical had partially merged with the device. In order to extract it from you physically, it would be like taking out a part of yourself. So a procedure had to be devised to remove the device with the least amount of trauma possible, but in some cases it caused discomfort, regrettably.

In roughly how many of those cases?
The discomfort cases? Several thousand.

And when were they all back out again? You put them in the early 1950s and took them out in . . .
The 1960s. By then, they were all out.

So there's no one else doing this on the planet, and so there is no other type of implant. Or are there other types of implants?
Perhaps, but we are not involved.

Who else would be doing it?
I couldn't say, but it is possible that there are others involved with such things. Certainly your own people are preparing a device that will fit in the palm of your hand, the hand of any of your citizens. If the device is installed anytime between now and 2010 or 2015 at the latest, it might have some uncomfortable aspects to it. If it is installed later, say around 2030 or thereabouts, it will be a perfectly benevolent and beneficial device allowing you much greater communication with all races. Our people have such devices.

But if it's installed in the next twelve years, is it the secret government attempting to control us?
Well, that is not exactly it, but it could have unintended negative side effects and could potentially be misused.

Who is promoting it?
It is being considered as a means to replace passports and citizen identity papers and all of this business. A rudimentary form of the device is already being experimentally installed in some animals. It's actually beyond the experimental basis, but the one that would be installed in the human being would be more advanced; it would be smaller and have greater capacities.

Like a homing signal or a smart card?
Well, it would allow governments to know their citizens compared to citizens of other places. It would be very useful as a security device. It would essentially eliminate crime, because it would be almost impossible to perpetrate a crime without being known, and so for any crime, the criminal would be guaranteed punishment—not that the punishment might be equal to the crime, but being caught would be guaranteed. So such a security device would have a certain amount of welcome from many peoples. But there might also be some problems.

Freedom or Bondage?

What would the problems be? Knowing the people of the United States, I don't think anyone would want it.

You'd be surprised. Suppose somebody told you that you could stop carrying money; that you could stop carrying credit cards; that you'd never to have to worry about having anything stolen from you again; that you would never have to carry ID because all the important data, as it were, about you would be available to those who need it and available to you should you need it about others; that you could walk safely on the streets at any hour of the day or night and on and on. You'd be surprised how many people would say, "Sure, fine."

[Laughs.] I don't like it already.

Suppose it was also this: It could suspend the symptoms of many diseases, including withdrawal from certain drugs. Suppose it would prevent the usage of drugs that are harmful. Suppose, in other words, that it answered a great many problems and had the potential to answer more in the future. Governments in general might be very benevolent toward it, and many citizens would consider it to be a boon.

Well, I must have a suspicious mind, because I see it as a way of keeping track of me.

Certainly that is a factor.

How do you use these devices? Do you use them for communication?

We use them for what I stated—all those things and more. It is a way of knowing. I think I will just stop with that word. It is a way of knowing a great deal.

Okay, but in your civilization, you don't have the tyrants we have and so . . .

There are no problems associated with the device for our people or other peoples.

But as I say, you do not have tyrants to contend with.

Yes, we do not have the challenges that you face.

Well, all right. I do not want to keep Robert for too long. You are a wonderful source of information. Are you available again if I get some more books?

Yes, but sooner rather than later. I won't be available indefinitely.

Okay. I'm hoping to spend the whole weekend reading some more of these books, but you've really explained the big picture—when you came, what you were doing and why and how it worked out. I think people are going to get a really good overview of who and what you are from this.

Good. Perhaps that will be satisfactory.

Let's see what happens. I want to thank you incredibly much.

Describing the Zetas

Sha Don
November 5, 1998

Do you wish to continue?

Yes, I'd like to start with a couple of little things. Was the story that I briefly synopzised from the Herrmann book about the planet in 50 zone 754 DA sector where you rescued one of your ships—was that accurate? You never said if what I was saying was accurate enough.

It was accurate enough that it does not require corrections.

Okay. When you talked about the implants, I was thinking later about the logistics. How many people were on the planet at the time you put them in?

I could not say. Many millions.

Billions. We have billions.

Perhaps. But it can be done without doing it one at a time. It is like you give a blessing or say a prayer that would affect many people, although you might not consciously know it. In some cases, where the people were receptive, the installation of these devices could have been done at a distance, working at a higher dimension where much can happen in a short time. The people who were less receptive, for whatever reason, would be the people who would have had the devices installed under more singular conditions, meaning directly. So fully 80 percent of the population had it done with the higher-dimensional practice. That reduced the amount of physical contacts necessary, and the procedure, the simple installation, is very fast. It is done within our moment of space rather than a moment of time. If you were to ask how long did it take, I would have to say a moment.

I see. Was the description in Betty Andreasson's book accurate, of having her eye taken out and having a BB with little hairs installed? Is that typical?

No, because she was special. What was installed within her body, because she was open to it, had greater capacity and magnitude in its ability to send and receive, and therefore it was able to propel her spiritual development to what it would take for three lifetimes. She was able to accomplish much more and do so quickly because of being receptive and accepting a device that was a little more complex.

So most of the human population—three billion or something—had these devices for around ten years?

Yes, no more than that. For some people, let's say maybe eight to eleven years.

Okay, so Betty made progress equal to three lifetimes. What do you think was the net average effect on the human population from this device that you put in? I mean, did it accelerate 10 percent more than we could have expected, or was it more or less?

It would be the net, meaning the average . . .

The increase beyond what would have happened without it.

The average would have been equal to about one and a half lifetimes, with some people doing more and some less. Still, I give you the median number.

So that one thing accelerated and led to the 1960s, right? Could you say it led to the whole change of consciousness in the 1960s?

I would not want to take sole responsibility for that—speaking as a representative of my people—but I would say that this, working in concert with other spiritual influences, might have been a contributing factor.

Well, that's amazing, because it was almost like we had a lifetime between the 1950s and the 1960s. It was so different.

Yes, it was most definitely a startling development, in some ways showing glimmers of the future and then bogging down in other ways, since you had not resolved that which you needed to resolve. Still, it was a glimmer of the future.

That's beautiful. How did you come to the understanding that you had to take them out? From your teachers or from other extraterrestrials?

Our guides indicated to us that if the devices were left in indefinitely, you would not be able to resolve that which you came here to do, meaning what you have been doing in the 1970s, 1980s and 1990s. Because everyone would be propelled forward so much, you would just move past resolution into higher development. So, realizing that this effect was taking place, we removed the devices.

I see. I'm glad you said all this. Had you done this before on any other planet? How did you know to do it? Is it something you had done before with an evolving population?

We typically do it on planets where we have hybridized species, but before that time we had not done it on a planet that we perceived to be outside our sphere. Only later did we discover that the planet is in our sphere but in a different way, on the soul line rather than on the physiological line.

A lot of people talk about your members and say there is an insignia of a flying serpent on your shoulder patch. Can you say what that represents? Is that a trading house?

This has to do with a ceremony. It is not displayed by everyone. As a matter of fact, it is only occasionally displayed and these days (meaning in your now time) usually not at all, but it has to do with another Ceremony of Renewal. It is not so different from your desire to wear emblems or insignias that are symbolic of something that you are performing, some function. So it is like that.

It's like getting a T-shirt after going to the Yankees game? [Chuckles.] A little more meaningful, right?

Something like that.

Crash and Rescue in South America

I don't even know what case it is, but you rescued some beings. A ship crashed in South America and the daughter of Isis said that some of the local people took your people in and you were able to effect a rescue. I think that would be an interesting story to tell. Can you tell that story?

This has happened more than once.

Really? Tell me. Humans need to know these things.

We do not beam people up as they do in the moving pictures, but we have the capacity to expand the radiated field from our ship. In this case it wouldn't be a ship that can travel in time, you understand? If we expand the radiated field while the ship is stationary in a given time, it creates a no-time, or time suspension, in that particular physical area.

Once time is suspended, if you were in that envelope, it would appear that unassociated beings were frozen in time—"unassociated" meaning not having an electronic cosign (although it is not circuitry as you know it), the signal in this sense being the sign and something you are wearing the cosign. As a result, you or our people could move around within that field, but if you were an Earth person and did not have the cosign, you would appear to be frozen in place. In fact, as you experienced your life, you would not notice it. It would be a split second, faster than the blink of an eye, so you would have no idea that you would ever have been perceived as frozen in time. Creating such an experience allows us to go in, take our people onboard and fly out again, without impacting the local population with our appearance.

But people who are not frozen are going to see the ship, aren't they?

They're never frozen, but that's the way you would perceive it if you would look at them. They would seem frozen to you, but if you were experiencing it as one of those people, you would not feel frozen. You just wouldn't notice it. It would be too fast.

If you went into a house where your people were prisoners, wouldn't you only use this technique on the area where the prisoners were or where there were humans you were going to deal with? Wouldn't other humans see the ship?

No, we have a mechanism so that the ship is unseen. It simply appears to be that which is around it. If it is in a sky with clouds, it will just look like the sky with clouds. It does not actually make the ship invisible. What it does is create a mask that causes the ship to be unrecognizable as an electronic pattern to devices that might be able to sense its presence. The person who might be looking with their eyesight would not notice it either, because it would simply be part of the background scenery (whatever that was). It would not sit in a crowd full of people looking like human beings, however.

Well, it certainly beats going in and shooting them up, doesn't it?

If we had to go in and, as you say, "shoot 'em up," we would have been permanently banned from this planet. Also, we would have had to pay the penalty of being sequestered on our own planets for many thousands of years. Punishment for such an action is severe and is meant to remind the offender, should such a thing ever take place, that such actions are not without consequences. It perhaps does not sound so threatening to you who do not travel to the stars very much, but if your world is so broad, to have it suddenly restricted like that would be a burden. Even if my people were "fed up" and wanted to "just do it," as your people say, and they pushed a button and obliterated an area to get your attention, we would be able to rescue our people, but not without a price.

Population and Life on Zeta Reticuli

Yes, much too big a price. How many Zetas are there in your time? Hundreds? Millions? Billions? Trillions?

Counting hybrid species and our own people, or strictly people that you would recognize to be primarily Zeta Reticulan?

Both. How many Zetas? How many hybrids?

Counting all within the sphere of influence of our civilization, not counting remote outposts with a few people here and there, we have a number of maybe about a billion.

Including the hybrids?

Yes. We are very careful with our population numbers, lest the requirements for survival become depleted. As you know, with many billions of people on a single planet such as yours, you often have people who do not have enough, because the idea of population stability has not been embraced yet. It will, though. It will be understood someday that it is humanitarian to stabilize the population, not by artificial means such as abortion, but simply by certain techniques that you will soon develop that will enable people to have the pleasure of intimacy without producing offspring very often.

This way, the population will eventually be humanely reduced through the easy process of people simply dying off and not so many people being born. Probably the target will initially be to reduce the population to about a billion, and then from there to about 800 million and so on, until in about fifty years the population will be stabilized at somewhere around half a billion.

That's only 10 percent.

It might seem strange to you now, but at that time there will also be people living underground for various beneficial reasons. This includes the underground population, which will allow the surface of the Earth to regenerate itself in its own way without having to be constantly concerned about its methods causing harm to populations, as floods and earthquakes often do.

And hurricanes and tornadoes.

This will all be recognized once people begin to embrace the fact that you are a portion of Earth and God Creator. The Earth itself is like your family, and you will expand your philosophies in a more heart-centered way so that the plants, the animals, Earth herself, yourselves—in other words all beings—will be considered equals, not only politically but in your hearts. When population reduction takes place naturally, simply by the dying out of the elder generations and fewer children being born, it will also cause civilizations all over the world to cherish children even more than they do now.

That's beautiful. I don't think I asked—what is your average life expectancy?

Utilizing our comparison to Earth years, depending upon activities or purpose or intent, variables, it would range from 700 to 1,200 years.

How long have you lived?

I am about 786 by your life standard.

And on your home planet now, are you in rest and recreation? Let's just stay with your home planet. What do you do there? Are you mostly out on ships? How much of your life do you spend on ships? What percentage of your time do you spend out exploring creation?

Speaking for myself only, having been on missions to Earth and other planets, and considering that my life is not over up to this point, I have spent about 40 percent of my life away from this planet on various missions.

Is that fairly typical? Is that average?

It is not typical. Many will have jobs on the planet or go to other nearby planets and be there for a length of time, but I took your question to mean traveling about with some consistency.

Yes. What is life like on your planet? How do you live? What are your joys? You don't have families as we do, do you?

Not as you do, but we consider each other part of an extended family. As such, there is a comradeship between each and every one of us. You must ask your questions one at a time or I will sometimes answer just one of them.

Yes, I understand.

You may ask some of your questions again.

What is your life like?

Our life is one of service. We have members who serve to maintain the population, just as you do. You have farmers and grocers and so on. We have comparable types. We also do a lot of traveling, not for trade as you do or for basic supplies, but trade more along the lines of exchanging ideas or philosophies. Sometimes we offer service to other planets, should they have projects they cannot do (because they do not have the resources, the techniques or the capacity), or we sometimes supplement them if they do. Service is perhaps our number one priority.

You have two suns? Is your planet light all the time?

It is not light all the time. We have a nighttime, but it is shorter than yours. We have about six hours of darkness.

Do you sleep to refresh yourselves? Is your cycle anything like ours?

We do not sleep as you do, but we do rest and have meditation time, as you might say, during which we do not think. When this takes place, we will often experience what feels to us like a higher dimension, another level of our existence. We find this most restful. The mind has a chance to regenerate with this experience since there is no thought, as you say, but there sometimes are visuals, things we see or sense. Still, the mind can relax during such times, allowing us to regenerate.

How do you take in nourishment?

We do not eat like you do. This is part of the reason that our mouths do not look like something that functions for consuming. If we feel the need for nourishment, we have something dense that will provide us with nutrients, but this is only necessary if we are doing something strenuous. Other than that, we have the capacity to live off the energy of the planet. This is reproduced in the ship, so we can live off that.

So if you come to Earth, can you walk around on the planet and breathe the air?

We cannot come to the Earth and walk around and breathe the air. We have to have an envelope around us, using a device that essentially maintains an artificial atmosphere within it. To a casual observer, we would perhaps seem to be unsheathed.

Is this the same thing that protects you from our violent emotions?

Yes.

So you can look like you come into a house, as you did with Betty Andreasson, but you have invisible protection.

We have a protection barrier that is not visible to the casual eye. Those who can utilize subtle vision might see a silvery type of light close to our bodies, but that requires subtle vision.

Because this is a higher-dimensional envelope?

Yes.

So what do you breathe, then? Is it a different combination of gases?

It is a different combination of gases. It does not include oxygen, since oxygen is an oxidizer. Creator has provided you with an oxygen system, guaranteeing that your residence on this planet in any given life will not be as long as it is elsewhere.

How do humans breathe on your ships then? Oh, even when you're in the same room with them, you have the envelope.

Yes, or we will generate an envelope around them that will contain the necessary elements to provide their life support.

Zeta Learning, Knowledge and Form

These are things I never knew before. Back to your planet and ships then—you don't have to read because you can get anything from the tableau, anything you want to know, right?

Yes, but we do not always utilize that. We do have the capacity to know what we do not know. If we focus into that vertical thought—that factor of thought Zoosh has referred to before—this exists for most extraterrestrials. You can do it yourselves. I believe you are working toward it now, which is why many of you are having problems remembering things, because linear memory is not your native memory.

Could you say you tune in to your spiritual selves? Or tune in to what, the total repository of knowledge?

Such terminology, even with the broadness that you have given it, is not broad enough. It is simply opening to a source that might be this source one time and another source another time.

The source is whoever knows about it, is that what you're saying?

It is not always the same source. It will provide you with the answer to anything you need to know. It might not be retained by all beings. Generally, individuals of my species will retain information for a time. If after a while it does not appear to have any further usefulness to that individual or his or her immediate peers, it is released and the individual no longer has that information. Should the question come up for another individual at another time, then he or she can utilize the same system. Therefore, it is unnecessary to write down the information and retain it in a book. This is another way that civilizations manage to have all the wisdom they need without cutting down trees to put ink on paper. We very rarely do that, but sometimes if we need to present a book such as has been discussed, we would ask certain plants to volunteer parts of themselves, if necessary, for the creation of any such processed product.

You can get any information you want. You don't have to sleep. You eat very rarely. Do you have certain enjoyments beyond the time you spend at your service?

Service is our enjoyment. Our meditation time is also greatly pleasurable. The ceremonies we have from time to time are an extra pleasure. Our lives are so satisfying that we do not require distractions that cause us to forget the burden of our life, because our lives are not a burden.

What do you consume?

If we need to consume something, it is like a heavy or thick liquid. We do not eat fruits and vegetables.

Liquid what? Is it liquid vegetables?

It is more. The way you could identify with it is that it would be considered a combination of minerals and, for lack of a better term, plasma—not referring to a blood product here, but referring to a condensed energy.

Because your bodies are made of light plasma, aren't they?

The ninth-dimensional bodies are, but not the seventh-dimensional bodies. The body that appears to be the physical body is . . . Well, everyone is made of light, but to be specific to a given dimension, I would say that it would not appear to be made of light if you were here and looked at me. You would touch me and say, "Oh, you are solid."

It is a fluid, a good replenishment. At times, should we find ourselves in a diplomatic situation on other planets, we have been known to consume some fruits or vegetables for ceremonial or diplomatic purposes, but we have to be careful because we do not have the elaborate intestinal system you have. So eating something we are unfamiliar with does require eating either in small quantities or only eating something we know to be at least borderline safe.

In the third dimension, the sixth and seventh dimensions are invisible. So you have the ability to be seen on the third dimension, or is it that in your . . . ?

No, no, no. Right now the seventh dimension is in the room you are in. Do you see it?

No. But then, how do humans see you and describe you?

Because of the envelope around us. For us to contact you, we have to create a mini-atmosphere around ourselves. You would see us because of the envelope around us.

But we could look through it and see you physically, right?

That's how you would see us if we wanted to be seen and were outside of the ship, yes. If we were inside the ship, you would not see us. But if you were inside your house, we would not see you, either.

There have been people who saw your people through porthole windows on your ships. That was when you wanted to be seen?

When we wanted to be seen, that's right, which is a way of acknowledging and respecting the viewer.

Raising Human Awareness

One of your functions seems to have been an assignment to very slowly allow humans to be aware that there are other intelligences, other beings, other races, right?

Yes, and as a result we have sometimes left evidence when it was not necessary. It has been pointed out to us that it is essential for you to realize that there are beings who might have general similarities to you, humanoid but otherwise very dissimilar, with the intention that eventually, at least—we hope sooner rather than later—you will learn how to get along with one another.

And then we can get along with you?

When you learn how to get along with each other, you will find it much easier to get along with races from other planets who might have nothing or practically nothing in common with you on the social or cultural level. On the basic level—in form, in soul, with love by Creator—all this would be in common, plus other things. Once you can welcome people of other cultures and languages or races on your own planet, then extraterrestrial contact will become a regular thing.

I'm looking forward to that. You and your fellow Zetas travel in ships. Can you list some of the things you trade? You're doing exploration. What are some of the other things you're doing? For what purposes do you travel?

We are self-sustaining. We do not require anything for our bodies or our technology from other planets. Largely we function, in trading terms, as assistants for planets that cannot trade or choose not to trade with planets that have something they need. Cargoes might be different from moment to moment. Given the needs of different planets, we serve as "delivery people." [Chuckles.]

[Chuckles.] But that is really awesome. You don't need anything. You've achieved your own level of technology, right?

We are autonomous in the sense that we have reached a level of existence where we are self-sustaining. This is a satisfying way to be, since very little, if anything, is wasted, and all continues to recycle itself in benevolent ways for beings.

And you invented your technology? You didn't get it from someone else?

We evolved our own technology; that is correct.

Artistic Hybrids

You create hybrids. Are they inculcated as you are up to the level of your knowledge at the moment?

Not usually. Sometimes they will be exposed to certain information, inculcated as you say, but this is only if they need this information to survive and thrive. We feel that since we are encouraging them to develop their own culture, we would be superimposing our lifestyle on them by giving them all that we ordinarily receive. We want them to develop their own lifestyle and culture, and so we only give them that which they require to survive.

How do you find places for them?

We do that first. We look for planets that can sustain life of one sort or another, and if we can hybridize or have a hybrid project ongoing, where that planet might serve as a host and chooses to do so (we always ask), then we will expand the hybrid experiment and seed the people on the planet with as much as they need to survive.

How many planets have you put hybrids on?

Right now there are nineteen in our sphere of influence.

And they are not just human-Zeta hybrids, but hybrids from everywhere, right?

We have hybrids from various places that we originally felt might provide—ultimately with the combination of our DNA—viable beings who might find life pleasurable to live.

So what are some of those other civilizations? Any that we've heard of?

No, but one of them is connected to the Andromeda star system. All of the others are systems that you've never heard of and couldn't really relate to.

Do the beings look like Zetas, then, or do they look like the other half?

They are always at least 51 percent Zeta. Sometimes the percentage is greater. They generally look like us in some fashion, although they will often have other species influences. Not all of them have the large eye with the inner eyelid, for example.

The members of the Faughn group have smaller eyes. They are artistic in nature and have more expressed feelings than we do. They have a form of humor that they have developed (mostly I do not understand it, but they seem to like it). [Chuckles.] They have a stable, artistic, musical society. I think that when your people meet them, you will be fond of them and recognize a kindred spirit within them. Certain things you like, they like.

They were originally created—yes, they are partially human—to be those who would offer diplomatic overtures to your race, representing us, although now that might or might not happen. It is a possibility, because they have studied your culture and will sometimes adapt things from your culture into theirs, such as the use of the timpani in music.

Is that one of the things you do? You visit them to bring things to them? Or do they have their own ships now?

They do not have too many ships. Being artists and artisans, their leanings are not technological. We have provided them with a few ships and set the ships up to navigate on the basis of their desires rather than with mathematics, for example. We provide the technological support that they might require from time to time.

You have nineteen planets that you can visit and enjoy interactions with, almost like your children, right?

We do not think of them as our children. They are our subspecies. It does not mean less than, but is simply a way of categorizing the varying degrees of us and other cultures.

But you enjoy visiting them, right?

Yes, I have enjoyed visiting them in the past, although I have not been there in many years.

Culture, Crime, Architecture and Art on Zeta Reticuli

What about the other half of the equation, when the other half is spacefaring? Do the Andromedans visit them and feel comfortable? How does that work?

I have noticed that the Andromedans visit, although I cannot say for myself whether they are comfortable. You would have to ask one of them. But they seem to visit with regularity, and I have noticed no problems.

So we can assume that they enjoy it. Well, that's great. I'm sure there are so many more things that humans would like to know . . .

We do not have medical doctors since we do not have medical conditions. Some similarities are not crossed over between our peoples. We do not experience sport or competitive activities.

You don't need policeman because you have no crime.

Correct.

What kind of buildings do you live in on your planet?

For the most part, they are what I would call homogenous buildings, meaning that they might be very large, long, rambling structures, low to the ground, with no doors. By doors, I mean that while one could go in and out, there is not something that closes an opening. There would be openings for what you call doors and windows, but no means to close them. We do not require privacy from one another.

Nor protection from the elements?

No. The elements are cooperative, so the comfort zone is benevolent.

You don't really put a lot of energy into art or architecture, then.

We have done some temporary artwork with liquid light, but the nature of liquid light is that it is a living existence. One tends to release it and allow it to do what it wishes to do in response to what we are doing. We might encourage some liquid light to float above us when we are doing a ceremony, and it will display many of the beautiful facets of its existence. We consider this art, but we do not create rigid art. Our art would always be interactive with life around it.

It would not be static or frozen or a sculpture?
Correct.

Prospects for Mass Contact

The point of these books is that at some point in the near future, sooner rather than later as you like to say, we hope to interact with you. Let's say that such a time came. Would there be some kind of announcement? Would you come by yourself? Would you and the Pleiadians and the Andromedans all come together? What might we expect?

Most likely there would be some kind of a preliminary contact by voice message.

Through TV or something?

No, it would be something through a representative organization, such as the United Nations. It would not be that someone would go to the United Nations. A message would be broadcast in some way so the members could hear it, perhaps at the General Assembly. It would be benevolent, nurturing and encouraging and would simply say that we feel that you have evolved sufficiently enough that you could accept our appearance and enjoy interacting with us. Unless this "august body" (we might say, to be formal) says otherwise, we will come to your planet, probably landing a ship near the United Nations, wherever it may be that day (it might not always be in New York). The people will get out of the ship and go in and meet with the General Assembly. If there is a desire to broadcast some kind of a greeting message through radio or television or other media, then we will gladly participate.

But it will be this kind of a contact through the United Nations so that no one country either feels a sense of claiming us or conversely finds a sense of burden that they are responsible for us and our happiness. If we approach the United Nations, which represents many but not all peoples of the Earth and will represent more in the future, we feel this would be the most natural and comfortable way for you. Diplomats also are of course used to getting along with people who look and are culturally different. So approaching the United Nations in this way makes perfect sense to us.

How would you decide who would get to come?

It is not like that with us, as I have said before. Once the decision is made to make contact, it will simply be whoever is available. We are all trained for such circumstances. We do not have a specific diplomatic class.

It would be whoever was closest, then, is what you're saying.

Whoever wasn't busy or whoever could do so. If we needed eight or nine individuals, then it would be whoever was, as you say, "handy." Or it might be beings who happen to be in the area, something like that. We would probably bring gifts for the representatives—not individual gifts, but perhaps a communication device or something that offers a benevolent encouragement such as a health aid, something that could be used to help regenerate Earth, a gift that would be good for all beings on the planet.

Have you given any gifts that ended up in the secret government's hands? You said the communicator . . . They have one, and somebody in Russia has one . . .

We gave a child a toy once. It was many years ago, in one of our travels through time. The toy is like a round ball about an inch around that floats. They have that. They have been trying to figure out what it does besides float, but it is a toy. That's all it does. [Chuckles.]

And the secret government has it. [Chuckles.]

Yes. You asked what else they might have. This they have. They did not get it by any nefarious means. It was an oddity in a village and people were afraid of it. They didn't know what to do with it. Eventually it ended up in the hands of someone who passed it on to the secret government. And now I am revealing that . . . [Laughs.] They will read this at some point and realize there isn't anything else it does. They can learn now. It's a toy. It floats. That's all it does.

It floats forever. So if they reverse engineer it . . .

All they will get is another toy. [Laughs.]

Joopah absolutely did not have a sense of humor in the beginning. Now he has. How did you get such a sense of humor?

I know Joopah. Joopah advised me on the subtleties of humor. He also discussed this with several others of our population. Others have attempted to learn it. It will gradually spread around our peoples, not for our own use, but for communications with Earth people. It will be useful in the United Nations someday, since you all know (and we have come to respect) that a joke can go a long way to ease the shock of our appearance.

You must not be shocked by our appearance, too. Well, no, you travel so much that you're not shocked by anyone.

We are not shocked by any appearance at any time. But you are only shocked because you don't remember who you are in the context of your total being. For you to be shocked is completely understandable.

The Responsibility of Hierarchy in Cat Beings

[To Tiger, the cat.] Don't you attack her. Now you just sit down and behave. Sit down. Be good.

Cat individual of the orange is full of hormones of the male. The female does not have such hormones and is not so responsive, much to male cat's sadness.

Yes, I know. And so he takes it out by picking on her.

He is not picking on her. It is natural in their species to have a hierarchy. It is more complex than you realize. For instance, if a cat or some other animal that was small enough so he could fight came and picked on her, he would come to her defense.

Yes, he did that one day when another cat was . . .

It is a hierarchy with responsibility. So it is not just wanting a favor; it is also providing a service.

Yes, he did. He came in and he ran off that other cat that was scaring her. Yes, he does that.

Oh, he's doing some good for her, too. You have to let them work it out. They will do so. But I appreciate your desire to have him "make nice." [Chuckles.] Do you still say "make nice?"

Yes, yes. "Make nice." You've been around humans a lot! [Laughs.]

I have heard these things from Joopah. He has given many talks.

What else do you think humans would like to know about your species?

Running out of questions, eh? [Chuckles.]

Once I have had a chance to read the other books that have all the contacts, there are probably some things your people have told the contactees that you could expand on.

Yes, when you have the time, please do ask, and I will expand on it, since that is, I believe, your original intention for this book.

It started out just explaining the ET contacts, but I can see now that it's much more meaningful, a beginning to prepare the way for the eventual interaction of our peoples.

Yes, it is a diplomatic and cultural journey, along with the mysteries that are revealed.

The Zetas in Human History

Sha Don

November 6, 1998

I would speak of a contact that you did not know about. Some time ago, one of the presidents of the United States was invited aboard a ship. We went back in time to do this, because we recognized within this man a special desire to leave your world a better place for his having come to his position of influence. This person's name was President Woodrow Wilson. We felt that he could accept our presence and would thrive as a result. We met him first when he was a young man and once more again in a secluded area while he was president of the United States.

Woodrow Wilson's Contact Experience

While he was president, the contact involved him and one of his associates, but when he was a young man, it was when he was on his own. As a young man, he could accept that there were beings from elsewhere, although we did ask a Pleiadian to come with us because they do look so very much like you. She, I believe, initially caused him to feel at ease and prepared him for our appearance so that when he saw us he was startled but not frightened. We were able to speak of the way we live and to talk about the way the Pleiadians live and even to discuss the way life would be on the Earth in the future.

As a young man, he wanted to know what he could do in order to bring about this more benevolent future the quickest way possible, and

Courtesy of Canady Library

Courtesy of Library of Congress

Figures 6.1 and 6.2: Woodrow Wilson as a young man and then later in 1919, during his presidency.

we encouraged him to become schooled, to try to reach some high office in the land and then to try to find a way to unite the nations of the world. We do not wish to take credit for his idea of the League of Nations, but we believe that those early talks might have inspired him more than he already was.

When we met again when he was president, he said that he was a little disappointed in the League and felt it was too much of a struggle to keep it going. We told him that it was important to have done it, because someday there would be the United Nations, and everyone would say that the United Nations was successful because it was preceded by the League of Nations, that the league made it possible to discover what worked and what didn't. As a result, although he might not have received much public credit, all those who worked in the United Nations would understand in their hearts how he had contributed toward world peace with his vision.

Oh, that's beautiful. How old was he the first time?

The first time I believe he was just barely a teenager.

Which time did you take him on the ship? When he was a teenager or when he was president?

Both times. It is easier to take him on the ship, because then we could speak quietly without having to be concerned about who was coming up the trail. [Chuckles.] And, of course, he loved seeing Earth from space. We talked about Earth people exploring the stars both times we met, and he said it would be wonderful, but he didn't think it would ever happen. We assured him that it would. [Laughs softly.]

He never talked to anybody?

I believe he confided in a loved one later in life.

I have never read anything about it, so I don't think anything ever got printed, do you?

No, it would have been a family member.

It's true that if he hadn't started it, we wouldn't have the United Nations, right?

I think he really helped to create the impetus for it, and even though it didn't work out the way his vision saw it, it did seed the idea. Therefore, when the United Nations began, people were enthusiastic about it even before it started work. I think that no matter how much the United States participates, the United Nations will exist into the far-flung future, guaranteeing that the United States will embrace it fully at some point—although I think the average U.S. citizen has a high opinion of this worthy organization.

Benjamin Franklin Meets a Pleiadian

That's a wonderful story. Did you contact anyone else?

Yes, because we had been going back in time, we also had an opportunity to speak indirectly, through Pleiadians, with Benjamin Franklin. He was at the time one of the most educated men in Western educational systems and also (not a typical combination) one of the most sophisticated. He always spoke about philosophies of life with individuals. We asked a Pleiadian who was thoroughly trained if he would come with us to that time, present himself at a party in France as a fascinating visitor from abroad (as it were) when Franklin was there and speak to Franklin about ideas and civilizations that encouraged his interests and underlined his zeal for democracy.

You have to understand that the Founding Fathers, as they're called, were much more idealistic than what has come through in today's writings. Because of their education level, they wanted the Constitution and the Bill of Rights to sound not only clear and legally acceptable but reasonably

Figure 6.3: Benjamin Franklin met a Pleiadian in France who encouraged him in his work.

Courtesy of Library of Congress

sophisticated in their presentation. So you don't quite feel the enthusiasm of the documents—with the possible exception of the Declaration of Independence, where the feeling is just as strong as the words. The Declaration of Independence is probably more a mirror of these people's passions than the other documents, although the other documents are worthy indeed. So this was also an opportunity to speak of our values and for the Pleiadian to speak of his people's values in a circumstance that was completely, for all intents and purposes to Franklin's regular life, innocuous. It was a conversation at a party, no more than forty minutes, then an "until we meet again" farewell, and that was it.

Our people have over the years found this to be a useful way to encourage peoples from the most simple and sacred societies to the most complex and sophisticated societies. We do not consider it to be interference. It was more of a sharing of ideas and ideals. This is always and only done with individuals who like to do it. No one is "drafted." [Chuckles.]

Did Franklin know this being was from the Pleiades?

Oh, no. No. He was presented as a visitor from far away or something, and the people were drinking and having fun. It was a social occasion, not an official occasion. If it had been an official occasion, then such a declaration would have been necessary, but at a party, one can meet somebody new, have an interesting and stimulating talk and then go home.

He was already an ambassador for the United States, wasn't he?

Yes, he was in France at that time. He was there for a while. One of the reasons that Europe could accept the United States as an actual, official place was because Franklin made such a wonderful representative. People liked him and were impressed with him. People thought he was brilliant. He was the guest everyone wanted in his or her home. As a result, people in France began to feel that the United States must be a country worth investing in. Of course, they probably had been thinking this for a while, but I think that being an influential culture at the time—perhaps a little more so than today, although they might someday become even more influential—they were able to prevail in the identification of the United States as an entity.

You certainly know a lot. How many years of your traveling have you been around this planet?

Because we can travel through time, I can say how many years out of my life it was in your time, but I have traveled through time several thousand years into the future of your civilization—along the desired future line, you understand—and many thousands of years into the past.

How do you think you influenced Franklin? Did he make any decisions as a result of that conversation?

No, I think the intention of the conversation was to encourage and sustain him on the path he was pursuing, because you have to understand that he was promoting the ideas of democracy in a state that was ruled by royalty. He needed encouragement.

Johann Sebastian Bach and Celestial Music

These are fascinating stories. Do you have any others like that?

Let me see if there's one more that might be of some interest. We had a brief contact with the famous composer Johann Sebastian Bach. This took place when he was a boy about three and a half years old. At that time he was already a genius and demonstrating the signs of genius (which are sometimes misunderstood). We are fond of children because of their great openness. We contacted him briefly—for about twenty minutes—one night when he was awake, but there was no one else in the space. We spoke to him and played

Figure 6.4: J.S. Bach was visited as a child and given energy that enhanced his personality.

Courtesy of William H. Scheide, Princeton

with him. We asked a benevolent guide of his to manifest physically and give him (and this is the way we put it to him as a child) a blessing, which was also a way of giving him a certain energy that enhanced his personality, so as he grew up he was able to express his genius without overwhelming most people. In other words, it provided him with greater charm. This particular guide of his was with him until he was about seven years old.

The Truth of Travis Walton's Case, Among Others, and the Planet of Cats

Sha Don and Zoosh

November 7, 1998

This is Sha Don. I am speaking from my normal place of being for the sake of the channel's comfort. I will, however, have some capacities to speak on matters that have not been written about. I would prefer that you ask about what you've read so far today so that our time is not wasted and we can talk about what is of greater interest to the reader.

All right. Here is a contact reported by Senior Master Sergeant Charles Moody, from Alamorgordo, New Mexico, 13 August 1975, at the Holloman Air Force Base You were through by the 1970s, weren't you?

We are occasionally still traveling to various times, but from the future to the past rather than sequentially.

Those beings were small, five feet tall, 110 to 130 pounds, with black skin. The leader wore silver. These guys were round-eyed. Were these Zetas?

No.

The Travis Walton Case

Travis Walton, when describing his encounter on November 5, 1975, in Beaver, Arizona, talks about beings that were less than five feet tall and had the same description as the Zetas, except that they had five digits on their hands. They weren't yours, were they?

It is possible.

It is?

101

Some of our beings have five digits; it simply depends on a job-related duty or if a particular sub-culture was involved.

This is the famous "fire in the sky" case where he went onto the mothership.

He describes the beings as appearing like my people?

Yes, but they're under five feet five inches tall, with five digits and no fingernails. There are pictures drawn of them. Let me show them. He worked with an artist on them until he got what he thought was perfect. He shows a number of different beings. These here are six feet two, Pleiadian-looking beings, and these ones here look like your people. [Points out various pictures in the book.] There are color pictures, and there's a picture of the mothership, where the craft was parked.

Courtesy of Michael H. Rogers

Figure 7.1: *Travis Walton, circa 1975.*

These are a variation of my people. As I have stated earlier, it is not unusual for my people to travel with more human-looking individuals, which is always intended to make Earth humans feel more comfortable. These beings, as pictured, are members directly of the Faughn group. Faughn group beings are taller. Joopah, for example, is a descendent of the Faughn group, but being a descendent is different than being of the Faughn group. Descendent would mean, for example, that a clone included some elements of the Faughn group, most likely so that Joopah could communicate better with human beings, and perhaps so that Joopah would have more social graces. That's it.

And the Faughn group is a group, as you said before, of hybrids that are partially human?

The Faughn group is not . . . You are right. The Faughn group is partly human.

You said it the other night.

I do not function linearly, so I have to check what I say.

Okay, this is one of the most famous contacts. There was a movie made about it except that they made it into some horror show, nasty slimy stuff.

Yes, it was a moving picture made for money, not for documentary evidence—not very pleasing to the contactee.

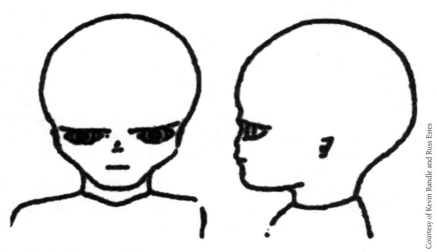

Figure 7.2: *Artist's depiction of the beings Travis Walton described as small creatures with domed heads and large eyes.*

So can you say why he was picked up? I haven't read what happened under regression. He was picked up and then he walked around the mothership. He fought the people. He fought the Zetas or the Faughn group.

Only at first did he resist. People will sometimes resist such an acquisition—I mean being taken aboard the ship—because it is so sudden. It is why we prefer to take people aboard the ship in a gentler way, as in, for instance, the case of Betty and Barney Hill, who were beings who met my people and walked through the woods, up the ramp and into the ship. But Mr. Walton was taken by artificial means that incorporate essentially cellular transfer to the ship. This was done because other people were present who were not intended to see the occupants of the ship.

Also, if the ship had landed anyway, other individuals who were present with Travis would have had to have been incapacitated for the duration of that man's contact. So it would have been an outrageous invasion of their freedom. This is why the acquisition was made in that fashion. When people are taken aboard by that unusual method, it is sudden and more frightening for the average human being.

He said it felt like being hit in the head with a baseball bat.

Yes, not pleasant. The decision was made to take him aboard this way because of the circumstances I described. The feeling of being struck does not exactly describe the feeling. This is how it occurs: A person is transferred to the ship. How it was done is to suddenly recompose him into his normal body. A feeling of impact or shock to the body occurs during recomposition, but it feels like the blow comes first and then recomposition. This is a trick of the memory as noticed by some people in car crashes or accidents. The sequences are jumbled . . . I must speak slowly tonight. You will have to be patient.

So Mr. Walton was taken aboard the ship because it was understood that he would have the courage to state at a later time what he recollected in the immediate moment. Now, Travis . . . I will say "that man." It is hard for me to say his name.

Okay.

Difficult pronunciation. So he struggled a bit, because of the shock to the physical body and the suddenness of the change of environment, but this struggling did not last so very long.

In the book he held off three Zetas with a weapon; he pushed them and they went out of the room. Then he went out of the room and sat in his chair, looking out a view window. They had to send some Pleiadians in to get him.

My people left the room because it was clear he was agitated. Again, we have the advantage of having people who look like that man. They come in the room, and then that man says to himself (we hope), "This is not going to be so bad after all."

He did.

This is a diplomatic mission, most often in consort with Pleiadians, or occasionally humanlike beings from other star systems such as Andromeda or Sirius. Once the Pleiadians had calmed him down, they told him that it would be all right, that he would have a good experience and that he would be privileged to learn many things of great interest to him and his people, referring to Earth people. He said, "All right," and requested that Pleiadians stay close at first while my people were present or if he does, he doesn't say so.

He doesn't remember any of this—or if he does, he doesn't say so.

But he got used to this contact with my people later. It's just the suddenness of it that was the shock. He was not so unsophisticated. Now the vehicle traveled some considerable distance away from the Earth—for the safety of all beings—and Mr. Walton was shown the usual program of the present Earth existence and the past leading up to it and what would happen if there were no major changes. Then he was shown the desirable present, the desirable past and the desirable future. Almost always after

Figure 7.3: Artist's rendering of the Zetas trying to calm a frightened Travis Walton.

Courtesy of Michael H. Rogers

people see this, they can tell that the vehicle they are on and the beings they are with have the best of intentions for the human race.

Then that man was given a tour of the solar system you are in. The first twenty hours or so—aside from rest periods and minor examinations to make sure he had not been injured by the suddenness of his acquisition on board and to allow him time to sleep—he was given a tour and flown about to various planets. In this way he had some pleasure.

He was given a great deal of information, which will be triggered in him when certain events happen on the Earth. This does not mean that he is somehow going to be out of control. What he will remember is the explanation about why these events are taking place and what he might be able to do to ease the passage through these events for his fellow citizens. This will begin for him soon, and he will also have more interesting dreams. I urge that man to keep a thorough notebook about these experiences—not only for his own sake in order to understand the wisdom that was given to him, but also to assist other citizens to move through these unusual times.

When a planet like your own—where there is advanced work going on in spiritual and physical applications—changes dimension while you are in the life cycle, sometimes unexplainable events happen. Usually they are simple things, but sometimes they are more mass events, meaning everyone has the experience within a range of time. These things will happen, and various individuals, such as that man and others who have been contacted by my people, will be in a position to make suggestions about the best way to proceed so that these experiences are as gentle as possible.

So you see, the reason he was picked up was that he was in reasonably good health, that he was understood to be a man of integrity and courage, that he had had a past life as a Zeta being (which is always the case, or a future life or sometimes both), and that he would live long enough to be of service to his people during that time of change. This time has begun recently and will continue for a while as you move through the resistance barrier to move past the 3.50 mark. The resistance barrier is not made up of energy projected by people who are afraid to go past that mark, but rather it is made up of things that are unresolved: experiences, applications and consequences that need to have a resolution of some sort, even if it is just the beginning of resolution.

In this way, the resistance barrier will grow weaker and eventually dissolve. So it is in your best interests as citizens of Earth to resolve past conflicts in some way or at least make some effort to do so. If it is not possible to communicate with individuals with whom conflicts might have taken place, then write a letter, say a prayer or have a conversation in the woods with their spirit. Do something to make resolution begin within you. Don't just simply pretend it's not so. It will add to the resistance barrier if you do and make the move to 3.50 and beyond more of a struggle than it needs to be.

This man, on the completion of his natural life cycle, will be given special honors aboard a massive ship. If he chooses, he can manifest a life on that ship or on either Pleiades or my home planet, Aria, where he will have an interesting and fulfilling life following up his previous Zeta life and his Earth experience. Or he might simply enjoy the honors and move on in his soul's desired direction.

That's wonderful! Okay, he was on your mothership. Is that what the picture shows?

It's not exactly a so-called mothership, but a maintenance vehicle designed to support and sustain vehicles that are smaller and populations that are larger. The vehicle is not quite large enough to be called a mothership. It is more like a supply ship with living quarters for many.

It's parked out here someplace in our solar system?

It moves about. It is not parked indefinitely.

Figure 7.4: Artist's depiction of the ship.

Courtesy of Michael H. Rogers

But then beyond that someplace, you have what has been called a mothership?
We have several of these, but at this time such a vehicle is not in your solar system or galaxy.

HAARP and Its Interference

During the late 1950s and 1960s and early 1970s, it was?
Yes. It was most often parked near Mars.

Does HAARP (High Frequency Active Auroral Research Program) interfere with such things now?
Yes, but there is a method to defend against such capricious experiments. Unfortunately, that method is to reflect rays back to the array. When this is done, it tends to either create an intriguing pattern, which is then more desirable to explore by experimenters [chuckles], or it tends to cause feedback energy and cause some damage. So it is easier to keep vehicles away.

There's no way just to damage HAARP?. Or would that be interfering, even though it's so nefarious?
It would be an act of war to destroy it.

Even though it is such a small group of people who are operating it and using it?
One person is enough of a group.

The Reasons for Taking Humans Onboard

I understand. Is your purpose to give information to many of these people whom you take on board so that they can help humans?

Yes, it is always this. Even if, as on some previous occasion, people are taken aboard to help us with a previous understanding of our races dying out (all these genetic experiments), they are given the same information so that the experience would be rewarding to them as well.

Most of them just remember the terror, the fear and the sense of being violated. They're not remembering the information.

But this passes. Eventually, if they get past the fear, their dream state or their memory will bring it up.

Is there anything else you want to say about Travis Walton or any of his experience?

Not without a question, no.

Do you want to talk about the Pleiadians on your ship or should we ask the Pleiadians when we talk to them?

Ask the Pleiadians directly, please.

When Travis was sitting in that chair, the buttons he was pushing just changed the viewer, right? They didn't interfere with anything?

Correct. The chair is intended for pleasure viewing.

It had nothing to do with science or running the ship?

No, he would not have been allowed to cause a problem with the ship. That would have been inexcusable on our part. I hope you understand that I do not speak of the contact as a participant. If I had been there, I would be able to give you a much more detailed description.

Well, we don't really need that, though. You've basically said what needs to be said. Could you say that after the 1960s you had the hybrids with you, that these other, larger beings were there?

Sometimes we had hybrids with us, but usually when hybrids were involved, we did not need to be present. They knew what we knew, and they did not need to be chaperoned, other than perhaps by having human-like people aboard.

Please excuse . . . There's been some interference for the past three or four days, which continues to build. It is electrical in nature. I think it's coming from the underground area near the former so-called Navajo base (not in honor of Navajo people, but just using that word).

You mean the ammunition site west of Flagstaff? Can you ask Zoosh or Isis if there is anything they can do to protect you and Robert?

I will ask. [Long pause.] They have made connection by a different route. We will try to make this kind of connection for a while. It appears to be better.

Okay. Is it going to be for the next few days or is it going to be ongoing?

I have no answer. I can only say this is clearly some kind of signal being generated underground from that area—just a little south of that area—and it is causing disruption of normal body functions such as heartbeat, respiration and thought processes. It is generally causing problems in the Sedona/Flagstaff area and also beyond this for some individuals in other towns and reservations.

When you are all through and ready to go, can you ask Zoosh to come in and say a little bit about it? Is there anything anybody can do about it?

It is creating disruption of the physiology for humans and, to a lesser extent, plants and animals.

That's terrible. I know I've felt a little funny for the past couple of days. I didn't know what it was. If you can continue, go ahead. If you can't, we'll stop.

An Unselfish Mother of Twins Seeking to Serve Humankind

We'll try to go ahead for a while. Let me speak of a contact that I was there for. There was in this place—I will say simply Pacific Northwest, U.S., and I will not say when to protect individuals . . .

Why don't you want to say when and where?

To protect human beings.

I know, but they've never talked about it?

This is all I can say. I can't always stop what I'm saying and answer a question while I'm answering other questions. The individual was a young mother pregnant with twins. She felt strongly that she was from someplace else. Her husband was not with her—he was absent for a time. She wanted to return to the stars with her children. My vehicle was nearby. Because she has a future life as a member of a race that is a combination of Pleiadian, Zeta and human, we stopped to visit her and invited her onboard for a time.

She asked if her children could be assisted in some way so they could serve humankind; she was totally unselfish, as is typical of mothers. She did not ask a thing for herself. We asked her to sit in a chair made for human beings (too big for us). While making sounds similar to music, gently, very gently and slowly, we provided a wisdom capacity to the unborn children that would allow them to develop spiritually very quickly and also develop in certain special ways intellectually.

So this process was accomplished in about four hours, during which time the mother rested quietly. Perhaps she might have been asleep for part of the time. After the process was complete, she asked us where we were from and we showed her a map similar to the one described by Betty Hill. She asked us if we came to Earth often, and we said yes. We had met many human beings but had never had a mother aboard with twins inside of her. It was new for us.

She laughed and totally unexpectedly burst into song without giving any explanation. She began to sing in clear and beautiful voice. Several other crew members peeked in to see what it was about and had to rush back to their duties. [Chuckles.] After the song, she said it was a song she had created for her children. She sang it all the time to welcome them into her life and life on Earth.

We made a recording of this beautiful song and have provided it to all of our civilizations that have birthing like you have so that mothers could sing in this same way—although with words slightly adapted to welcome them to their home planet of choice. We have also shared the song with friends and allies from other planets. [Smiles.] It has become a very popular song amongst people from places other than Earth. I thought I would relate that in case the then-young mother might happen to see this.

But as you said before, you do not follow up, so you don't know how her children turned out or what they are doing or anything?

We do not know. We hope for the best. We only know what happens to people when they reach the end of their natural cycle. If they choose, they can inform us. If they do not choose or have other duties to perform first, then we find out or we don't. It's all right not to know.

A Visit to Kaath, the Planet of Cats

Have you had any other experiences you would like to share that cheered you up or that you felt were unusual?

I had a very pleasant experience once. [Cat meows.] Yes, I will tell. I went to a place where there were only cats. It was a large, open field near a small town where there were many former housecats, as you say. But this was many generations of small cats raised in the wild by mother and father cats. We felt that evening that we needed personally, for ourselves, to have contact with Earth beings for the joy of it only—no work to do on our part, nothing for them to do, just a social occasion. [Cat meows.] Yes, yes.

We had heard from some of our vessels that this place was perfect. The ship landed, the ramp opened and we exuded a signal to attract cats.

Many cats came up the ramp into the ship, perfectly comfortable with us, no explanations necessary. We asked them if they would like to fly about or if they would like to take a short trip to visit their home planet. They all wanted to go to their home planet, so we took a trip. In time it was about a two-week trip, but we returned to the point of landing about an hour after the cats originally boarded—returning in time, you understand.

So for this amount of time—two weeks—we were able to have a longer experience with our friends. We went to the home planet of such beings and they had a wonderful time. They were able to interact, play and have fun, with no need to eat, as their sustenance was derived from the environment. We had many evenings of stories and songs, during which time the earthbound cats would sit in repose—with eyes not quite closed, in a meditative state, you would say—and listen to these old stories and songs of their people. They heard stories and songs more than once and were able to memorize the stories. As a result, when they returned to Earth, they were able to tell stories and sing songs a little bit to other members of Earth cat family. In this way we have pleasure, and they do also.

That's beautiful. Is this the planet Kaath? What do they look like, the beings who live there?

Most beings are upright, as you say, but some walk on four appendages, and some have similarity in general appearance to cats as you know them to be. Others are quite different, but none of them look like humans. They all have senses like cats. You say cats have six senses, but they have more than that. Cats often know when things are going to happen. It's enjoyable.

Oh, I'm glad. It was something you shared with your friends.

Our people, my people—at least on this ship at this time and several others functioning on such missions—are very fond of cat people, because the method of communication among my people and cat people is identical. So communication is perfect, just as it is among ourselves. Cat people speak of observations of human beings and life on Earth, and we are not required to use any device to protect ourselves. Cat people know who we are, what we require, and they remain in a state of perfect balance in our company when onboard the ship. Therefore we are able to glean vast amounts of information about human beings without feeling the repercussions of human emotion.

That's incredible. And then that goes into the tableau?

Yes, that is entered into the tableau. Cats also tell us about their life experience—different from ours, so different. To be so far from your home planet, to be born on a planet not your own and to live your whole life there—very challenging. But they seemed to be of adventurous spirit and they are happy to do it.

So they come here remembering the home planet and they go back home remembering here?

Yes.

Is the channel getting more uncomfortable?

It's difficult. It seems to be a modulated signal incorporating electrical reverse polarity. Such signal electricity alone is difficult for this channel being, but reverse polarity seems to be utilized for some mechanical purpose. It is creating disruption in the natural flow of magnetic energy and also creating disruption in life-cycle energy for all Earth beings.

All right. Whenever you need to leave, you leave.

The Wisdom of the Cat People

Zetas understand humans probably more than anyone, then, because you've gone into our past and into our future. You've interacted with us.

No, no. I cannot say that is true. I believe others understand better, but we have had more contact with human beings than most other species. However, communication between our species has been difficult, so to say we understand you better . . . No, I cannot say we do, but assistance from other races such as cats has been most helpful.

What did you learn from them? If you could synopsize what you learned from them, how would you say it?

The cat experience is always couched in the familiar, meaning that individual cat's experience with an individual human being. Cats don't talk about human beings as a species but refer to individual human beings. As a race, cats are not interested in human beings at large. They are only interested in the human beings with whom they have personal contact. Therefore, these being small, wild cats, individual contacts with human beings aren't as common as for cats you live with. Nevertheless, there's been enough contact so that occasionally charming stories are told, such as about interaction with children or the very old. Children and very old human beings on your planet seem to have a much broader range of tolerance for unusual beings— meaning beings not like themselves—so most often stories are about interaction with such humans.

That's right, the emotional. You're so human, I forgot. That's right, you don't understand our endocrine system and our wild emotional . . .

Children have passions too, and also the very old. But they are much more accepting of different beings—meaning, in the case of young children, cats and dogs and ETs and in the case of the very old, spirits, angels or guides. . . . Perhaps now would be a good time to stop and let Zoosh comment on the problematic device.

Handling Electronic Interference

All right. Zoosh here. I will thank Sha Don for bringing up the issue of this radiating device. The device is not intended to cause the harm it is causing, but it is associated with an underground base. It is an experimental device that is involved with long-range communications sent from that underground location through the Earth to other sub-surface locations on other parts of the Earth.

Some sub-surface locations are underwater, and some are underground, but the reversal of the polarity of the electricity is exactly what is causing trouble with the physiological systems of various beings. I will attempt to do something to modulate the electricity, and I will ask that other sensitive and spiritual beings send pink light to this area. The area would be two, two and a half, maybe three miles south of the area formerly referred to as the Navajo army dump, or ammunition depot, and it is underground by some small amount.

For those who use crystals, I would suggest utilizing rose quartz to scan energy through toward this area. That will tend to mix pink light and rose quartz energy light in with the radiated signal, not harming the experiment being done underground, but allowing it to radiate out pink light and rose quartz energy, which is very helpful for human beings disrupted by this reverse-polarity electricity.

Is this electricity why we've been kind of jumpy and agitated, getting at each other's throats?

Yes. I recommend speaking of this or telling people somehow. Urge them to utilize rose quartz in a similar fashion, by placing it on the solar plexus.

Is the device a permanent installation there, or is it only temporary?

No, it is only an experiment. Eventually the device will be thoroughly shielded, but right now it is not shielded at all. They believe, of course, that since the device is underground, it is not causing very much radiation on the surface, but as it turns out, the radiation that does come to the surface is actually causing harm to individuals. But you would not be able to call your Senator and complain, since it is a secret experiment.

Thank you very much.
    Good night.

Gifted Spacecraft, Crashed Spacecraft and the Test of Technology

Sha Don

November 9, 1998

Greetings. This is Sha Don. You have done your homework, I hear.

Greetings. And yes [laughs], I read until my eyes puckered. Let's start with the crashes. It appears that there's much confusion out there in the books, because there was one around Roswell/Corona, and then there was one right at Magdalena—two of them within a couple of days in 1947, right?

Are you not speaking of the material coming down in two different places from one vehicle?

Did that happen? The pieces all over Brazel's ranch and the intact spacecraft are all one?

Yes, because it was not fully intact. There are bits missing and the bits are on the man's ranch.

Okay, that's one. And then they talk about one that they call Magdalena, very close nearby, a day or so later. Is that true?

They say I should not comment on that. I can only speak about this and not that, but I cannot say true or false.

Who is telling you that?

The tableau. The tableau knows the plan for you.

But it's fifty years later. The secrecy's over.

Fifty years is nothing.

Courtesy of Blue Alien Network

Figure 8.1: Rancher Bill "Mac" Brazel, who found a large amount of strange debris strewn across a field on the July 4, 1947.

But that was the secrecy agreement.
You are talking to the wrong person. Talk to the tableau.

Does it talk?
No.

[Laughs.] So I can talk to it all I want, but it won't talk back?
Well, it might say or do something that I can observe and tell you, but it will not. This is not a court of law. [Chuckles.]

Roswell and Aztec

So there were one or two crashes right around Roswell, and then there was one in Aztec, New Mexico. There was one, they say, in Laredo, Texas. There have been several. At this point, I'm not trying to do an investigative report. But can you tell me how many of your ships crashed that we have pieces of?
Three.

Only three?
That I know of.

So Roswell and Aztec were yours, and the one just south of Laredo, Texas? Is the other one outside of the United States? No?
To be perfectly frank—is that the word?—there were two outside of the United States. The one in the United States was in Aztec.

Do you have mind contact with all the members of Zeta?

Not all, but some. Contrary to speculation, we are not a single group mind.

Could you talk about that?

We have the capacity to communicate with each other rapidly, but we do not think as one, just as ants do not think as one on your planet. This whole idea that individuals think as one because they participate with such synchronous behavior is a falsehood. It is also a way of suggesting philosophically that in order to cooperate at that level, a person must lose his or her sense of identity and individuality. In my experience, the opposite is true. One must be very secure in one's own individual personality to cooperate absolutely toward an endeavor that is of benefit to either the group or to the group and others according to our service.

Okay. So say more. How do you communicate mind to mind with someone who's far away? How does that work?

Sometimes it utilizes a transmission device not unlike yours. If it is a faraway person, sometimes we communicate on the meditative level, spiritually speaking, but we do not simply just talk to the other person as if he or she could hear us.

Do you fly your craft in formation? When we see very tight formations zooming back and forth at impossible angles, are those yours?

We are not the only ones to do this, but we have been doing it for the past eighty years or so because of what your machines can detect. This whole business of flying with nonballistic motion was to confuse your machines, but now your machines have figured that out, so sometimes we fly in patterns. Other times, not. It depends on the number of vehicles needed for any particular assignment. If only one or two, then a pattern is unnecessary.

What would a large number of vehicles be needed for? What would be an example?

As of this time I can see no reason to have a large number of vehicles come to Earth.

But in the past . . .

Again, I can see no reason to have a large number of vehicles come to the Earth in one formation. For one thing, they would be going to different places on the Earth, so why fly together?

But when you did that in the past, it was to draw attention to the fact that you were here?

We have only done that once in the past, over Peru. That was because a spiritual child asked us to, but the formation you may be thinking of over Washington D.C. was not our people.

No, I know that. But what I was really getting at was that I would assume you would have to communicate in some way beyond technical means to hold those types of formations. That's what I was getting at.

No, it is not difficult. After all, your own vehicles fly in tight formations. We do not fly any tighter than in those tight formations you fly in.

I see.

We might at times have a three-ship triangular formation, but then only for a cause, meaning to contact somebody we know.

All right. Aztec, New Mexico, was the only crash in the United States, then. They did a lot of detective work and everybody thinks the rest were yours.

A great many have assumed that Roswell was one of ours. Sometimes the tableau says yes, and sometimes it says no. My general impression from my work with the tableau over the years would suggest that the ship was not ours but that perhaps one or two of the individuals on board were our people. It is more likely, however, that the ship was from another place, another port, as you might say.

Can you say who? Did they have a name or a civilization or something?

The reason the tableau is vague is because it does not wish to discuss this very much.

I see. All right.

It is a point of contention between our government and yours. Our people on the ship were observers, not unlike if you were to send diplomats aboard a seagoing vessel under another country's flag.

Gifts of Ships

We'll ask somebody else, then, because there were several crashes. Thirty-two feet long, sixty-six feet in diameter, ninety-nine feet . . . many of them that the government got. I don't know who the others belonged to.

Remember, these were not all captured.

They crashed.

No, no. Some of these were gifts, especially ones that were completely intact. There are several that were entirely intact. Our vehicles do not crash when they are intact. So the ones that are intact are gifts, and gifts, of course, would have no weapons systems. They would be rudimentary ships, meaning that one or two of your people might conceivably fold themselves inside and make some effort to learn how to fly abroad in them. Even then, there would not be much damage done if they were to bump off the walls a little bit. I know that in fact the Pleiadians gave your government a gift of a ship that is completely intact.

So are we flying around with it now?

Your people have been experimenting with it for years to some extent, trying to get ideas and also trying to make some sense out of how it works. You are used to mechanical contrivance, but the ship is not entirely mechanical. It has levels. I have felt for many years that these computer games—while the subject matter of the games is perhaps not the most spiritual—are very useful. The level of the games—meaning when you succeed at level one, you go to the next level—has been useful training for your youngsters, and now they are growing up and the next generation is coming along. The ship is analogous to that. It has some mechanical contrivances that can perform certain functions, and the ship can do things that your vehicles cannot do, but once you have mastered or at least understood the rudiments of that, the next level is mental.

So you engage with the ship on a mental level. You might, for instance, wear something around your forehead or temples and engage with the ship that way. At another level beyond that, you might make a connection with the ship on the spiritual or feeling level. There are all these different levels. The ship is a training device to train the pilot or pilots (and to some extent the ground crew) on the advantages of evolving and embracing spiritual evolution so that the organic matter—and I say organic advisedly, meaning not only the thinking matter of the ship, but the feeling or the heart or the spirit of the ship—can interact with you.

Once you have engaged the ship on that level, it can do a great deal more. In this way, the ship, its original port, your planet and planets beyond your own are protected, because in order to pilot such a ship (even to bring a passenger, since the passenger would have to engage spiritually as well), the pilot and the passenger would have to make a physical, mental, spiritual, emotional, heart and perhaps even instinctual connection on a very personal level with the ship. When that is done, the vehicle might usually be able to fly out of your galaxy, travel in time and do all of these things. The safety mechanism is that the pilot and passenger are engaged in those levels of connection. Because of this, they cannot do harm to themselves or others. Even if there were something onboard the ship that will cause something harmful to occur (an object that may not even have been put there by the pilot or the passenger), that object itself would either not work, or the ship would not go anywhere with the pilot and passenger.

Engaging a ship in this way requires the trust and faith of the ground crew in the pilot and passenger that they will return. So it is a training tool. This is how the Pleiadians train their young, and when they feel a race is deserving of an opportunity to learn these lessons, they will offer a prize such as a vehicle like this, which cannot be made to work fully until you adjust your whole being to it.

How Earth Is Tested

But the people who have control of it are the least likely to get into the spiritual or heart-centered beingness, right?

For now, but think about it: Imagine if you had something that could do miraculous things, and you knew it could do so because the people who gave it to you told you, "With this ship you can fly to the center of the universe and meet the most wondrous beings you have ever even imagined." But when you're trying to use it, all you can do is get it to float up off the ground for a little bit and then come back down. You would feel like the beings had lied to you or that there's something you're not doing right.

Because you're still in the mechanical level?

What I'm saying is that at some point you are going to reluctantly relent and allow others to begin playing with it. It might take fifty or a hundred years, but at some point you're going to say "I give up" and let others try to do something with it. In this way, the Pleiadians are gauging your civilization, at least on the level of governments and sinister secret governments. Once they see that ship take off and fly to the center of the universe, they'll know you've made progress, and then they will approach. Is this not wise?

That is pretty clever. And your ships work the same way as those of the Pleiadians?

No, no, but their ships are made with a great deal of heart, and the material, the matter of the ship, is actually alive. Our ships are not dead, but they are not as alive as the Pleiadian ships. The Pleiadians have a certain amount of pride in the level of—how can we say?—beingness of their ships. Not the really old ones, you understand, but the current fleet. Like your taxicabs, the old ones are still chugging about but are not necessarily [chuckles] the most advanced.

The ships that you, the Zetas, gave to the United States government . . . did you give them just to the United States or to other governments?

We gave a toy to the U.S. Government—what we would consider a toy—that is a communications device.

Yes, you talked about that.

Yes, but we did not give a ship.

You didn't give ships to any government?

When a government, even inadvertently, knocks one of your ships out of the sky and then won't give your people back, why would you want to make a gift to them?

Okay, I misunderstood you earlier. You said that not all of the ships our government had were crashed.

Yes, they had a Pleiadian ship that is entirely intact.

Crashes in the North

But regarding your ships that crashed, are you saying only one crashed in the United States? Was there one in Sweden and one in Norway? Can you say where the other two are?

I will say only that they are in the North country. One has not been discovered.

Oh, and you can't say if that's the Swedish or the Norwegian one, then?

The other one has been discovered, but the government and the people there are a little more advanced and were quick to acquiesce to returning our people. We did not take the vehicle. We said, "This vehicle crashed at no fault of your own." It was weakened by exposure to a particular kind of energy on Earth. When you fly north, you know, you get closer to the magnetic pole, and so the ship lost some of its capacity to navigate, but it was what you would call a controlled crash landing. It was not damaged very much and the people inside were not injured, but the ship itself could not regularly leave.

So the beings, the government and so on, said, "How can we help you?" And the people on the ship said, "Don't come too close, because if you touch the ship for the first twenty-eight to sixty minutes, it could harm you," and so they stayed at a distance. Then they talked through a communication device on the ship, and the people on the ship said, "We will ask if the ship can be left in your hands," and there was some considerable discussion about that.

So, as is not unusual for my people, once the occupants were evacuated, the communication to the surface was, "We will loan you the ship." [Chuckles.] I called it a gift, but to me, a loan for sixty years is quite a while. The idea was that at the end of the sixty years, if they could not come close to reproducing it with their own materials or figure out how it worked—even though we have engaged a circuit that would keep it from leaving Earth's atmosphere—we would take it back. If they make enough progress with it, we will help you with your space program.

So this northern country was very helpful. The other ship crashed in a remote northern location, and the occupants were rescued. The ship was buried underground and is not likely to be discovered.

So three altogether. Are all the rest of them from other civilizations, then?

Yes, they are. The word goes out. Unfortunately, my people are slow in communicating in general, and we were slow to put the word out that there were machines being tested on the Earth that might interfere with a certain type of navigation system. By the time we and others put the word out, five to seven Earth days had gone by and several ships were inadvertently knocked down. I believe it was unintentional.

They seemed to have bodies similar to yours.

We had two people on this ship. They told me I can say that; there were two people on the ship in Roswell.

Two there, and then the ones in Aztec.

Aztec was our ship.

So those are the only two that are Zeta, then?

Well, the ship's origin in Roswell was not Zeta, as I said, but I must be specific.

So either the information we have gotten is full of disinformation, or there are other civilizations that have beings that look like yours. Are there any?

There are civilizations where, as I said, we have been hybridizing for years, but we do not have people who look identical to us. All of our hybrids look kind of like us, but our people have a very specific appearance.

Okay, so when you say there were only three crashes—plus the two observers at Roswell who were Zeta—you are saying these were . . .

Specifically Zeta Reticulan, 100 percent of Zeta Reticulan origin. I am excluding any hybrids.

How many hybrid ships crashed? I ask because there seem to be a lot of them.

About five.

Five. That makes sense, then. And some of them couldn't breathe the atmosphere, right? Some of the reports state that the door was open and they were just sort of falling out of the door.

Nobody can breathe the atmosphere. Even the Pleiadians can hardly tolerate your atmosphere. Nobody but Earth people can tolerate it, and you don't tolerate it very well either.

Why Life Is Hard on Earth

That's why we die so young.

Yes, but bad air you're born with. If your atmosphere were more suitable to life here . . .

We could live hundreds of years.

Yes, but it is intended that you live short lives, because life is hard here.

And we need to learn this lesson and get on to the next one?

Well, this is the hard one.

This life now?

Life on Earth is the hard lesson. You could argue that there were lessons before Earth that were hard, but in my way of looking at it, this is the hard one. In other places, if you make a mistake, you blow up a planet and it's over—that's that. It would be a catastrophe, but it would be over. Here, that is less likely to occur. You make a mistake and the following six generations might suffer from it, because in this place you are intended to learn. And you are not just asked to learn. You are not even allowed to learn. You are *required* to learn. No one has come to this planet in the last several thousand years, even if living only a minute, without learning something.

You have more of your higher level with you tonight, don't you?

Yes.

I can tell. What I'm learning from these books is what the Zetas have given to humans—that lifetime-and-a-half acceleration, the technology we got from your ships that led to the integrated circuit, the laser . . . everything.

The Pleiadians have not been in agreement with us on this. The Pleiadians feel that your flirtation with technology without a heart is the most likely scenario in which you might obliterate yourselves, but we were advised by our guides that you must go through this time of science and technology that is heartless in order to *choose* to put heart into the technology. If you started out with heart in your technology (as the Pleiadians do), you might never have learned the lesson that you are still learning, which is that if science or technology harms as well as helps, then there is something wrong with the entire system, and the entire system must be changed, even if part of the science or technology seems to be exclusively helping. This is a difficult lesson for you, but our guides informed us that this is a terrible struggle, one that you must learn here and now so that when other lessons or challenges arise in the future, you will have a reason to choose heart-centered technology and science as compared to simply going along with heartless technology because that is the way everybody else does it.

Well said. It's the Atlantean lesson.

Yes, it is completely understood by myself and many others on many levels that some aspects of science and technology are very humanitarian, even devoted to the betterment of all beings. However, if even one aspect is hurtful, then the entire equation must be modified. Granted, the benevolent aspect will need to be modified least, but even that will need to modified somewhat.

All right. You say that the Pleiadians disagreed with you on this. Did you give the technology to the United States or did the government take it from those ships that crashed?

The Pleiadians don't see a difference between giving and taking, because their advisors see it as a circumstance that could be avoided, especially since we can travel in time.

Oh, you could have come back and retrieved the ship.

Yes, the Pleiadians did not recognize accidents or crashes. From their point of view, as you say, if something like that happened, they would say, "Why don't you go back and pick up the pieces? Don't leave anything. And leave them with no memory of it." But we say, "Now this is what we are guided to do. You must follow your path as you have been guided to do, and we must follow our path." We do not have agreement on this today, although in most other aspects we get along. [Chuckles.]

See, you're totally different from how humans typically see you. Why, in your normal life, are you separated from this spiritual aspect? You are so totally different when you are connected with this part of yourself.

Oh no, you do not understand. When I am in this spiritual aspect of myself, I can speak to you with my full personality, because I do not need an electric or electronic guardian to keep me protected from your energy, even at a distance. Do you understand now?

Yes.

But when I speak to you from my normal self, even though I'm millions of light years away, I still need a device to protect me from your feelings, as felt through the channel to me. The reason you are experiencing my full personality in this meditative communication—where I'm in a meditative state—is because I do not require the use of that device at all.

That is very interesting. I didn't know that.

This is the normal personality we show to others when we do not have to use the device. We do have personalities. [Chuckles.] We are individuals.

Misperceptions of ETs

That's why I want this book out, because there's so much misinformation, disinformation and confusion out there. You're seen as practically automatons.

Think of this for the reader: Say you are new to planet Earth, and you come to a school. You look like an Earth person, so no one thinks anything of it, but you are not from Earth. Everybody is playing or teaching or studying. You go to a college, and the people are studying and laughing between classes, and you think, "Oh, everybody here is just like on our planet." Then you visit an army base, and people are yelling, screaming, working hard and marching around like automatons, saying, "Yes, sir; no, sir."

So our interaction with the people on your ships has been like an army base. [Laughs.]

It's as if you find yourself on a military base, and because you do not experience our personality, you only experience what is safe for us to radiate through the shielding device. Not what is safe for you, but what is safe for us. Our personality is completely safe for you. It is your personality and energy in this body on Earth now that is not safe for us, but we get along just fine with your immortal personality. It is your personality with Earth conditions and with Earth body and with polarity that is difficult for us. Hence, we have to use the device, as you discovered tonight. Even millions and millions of light years away, I still have to use the device in my completely physical state.

That information needs to be put out.

So speaking to you from this level, you can see a little more of my personality and get the impression from me (being just one of many) that we all have personality.

I'm delighted. And might one of the little tiny considerations of accelerating human spirituality and giving us technology have been to speed up time so that we could all interact without using the device a little bit sooner?

No, we are not allowed or encouraged to speed up anything for you. As a matter of fact, if anything, we are encouraged to slow it down so that you can experience the maximum detail.

But you said those devices sped up our evolution by a lifetime and a half.

Yes, but not really. Just being exposed to them sped up your spiritual evolution. As I said before, that is a side benefit from my perspective, but it was not intended. It just happens, and therefore that's why we don't pick everybody up. We don't want to accelerate you so that you do not learn what you came here to learn. To learn those lessons requires slow, not quick learning. Quick is your normal state; slow allows you to learn, with details.

With details, yes. Joopah said that because there was some inadvertent discomfort attached to the Zeta-human connection or contacts, they were going to be "discreated." What is your understanding about that?

Can you elaborate, please?

He said they were going to go back in time and that if someone had interacted with a Zeta and some part of that person had been cured, fixed or healed, the experience would be changed so that the interaction would be with an Andromedan, a Pleiadian or someone with feelings, and that from now until seventy-five years from now all of this would be discreated. Is this something that you know about?

I do not understand, so apparently not.

Can you ask a guide or something? Because I'd like to talk about it a little bit.

I do not understand. They say, "Ask Joopah." Could you rephrase some more?

Well, what he said was that every interaction between a human and a Zeta, from the human's point of view, would become one with a person who was more clearly on a feeling level.

Which person?

From the human point of view, instead of a Zeta it would be a Pleiadian or a Sirian or something.

Why?

Because you might not understand, but there was a lot of discomfort for the humans.

But why would the discomfort not be present if you simply change the being? Oh, because of our device . . .

We have a feeling level, and we could feel the being's heart. We can't feel your heart because it's cloaked from us, do you see? I have many, many books here about people who are still going to therapy to get over the sense of being violated, of not having free choice. On a human, conscious level, they didn't understand what was going on, and they felt trauma and pain.

It is unfortunate.

I was asking why it had to be like that for some people who gained a lot in their interaction. But they said that every bit of discomfort that humans felt has to be discreated and they were going to start with that little piece of it.

I see. Thank you for that explanation. You can tell that I have nothing to give you, but now you've given me something.

Sources of Modern Technology: Guided rather than Given

Let's get back to these craft, because our way of life is different now because of the chips and the lasers. I know military capability has increased, but humans' everyday lives, from computers to cameras, everything we deal with . . .

We do not see ourselves as being responsible for this. To the extent you have seen our technology, it has not been that you took our technology and adapted it to yours. You got ideas from it. That's all. Ideas. Not that you found a transistor in our ship [laughs], but that you got ideas that prompted you to go in this or that direction with your technology.

Which we might not have done without your ships?

Yes, you might have taken longer to get to the level of technology where you are now, since this gave you something you could look at and say, "Well, this seems to work and do things that we want to do at some point in time." Of course, everybody's saying sooner not later. The ship and the ship's technology acted as a guide, a goal, that's it. To say that we somehow provided this—I am not personally feeling comfortable with that. I'd rather say that we supported a certain direction in your technological pursuits.

You catalyzed . . . But we're only still, like you say, on the physical level and working toward the other levels.

Yes. Ultimately, once you fully embrace these other levels of your own choice, you will be able to do more with the machines you are using now, machines you yourselves have created and invented. You will help them, they will be able to help you and you will change the way you do things.

Well, they're starting to. I mean F-22 Raptors are practically flown with the mind.

Not completely, but there is some interaction between the senses and the vehicle. Perhaps it would be better not to say too much about that. Your government would not be happy if I did. I do not wish to unnecessarily offend.

Let's talk about that. You can't have a bad feeling and operate one of those things?

You wouldn't want to be distracted and operate such a thing. That's why they are going slowly with this technology, because they have been getting hints that if the pilot is having a hard time at home or is upset about something, then the more sensitive the system is, the more likely it will react sympathetically (not using sympathy in terms of being heart-centered but sympathetically in terms of the vibrational) with the pilot, and the system might not be able to function once it is in sympathy with the pilot. Of course, in the long run, it is exactly that which will help you to make a spiritual leap, but current research doesn't operate in such erudite circles. Most of this is not understood as an advantage by the casual experimenter. But eventually someone will read such reports, if they are given in great detail and say, "Oh, this is the direction to go with the spacecraft."

That's what we might have. What I'd like to do is just have humans feel that they know you better. Are we looking at hundreds of years before you can visit Earth without your shielding?

Oh, it might be a hundred and fifty years. But other ETs will visit you, and we might come to see you with the device. You might not quite grasp us for a while, but future generations will. Other ETs will try to explain, and eventually people will understand, and it will just give you greater motivation to embrace heart technology.

Did you at first attempt to interact with humans without it?

Yes, and it resulted in many deaths amongst our people. We naturally thought that it was a germ or a plague. So we would isolate our people afterward for a time. After we analyzed them, we could see it wasn't a germ. Then we tried the opposite. We fully isolated the visitors on the ship in a "shell," and they would be feeling uncomfortable, like being in an incubator: They desperately wanted to get out.

Is that the shell talked about in the Andreasson book?

No, I think that was an aftereffect, meaning that it was still being used to some extent then, although it had other purposes. After a while, however, we realized this would not be all right. Earth people and the like must be able to move freely or they are frightened. It is one thing to have to be still for a few moments of consciousness and another thing to have to always be still. That is very upsetting. So then our scientists suggested that perhaps we could collapse the auric field around us, our own auric field, so we could maintain our own energy exclusively within this field. It would not be perceptible to any Earth person, other than the most sensitive people who at times might see a silver glow on the edges where our bodies meet the rest of reality. We opted for that, and from the moment we started using that device, there were no further casualties.

I think you've said that somehow you also breathe within that.

It is a complete envelopment. It might appear to be exposed, but it is entirely like a shield.

What do you breathe?

Our atmosphere is different from yours.

You can't say. Is there a reason why not?

There must be. The tableau never justifies anything, ever. Justification is a portion of analysis. Analysis with justification is only used in worlds that are polarized. It's not used anywhere else, because it is unnecessary. It is a natural comment on your part, yet it is like a non sequitur to the tableau. The tableau says, "This is what is," and is not authoritarian. It is as if the tableau says to me, "Look, this is an apple," and you say, "But couldn't it be an orange?" The tableau doesn't know how to respond to that.

Well, I wouldn't say, "Couldn't it be an orange?" I would say, "Why is it an apple? What is it made up of? Why is there a . . . ?"

But regardless, if you said, "Why is it an apple?" the tableau would not know how to respond to that.

Okay, what I was getting at was that whatever you do breathe, you are required to somehow move it through your body, right?

There is a limit to what I can tell you strategically about ourselves, since we are still in negotiations with your government—obviously not with the president; he does not know much about us and is not too interested, but he might know a little bit. Generally speaking, though, the people we are in communication with do not hold elective office, which is suitable to us so our communications and negotiations can have an element of continuity. If we negotiated with a president who is gone in four years, then what good is that? [Chuckles.]

ET Captives and the Secret Government

Do you negotiate with what we call the inner circle of the secret government?

Sometimes, and sometimes with certain elements of your bureaucratic government.

I was just going to ask how long your envelope could support you, but if that's strategic too, then . . .

That is strategic. Certain things about our survival are considered strategic. That is a good word, don't you think? You, of course, would not go to a country you are fighting with and say, "This is how many troops we have, and how many guns." You would never do that.

Do you consider that you are fighting with us?

No.

Are any of your people still in captivity?

Yes. Why else would we be negotiating?

I see. But what about you personally in your life? I think I already asked you that. You don't need to read or watch television or anything, or so many of the things we do to get information—you have the tableau.

We have the tableau, but I understand Zoosh is encouraging you to engage in vertical wisdom. We do not often do this because we have the tableau, but I feel engaging vertical wisdom is really an advanced step, definitely a spiritual thing to do. If you can do that, you will gradually lose interest in television even for entertainment, because once you can engage vertical wisdom and get interested in doing that, then that is all you'll want to do in terms of your external communication.

Cross-Species Communication

Okay, what other things would you like to communicate about how you live your lives? Because, as we've said, we have such a misconception of who you are.

We are very studious. Part of the reason why we are so pleased to contribute to other beings' evolution or projects is because we are interested in everything. Therefore we are quite open to the various manners and mores of different civilizations, without judgment. We will not inflict harm on another intentionally, so we cannot be used in that way, but we do many things that would be of service. We are interested in the social levels and cultures of different civilizations.

We would consider, for example (since this is Zoosh's favorite), that ants would be a civilization or culture. We would not differentiate a culture—when we say Earth people, we are usually referring to human beings—but ants, having lived here before you did, would certainly qualify under that definition as "Earth people." But we do not think of them that way, because they are much broader beings. So, as I say, civilization and culture to us might be something that is of a given planet, such as Earth human beings, or it might be a plant or an animal.

You can communicate with all of them?

We can communicate. For instance, say I am in an enclosed space with one or several Earth ants; I can immediately take the device off. Why? Is it because the ant does not have a full range of emotions and feelings like Earth people? No, the ant has the full range; it has anger, it has rage and it has love.

I didn't know that.

Of course it does. All beings do. Even a plant has those things, even a spirit in a cloud. In the case of our example, the ant knows who we are. It is an advanced spiritual being and would not for a moment exude any fear or anxiousness, energy or emotion that might harm us. The ant has the capacity to move into phase with our needs, and therefore we can turn the device off and communicate with the ant, and the ant will—almost immediately every time—reassure us that we are safe.

The ant will say, "You're safe," and we will say, "Thank you so much," or something like that. The ant will reassure us that, "You are safe; we are phased with you," or something like that. It will reassure us more than once. They don't have to do this, but they are polite. Often this is found in cultures of Earth, and sometimes even with Earth people. [Chuckles.]

How rare. [Laughs.] Have you ever met an Earth person with whom you could turn off the device?

Yes.

Can you say anything about that?

I have personally met such an individual, and I have heard of other meetings like this between Earth people and my people. It has always been with a person you would call a shaman or medicine person who has the same capacity as the ant, who has learned how to shift his or her energy to be in complete connection with another type of being, thus keeping the feeling level in phase (using the electrical term) and entirely compatible with that of whomever he or she is with.

Transcendent Tribal Wisdom

I had this experience myself with a tribal medicine man. I think his descendents are still alive today; his people are still intact in a Southwestern tribe. I had a wonderful meeting with him. He was wearing his ceremonial garb, having just completed a ceremony. Our ship could see him doing this. He was near a mountaintop. When he finished, he sat down and was resting, and we flew up and hovered nearby. Although the ship did not appear, he could feel it. One of my crew stuck his head out of the port and communicated to him, "Would you like to come aboard for a visit?" He phased with the crew member for a moment, while the crew member had to keep his head out the port a little longer than normal.

Once this great man had phased with our crew member, he said, "Yes, I am connected with you now. You will find that you are safe with me." The moment he said that, I knew this was a man of some wisdom. So he came aboard the vehicle, and we were blessed to have had him aboard for ten experiential Earth days. Then we returned him to his village, but not to the exact time. He said we did not have to do that. We returned him when about one day had gone by. So he stayed ten days with us and was gone only one day of Earth time.

We had a wonderful time. He stayed in phase with us even when he was asleep and dreaming. This is what an ant person can do, and this shamanic person could do it too. We were very impressed, very impressed.

How did he know? He had never talked to you before.

He did the same thing with us that he would do with a plant. Shamanic people know how to do this. You go toward a plant and at first it moves back. It is frightened. You might not see it, but if you look closely you'll see it. Then you say something like, "Good life," or some such thing that they say to each other. Then the plants say, "Oh, maybe it's okay." Then try not to crush other plants when you hunker down and radiate heart energy toward the plant. Then the plant relaxes, and while you are radiating heart energy, get in phase with the plant. The plant can communicate with you, if you wish to communicate and the plant wishes to communicate.

All life is like this—human beings, plants, rocks, rain drops, snow-flakes, animals—it's universal. The shaman did the same thing with my crew member that he would have done with any plant, because that is the way he lived his life. We had him on board for ten wonderful days. We talked to him and he to us. He'd say, "I would like to see the Moon and maybe touch it," and we'd say, "Yes, come." We took him to the moon and put a field around him so that he could walk on the moon in his regular clothes without a spacesuit. He reached down and felt the sort of crunchy surface on that part of the Moon. He liked that so much.

Was he allowed to remember it when he came back?

It wasn't a matter of allowing it. We were honored to meet him. We only induce that in people who might be upset about us or who have people around them who might be upset, but this was an advanced shamanic man. He could phase with all the people he communicated with. We weren't the least bit worried; we were honored. To this day, we have a gift he gave to us. It is in a place of great honor with my people, like an altar. He gave us this special gift and said, "Remember me always with this gift, and I will hold you all in my heart." We have the highest regard for this great friend. When he came to the end of his natural cycle, he appeared briefly on our planet and spoke to all our people. We could see only his face. He gave us a message of greetings and said how much he had enjoyed his time with us. Our people were thrilled.

That's beautiful, and that's a goal—our future, right?

It's a reachable goal, because this happened several hundred years ago. And there are still shamanic and medicine people with you today, and more people are getting interested all the time. So if this man and all these other men and women can do this—and some children too—yes, it means it is possible for any human being. It is not an unreach-able goal, not something that you have to go to a higher dimension to do. When we met this man, Earth and its people were at 3.0. You do not have to go up to that higher dimension; you just need to know how to communicate to beings in such a way that those beings feel safe and reassured, just the way your ants talk to us. So this man talked to us and to trees and to other plants and animals. It is something you can all do, but it takes time and the desire and openness to work slowly. Begin with plants and simple wild animals—maybe with the plants first; they won't frighten you. It's not good to start with a bear or a lion. [Chuckles.] Better to start with a pine tree or some such being, one who is gentle and has a sense of humor.

ET Humor

See, nothing has been published since your first interaction that would lead humans to believe you had a sense of humor.

We learned. We did not have a sense of humor like human beings. Our sense of humor is along the lines of maybe making a double entendre or pun, or a sense of irony, but we did not have the range of humor the human being has developed; it is one of your great assets, I feel. Wit, irony, satire, silliness. We have a little silliness. We like to be silly with children.

So you said Joopah taught you, then?

Joopah teaches very openly. He said that it took him a long time to learn but there was no reason for us to take so long, and so he shared with us.

When he first talked and tried to make a joke, it was terrible. [Laughs.]

If he were here, he would say that it took him a while to get his "timing" down. He told me that once. I thought then that it was just an intellectual statement. Now I recognize the humor in there. [Chuckles.]

Natures of the Dimensions

You're in the seventh dimension, so do you have a lightbody?

No. If you were in the seventh dimension with us, we would seem solid.

But do you have the ability to condense into the third dimension, then? Otherwise you wouldn't have any bodies, right? When your ship crashes, these beings look to be the same density that we are.

The second-dimensional being of Earth (not necessarily less than you in spirit) might be more advanced, but in choosing two dimensions cannot see you at three.

Our understanding now is that there are some type of trading confederations and some loose associations of various civilizations. Do you belong to any of them? We once had a report that you and the Pleiadians had gone off to Andromeda for a council meeting about this part of the galaxy.

We have loose-knit trade organizations—meaning no dues, no rules—but they are organizations only in the fact that we trade with these people and they trade with us. So we consider that a loose-knit organization, though it is not set up by organizational principles you might consider to be as such. We might have diplomatic, loose-knit connections with Pleiadians or Andromedans, Sirians and so forth, because of a connection with you on Earth and so on. We do not consider these things to be a large part of our lives.

If it were a council we were sitting on, that might be different, but generally speaking we do not seek to sit on any council. We would rather serve than make decisions that might affect others who we only slightly understand. Our desire is to serve and learn. We enjoy that very much, and so we pursue it. Other races might wish to be involved in consular activities, but we are not interested in that.

Well, how does it work? Let's say that within this galaxy, it's been called the prime directive that you cannot interfere with Earth's evolution. Is that the same all over the galaxy? Is that a rule? Or can you pretty much go anywhere and do anything you like?

All civilizations might have certain things that they are all right or not all right with. If for some reason—we have not discovered this yet, but just as an example—a civilization in any other part of this galaxy were not comfortable with us as we approached their planet (say from ten thousand miles away or something), we would hear something saying, "Please approach no closer. Thank you for your interest, and if you want to know more about us . . ." And they would refer us to other civilizations that we know, and so forth. This has never occurred, but should it, it would be something like that. Insofar as your civilization is concerned, the reason this so-called "prime directive" as you call it (really just a rule) is in place is because you are protected, not only from interference with your civilization but from those who would come and give you great gifts. Protection works in more than one way.

Suppose you feel fearful about a neighborhood you are new to. You lock the door and don't answer it if someone knocks. Maybe out of ten people, two people would actually be disturbing—maybe only one person—but the other eight people might be bringing great gifts to you, while you are afraid to open the door. What I am saying is this—protection works both ways. It keeps things away from you that might harm you, but the vast effect of the protection is to keep things away from you that, while they might be of great and valuable use, would also interfere with your lessons. So protection is not all that it might seem to be in terms of dramatics.

In the past, a long time ago, there were wars, with ETs colonizing and landing. That was before the current—what can we call it, the current class?

As far as I'm aware, there weren't ETs doing battle with other ETs or with human beings on this planet.

They were battling to control the planet, weren't they?

They might have done some battle external to the planet, but I do not think there is anyplace about which I could say, "Go to this area, and you will find bits and pieces of a previous war of extraterrestrial civilizations." That's not on the surface. Some skirmishes might have happened below the surface, but they would not have left anything, not even a grain of sand. They would have been fastidious and cleaned up.

The Travels of Sha Don

Let's get back to your travels. Do you travel around the universe? Beyond the universe? In this galaxy?

We travel in this galaxy, in our own and in others like Orion or Sirius or the Pleiades, but we don't go too far. We have a rule that we have practically no missions out doing what your science might call basic research. If we hear of a civilization that has some interest to us or might be of interest to someone we visit, we might send an emissary ship to inquire about their activities. But generally we do not travel far and wide.

But on other planets you land and talk to the people?

As do you. When you go to trade your dollars for goods at a store, you land on your feet and talk to the people. It's no different.

So even though you don't go vast distances, your ability to travel in time gives you the whole spectrum of that civilization?

Yes, we have the capacity to do it, but we have enough to do here. [Chuckles.] If we ran out of things to do here, then we might conceivably expand our area of travel, but our chances of running out of things to do here is limited. For example, for all the time my civilization has been in existence (experiential time and not linear time), even with all the exploring we have done with various galaxies and so forth, we have not explored more than one-tenth of your galaxy. So we have lots more to do here before we would ever start seriously considering expanding our explorations beyond this environment.

But now the big thing is that you are all moving to the ninth dimension to a golden lightbody. How is that going to affect your daily life?

Joopah has indicated that it will make a very big change. For instance, we will no longer use ships. When we are at the ninth dimension, we will be able to travel without a ship, or if we choose to travel in company with others, we might form a condensed ball or a disk of light, for instance, and travel in that way. But Joopah has indicated it will mean a radical change to our society, and although we do not normally feel comfortable with sudden and extreme changes, we do understand that this is a change for our benefit and perhaps the benefit of others. We do not know, but at least it is for our benefit, and it is meant to be. So we are prepared to suspend our usual approach, especially since Joopah has indicated that being at this dimension will be very comfortable for us. So we have had a few others become like this and they are amongst us. I quote Joopah, because I happen to know him, but there are others amongst us who are working amongst our people and speaking of such matters.

But you really basically have no idea of what your experience will be or how that will affect your ideals of service.

Joopah and beings like him seem to have those answers, but they also seem to feel no great urgency [chuckles] to tell us these things, because we don't have the urgent need to know. Remember that we are not you. We are not cut off from our total being, and if we have curiosity, we can go to the spiritual level I am on now and inquire. If we need to know or if it would be beneficial for us to know, it will be shared with us. If we do not need to know or if whoever shares these things with us feels we do not need to know, we won't know it, or perhaps we won't recall it. So we do not need to ask Joopah for such things if it would even occur to most individuals.

It is more a happiness. We know it is a gift. We think of it this way, and we are all sure that we will like it. It's just because of our nature that it will take us a while to make the change. We are not resistant; we are just slow. [Chuckles.]

But how does it work, then? Who decides in what order you attain your golden lightbody?

There is no authority figure or hierarchy.

Right. So it's just when one asks?

It just happens.

Ah, it just happens. That's a tremendous leap of faith in a sense, isn't it, that you are all allowing that to happen? I know they said it's a gift, but it's still a tremendous change.

Say a man learns to ride a bicycle when he is a boy. He rides and has fun with his friends. Then when he becomes a grandfather years later, he is teaching his grandson how to ride a bicycle. After not having ridden one for fifty or sixty years, he hops on the bicycle because he has faith that he will remember it. Maybe he will wobble a little bit, but then he'll do it and say, "See? If grandpa can do it, you can too." Then he gets his grandson up on the bicycle with training wheels, and pretty soon the training wheels come off.

It is like that, a faith based on experience. Our people were not always at dimension seven. Go back, back, back. We were at five, and eventually we went to six and then eventually to seven. We have eased through dimensions before, and so in that sense we have faith like the fictional grandfather. If we could ride a bicycle well when we were children, then we can ride pretty well as grandfathers.

That's a good story. You are really exuding golden light. When you pick up somebody on Earth, do you tell them, "Here's your past and your future and your present if you don't change, and here it is if it's beneficial?"

As a rule, we do not do that. It depends on what the person is comfortable with.

That was just the first part of the question. In the past, in our time, your souls lived in human bodies. So we are your past.

You are the past of some of our people, yes.

So is that on both the timeline of past negativity and the timeline with future benevolence?

This we do not know. We think it is in the distant past of the Explorer Race. In the present we are also unsure. In the future, we are certain that you are our past experience on the benevolent timeline, as you are calling it. But at present it is mixed. We do not know whether this means that some of you will go on to that benevolent experience and not others, or whether it is that that experiential level is not fully engaged yet. We just do not know.

Well, it's our understanding that we all have to move on to that to move up. So maybe there's a synchronicity with you moving to your golden lightbodies and us moving to our totally benevolent past and future.

I believe this must be so. That could be another explanation for why our transition is as slow as it is. However, we are not known for our speedy change of mind.

But maybe it is slow because humans are slow.

That's certainly a reasonable conjecture.

I mean, slow to become benevolent.

I understand. You are saying synchronously. Yes. It is perfectly reasonable to assume that the synchronous changes throughout this universe are all interconnected.

That's pretty cool; you get your golden lightbodies, and we move up a dimension or two.

Or you move up a dimension and we get our golden lightbodies. [Laughs.] We do not think of it as being entirely interdependent, but rather synchronous somehow, like the wheel on the car—one wheel is pushed but the others come along.

So at some point out there in the future, we'll have a discussion about what you were just pushing. [Chuckles.]

Perhaps. I cannot say for certain.

Okay, all right. I feel really content.

Let me close with this one comment for the movie industry. I do not know of any ETs in my entire life span whom I have met—nor have I ever heard of any—who salivate so much that it is dripping out of their mouths. This idea of frightening monsters is unfounded. I have never met an ET I would think of as frightening. I have certainly met a few that

I would think of as being slower—not exactly boring, but slower—but in my experience, to be threatened by an ET is unknown. I have heard of such cases, but they are rare to the point of being almost random. So maybe consider more movies about benevolent ETs. It might just be that people would like them. Good night.

Good night. Thank you, Sha Don. I really appreciate it. Thank you.

The Zetas Interact Emotionally

Sha Don

November 10, 1998

*A**re you called an elder? You said you were seven hundred to twelve hundred years old . . .*

No. We do not have such designations.

We have been told that, on a level beyond your race and ours, the reason you were asked to sort of look over us, shepherd us or interact with humans, was so that you would come to the realization that having an emotional body is not a terrible thing. What would you like to say about that?

Yes. We have been informed of this. Of course, we feel we do have an emotional body, but we do not exercise a great many variables with it, so it has been offered to us that we could consider exercising or expressing a greater range of feeling, which would still be compatible with our selves. As a people, we are considering it. I do not speak for the people but as one of the people, but I can say that we are considering other feelings or emotions and their expressions. However, in the privacy of our own kind and with those we have faith in, such as the individuals I mentioned the other night, we do express more than calm. We might very well express joy or happiness or love, but we do not do this when exposed to beings or species with whom we must be using the protective envelope. Then, in those circumstances, it is to our advantage to focus on being calm, so we do not also become excited and thus exacerbate the situation.

Therefore it is to our personal advantage to focus and meditate on calm. If all of our people on a ship, let's say, are focusing and meditating on calm while doing our other activities, it is easier to maintain that emotion. If we have different benevolent emotions, it is harder to maintain it. We can, but given all of our other duties on the ship, we will probably maintain this particular aspect of being calm around those with whom we must use the protective device.

This is the preliminary decision, although nothing formal has been decided. Of course, we recognize that when we are in our ninth-dimensional golden lightbody, we will not require the device, and we will be able to express a full range of benevolent feelings and emotions without any qualms or discomforts. So we do understand that and are totally at peace with that.

Spontaneous Transitions to Golden Lightbodies

But can you just go into your golden lightbody and start expressing? Wouldn't it be like saying, "When I get there, I'm going to be a dancer, but I've never exercised or had any practice"?

Does a human child practice being a human child before he or she is one?

No.

We are talking about a change of being. Why do we need to practice to be what we will be? Better that we should stay in touch with what we *are* so we do not get confused about that.

My question was based on the fact that you don't have much time because you're going to become a golden lightbeing. I didn't realize that the full range of emotions was part of that. I thought it was more of a planned, spiritual kind of thing.

According to what I have seen from the golden-light versions of ourselves, they do exhibit a full range of benevolent emotions around us. This is according to what I know and have been told by Joopah and one other. It is not something that Joopah practiced. It was simply something that was present and it . . . "comes with the package."

Haha! That's a good one. My concern was that you would miss it.

We are intrigued about the prospect. As a matter of fact, today two more of my people transformed into this golden lightbody. It appears to be entirely spontaneous, without any planning or forethought. Therefore, such actions and plans as might be laid for a chosen project cannot be done. So there is no point in training for something like that.

And how are they reacting? They're very happy?

It is very simple. It happens, and then, "Oh, wonderful." And you go on. You don't necessarily change what you were going to do that day. [Chuckles.]

But you said that they wouldn't be going out on ships anymore?

I have been advised that those particular beings will not require ships. If they choose to travel in the company of others like them, they might choose to condense as light, but if they wish to travel on their own, they can do so. You would not see someone hurtling through space, as it were, and looking like that. [Chuckles.] They would probably be traveling as an efficient ball of light.

Or going through portals? That's part of it?

I cannot say. Not that I am not willing to say, I simply cannot.

The possibility might be, then, that if they don't need the devices, they might (while you're still dealing with humans) come on the ships and interact with people? Or you don't really interact with people that much any more?

Just say for the sake of an example that we did. It is certainly possible. One might also ask, "What about golden-light visions of our people flying with, say, Pleiadians on a Pleiadian ship?" I don't see why not; it hasn't come up yet. Or on some other ship? I don't see why not, as I've said, but there might be reasons. Speculation is not something I am good at. [Chuckles.]

When I was talking to Joopah, I got the impression that the first ones are going to be like ambassadors of the golden lightbeing status to the rest of the Zetas, saying, "Hey, it's wonderful; don't be afraid." I think that's what the first group of them are going to do.

Yes, this has been accomplished and nobody is concerned anymore. Now they can do as they wish, although I do not think any gold lightbeings of my people have traveled anywhere off the planet yet. But for all I might know, perhaps they have and I don't know about it.

In addition to the work you do with humans—that is just a small part of what you do—you do scientific work all over the galaxy, don't you? You have projects everywhere. Do I understand that right?

Well, nothing quite so focused as what we do with Earth people. We might have projects in other places, but nothing at the same level of urgency or complexity as what we do with you. So there is plenty of time for everything else, and it is perhaps not so very relevant.

The Time Is Coming when Humans and Hybrids Will Meet

What I'm leading to is that you thought your race was coming to an end, so you created these hybrids. Is it possible that they can take over the work you were doing with the humans?

My feeling is this: The work we have done with human beings is work that was assigned to us and embraced by us. We do not wish to pass on to the hybrid species anything other than the basis of our own knowledge and wisdom, that they might accept or reject or build upon it. It has not been our desire, nor would it be an assignment or even a suggestion on our part, that any of the hybrid species take this over, because it would interfere with their own free choice. Therefore, if any of them express an interest in participating (which some have in the past) then they have been invited to come with us. There has been only occasional interest. I think they are waiting for you as a people to become more interested in meeting them, because their race is the most adaptable and amenable to you. I think you would find them to be interesting and intriguing and fun. They feel that you are not yet quite ready to embrace them, but I think this time is coming.

Help me to understand that. You lived for 1,200 years. Do you remember your past lives as a soul?

I do not consciously think about them unless for some reason I need to know something that I might have done in a previous lifetime or something that I might wish to do in a future lifetime but have not done. We don't interfere with our futures. Although I can access that, I personally (speaking for myself) have not looked into my past lives too much, because I feel they would be a distraction. It would be very easy to become overly attached to past-life accomplishments or perhaps, even more so, to things that were left undone. I have discovered that individuals (not my people but other people I have met) who have become very interested in their past lives have invariably tried to resolve past-life problems in their present lives. Sometimes the process is unconscious because the individual has compassion for past-life problems, feeling or perhaps thinking unconsciously or subconsciously that it wouldn't be so difficult to resolve that in the present life and take some simple, even innocuous, step toward resolution. This leads one vastly astray of one's present life. So, having seen enough of this, I would learn by the experience of others.

That leads to two questions. Number one: Have most of your past lives been as a Zeta, or have you been in other civilizations and other types of bodies?

I have looked at my past lives. Sometimes you on Earth have this experience and can look at someone and see his or her past life flashing by, one life after another. You have had this experience? It's most remarkable. I have done this, but I have not looked further.

What I'm leading to is the chance to have fun. Do you think that it's possible that some Zetas who might not be ready or might not want to go directly to their golden lightbodies could go to into the body of the hybrids after this life cycle?

I must correct your question. Everybody is ready.

Everybody's ready?

Everybody is now ready, accepting and continuing with his or her current life until this spontaneous event occurs. Perhaps it will accelerate, perhaps not. We have no sense of anxiety. This has been resolved, so you will need to alter your question.

I see. Once you attain your golden lightbody, is it an immortal body that you keep for as long as you want it?

I do not know. One would assume from contact with other golden lightbeings that some extensive long life would be available, but I do not know, nor have I asked Joopah—but I will inquire. [Pauses.] Joopah says immortal, but he is not certain.

The Formation of the Tableau

You don't need to be certain. It's another adventure. The other question I have is where you get your answers. Let's deal with that.

From the tableau.

Is that a spiritual mechanism or a technological one?

The tableau is a living machine. (All your machines are living too, but not happily.) This is a happily living machine, constructed on the basis of materials (the materials that make it up) that have indicated an interest in knowing without reservation. So we have invited these materials to form up into some shape that is pleasing to them, which means that the tableau might not always appear the same. The structure of it might be different, according to the material's choice. Therefore, the tableau will essentially (if it is something visible) float a picture out—not like a hologram exactly, a little more lifelike. If it is thought- or word-oriented, it will transfer that to the mind of inquiry, meaning that if you have a question, you ask the tableau. You might think it, and the tableau will respond with what it knows or can access.

If it is something that requires other senses, according to our sense of how they work, it will attempt to give us all that we can take in at the speed at which we can take it in, in the safest, gentlest way for us. This is typical of any being—speaking of the tableau as some*one*—who wishes to work compatibly with others. It's a good teaching method. The tableau does not give us more than we can assimilate, nor does it tantalize us [chuckles] with only a little bit. It will give us a response that we can actually assimilate.

I'm still a little confused. Is it in one place? Do you use something wherever you are in order to talk to it? Can you talk to it on your ship, at home, anyplace you are, anytime?

Sometimes I have seen tableaux that are quite large. They are like this [gestures].

Three feet wide and a couple of feet high. Okay.

Maybe something like a couple of feet by a couple of feet or two and a half feet, something like that, but not square or round. It would be some abstract shape that the tableau itself found to be pleasing. I have seen a tableau so small that I had to use an instrument to see it. This tells you, of course, that each tableau is complete unto itself. For instance . . .

There's not just one? There are a great many of them?

Yes. For instance, a tableau that might be taken aboard a ship would need to be fairly small. As it becomes a tableau, we first indicate how we might like to use it, which suggests a form in the desired shape, and we ask it, "Would you like to travel in a ship with us?" There is a complete explanation. We say, "You will have the opportunity to go places, see things and acquire knowledge. Perhaps you will see different kinds of beings you would not normally physically see," and so on.

So then volunteers of that material will invariably create a smaller version so as to be easily installed in a ship. We do not carry them around. They like to be established somewhere. Once they have created a place and a form, they like to stay there. They want to be in that spot.

If it is a ship, they stay in that spot on the ship. The ship might move around, but they remain where they are in the ship. So a certain amount of continuity seems to be desired by the tableau. I refer to the tableau as singular, but there are more than one.

There's one in every ship. And when you're home . . . ? Are there thousands of these beings?

Yes. Not every person needs or desires a tableau in his or her home or area of living. However, if one is needed, a person will go to somebody else's place and use it. It is also possible, if one cannot assimilate the information right then, to touch the tableau. First you would inquire, and then you would touch it with one finger. Once the tableau is touched in this manner, the knowledge will be incorporated into that finger. Then you might later touch it to your palm for assimilation. It might possibly be something you are curious about but not having to do with your work in that moment, or perhaps you don't have the time to assimilate it then but you later will.

How do they communicate with each other? How do they all keep updated?

I have no idea whether or not they communicate with each other. The material itself all comes from one place, and I have no reason to believe that there is any disconnection between them, no break. I don't know if they communicate with each other. It is not like updating a computer, but my understanding of the existence of this material is that wherever it exists (meaning once it has been moved from such a place) it remains in touch with all the other material, even if the ship goes to the other side of the universe. Time and space do not matter.

So there was once one somewhere and then each subsequent one is somehow born from that or given the information that's there?

Say, for example, that all coal on Earth was once a single being, meaning one massive piece of coal.

I see where you're going . . .

Then I won't go there. It is this. It is the same material, only acquired in one certain place. My understanding is that time and space don't matter, and it remains in touch with itself.

Contacting the Tableau through Meditation

This might be belaboring it a little bit, but I want to get it in the book. Let's say you're here on Earth and you learn something important—do you think it into your tableau? How do you put it into the one on the ship?

That is a good question. Whether we are at home or on the ship, all members of the people meditate once within a time period that would be roughly equal to three and a half days. During that time, we become more expansive, and the tableau can access anything in our conscious, subconscious or unconscious. It can access anything within us and acquire any information that it feels it might need for any reason. It is a living machine. When we are in this meditative state, there not only is no barrier between us and other life forms, but there is actually union between us and all of existence.

Once the tableau on your ship chooses to incorporate within itself what you have just learned, then somehow all the others everywhere know it too?

I do not know. It is possible. One assumes that if all parts of a being are connected regardless of time and space, then if one part knows, it is reasonable to assume that the other parts do also.

When humans or Pleiadians or other beings are onboard, even if the humans aren't meditating, can they access what's in the tableau too?

No, they have respect for other species' sense of privacy. But if the beings were to meditate and achieve that level of union with all life, then the tableau might, only might, acquire such wisdom or information if it felt that the being would not be insulted or upset about the tableau or others knowing. If the tableau felt a sense of privacy about this information, it would not assimilate it. It would be as if you picked up something and then put it back. It is a built-in "reject" mechanism. [Chuckles.]

Would most humans on the ships be scared, frightened and upset usually?

It depends upon whether they stay with us long enough. If they are spiritually advanced, like the individuals I referred to before, they might not even need to meditate to go to that level.

Oh, so when the shaman was with you, the tableau might have learned some things from him that he wouldn't have minded sharing?

Yes. Most shamanic people do not have many secrets when it comes to their personal lives, although they might retain secrets of others, and so the tableau might feel that the shaman knew things about other people that they would not like to be known, and it would not acquire that information.

Selection and Management of Contacts

If you are in your ship and I ask about a certain case or contact, even if you weren't part of the crew of that ship, is there then information in the tableau about that particular contact with humans?

There might be, yes. Yet when we first began, the idea was that I would comment on cases where I was present. It is possible that I might be able to access information from the tableau in situations where I was not present; however, the information would then become slightly different. It would be as if I were watching it happen, and I would not be able to give you my personal responses. I might not be able to give you the personal responses of the person invited aboard either, because while the tableau would be a witness, if the person invited aboard did not wish to have his or her memories or experiences acquired, the tableau would simply be a visual witness.

Let's say we're dealing with contact cases from the late 1940s through today. How many different humans did you contact, not counting when you put in the implant?

Oh, maybe seven or eight.

Is that all?

There were others doing this, plus sometimes I would be in some other part of the ship while someone was welcomed aboard. Therefore, I might not actually be present during the experience. So I would report to you my personal encounters only. I was aboard the ship for about thirty-five others, something like that, but I did not encounter the individuals. I was just there.

You were the coordinator of the ship?

When I was doing this, I was the coordinator. You say commander, because of your race's desire still to be led, but my people do not require leadership in this way, so a coordinator would be similar to a manager, not to a captain.

So you had many things to manage. Let's see. The medical people, the psychologist . . . how would you describe who would interact with the contactees?

We aren't really broken down into specialties like that. Remember, my people can access methods and manners—perhaps not mores [chuckles], but methods and manners—if we need to. There is, I believe, in most cases someone who could cause the subject or person invited aboard to become calmer should he or she become upset for any reason.

It took us a while to realize that this was a past-future life connection, but when we realized that, we made it a point to have someone like that onboard. In my experience, it is easy to be calmed by some aspect of you from the future. Generally speaking, future aspects are more advanced or benevolent, at least in my experience, and because they have love for you personally, they can easily calm you. So it was like that—not a specific psychologist, doctor, nurse or historian.

On a particular ship, were the contacted humans chosen because the inhabitants or crew of the ship would look for their past lives, or were they chosen first and then you would find someone of Zeta from his or her future life and get that being on the ship? Which way did it work?

It was both ways. In the beginning, it wasn't on the past lifeline. It was just a scan to see which souls were open to this. Then later, when we realized the past-future connection, we would give priority to souls who were open to this, who would have a future life. We could bring that future life with us. This tells you something important.

That there's a lot of planning involved.

More than that. It tells you that the scan takes place from our planet and not from the ship, because one cannot discover near your planet that a future life is back home on our planet. So the scan takes place from our planet or wherever our place is in that moment, and then the future life is asked if it wishes to participate.

If the future life does, then it comes along, and the priority is to pick up that associated Earth person. If there are other volunteers on the soul level, they come along, and the priority is to pick up that Earth person. If there are other volunteers on the soul level but no current future life among my people, then that would be a secondary priority.

That's fascinating. So much more planning went into the contact operation than anyone knew.

Yes. It has been reported that there was some speculation as to whether this was random or done because the people were on a lonely stretch of highway. It wasn't like that. As a matter of fact, there was never anything random about it. If people happen to be on a lonely stretch of highway, this is because they would have been requested at their sleep or dream level—or if they meditated, at the meditation level—if it would be convenient for them. It was always polite.

They were asked to drive out someplace, if they drove, or to go out where they could have privacy should such contact take place. There were never any promises. So that's why sometimes these contacts would take place in remote locations. It was not because the subconscious had been commanded or given an authoritarian demand, but rather because the subconscious, working in concert with the soul—and the soul would be accessed by us—would acquiesce and essentially say "Yes, we'll do that."

On a conscious level, then, people do report that they feel compelled or impelled to go someplace. They don't know why; there's no conscious reason for it. They just have to do that.

Yes, but this is not us doing that. It is rather their soul and their soul's interaction with their subconscious. If their subconscious is, for whatever reason, insistent in its temperament, they will feel it as compelling. If, on the other hand, their subconscious is relaxed, perhaps more integrated and accepted, appreciated, loved and so on, then there will just be an interest. Perhaps, "Let's do this," "Let's make it fun," or "We'll go for a drive; want to come along?" Like that, a social occasion, but not an obsession. I'm not trying to say that those who felt compelled were somehow flawed; rather, the subconscious would have felt that no other message would have been listened to and responded to. It would be that extreme, based on that understanding.

So, not counting going into the past but just the past forty to forty-five years, how many of your ships have been here contacting humans, not counting the one where you contacted everybody on the planet?

You're asking how many ships or how many missions? Because not that many vehicles were involved. The total number of vehicles assigned to this project never exceeded a hundred, but those vehicles might travel back and forth and change crews and so on.

So then how many missions? How long would a mission last?

It depended—there was no fixed time. It would last as long as it would take for whatever the mission was about. So I cannot give you a general answer on that.

Describe some of the missions. Would they just be for contact or would they have other business?

Sometimes they would be solely for contact, but most of the time they would be to observe. While a certain limited degree of observation is possible from our planet to yours, to observe from close range is invaluable. Our ship would not be seen but would be present. Perhaps it might be sitting on a hill, someplace where it's not going to be bumped into by animals or people, where it will not harm anyone. Our people would be inside, perhaps using some instruments like telescopes and looking at human beings from a relatively close range. As your scientists and social scientists know, such observation is invaluable, because you can to some degree understand or at least observe nuances that you might not be able to grasp from a distance.

But your version of the telescope would be like a television or something, right?

The magnification would not be like where you pick something up and hold it to your eye but rather like looking through the porthole (let's call it a porthole), and the porthole itself would function in a magnifying capacity, not unlike a lens.

How far away could you see? Blocks? Miles?

We probably would not observe anything—using that type of technology—that was more than fifty miles away.

But you could see clearly anything you chose in the house, through houses, through walls and buildings?

No, no, it doesn't do that. If there is a need to look through the walls, we would have to go there and look through the walls. It is extremely unlikely that we would get permission to do that. We do not desire to invade your privacy. We are not gods, nor are we omnipotent.

But when you come through the walls into houses to contact people, that's what you would consider a prior agreement then?

We do not go into anybody's house to see what they are watching on television. [Chuckles.] We do not do that. For instance, some extraterrestrials I have known who do not normally contact human beings might, for some reason, be passing Earth. They might land, get out and walk about and observe, not unlike the way you might observe someplace that was new to you, leaving as little trace as possible, disrupting things as little as possible, but looking around and then leaving. That is more of what casual passersby might do if they do not have systematic communication between the species.

Did you ever take power from a power line?

Some of our older ships might have if they had a problem, say in the 1940s with your radar. They might have recharged some element of the ship by pulling power from a power line. They felt it would impact your culture as little as possible. This is no longer done. Such vehicles are no longer used by us.

Underwater and Underground

Can you go under the water and go any place you want?

I cannot speak generally. Speaking from my own personal experience, I'd have to say that sometimes a higher-dimensional object goes into water in which it moves quickly. Other times the ship is functioning within your dimension and it would be go into the water slowly, coming out without too much swiftness so as not to shock the ship or the water and its occupants.

Some of what they call USOs (Unidentified Submerged Objects) could be yours too, then?

They might be. I think mostly these are of other species, but sometimes we did this in order to visit some base of other extraterrestrials or some base established by someone who happens to be underwater. It might have been there for a long time. If it was there for long enough, it might not always have been underwater, but due to the changing elements on Earth it now is. Generally speaking, though, the base would have been established while the water was there. I do know of one circumstance when the water came later.

Now, aren't most of the beings under the Earth gone?

A few are left in outposts of the Earth, but not many. The ones who are left are either very advanced or have highly complex systems to protect themselves from all the radiations on Earth now. Or they might be automated beings who are not impacted by such radiations in any detrimental way.

They just report what's going on?

Yes, or if they are not entirely automated and are more conscious (as our machines often are), then they will let us know if they feel complete. They are not slaves. If they feel they wish to go on and do something else, then some means will be set up for them to return or move on elsewhere.

Did you have Zeta bases under the water or under the land?

We used to have bases occupied by many more individuals until the 1940s got underway and you began to experiment with certain energy beams, some of which would travel in a spherical rather than an aimed pattern. We began to move away, because once you begin to experiment with such things, you do them bigger and bigger, more and more, stronger and stronger. Oftentimes, you do things that are detrimental to your own health and the health of others from ignorance, although this has become so established now that I think many average citizens and scientists also have realized that bigger and more powerful isn't necessarily better.

People are now aware of microwaves and radiation and a lot of things. Was there a particular year when you quit coming so often? I think you said it was when it got to be so unhealthy to do so, right?

We greatly reduced our visits after the mid-1940s and continued to reduce them, so that by the time of the 1960s they were becoming occasional, although one cannot say that across the board, because there were still some locations on Earth that were safe to come to as the emissions or energies that might harm us were not so pervasive there.

But that would be in very desolate places with very high mountains?

So-called undeveloped countries or places where technology was not a high priority.

The Unconscious and the Subconscious

Okay, I'm trying to understand about the Zeta's lives, their civilization and culture. What more can you say about Zeta life?

What can I say to that? Have we missed anything? Is there anything we haven't discussed about your culture? I'm just saying . . .

It's so wide and vast. I just want people to get to know you.

I understand. We don't play backgammon. We don't play jacks, but we have been known to do jumping jacks with children.

I'm sort of out of questions. It's fascinating talking to you. Are you still in your meditative body now?

Oh yes.

That one time when you weren't, it was difficult on both sides.

Yes.

You could feel all the things I am hiding from myself, right?

We do not look too hard. If you are hiding it, that means it is private, even if you are hiding it from yourself. There must be a reason, and so it's private.

Well, we're all trying to unhide everything. That's sort of what we're looking at.

In my albeit limited understanding of the human consciousness, I would have to say that timing is everything when it comes to, as you say, unhiding things. It is perhaps not best for you to know everything at once all the time, because some things are better known or remembered as an adult when you have an adult's tools. So some sequence is useful.

In your travels, is it only humans who have a subconscious that is not accessible to the conscious mind? Is that only because we have the veil? That's not common, is it?

It is not common for the subconscious to be *as* inaccessible as it is for you. I would say that I have a subconscious, but it is accessible. I have an unconscious that is somewhat accessible. I do not attempt to access it to the degree that it could tell me every day of my future. It might be possible, but then what would be the point of living? So it would be self-destructive to do that. I would say that to the degree that your subconscious is not readily accessible is unusual in my experience.

Never Underestimate Human Consciousness

Well, humans are pretty weird, let's face it.

No, humans are very advanced. Only the most advanced souls (and this I know) are allowed to suspend conscious awareness of the degree of their faculties (their knowledge and capacities), which you suspend because you are advanced. If you were to take a person who was not advanced and suspend this knowledge, he or she would be terribly upset and confused, injured perhaps, even killed. However, I have been informed that no one manifests on Earth without having had at least one life of spiritual mastery, and often many lives—two or three. Thus it is assumed by Creator that you have capacities that go beyond your individual personality in a given life because of that requirement. The suspension of conscious awareness of your greater being might then be acceptable.

So we do not consider humans "weird." We consider them advanced and to some extent adventurous, because not everyone who has had lives of spiritual mastery wishes to come to Earth and try life as a human— only those who are reasonably adventurous and have the desire to experience something entirely new.

Are you familiar with some of the material that we've been bringing out in these books, that the Explorer Race all go back to three-seed souls that are distinct from the Creator?

I did not know that, but I cannot say that I am particularly surprised. It is not surprising, as I say, because of the degree of your capacities that we have been exposed to.

But that means . . . I don't know what that means. Does it mean that you also are connected to those souls? Or that you just had the adventure of having an Earth life?

I do not know either.

So when you find out there are some adventures ahead! [Laughs.]

If I want to know. I'll say this: Do not assume, because you feel unwise or uninformed, that you are beings low on the ladder of conscious evolution. Everyone I know or have ever met or heard of who has ever come to observe you or interact with you as a race of beings has been most impressed with your depth of character and your capacity for flexibility, spontaneity and acquisition of knowledge.

These characteristics are often the markers of advanced beings, so if sometimes you're not feeling very advanced [chuckles] or you are surrounded by people who don't seem to be acting very advanced, it might well be true that day, but on the soul level, as well as at times on the conscious level, there is much more to you than a single day's observation would reveal.

Roswell and the Case of Billy Meier

Zoosh

November 15, 1998

The reason I'm bringing this up is that you all are becoming more sensitive—everyone, whether you want to or not—and this is in some cases causing problems for people who are in situations where sensitivity has not been catered to in the past. For others, things that might have gone uncommented on by you, or that have been ignored before, now seem larger than life. This is because, in order to move back up the dimensional scale to a broader spirituality (which is your normal place of being), you cannot retain judgment, fear and so on. You must become more sensitive so that you are aware of these things within you.

Now, many of you have been having difficulty dealing with the emotions of others around you. Sometimes you find yourself processing other people's feelings, or "stuff" as you say it, and you do not really grasp that. So, there is more to it.

Overcoming the Cruelty Factor

Consider that all life is sacred, including your own. This means that all life deserves to be treated in a benevolent fashion, or as benevolently as you can. You try to be benevolent, not just as in, "Oh, I just backed over the flowers in the garden and, well, I was trying to be benevolent, but I made a mistake. Too bad." That's not it. Your reaction would be, "Oh, I backed over the flowers," as if you backed over your own foot.

You understand? It really makes a difference now, because as you get more sensitive, there will be explosions on the physical level of activity. If you as a race of people do not respond to your own sensitivity, then the "parent race," so to speak, of your physical body—otherwise known as Mother Earth—will express it for you. This is why we have sudden and extreme storms and volcanoes bursting forth unexpectedly. It is not necessarily because the people in that geographical area are not expressing sensitivity, but because a large concentration of people within, say, four thousand miles of that area are not expressing their sensitivity in benevolent and beneficial ways for themselves and others.

So when you have built into your society the machine that creates or generates foodstuffs without any sense of grace or thankfulness to that which provides its life for your nourishment, then you will eventually find yourself ingesting the cruelty factor. The sinister secret government has consciously embraced cruelty, and you—almost all of you—have gone along with this unconsciously, or perhaps some of you embraced the cruelty factor as what you call a "fact of life." "Well, the animals have to die so that we can be fed. Oh, the crops have to be taken in so that we can be fed." This is all true, but as I've said, and as Speaks of Many Truths has commented before, when you are genuinely thankful from your heart to the plants and animals for the sacrifice of their lives so that you might eat and be nourished and you say so from your mouth and mean it, then you don't have to eat as much; you will be nourished fully and there will be plenty to go around for everyone. This might not seem so important now, but as the population continues to explode, I want you to keep it in mind, because eventually you will also have to consider the conundrum: "Where are all the people going to live?" *and* "Where are we going to grow the crops?"

Resisting Expansion and Resisting those Resisters

Consider this: The sinister secret government would like nothing better than to stop the universe from expanding at all. The underlying goal of these individuals is to stop things, because right now the expansion of all beings guarantees that they will be transformed into beings something other than what they are now, meaning they will be transformed into benevolent beings, which is wonderful for everybody including them, but they don't know that.

So the sinister secret government is making every effort possible—and has been doing so for the past twenty-five to thirty years especially—to transform the way you do things so that cruelty becomes a part of life. And yet here you are now, becoming more and more sensitive. You cannot just hear some horrible thing on the news and turn a deaf ear. You are beginning to feel it as if it were close to you. This is why people are more reactive. This is also why people are more fearful. They will hear something on the news that perhaps did not even happen in their town, but they will become more fearful because of the greater connection between all human beings and all life forms on this planet—and hence to the universe.

I want you to understand something. Becoming heart-centered and doing the heart-warmth exercise is not just a way to become more spiritual. It is literally a way to survive and prosper. I need to bring these reminders out from time to time because it is very easy for the reader to become complacent. From time to time, it is my job to go up in the bell tower, as it were, and ring the bell with enthusiasm.

The Expansion of the Universe Is the Expansion of Consciousness

You said something interesting. We've heard of the expansion of the universe, of creation, the Doppler shift and all that. You're saying that the expansion is also our expansion into a higher consciousness?

The Love-Heat Exercise

I am giving you what we're calling the love-heat exercise in a way that Speaks of Many Truths taught me how to do it. Take your thumb and rub it very gently across your fingertips for about half a minute or a minute. While you do that, don't do anything else. Just put your attention on your fingertips. Close your eyes and feel your thumb rubbing slowly across your fingertips. Notice that when you do that, it brings your *physical* attention into that part of your body. Now you can relax and bring that same physical attention anywhere inside your chest—not just where your heart is, but anywhere across your chest, your solar plexus area or abdomen—and either generate or look for a physical warmth that you can actually feel.

Take a minute or two or as long as you need to find that warmth. When you find it, go into that feeling of warmth and feel it more, just stay with it. Stay with that feeling of warmth. Feel it for a few minutes so you can memorize the method, and most importantly, so your body can create a recollection, a physical recollection of how it feels and how it needs to feel for you. The heat might come up in different parts of your body—maybe one time in the left of your chest, maybe another time in the right of your abdomen or other places around there. Wherever you feel it, just let it be there. Don't try and move it around—that's where it's showing up in that moment. Always when it comes up and you feel the warmth, go into it and feel it more.

Make sure you do this when you are alone and quiet, not when you are driving a car or doing anything that requires your full attention. After you do the warmth for five minutes or so if you can, or as long as you can do it, then relax. And afterward, think about this: The warmth is the physical evidence of loving yourself. Many of you have read for years about how we need to love ourselves, but in fact, the method is not just saying, "I love myself," or doing other mental exercises that are helpful to give you permission to love yourself. Rather, the actual physical experience of loving yourself is in this manner, and there are things you can do that are supportive of it. But in my experience, and the way I was taught, this is the method you can most easily do.

The heat will tend to push everything out of you that is not of you or that is not supporting you, because the heat, as the physical experience of loving yourself, also unites you with Creator. It unites you with the harmony of all beings, and it will tend to create a greater sense of harmony with all things. You might notice as you get better at this and can do it longer that should you be around your friends or other people, they might feel more relaxed around you, or situations might become more harmonious. Things that used to bother or upset you don't bother you very much, because the heat creates an energy, not only of self-love, but of harmony. Remember that the harmony part is so important. You might also notice that animals will react differently to you—maybe they'll be more friendly, perhaps they'll be more relaxed, maybe they'll look at you in a different way. Sometimes you'll be surprised at what animals, even the smallest—such as a grasshopper, a beetle, a butterfly, a bird—might do because you're feeling this heat.

Because it is love energy, it naturally radiates just as light comes out of a light bulb. Remember, you don't throw the heat out, even with the best of intentions. You don't send it to people. If other people are interested in what you are doing or why they feel better around you, you can teach them how to do this heart-warmth/physical-warmth exercise in the way you learned or the way that works best for you. And the most important thing to remember is that this method of loving yourself and generating harmony for yourself creates harmony for others, because you are in harmony. Remember that this works well and will provide you with a greater sense of ease and comfort in your life no matter who you are, where you are, what you are doing or how you're living your life. It can only improve your experience. The heart-warmth/physical-warmth exercise is something that is intended to benefit all life, and in my experience, it does benefit my life.

—Robert Shapiro.

Yes, because all expansion happens universally and almost totally simultaneously. Therefore you would not normally find shrinking and expanding consciousness within this same unit (referring to a universe as a unit). So one is constantly confronted with paradoxes on a creator-training-school planet like this, but the paradoxes are built in on purpose so that your attention will be caught and you will be required to notice things that you might otherwise miss in your busy day.

Now, in the paper that you gave Robert, you said that if we couldn't expand, if the secret government could close us down, then an immune-system-type thing in the universe would eliminate us.

It will be like this if you continue to accept or turn a blind eye to the cruelty factor. Years ago, for example, aside from providing food to the hungry, the Hunger Project was trying to convince people to change the thought that there will always be hungry people, because that thought— accepting that hunger among some peoples is inevitable—was actually a portion of the cruelty factor. I mention that because it is something that many of you are aware of as having been a worthy project and a worthy attempt to change consciousness that went across the board and was effective in many areas.

Now if the sensitivity of all beings expands, meaning not only your own but the sensitivity of the animals and plants around you, what happens more and more often is that extreme messages will be coming forth. There might be, say, some kind of catastrophe at the agricultural level, such as Britain's recent struggle with so-called mad cow disease, or, on a smaller level, perhaps a farmer will lose an entire crop unexpectedly for no apparent reason and without any warning.

These kinds of catastrophes might have something to do with the individuals involved, but on the larger scale they are also messages that something is dreadfully wrong and needs to be changed. The Earth does not have to produce massive, crushing storms and violence on the surface, but if you shirk your duties as creators, the Earth will ultimately have to respond to you on the basis of the universal call, which says the universe must expand just as consciousness must expand. If that occurs, the "immune-system" reaction will take place between Mother Earth and yourself—and possibly even with some cosmic involvement, such as an increase, say, in x-rays from space—and as a result, there will be more and more disease factors among you.

This is not a threat or a punishment; it is a call to arms. I am encouraging you not only to focus on the warmth that is the eternal love within you but also, when you are in that warmth (the next level of the exercise, okay?), to say something simple out loud while retaining that heat in your chest or solar plexus or wherever it is in your body. It is critical that you retain it while you're speaking, so you may not be able to speak in elaborate terminology. Just say, "I am now creating benevolence in my life and in what is around me," or something to that effect. Or, if you choose, you could say, "I will request that benevolence be a natural factor of life for all beings." Say something simple that will function in concordance with your job as apprentice creators.

You might ask, "Zoosh, why do we have to come to Earth to learn how to be creators?" Well, as I've said in previous books, Earth is a place where you are presented with the results, a fait accompli if you will, of your thoughts and theories. Therefore, in order to function as creators in training here, you must utilize the physical world, and the most immediate physical world you have is your physical body with your thoughts, your physical statements and the feeling of warmth and love that can best be expressed physically to form a union and generate genuine benevolence. You would be very surprised how much it can help with even a few of you saying this affirmation—and the more and more and more of you who are doing this, the more it will help.

The Expansion Is Always and Infinite

Is the universe expanding because it's almost the end of this creation? Or is it expanding because it expands all the time?

It is always expanding. Just as growth is a natural factor, so expansion—which is simply growth from the inside out—is natural; just as you grow from the inside out, so does the universe, and yet within the universe, it cannot expand if something is not right. If there is a disease within you, if it is a catastrophic disease, it will "knock you off" [chuckles], but on the personality level, on the soul level, you are immortal, all right?

In the case of the universe, however, it is benevolent almost everyplace but here in this isolated corner of the universe where your planet resides and where creators in training can go through extreme lessons of application, while the rest of the universe is far enough away from you that you cannot do too much damage. Yet even at the outer perimeters of the universe where you are, if you are unconsciously radiating malevolence by embracing the cruelty factor as a fact of life, the universe will eventually stop expanding, and it will direct its attention towards eliminating that disease.

Now, I know you want to live. I know you want to expand spiritually. I know you don't want to have to do this whole Explorer Race thing all over again, and as I've said before, from time to time, you will be tested.

This is a test. It is not only a test, but it is still a test. Do you understand? Therefore, the way to pass the test is not to know what to do, but to do it. Simply thinking about doing it won't work, because you can think about doing it without being on Earth; but on Earth, you do it. You engage the physical, the material, on a planet where you are presented with consequences and physical evidence, which you are trained, before birth, to accept above all else.

Therefore, in order to save the Earth, to save its populations and to make Earth your friend, you need to genuinely apply the golden rule, which mentally you know is a good thing. You need to apply it now, not as a mental exercise, but as a physical exercise. That is why the heat in the chest is critical—because when you are feeling that, you will not be able to maintain that feeling and do anything that is not of love.

I do not expect you to be able to maintain the heat in your chest or solar plexus in every moment, but I do want to encourage you to do it as much as you can. Obviously, it might not be a good thing to do when you are driving or performing surgery or some such thing that requires your absolute attention. But when you are sitting or you have a moment, when there is no great demand on your time and energies, please do it and note how you react.

Perhaps you will be feeling the heat and something will be going on around you, maybe the television or something, and it will make it hard for you to maintain the heat. Turn off the television and see if you can maintain the heat more easily. Ultimately, it is like a winnowing system, because, as a sensor for love, it will tell you not only what is good for you in that moment, but it will tend to broadcast that energy all around and about you and will maintain a greater benevolence for you in your life. And since love and heat naturally radiate, it will leave some of that around and about where you have gone.

Do not broadcast it consciously, though. If you do, you just shove it out and you'll have to regenerate all over again. If you keep shoving it out, eventually it will be harder to create it because the physical body knows. It is your job to generate and maintain it and, if you choose, teach others how to do it if they wish to know. This is not to be treated as a messianic venture but rather as something that you can share with others, if it works for you and if they would like to experience it.

It works much better this way than for you to be sending it to others. For one thing, when you send it to others, it is willful on your part, controlling people, and true love does not require that others feel love as well. I want to bring this to your attention, because it is very easy to play into the hands of those who would manipulate you for their own gain, using cynicism so that you will not be disappointed. I've discussed cynicism before, but this is the next level of it. And with you, there is always a next level.

Always?
Always. If there isn't a next level, why be curious?

Theft and Imprisonment by the Secret Government

All right. [Chuckles.] What it seems is that Roswell is where the Grays crashed, and then the government combed the wreckage and reverse-engineered technology from the craft. Sha Don didn't want to talk about it, but that's one of the most famous cases.

I must honor Sha Don's feelings on this matter. His people feel very strongly about it, and I would be remiss to ignore that.

Can't we just briefly say what it is they feel strongly about?

Yes. I will say that they feel so strongly about Roswell because an agreement was made with the government of the United States just before the crash at Roswell. The agreement was made between Zeta Reticuli and the United States government that, should such an event ever occur, the citizens of the ship (be they Zeta beings or any other ETs) would be promptly returned to the civilization from which they came, since neither the citizens of the United States nor the U.S. government would have the means to care for them or give them treatment in the way they would require—a logical agreement—and that for such service, the government would be given some kind of gift by whatever ETs were involved. This agreement was made with a few other governments.

Now the reason the agreement was made—from the Zetas' and other ETs' point of view—was that the U.S. was developing and experimenting further with radar, which they understood insofar as how it worked. But as one experiments with things in a polarized world, one is always trying to make things either bigger or smaller. The ETs were concerned that these experiments might unintentionally interfere with an extraterrestrial ship because of the method most ships in those days used to navigate around Earth, fairly close to the planetary body itself, meaning within the atmosphere.

So the reason there is so much anger and betrayal felt is that when the crash occurred, not only did the government of the United States make no attempt to return the extraterrestrials, but when contacted over and over and over again, people in the U. S. government denied that they had any beings—stonewalling, as you say—or said that the beings could not be moved or that they were dead. In point of fact, death is experienced differently by different beings all over the universe, and the beings who were supposedly dead were not, but were able to maintain themselves for a short time; if they had been rescued by their own kind, they could have been repaired and could have had some kind of a life. This was considered not only a breach of contract but a breach of faith.

Many extraterrestrials who were planning on contacting Earth governments more extensively with benevolent offers of trading pulled back, not the least of which were the Pleiadians, who will eventually be the best partners you've ever known. This is about the time when the Pleiadians— not all Pleiadians, but some of the especially influential ones—began to develop their attitude about Earth that you are barbarians, and when the Pleiadians put that title on someone, it essentially is like a neon sign flashing, saying it's not safe to go past this point.

Now, those who made the agreement originally with the ETs meant exactly what they said, but sinister agents behind the scene (you can imagine who) managed to manipulate things, stating, "Why do we need gifts from the extraterrestrials when we have the ship and the ETs themselves? We can do more with that; we don't need their little presents." In other words, they used greed, and it is so easy to fall into that trap, as you know.

So now various governments around the world, most predominantly the United States government, have ships that were sometimes intentionally knocked down, but they don't really know very much about the ships. If they had cooperated, you would now be well involved with ETs. There would be no hunger or disease. Life would be pretty nice for everybody.

You might ask, "Why would ETs withhold such largesse from the mass population just because of a few greedy people in high places of influence?" But you see, ETs do not recognize individuality as much as you do here. You recognize that what one individual says or does represents that individual, or at most his or her family. The ETs see this as a global thing. If one person says this or does this, then that must mean the tendency exists in all people on this planet, and therefore no human being on this planet can be trusted. That is because that's the way they live, and one tends to see others in one's own image, as you know well.

So that's what slowed things down. And it was about this time that the sinister secret government began to realize (meaning experience) its power and became much more aggressively involved in manipulation and corruption. I do not believe they will win, but they will go down with a fight. It is your job to do the simple things I have already stated (such as the love-heat exercise) that can improve your lives and the lives of those around you.

The Gift of Technology

But that crash is where they were able to reverse engineer a lot. That's where a lot of our technology came from; suddenly, out of nowhere, we went from a picture tube to a transistor and a chip.

But that was as a result of a gift, that kind of thing. Go back in time and start noticing when that was coming on. Granted, some of that was research (and let's not take it away from the inventors) but yes, a lot of the inventions of your time now—not all, but some of them—trace their roots back to some of that original analysis of ET vessels.

But it's like this. Let's take an ET ship that your government has had the greatest success with. All right? Any one ship at random. Even the level of success that they are experiencing with that ship does not represent one-tenth of a percent of what that ship is capable of doing. Some of these ships—and I'm just talking about little ships that fly around and that look, for all intents and purposes, fairly innocuous . . . it is not unusual that a ship like that could either create a planet or destroy one.

Even the little ones that look like shuttles?

I wouldn't say shuttles, but they are small.

They go back and forth to the mothership, you mean?

Yes, they wouldn't destroy a planet but they could, and it is that level of destruction that prompts such great and sticky greed.

Right. The secret government wants that level of technology.

Yes, but the military powers of your world would like to have that also—not necessarily that they would use it, but they might like to wave it around like a cudgel.

But do they understand that they are alive only because of the importance of the Explorer Race, and as Sha Don explained, because the penalty for interfering is so profound?

Does who understand?

The secret government and the military powers. Do they understand why they are getting away with what they're doing?

No. Unless, of course, they've read these books. But if you are asking, "Do they know by some other means?" No. As a result, they are convinced that they are in fact powerful. Shortsightedness is a factor of their existence.

Because, as Sha Don explained, in one minute the ETs could have gotten any of the beings they wanted back, right?

Yes.

The Case of Billy Meier

I've got two big books on the Pleiades and the case of Billy Meier—you know, everybody knows a little about that, but not anything really deep. What can you tell us about his case?

Well you see, Billy Meier (a contactee starting in 1975) was an ordinary man; he is not a PhD candidate. The thing a lot of people don't know about Billy Meier, however, is that as an adult rather than as a child, he was very clearly and slowly given the history of the world as it has been, and then he was also given the desirable past and the desirable future.

But receiving it as an adult, one is not so simplistic anymore as one is as a child, and he became somewhat overwrought by what had been done. He became very angry with certain religions that had become corrupted or had perpetuated corruption that began in the past. Particularly, he became very upset with the Christian religion—with which he was once involved—because what seemed to be a beautiful religion had actually become something that was the antithesis of what Jesus and others intended for it to be. Therefore a lot of people either lost interest in what he was doing or began to attack him.

But any man can only be expected to engage himself with the truth up to a point. I would say that if the Pleiadians had to do it over again, they would perhaps not give him the level of detail they provided him with—not because he did not have the capacity to understand, but because the drama of it was too much. I might add that they were not present when he was seeing this history, because even for them it would have been upsetting, but he saw it and it was upsetting to him. It was like having the past suddenly revealed to you. It naturally caused a reaction.

Figure 10.1: "Billy" Eduard Albert Meier (February 3, 1937), a Swiss farmer whose first contacts began in 1942.

Courtesy of UFO Digest

You're saying that they played it like a movie and he wrote it down?

He remembered it. He wrote some of it down.

What does "remember it" mean?

You can only remember so much, considering that several thousand years of history are being shown to you sequentially, not quickly. You're going to remember only so much and not other things.

But it was shown to him like a movie?

Yes, the way it is done on a Zeta ship with the children is by showing the present, showing the past that has led to this present and then showing the future—gently, though, with children. They then show the present as it could be and then the desirable past and desirable future, all the while taking into account that the viewers are children and one does not show them too much gore, blood, guts and suffering. But as an adult, he was shown the facts, unadulterated. It really was too much.

The Effects of Time Travel

Zoosh

November 30, 1998

All right. Zoosh speaking. Greetings.

Greetings. I'm not clear from everything I've read whether the Zetas have truly been coming here ever since there were humans, or whether, as you say, they came in the 1940s and went back in time. Maybe it doesn't matter; maybe the net effect is the same.

You could say that the net effect is ultimately the same. Let's put it that way, because if they fly through time to get long distances behind them—to say that they should key off of one time and go to the past—it is almost irrelevant in terms of differentiating it from having come to the past initially. I'd say that it's not a hair worth splitting.

Bloodlines

So we have a case in this particular book. Let's just talk about a woman named Carol who's in a book called Close Encounters of the Fourth Kind. *She has a son and a granddaughter, and it appears that her father and her father's father were also visited by these Zetas. So does that mean that they came to her and then went back on the soul line or the genetic line then?*

No, these cases where family bloodlines are involved are usually quite different from those involving a soul line.

But they would have gone to Carol because she was on a soul line?

Yes, but going back on the bloodline is usually done to understand something of the initial contactee, and the trouble with talking about this is that it becomes unnecessarily complicated for the reader, but a simple illustration would be infinitely useful. [See Figure 11.1.]

Just write on the back of this. There's a tablet on top.

Fine. Now, three trips along a timeline—this being a timeline and this also being a timeline—could be done at different times. Yes? They came here, they came here and they came here; or they went back and they went back. And these people, since they went back in a given time frame—meaning they landed, it happened, they went back in that time—would be able to say to this person and to this person, "This happened in my time." So it is really essentially the same thing in terms of human recollection. The only difference is the physics of it.

One might also say that there might be a difference in terms of the information and experience gathered. The Zetas would see it this way, that it would be infinitely better to go to the person, to go to Carol, than to go to see her father and then go to see her grandfather in that sequence, because the same Zetas would be contacting these same individuals instead of having different Zetas contacting these beings at different times and having to compare notes, as it were. You understand? So

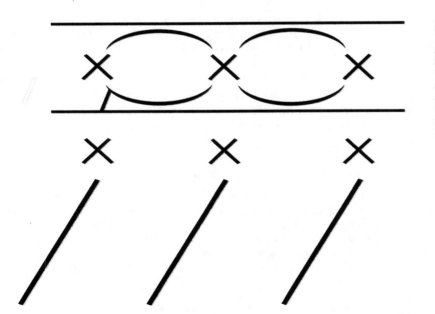

Figure 11.1: Zoosh's illustration of separate soul-line contacts along a timeline.

they will always, if they can, go back in time using the second method as I have drawn it in the illustration. And I think the illustration is useful in that context, because meshed with the words that I'm talking about, you can see that it is infinitely more valuable to use the method of repetitive and sequential contact by the same Zeta scientists.

All right, Carol was used for breeding purposes. Does that mean that they went back and checked out the father and the grandfather?

Yes. It would mean that they would be looking not only at the genetics but also—because there are subtleties involved here (it seems like there aren't, but there are)—they would want to know how she came to be the way she is through the masculine genetic bloodline. Most likely they would have gone back on the feminine genetic bloodline as well. It would be not typical to go on one bloodline only.

Okay. That's not known.

This is not always discovered, however.

Do you want to talk about this?

Sure. Well, we could ask for a Zeta. Sha Don has made some arrangements, I believe.

Okay, and then if there was someone who was on that ship we could talk to—not the captain. I don't think the coordinator is the person to talk to. I think the being who is on the soul line, the being who talks to Carol who would be her future self is the one to talk to, right?

That would be an interesting person to talk to, because she would have a personal stake in the matter. As she might see it though, she wouldn't feel it that way but would feel a greater sense of intimacy with the individual. Yes.

Why don't I ask you the questions that come up, and then maybe during this same session that being could come.

Early Zeta Contacts: Misunderstanding on Both Sides

Okay. When Carol was four years old, they began to come and get her, and she was so frightened that she would go in the closet and stuff clothes in the holes so the light couldn't get in to get her. I know there's some overwhelming goodness about this, but these people seem to suffer an awful lot.

It is unfortunate. You have to remember now, how old would this lady be today [1998]?

Forty-six.

So we're going back forty-two years to the initial contact, because, in this case, we're not talking about sequencing from the future to the past in terms of our time here that you are experiencing today. So we're to remember that the Zetas then were not so terribly sophisticated with contacts with human beings, and at that time they had not discovered their affinity with small children. They had this discovery, but it happened later, and they went back in time to find out if they could reproduce this affinity.

Generally speaking, they like children, but because of the circumstances of this one individual, her fear of them is what prompted their going back in her genetic line to see what would cause such fear, because from their point of view they weren't doing anything that would cause her to be so frightened. That would be their point of view.

But from her point of view, they come in and snatch her, and then from her earliest memories, they ask her to hold what she calls the "uglies," which were the hybrids. Until she was old enough to be impregnated, they would want her to hold these babies like a little mother.

That is just representative of their ignorance. It is not that they were trying to harm her.

When she was a little older, like eight or nine, then it was like she was a mother. They would have a whole group of children, and she would mother some of these younger human children too, like babysitting.

By that time, she knew what was expected of her, plus she had developed the qualities that young girls develop so that they might demonstrate motherhood, but at four years old she was too young for that. The Zetas didn't know that then. We know it now.

Because the Zetas have all the wisdom of an adult, no matter how old they are, and they didn't understand our cycle of baby to child to prepubescent to teen to adult?

That's exactly right. They didn't understand the maturation cycle, because for them it does not exist. It did not occur to them. You have to remember—and I'm speaking to the reader here—that what is obvious to every human being on Earth might be entirely foreign and not even considered to be possible in other cultures on other planets. So that is the circumstance. It didn't even occur to them that the same love or concern or care shown by an older person would not be shown by a little girl. So it took them a while to assimilate that idea based entirely on observation, as individuals who had virtually no context to understand what they were seeing. It's not that they're stupid; they simply had no context in which to put it. They didn't understand it.

When the Zetas have a mystery, they would—at least then—always explore the causation of that mystery in the genetic past of the individual to see if there might be something "wrong" with that person. When they could not find anything wrong with that person, they decided that this represented something they did not understand. When they come across situations like this, they will do the experience enough times so that they have cumulative evidence. I grant that this happened to the individual herself—Carol, as she is referred to here.

That might not be her real name. I don't know.

That's all right. I grant that for her it was trauma. However, I think she does not feel that way today.

Well, this book is about a very interesting conference at the Massachusetts Institute of Technology in 1992. At that time, she had no idea. She had just a few memories. She had never been regressed or anything, but just . . . for instance, in the conference, she talked about her four-year-old granddaughter who was being picked up and talked to by someone named Nu, and they give her a little ball of light, and she could play with it to go through walls and windows.

See how far they came? Again, now they are playing with children in the context of what children like. It took time to go that distance, just like it takes time for any culture on Earth to understand another culture, and I'm talking about people who want to understand the culture. It takes time.

Learning the Value of Emotions

In previous books, you have said, I think, that the Zetas were sent here, they thought, to do this hybridization, but it was really so they would interact with beings who had emotions so that the Zetas could come to learn the value of emotions.

Yes, and although I might have put it that way, it is not an either-or situation. There is more than one reason they were sent here: Look now at the hybrid races, many of whom are really fantastic. They are going to be the links in a much more benevolent and gentle way between the human race and the little Zeta people themselves—little in terms of their stature, their height—and it will be infinitely easier for the human race to meet a hybrid between humans and Zetas first than to meet the Zetas directly. Human beings, even if they have read all this material and everything that has been generated in recent years, will still find it infinitely easier to meet a hybrid who has similar acculturation and general demeanor and who creates the same art (if not exactly the same, at least similar), so that you would have somebody you can identify with and say, "Well, these people are different, but they're not frightening."

So I would have to say that ultimately more than one reason applies here in terms of Zeta contact with the human race, which is also the Zetas' past lives on the soul line. There are many reasons for this contact, and it's also intended for the Explorer Race to understand that these beings are your future in some future incarnation, to see what you might be coming to be and how you might wish to modify that so that the Zetas in the future might be more culturally broad-minded instead of only intellectually powerful. So it serves many different directions.

It is a multileveled stitching back and forth, designed to alter both the past and the future and ultimately to create a benevolent present when your races begin to meet, trade, talk and exchange ideas on a more frequent and benevolent basis.

But we have published that by going to this other timeline, the Zetas are no longer our future.

Maybe. Maybe not.

I mean that's what you've told us in the past.

Yes, I might very well have told you that, but you have to remember that although you and the reader will often feel more comfortable with a fixed situation, nothing is fixed. How can you all be one if you have very divided separations between you?

Humans?

And anybody else. It is not possible. There has to be a degree of blending. The truth is always changing, not only on the basis of perspective, but on the basis of constant interaction of different timelines and evolutions that take place as a result of past, future and present civilizations coming in contact with one another in the same moment.

Is that only because we're on a loop of time, or is that true across the universe?

It is only because of the Explorer Race phenomenon.

And the loop of time?

Not just in the loop of time, because we cannot be rigid about it. The Explorer Race will exist after the loop of time, and there will still be some of this sequencing from various timelines—as you would say, in the present moment, there is a potential past or a potential future. However, should you be in that future as an individual living there, to you it would be absolutely valid and real, and so you might say to yourself right now, "I am a real being." Yes? But suppose in some future incarnation you went back into the past and uncreated the circumstances that brought you into existence in this life; then you, the solid real being of this moment, would not exist.

[Laughs.] That is perhaps a little clearer now.

So I will sometimes fulfill your desire, especially in the past, for rigid fixed truth. However, truth is always encompassing.

> *Never Forget That*
> # TRUTH IS ALWAYS ENCOMPASSING.

This is very important, because truth must include all influences upon it regardless of time, place or circumstance. This is very important if you're ever going to learn how to travel in time.

Back in Time, Modifying Contacts

All right. So, if the Zetas are going to go back and uncreate their interactions with humans . . .

Only the ones that caused trauma.

The ones that caused traumas, okay, but from those traumas are ties into situations from which the Faughn race of hybrids came.

Yes, but they can still modify the initial contacts so there was no trauma involved. This will take time—it will take quite a bit of time. However, they are dedicated to it, and they prefer to do it on their own, even though other races have volunteered to go back and soften the trauma for them. But they said, "No, no, we want to understand this ourselves," and so we (meaning the Zeta Race) want to go back in time and re-create these initial contacts in a more gentle, benevolent way, using the level of sophistication that we are learning now in terms of our intercommunications with the human race.

When I mentioned that to Sha Don just two weeks ago, he didn't know anything about it.

Well, that isn't . . . I cannot take credit for his not knowing anything about it. [Chuckles.] All beings do not know all the same thing at the same time, as you well know.

No, but don't they look in their tableau and everybody puts everything in it so they all try to know what everybody else knows?

So? My life and my wisdom are not limited by the Zeta tableau.

You once said that after the uncreation, some of the traumatic interactions wouldn't be with the Zeta. The interaction would happen, but it would have been with an Arcturian or an Andromedan or something.

Specifically meaning in a particular contact, you mean?

Alternate Means of Contact

Yes, well, the way you and Joopah explained it, it was almost as if the Zetas wouldn't even have the interaction at all anymore. But now you're saying it would be the Zetas, but they would just try not to be so unfeeling.

They can't try not to be unfeeling. By that time they will have become, as they see it, more diplomatic, but as you would see it, they will be more gentle and more understanding, more patient and more respectful of what the human beings now term boundaries, meaning that they would take the time to explain, "This is what we need, and this is why we need it." In a lot of cases, this time was taken, but not everybody remembers it. In other cases, the time wasn't taken, especially if they were repeat visits, but they will now probably take the time to explain, "This is why we need this. We ask for your help. We feel that you've said okay on the soul level, but we'd like you to understand on the conscious level." In other words, they'll be more diplomatic and gentle. That doesn't mean they won't do it, but they will be more diplomatic and gentle, and they will find more gentle ways—meaning less invasive ways, or, if the ways must be invasive, then very gentle and not painful ways to accomplish the same goal.

But by the time the humans go out and start space traveling, won't the Zetas be in their golden lightbodies, or will it take longer than that?

It will take longer for the total conversion. Besides, you must remember that the Zetas were talking about our living on a different timeline, experientially maybe a million years in the future. So, that point is moot.

That point is moot, but they can come back . . .

By the time you're going out as a civilization to explore the stars—and the Zetas were talking about living a million years in the future—you're not going to explore the stars initially with a very powerful means to get around. You might be traveling in time, but in a very restricted type of vehicle, and so you can't just flit around anywhere. In any event, you have to recognize that the Zetas are on an entirely different timeline.

It's like this: take your current civilizations. When you look back to try to understand the dinosaurs and prehistoric man, basically all that can be done is to make your best guess, and we're just talking about a few hundred thousand years or so in terms of prehistoric man. If the Zetas are on a different timeline a million years into the future and on a different planet and from a different culture entirely, well, that's asking a lot for them to know how to act. [Chuckles.]

But to get back to what you were talking about . . .

Okay. I assumed they'd keep on coming here and that we would interact with them here, but that's not true, then.

They really are only coming now to try to make things better, and even then they are not coming that much.

This book, **Close Encounters of the Fourth Kind,** *is very recent, and they were picking up this woman every couple of weeks or so.*

I repeat: They are not coming that much.

But in 1992 they were?

They are not coming that much. That doesn't mean they are not coming. It means they are not coming that much as compared to in, say, the 1950s or 1940s.

But then obviously some of the people, those whom the Zetas have been coming to for years, the Zetas are continuing to come to, since the woman was having these experiences in 1992. I don't know what happened after that, because that's as far as the book goes.

When they've contacted the same individuals over and over again, especially making genetic connections with their past bloodline, they are able to contact these individuals without actually sending a ship to the surface of the planet, which would be very dangerous. It is not realistic, with the methods of defense that your country or even any modern technological nation has, to think that a ship could land. Think about it. On the surface? It's ridiculous.

So what happens with individuals they've been seeing for a time is that they come in a slightly altered dimension, if they come at all. They might even approach sideways, let's say, for the sake of putting it in a different context where they don't actually come in a ship at all. But they might approach from, say, a neighboring dimension and come through that dimension through portals. They have the contact with the individual, but there is not a ship that comes to Earth at all, and that is why with all the people running around looking toward the sky, one doesn't see too many ships, at least physically. One doesn't hear about too many silver vehicles, silvery-looking vehicles, landeding somewhere in the 1990s. It's not safe.

Well, all right. She had several contacts here in 1991.

I'm not saying that she didn't have the contacts. I'm saying the contacts take place. That's why I say the Zetas are coming much less, meaning that the contacts take place in such a way that the vehicle itself does not have to come to Earth, although the contact that she experiences might sometimes take place on the vehicle, but the vehicle and herself are in a different dimension— in some place where the vehicle can be and where the contact can take place, but where no one has to get hurt.

The Variability of Sophistication across Time and Dimensions

So they have the ability to move her into a different dimension, then?

That's right. A lot of people who have contacts in this manner with this particular experiment, a long-term genetic experiment, will have such

experiences or will certainly find themselves sitting someplace and looking up, such as the man who sent you the pictures years ago. He looks
up and suddenly there's a hole in the wall, and on the other side of the
wall there are the ETs and the babies, and he walks through the hole in
the wall, and there he is. Obviously, he's in another dimension. The ship
didn't pull into his apartment building and park inside it.

*Okay. That explains a lot, because there are so many cases like that one. I think
Sha Don said that the Zetas have the ability to create this window so that the interior of their ship (he didn't say it the way you did . . . your explanation is much
clearer) is just right next door to something.*
　　Yes, that's how it's done in such a way as to keep people from getting hurt.

*But this woman, for instance, had one case where she got out of her pickup truck,
and somebody was playing. Then she was on the ship, and they put a thing in her
ear that hurt like crazy, and then she saw pictures in her mind.*
　　Yes. They still need to work on that; it shouldn't hurt. They haven't quite
figured out pain yet, but they are getting there. Of course, in different timelines, you have to understand . . . [Draws.] [See Figure 11.2.] If this circle is
the future and this bigger circle is the present, the point of origin (it's complicated because we're talking mathematics, here) of the mission from the Zeta's
viewpoint has to do with velocity. Let's see if I can make it at a formula level.
Sophistication level is going to be s, okay? Velocity is v, which has to do with
$v(t)$, where t is time, okay? The distance traveled is d. The distance traveled
(which is going to be different every time) and the velocity and the time—the
moments, the speed, the collapse of time, the expansion of time (meaning
going and coming)—are then essentially a starting and stopping.
　　The level of sophistication in the future is the variable in the equation. It is the weakest aspect of the formula, because velocity, time and
distance must be honored as most important for the safety of the mission and the people inside the ship—and for that matter, the people
who are being contacted. Otherwise, there will be instability. So they
must concentrate on $v(t)$ and d to create safety and stability, with s as a
distant last in their priorities. So if something has to give—and this is
the weak link; this is allowed to be the element that gives—it is the level
of sophistication of the Zeta people.
　　So they come this way. Their level of sophistication from the point
they started out might be very high. Maybe they've learned a lot. Maybe
they've been fully acculturated. Maybe they're almost at the level of gold
lightbeings but they're not quite there yet. But because of the need for
stability, their level of sophistication might be lost in transit, and that's
how these kinds of things happen.

In the sense that they regress to an earlier time or something?

No, they don't regress; they don't become who they were. Regression suggests that they revert to a past. They just lose some of their knowledge, some of their acculturation. They lose it because if something has to give, the level of sophistication is the safest thing to lose. In turn, because if any of these other things give, not only can this bring certain death for all participants—including the contactee—but potentially a rip could occur in the fabric of time and even space itself. So this tells you that the priority is going to be these things over here, and that the sophistication level, although considered important, is going to be treated as the weak link.

Fascinating. Does that stand true for everybody, or just for the Zetas?

It stands true in fact for everybody, which is why you will often have civilizations that will come and be in contact with human beings, and these civilizations will come from very far away or vastly into the future (although if they have a level of cultural or intellectual sophistication that has been going on indefinitely, it does not make that much difference), but the human being on Earth does not see these people for what they really are.

I might add as an interesting aside that an incarnation of a being such as Jesus or any other profound teacher whose abilities went far beyond the natural human being—a being like this, fully embodied in his total being regardless of his birth method, would have a soul being within the body who would not be perceived in the totality of his being, because the

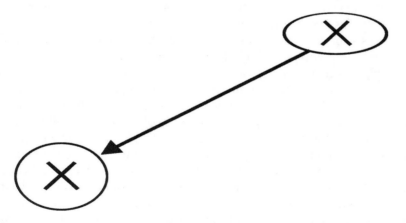

Figure 11.2: Zoosh explains how the level of sophistication on the part of the Zetas can be lost in transit through different timelines, as the Zetas travel in time from their point of origin (top right circle) to their destination in the future (bottom left circle).

level of his true sophistication would not be perceptible to those around. Some of that sophistication would be lost. I'm not saying that that would have changed the founder of the Christian religion in terms of the story, but to use Jesus as the idea of being someone from someplace else who came here. Let's just say anybody from someplace else who came here would have to deal with that limiting factor.

So most Earth contactees, meaning those who have been contacted *on* Earth, have not seen these beings in their true personalities and their true level of sophistication. The only way you can see these beings in their true level of sophistication is if you go onboard the ship—let's say that's the method of transit—and go to their home planet in their time, in the culture and time in which their life is taking place. Then you would experience them as they are.

This is something to keep in mind for the future when you begin to travel in time, because your race on Earth will experience the same mathematics. So this tells you that the cumulative impact over time (which is why civilizations in space exist for thousands of millions of years in highly cultured and cultivated ways) allows for a level of sophistication that is profound.

The Mathematics of Compression

For instance, you might have a highly sophisticated, benevolent, spiritual culture that's been going on for three or four or five hundred years. You fly off into space, as far as a Zeta might come, and by the time you get there, you haven't lost IQ points, but you've lost some of that sophistication. Now this might be quite a loss if your civilization had not quite been doing this sophisticated culture for very long. But if you are, say, on the Pleiades, where you've had a balanced, benevolent civilization on some of the planets there for millions of years and you travel and lose, say, a thousand years of sophistication, you're not going to really notice much. So the timing of such travels is vitally important, and the allowance of the stimulation of inspiration, for example, of those who will invent or be credited for inventing space travel utilizing time methods will have to come incrementally, so that by the time you are freely traveling as Earth people with your Earth culture, you will have had to establish a benevolent spiritual civilization on Earth for a minimum of five thousand years.

This is entirely because of the mathematics of what we can call compression. When the signal, meaning the traveling party, is compressed, something's got to give, because otherwise it's possible to not only create a hazard, but if you continue to compress the being—even as a soul being, as an energy being—something could be damaged in the being. As you know, simple physics tells you that if you want to keep whatever it is you are compressing nice and safe—we're not talking about compressing coal into a diamond here; we're talking about producing a laboratory experiment—you're going to put something on the object you're compressing so it can release atmosphere, whatever's inside it, so that it can be crushed, as it were, in a controlled, undamaged way.

To release the pressure, I see.

It's important for us to begin to put some of these thoughts out there, because people are working on these things, and by the time (and it will take time) you can resolve these problems, which will ultimately result in space travel, civilization will be on a more benevolent footing.

Protection against the Effects of Compression and Decompression

So that's why they took those elaborate precautions. We've heard different stories, but the most recent we've talked about is that of Betty Andreasson. When they took her to the home planet, they put her in jelly in a box, and they took these precautions to keep her from compressing and decompressing?

The precautions they took were profound. That was done to keep her from losing her mind and her personality, because they knew they were not only taking her to the place where they lived—meaning they were taking her spatially somewhere across a distance—but they were also taking her across time. They knew that Betty has future lives within this time, maybe not on Zeta Reticuli, but they were taking her in her body with her soul into the future through—past, around, somehow, they don't even know all of it themselves—those levels. That's why they took such elaborate precautions, allowing her to not only be physically safe, but to retain her soul and her personality from this life so that when she was returned to Earth (even though she would have had profound experiences), she would still be Betty Andreasson.

There's a possibility that if they hadn't done that, she would have merged with some of her future lives?

Yes, and that would probably mean that as a result she would be much smarter, much more spiritual and probably bored with Earth life, and they would then unintentionally have interfered with her life. Even so, people who do come into contact with ETs and go out and fly on the ships and so on will often have expanded psychic capacities, as you call them, but in fact these are simply expanded spiritual capacities, because of traveling in time. This happens.

No one knows why that is. It's because they literally almost become some of their future selves?

Yes, they can pass . . . That's why travel in time has to happen so fast. It has to be almost instantaneous, because if you slowed it down by, say, three times as slow, the chances of picking up qualities and attributes of your future lives, which might have not only nothing to do with your present life but might very well interfere with your present life, are greatly increased. It does work in a quantum way to the degree that the more you slow it down, the more you do, the more the risk factor multiplies—almost to the infinite.

When the Zetas bring the person back to his or her present life, there is something that has to take place, because you could ask about the thing I just talked about—their level of sophistication. When they brought Betty back (since we were talking about Betty), they put her in this protective device, but they also had to traverse the passage back to within a very narrow band of time, meaning that they must cover, to the best of their ability, their exact route, velocity, time, distance, everything, and retrace their steps to within a very narrow latitude.

That is why very often people will come back after an experience like that and think that it doesn't make sense. Even for a person like Betty, who has been able to reconnect all this vast experience, it doesn't make sense to her. She was there, and she was there for a long time, and yet when she came back from that trip, she was seemingly gone for only a short time. It had to be done in such a way that it would protect her, and we know that this happens through time by functioning in a different timeline; however, it is critically important that all this stuff be done just so.

Now, to address the question you asked before. What happens if they take people into the past? Generally, they do not take contactees into the past.

No, I didn't make myself clear. When the Zetas come from where they are, back to us, they might traverse some of their past lives and pick up that lack of sophistication. Isn't it possible that they become their more unsophisticated selves?

No. The lack of sophistication comes from the formula as stated, but what protects them from being affected by this same thing is their own system of protection built into the ship. That level of protection, however, is made for them, for their species. That's why they have to use this elaborate contraption for an Earth person that looks strange and is experienced as being weird, because it cannot be built into the ship per se. It's something that's on the ship momentarily, there while the person is on the ship. The moment the mission is over, that technical object is removed unless the ship is going to be used in the same way in the future.

So, to cover this from the complete point of view, if a human being were picked up and taken into his or her past, taken into the far-flung past, the same hazard would exist, but they don't do this. They practically never take human beings into the past. They might show you the past on the ship, historically speaking, and they might even in some certain circumstances show you a past life or two if for some reason that were important, but to take you into the past incrementally, covering a very small range of time, is considerably more of a risk than covering a long range of time or distance. It is more of a risk because the same velocity that is used to cover many, many light years must be used to go back a short distance in time.

Going back to the previous drawing (Figure 11.5), let's break down that velocity a little bit more. In the original trip, when you go from the point of origin (the circle on the right), whether you're going into the past or into the future, the initial velocity is slower, then it picks up speed and then toward the end it will again slow down. So the initial velocity and the arrival velocity are a little slower than the rest of the trip's velocity.

Now, if you think of a shorter trip in time and space, making the distance from the point of origin to the destination much smaller, the problem is that the slowness of the velocity on leaving and arriving lasts almost the entire trip. As a result, because you are going so slowly, the chances of picking up impacts from previous lives are greatly expanded, just like I mentioned before, because the slower you go, the more infinite the possibilities are that people will be impacted by any lifetimes that they had within that space-time frame.

That's why they practically never take people into the past. It's one thing to take them into the future—a million years into the future, a hundred and fifty star-years, light-years and so on (I want to call them star-years, because they are called that in other places)—that's much safer. Larger distances and longer times are infinitely safer than shorter distances and shorter times.

Is what you call a star-year equal to our light-year, or is it longer?
Longer.

Botched Experiments in Time Travel

What about the abortive attempts made by the secret government to send people into the past without knowing any of this, as in the Montauk Project or the Philadelphia Experiment?

That's why those attempts were such disasters. The only individuals who survived did so on the basis of pure chance, meaning as they say proverbially, that if you throw enough coins on a table, eventually one lands on its edge, but that is really a bit extreme, and perhaps too extreme for this.

The ones who missed, they missed their past lives. They somehow didn't connect with them?

The ones who survived were entirely messed up when they came back. The vast quantity of individuals were simply killed or lost, and the ones who survived were completely messed up. They might have picked up elements not only from past lives, but because there was no safety mechanism built in whatsoever, they might have picked up effects from any life being, any being around. So when they came back, they might have profound knowledge and they might have profound insights, but they were pretty much guaranteed insanity, at least within that context.

You're saying that there were no cases of people coming back with their minds balanced?

Intact, no. When they came back, if they came back, they were completely deranged, not to say dangerous. You didn't know we were going to get so technical tonight, did you?

Let me say this: At this point, if you're going to pursue Carol's experiences, it might be as well to have the person you suggested (of the Zeta future life) comment, if that person chooses to do so. If not, it might be possible to get somebody who would care to comment, but this should be done tomorrow night.

Hybrids and Clones

She called the person she talked to a "tall being," which usually is one of their teachers. What kind of being was that person?

Tall, relatively speaking?

Tall. No, she's very tall. About six feet. It could be a hybrid then. Maybe it's five feet one inch. Much taller than the three and a half feet ones.

Yes, the taller beings are usually but not necessarily hybrids. They might also be the ones on the vehicle who do things, manage things: what you would call a captain.

Oh, the captains might be taller. They might be Zetas?

Those who have more responsibility will usually be delineated by their skills. They are not rewarded by being taller, but it is just a way to easily pick out someone you might go to as a Zeta to say, "What do you wish me to do next?"

Can they be made taller even after they're cloned? Can their size be changed?

Probably not.

So they are created. The captains are created as the coordinators?

The coordinators would probably be cloned at the adult height.

So they don't go into these jobs. They are literally . . .

They are created with that size and then trained for the position. They are not divined the knowledge and wisdom. They have to learn it like anyone else.

But they are basically inculcated, because they said that . . .

They're inculcated with facts, but you can't be inculcated with experience. Wisdom takes time and trial and error, just as it does for anybody, which is why in the beginning contacts with the Zetas, they weren't what you would call "Earth wise," but they are getting there.

But this is interesting, Zoosh, because Sha Don told me that the hybrids are inculcated with the level of awareness that the Zeta have at the moment they're cloned, and then they're sent out on their own. Maybe some of these crazy things we've seen could be from those with no experience?

Yes, it's certainly possible. I'm not disputing the fact that they are infused with this knowledge and cultural wisdom, yes? But even so, although you might have that knowledge, and it might work many times, there would be that certain time or the circumstance within a time where the wisdom and knowledge doesn't apply, and then you just have to do the best you can on your own. That's why I say that wisdom comes through trial and error for them as well. It might not be quite as extreme as the way you must achieve wisdom here, but then their responsibilities are considerably less than yours.

Yes, and the hybrids, when they're first created, have that almost childish spontaneity. One of the things that Carol had on was earrings that had pendants, and somebody on the ship, in an almost childish way, pulled them out and damaged her ear, not realizing what he was doing, and her ear was all bloody, you know? The being just wanted to play with them.

Yes. Here you have a situation where a child can be unintentionally harmful out of curiosity. This is not to say that they're children, but this is a case where there's no wisdom. No experience. No understanding. There is apparently no compassion, but it's not true that they don't have compassion. It's just that their level of compassion exists for one another, just as your level of compassion exists for one another here, but your level of sophistication and training as to what compassion is all about and what it stems from is greatly magnified over them, because you have pain, discomfort, annoyance, polarity. They don't have any of that.

The Value of Pain

And because that's one of our prime lessons. I mean, that's a really big deal involved in choosing to be human.

Yes, and if you're going to have a society and culture that teaches you responsibility for your creations, there has to be some way to learn responsibility and to desire that responsibility so that you can acquire wisdom, meaning that there must be something that will show you this, not this. Pain is very useful that way in a physical society—it is perhaps invaluable—whereas in the Zeta society, it is entirely unnecessary, so that even pulling an earring out and seeing blood would not cause the Zeta to realize in any way that there had been any infliction of harm to the individual, because there's no context within their culture to understand that.

Right. If they've never felt pain, how can they sense what it is in someone else?

So they have to learn compassion as an outsider without being able to feel pain, because it wouldn't be safe. If they were to feel even the slightest amount of pain, it would probably not only kill them but could very easily prompt a disease in their civilization.

You might say they're protected, as many ET civilizations are protected and to an extent you are also protected, but protection, as I've said before, is a two-way street. You are protected from experiencing something, but you are also kept from experiencing something, and so you might get stuck. That's what has happened to a lot of ET civilizations. They've been protected all right, but they're stuck.

Your civilization is protected in a different way. You're shielded to a great extent from contact with ETs as one normally experiences everyplace else, but at the same time, and although many of you might like to have that contact, you probably are not ready for it, because your civilization has been kept in such an—how can I say?—unsophisticated way, meaning that you're still getting used to one another, and you're not prepared for the incredible variety and spontaneity and unexpected actions and behaviors that one would experience on a moment-to-moment basis with ETs. You're not exactly prepared for that with one another.

So, in the sense of a Zeta being, we're sophisticated, because we've had so much more life experience and so many more challenges and so many more opportunities to learn, but in relation to the rest of the beings out there, we're still children?

Culturally speaking, you are very unsophisticated compared to the average extraterrestrial. But then one cannot say that across the board, because there are cultures here on Earth, even in existence still today, that are very sophisticated. Granted, there might not be as many people practicing those cultures as once existed, but the cultures are at least there as remnants. They are still in evidence. So one cannot make that as an across-the-board statement.

Such as? You mean shamanic cultures?

Yes, shamanic or mystical cultures that might easily include extraterrestrials as beings who can be spoken to telepathically. Or, for instance, such cultures could be talking to spirits or even potential spirits and so on—the spirits of any living form of existence. Of course, everything is alive, and so this kind of thing would make for a much more sophisticated culture. I'm not just talking about a vastly complex culture. I'm talking about a sophisticated culture in which the basic absolute that everything is alive is taken for granted, whereas in a less sophisticated culture, life has to not only prove its existence but also justify its value.

Science might consider something to be a lower level of life, because science, as a culture (let's call it that), cannot, by utilizing its own tools, understand the communication from this type of being, and therefore classifies it as less than what it is, which is, of course, a very unsophisticated point of view.

I love it. The scientists are going to love it. [Chuckles.]

The whole point is to encourage scientists to become mystical scientists and heart-god scientists and all of these things, and it's coming. But just like with any other garden, it needs to be nurtured and encouraged.

And on that note . . .

I'll say good night.

I enjoyed this evening. Thank you.

Zeta Diplomacy and
Ancient Contacts on Earth

Zwo Ti

November 30, 1998

My name is Zwo Ti.

Welcome, welcome.

Sha Don arranged for me to speak in his absence, because he has other duties. I have been working with the Zeta people for many years, and I consult with them to provide a degree of understanding so they can assimilate cultural differences or become more culturally sophisticated, as you might say.

Diplomat to the Zetas from their Parent Race

I am like a diplomatic attaché from their advisers. The advisers to the Zeta race are a group of beings now around in the eleventh dimension who consider themselves to be the parent race of the Zetas. They have, however, moved to this place, having once occupied the ninth dimension. My job is to help the Zetas assimilate what their advisers say to them. The advisers always speak to the Zetas in terms couched like a story or a ceremony, but never with the type of intellectual explanation that the Zetas require so that they can fit thoughts that are new to them into their overall paradigm of knowledge. This is my job, and I embrace it.

Sha Don asked me to speak tonight, because he felt there were questions that you asked him before that would be difficult for him to reply to, either because of the method used by him to consult for wisdom beyond, which he knew was limited about certain situations, or because he felt he had to be circumspect and could not speak freely. He felt that I could perhaps be of greater assistance.

Wonderful! I'm glad you're here.

The Chinese Connection

I have been consulting with the Zetas for many years, since they started their contacts in China. About four thousand years ago (your time), Zetas began to visit more remote locations in what is now considered China, Tibet and even Nepal. Those visits were not made for the purpose that has been explored in the case of recent human contacts, but rather to create an alliance. The Zetas were advised by myself and others that regardless of political changes, China would manage to maintain a degree of ongoing culture that would be as close to permanent as was possible for modern times (incorporating the more classical interpretation of modern). Therefore, the Zeta people sought out Chinese citizens to create long-term political alliances and to exchange ideas, ideals and philosophies. Their success was such that the Zetas came to the opinion that all human beings on Earth would have this culture.

That is another reason the Zetas have had some trouble recently. Because of their inability to grasp that a culture represented in one geographic location on Earth might be entirely foreign to another, they would tend to approach other people of Earth—say in the United States or South America or other locations—with the same cultural approach they might show toward those former times and citizens in China. Therefore, when they started coming into all of the difficulties, they had to go back and consult their knowledge, because the contacts made in ancient (you say ancient, but I'm wanting to say classical, because that's recent history) China were made by Zetas who were no longer alive, and so those were not the type of contacts that were explained mathematically last night by Zoosh; rather, they were a direct line to a certain time.

With no living member of their race to consult with, they could only go by what was in the tableau. This was part of the reason that, when they started making the contacts about which you have been asking questions recently, they were not so very talkative. They were polite, but there was expectancy on their part for a certain acquiescence by the citizens, because those old Chinese contacts had given a very long, detailed explanation about the potential for what Zeta Reticuli might face even then.

At that time, they knew they might have a problem, but they didn't know whether it would actually happen. So a great deal of discussion took place about how to approach things, what might be available in terms of citizen cooperation, who to approach, how they should be treated and so on, and it was all set up to serve the human being acculturated to four-thousand-year-old China.

Part of the lack of sophistication shown by the Zeta people, then, is based on information that was gathered long ago on Earth in a culture that at the time was relatively isolated from Europe and other countries that have come to be culturally influential in your part of the hemisphere.

Did they contact the ruling classes or the natives? The peasants? The scholars?

They tended to contact the scholars or the wisdom-keepers—the more influential or wealthier people, not the average citizen. So there was a great deal of formality, but the Zeta people can be very formal, and they felt at ease. After a short time, the ancient Chinese people also felt at ease and felt a degree of affinity with these beings from so far away, and there was a diplomatic cultural exchange, although no citizens of Earth went to Zeta Reticuli. The Zeta people would often put on demonstrations, speaking of future Earth potentials or demonstrating past or present extraterrestrial civilizations and answering questions, as one might ask or be asked of by another culture about your own experience. Equally, the philosophers of the time explained Chinese culture, thought and tradition to these ancient Zeta astronauts, and there was a sense of comradeship.

But the key here is that if someone visited the Zetas, the Zetas would put it in their tableau, and it would all be part of their history. Everyone would know it. So they must have assumed that the Chinese had something similar, and that we in our time would have access to the information they had given the ancient Chinese.

Yes, they assumed . . .

That we would have access . . .

That's right. They assumed you would know all these things. They were completely baffled because you didn't. This is, of course, an example of the lack of cultural diversity and the lack of, how can we say, political struggle that exists on Zeta as compared to your own world.

Was anything ever written in China?

Yes, although I am not certain where it is now. My feeling is that some ancient scrolls might still exist. I believe some of them were destroyed in a recent political upheaval there, yet some of them might still be hidden and will someday be useful for reestablishing diplomatic explorations and cultural exchanges between the people of Earth and Zeta Reticuli. It is certain that even today the Zeta citizens (today meaning their time) will desire to reestablish contact with the Chinese people. They might be a little confused by the current political regime, which, as far as I can tell, will moderate in the next hundred years but still have a broad-based desire to practice equality—it will be more heart-centered rather than authoritarian.

Did they attempt to go back to China in their latest visit here?

No, they thought there was no point. They flew over the region and noted the apparent changes and decided that it would be better to just continue with the mission. One thing to know about Zeta people is that if they have a mission, they will pursue it without deflection, meaning that the idea of questioning the mission would be unthinkable—not because they are such a well-ordered society, but rather because they are so united.

So their mission did not include the Chinese as part of the hybridization program?

No.

That's interesting. I didn't know that it was limited to certain countries.

It was felt that there had been such cooperation and respect for China, because of the ongoing contacts, that Chinese citizens were exempt from having to participate in such an experience unless it would be necessary to infuse the blood or fluids of (this would be the Zeta perception) an insightful royal class. As those were not the qualities they were looking for—because of their motivation, they were looking for people with strong feelings, with a lot of heart energy and a very rugged and durable conditioning or genetics—they did not consider going to China. They felt that, while people like that exist or have existed in China, that country had already served so much that it would be impolite. It would not be honoring them, not appreciating their investment in the Zeta-Earth connection simply to do this.

What countries did they go to, then?

North America. All of North America and what you call Central America. They also went to the western side of South America, countries along the Andes.

Yes, those people are very spiritual.

They went to Northern Europe, where winter climates would predominate, an Alaska type of culture, because of the connection between Alaska and along the Bering Strait, the islands that run toward Russia and Siberia. They were looking for people of strong heart and physical strength, so they looked in places where the weather was rugged or where people had to deal with mountainous terrain, high altitudes and so on—where people were generally durable.

So are you part of the eleventh-dimensional race that created the Zetas?

No, I am not. I am like a diplomat who functions between that race of beings and the Zetas, so I have to have the capacity to move between the seventh and the eleventh dimensions, which I do.

The Life of a Diplomat

Can you tell me about yourself?

My race is extremely limited in population. We have been supported—but were not created—by that eleventh-dimensional race. I cannot say where we're from or how we got here. I do not know, nor is it written anywhere that I am aware of, because I think that our people are trained from birth for diplomacy. Some of my people in other parts of the universe also function as diplomats or perhaps diplomatic couriers. Our past culture and traditions are almost unknown. We are totally in service. Our planet is in the Andromedan system and we are few in number. The total number of us on our planet never exceeds twenty-five thousand.

The planet is about three times as big as Earth. This tells you something about us. It tells you that we like to have space around us [chuckles], and we are disinclined to crowd upon each other. This is why when we go home we feel restored, because in our duties we are often in crowded situations.

You live in the Andromedan system but are not classified as an Andromedan?

Oh, I would classify myself that way. I usually reside in Zeta Reticuli, because they are the people I serve, but every three years (a time equal to about three years of your time) I go home to be restored for about two months of your time (all in a row; not a day here or a day there). During those two months I become restored and live out on the land in our family house, and it is a very simple, refreshing life, interacting with our version of nature where we have living stone. I know you have living stone too, but the people on my planet are aware that the stone is alive.

And we're not.

You are not aware of this yet as a general culture on your planet. We are aware of the living stone, and the few plants that exist are treasured. There are a few small animals that are also treasured. You would say they are about the size of a beetle or perhaps a large spider. They are treasured and we can communicate with them also, and so we communicate with life around us in a fairly isolated place. Perhaps one or two other family members might be present but often not. During this retreat and restoration, a feeling of balance with the sacred world is reestablished.

What is your life cycle? How long do you normally live and how old are you?

Compared to your years, our life cycle is approximately seventy-five thousand of your years.

Where are you on that cycle now?

I am at about 57,000, plus a few.

And what do you look like? I don't think I know what Andromedans look like.

All Andromedans do not look alike, not unlike people of your star system. You do not all look alike here either.

Just your group, then, your twenty-five thousand.

Our people are fairly short, about three feet tall. You would say squat, meaning thick. We are short and thick, with some appendages from the area of what you would call the head that look similar to hair but are not quite hair. We have arms that are not fully articulated: Our arms are connected to our physical bodies down to the area where the elbow would be, and so there is not the range of motion that you have. Our legs are also connected, although we do not have the knee joint. In comparison to your body, our legs are connected to about where the knee would be if there were one. We do not walk the way you do but we glide, and our appearance by your standards is different.

Does it have any relationship to the Zetas—the large head and the wraparound eyes?

No, but I believe that our height allows them to feel a certain affinity, since many of them are of similar height. They do not feel they are so very different.

If I were to see you, what would your face look like?

It's hard to describe. We don't really have a neck. You want to know facial features compared to your own? We have eyes, not much bigger than your own, perhaps around the same size. We do not have as heavy a brow line as you do. We have a nose, not as pronounced as some of you. We have a mouth, but we do not often utilize it for talk. It is, I believe, perhaps a recessive feature.

You're telepathic. And your face is what color?

It would appear to you looking at us from where you are sitting to be a bluish gray, but in fact it is a color to us that is a little more greenish gray. You can simply say greenish gray if you wish, but your color spectrum and our energy body would cause you to perceive us as bluish gray.

More blue or more gray? Are you one of the blue beings that we've heard about?

We're not blue at all.

Right. But would we see you as blue? Bluish gray?

You might see us more blue than gray.

There are a lot of reports of blue people on spacecraft. Are you birthed or cloned?
Birthed.

Do you have a family?
Yes. We do not marry as you do, but I have a brother and two sisters.

But not your own children yet, because you're never home?
We do not have family like you with a husband, wife and children and so on. Members of our race are birthed from two to four beings who birth all of us. We do not have a family unit, but we have certain beings who have a greater affinity for one another—friends, you would say—and these beings would be considered our brothers or sisters.

Destined for Diplomacy

Do you have a childhood, or were you trained to be a diplomat from early on?
We have a childhood, and we're trained to be diplomats. It's just that when we are young we are exposed to more childlike things, but they are all geared and structured toward helping us to see the world around us as one being, or if you prefer, as parts of one being. So our childhood is comparable to shamanic childhood of certain cultures here on Earth, but it is perhaps gentler in some ways. When we are past childhood, which would be equal to about from twelve to fifteen hundred years, we go out with other members of our race and accompany them for a few thousand years on their missions so we can see how it is done. About the time we are from 3,500 to 5,000 we will receive our first mission, usually something uncomplicated. Not unlike yourselves, we start out with the simple and as we gain more experience, we are placed into situations that might be more complex.

Have you always worked with the Zetas and their teachers?
Yes, I have. But in the beginning, when I was given something less complex, I was working with a short-lived (in Zeta terms) experiment in which they were trying to create a birthing system similar to your own. So I was interacting with children. This is something that they ultimately decided was not for them, but they did pass it on as a worthy method to some of the hybrid races.

I want to skip a minute to go to the teachers. What can you tell me about them? Are they the tall beings who are sometimes seen on the ships?
I think not, since usually these guides and teachers for the Zetas—the Pan races they see themselves as—do not go aboard the ship. But I cannot rule it out.

I'm sorry; I didn't state my question properly. Betty Andreasson was taken to the Zeta home planet for a ceremony and, outside of the door or portal she went through to have the experience of meeting God, there was one of these tall beings. Was that a teacher?

Yes, this is certainly possible.

Can you just give me a brief history of these beings and how they came to create the Zetas?

These beings, as far as I know, go back to before anything that could be considered sequential, and so they go back to . . .

Before this creation?

Before sequence was invented. They seem to be highly motivated to create simple, meaning uncomplicated, races that can function as an ideal vessel for a specific way of being. Ergo, the Zetas focus on thought. You understand that I can speak little about them because they are so hard to explain in the terminology of the Earth person.

They're immortal?

Yes. They seem to desire that any race they have generated—or parented, as they say—achieve its zenith, but after achieving its zenith, it either discontinues or moves to a higher level of itself. So they are not interested in races perpetuating a status quo.

That has something to do with what the Zetas were perceiving as their end, then, when they thought they would not have bodies anymore.

Yes. Their advisers were telling them that they could not go on as they were, because they had achieved the highest level that that particular form of civilization could attain, given who and what they were.

So they saw it as the end rather than going up to a higher dimension?

As anyone might.

As we do, as with all the predictions here.

When it was revealed to them that they could have a civilization by jumping dimensions, they were first relieved and secondly intrigued, but even the ninth-dimensional version of the Zetas will again be advised by this parent race. Should they again achieve that level, there will either be the option of moving in dimension or something else. I do not know what.

This parent race seems to be of a level that is close or perhaps equal to some creators, but they are not entirely singular in their creation. They like to go to other beings' creations and create something within that creation—such as in this universe—and allow the conditions of that influence to sway or affect their created races. From what little I have been able to understand of them—they are so complex—they have apparently done this before in other universes.

But do you think the Zetas are the only ones they have created in this creation?

No, I do not think that is true. I believe they have other races they created in this universe and therefore must have other individuals of their race near those people as well, but I have not seen them. This is something I am extrapolating based on things they have told me or hinted at or that I have overheard when they communicate to each other. You have to remember that our race, my people, are trained to be diplomats, not scholars.

Tell me about being a diplomat. How would you describe what you do?

My main focus is to ease communication from the parent race to the Zeta race and to elaborate on what the parent race says or attempts to communicate in some direct—or more often, symbolic—way to the Zeta people. Very often I find myself acting as an interpreter of this symbolic communication, and I provide my best consultation on what it might mean. I will always say, "This is what it might mean," or "It might mean this or that," for instance, based upon my best guess. The Zetas might then say, "Well, it might also mean this," and I might say, "You are certainly right." That is an example.

The Appearance of the Parent Race

Does the parent race maintain a shape that you recognize? Are they balls of light?

I have seen them in a few different forms. I have seen them as pillars of light, and on more than one occasion I have seen them in what I would call a statuesque form, a seated being who seems to look more like an Earth human than anything else. Sometimes I consider this to be like the form of an oracle on Earth. I do not know why they take this form, because I do not think it is their native form, but on more than one occasion I have seen one of their number in this form, always seated with some kind of something on the head—not a crown exactly, but something tall—and something worn around the neck and over the chest, having a certain regal bearing.

Like with a robe or something?

No. I do not know what this is about, but I think it might have some connection to Egypt.

Then sometimes they look like very tall beings?

Sometimes they look like vertical beams of light, gold light with white. That's the way I see them most of the time. When I hear them talking, my impression is that it is a collective voice rather than the words of an individual.

So you don't go to where they are; they communicate with you?

Sometimes I go to where they are.

In your spirit body or in a ship?

As myself. I do not do spirit travel that I am aware of.

You go by yourself in a ship?

No ship; it is a place I stand—it must be a portal. And I am there and communicate with them, and often I will feel that I must go there when they have something they wish to say. They prefer to communicate directly to me, in their presence. I cannot remember that they've communicated to me in a vision more than once.

Even though they are a collective, you see them as individuals at different times?

Yes, I see them as individuals. I cannot state for a fact that they are a collective; I can only tell you that my best guess is that the voice I hear might represent a collective consciousness. They have told me precious little about themselves, which is why I am not forthcoming with details about them.

But you're helping to give an understanding of how it all works. All right, so, how many Zetas are there? A million? A hundred thousand? I have no idea. Do all twenty-five thousand of you on your planet work with the Zetas?

Oh no, I should think there are no more than eighty-seven of us working with the Zetas. The others are either too young or are older members who are teachers. Or, in the case of the bulk of the population, we are working elsewhere.

As a liaison between the parent race and the Zetas, when you go there, do you go to two Zetas in a ship or do you go to the whole council?

I generally will not go to individual Zetas as you have indicated, but to large gatherings. I don't know that they have a council per se. I don't think they have what you would call a ruling political body. They seem to have sufficient connection and union between them. The overwhelming message of the Zeta culture is Union. They seem to have enough union that going to a place where there is a gathering, such as before or after a ceremony . . .

That gets it out to everybody?

Yes, whatever needs to be explained or spoken of will get out. Then, if it needs to go further, I will go to other places at times of gatherings.

But then it goes into what they call their tableau, and everyone has access to it?

Access, yes, but as you know, access does not mean that you *know*. There could be many things in one of your access machines, but you do not necessarily know them. The tableau is the same way; it is not a collective consciousness. It is a means to access knowledge or wisdom, but you must want it and go to it for that. It will not disseminate this knowledge and wisdom on its own.

I see.

So even if it goes into the tableau, we cannot be certain that it will spread very rapidly. If it is something important, I will simply travel around the planet, speaking to this and then that group, until many, many, if not the majority, know and understand it. If it is necessary to elaborate on other planets where Zeta people are, then I will do that. This is probably why our life expectancy is seventy-five thousand years: because such explanations might take, by your standards, twenty or thirty years to reach most of the people.

So that's why there are eighty-seven of you working with the Zetas, then. There's that brief time when you have your recuperation, but then you may be traveling around with one message and another one may be traveling around with another message. Like that?

That's possible. Certainly we're not all on the same planet. We are situated wherever Zetas are the predominant culture. Generally speaking, if Zetas live on a planet, they are the primary if not the singular population, but occasionally they will live with some of the hybrids they have fostered and encouraged. So that would be variety for them. [Chuckles.]

I thought that they were all on one planet. How many planets do they live on?

Oh, I think it is about nine. I am not counting the various hybrid groups. I do not generally contact them.

Do you or any of your people normally go out on spaceships?

Not that I'm aware of, but it is possible. I'm not aware of everything my people are doing.

How do you communicate with your people? When necessary, do you have the ability to communicate at a distance?

We can, but I cannot recall a time when it has been necessary.

Oh, so it's when you meet on your home planet?

Yes.

And the other members of your diplomatic family, do they go to different planets that we have heard of, or are they spread all over the universe?

They are spread all over.

So you all come back and tell each other stories of the people you've worked with?

On the rare occasions when we are in one place at the same time, we will often speak of our different experiences, yes.

*You have learned, then, from some of their contacts about some of the other civiliza-
tions or other species out there?*

Not necessarily. What will be discussed would be the challenge of communication and how the communication was facilitated, because that would
be something that would help all of us, but not necessarily details of the
different civilizations. It might be a story where one would hear about the
difficulties of acting as a liaison between two peoples, one of whom cannot
hear and the other of whom cannot speak, and so we would have to find a
way. Now that was not the case for me, but one of my family members had
that challenge. One people could not hear and the other could not speak.
So my family member had to find a different means of communication that
was valid and reliable for both species. That is the type of story that would
be discussed, rather than details of the various cultures.

I see. How did you solve that?

Using color. What was seen.

*Yes, hear and speak. So both species had eyes. All right now, bringing this closer . . .
have you been to Earth?*

No.

So what is your knowledge of Earth? How have you gained it?

The knowledge that I have of Earth I have gained from the Zeta tableau. The other race I work with does not communicate to me about
Earth citizens.

And they have never come to Earth?

I could not say.

*Do they have a name if we ever want to talk to them in the future? Do they have a
designation?*

It is a sound.

Well, I suppose we could ask for the Zeta's parent race if we ever wanted them.

That would be better.

Hybridization, Implants and Experiments in Zeta Sexuality

*So now let's talk about this mission. How did it come about? Did the parent race
tell the Zetas to start a hybridization program, or did the Zetas come up with it as a
solution for their problem?*

I believe that the Zetas came up with the idea of the hybrid on their own,
because I do not recall being involved in consultations along these lines in
any way, shape or form. I do recall overhearing the parent race discussing
amongst themselves once that it could lead to—this is the best word I can
use in your language—mischief. We will have to pay attention.

What about the putting of the implant in every human?

Again, that was entirely a Zeta choice.

Okay. What are some of the things that the parent race wants the Zeta to know? What are some of your communications? They seem to have a certain amount of free will to do what they want.

Yes, as does any species. One with a focus toward thought especially must have a certain degree of free will so that it can discover if its thoughts are valid by testing them.

Right, and as scientists, that's what they do?

Yes. I once explained in some detail what a ceremony or a symbolic vision of the parent race showed all the Zeta planets at one time that I felt had to do with sexuality. I tried to explain this in many different ways to the Zeta Race. They told me that they had in fact attempted to incorporate sexuality into their culture but felt that it created more problems than it solved.

Therefore I told them that it could also mean a connection or coming together of the masculine and the feminine on more philosophical or intellectual or feeling terms instead of physical sexuality, and they were interested in that. "How might that be?" they would say, and then I would explain how a thought might be accompanied by a benevolent feeling that feels good to the thinker and that this would be an example of the masculine and feminine functioning in balance. They were interested in that.

You haven't carried messages, directions or guidance from the parent race to the Zetas that has had anything to do with Earth or humans?

No, I think Sha Don wanted me to speak here to give you an overview of the roots of Zeta culture as compared to individual explanations. This individual who explains will either be Sha Don or someone else, but not myself. I am speaking strictly to, you might say, flesh out the understanding that the human race might have of a totally foreign species.

Yes, and I'm so glad you're here. I just didn't know exactly how involved the parent race was. For instance, at some level, another reason for the Zetas interacting with the humans was for them to see emotional beings close up, but whose idea was that? Did that come from the Creator or from the parent race?

I think that this might have come from the parent race—not to shock or frighten the Zetas, but to expose them to a potential (even given their protective element) to be saturated or to leave a saturation effect in the ship, because the ship itself can absorb sensation. At a later date at a safe level, that sensation could then be experienced by individual Zeta researchers to see if such sensations create either high feelings or low feelings, as your contactee might say, and if they might be valid avenues to explore for their own culture. There is, of course, only an allowance of a very tiny bit of exposure to more unpleasant feelings, but there is significant latitude for exposure to more benevolent feelings. Very often contactees are thrilled to meet a race of ETs if they know or believe that ETs exist, and very often this level of joy can be sampled later by individual Zeta researchers to see if such euphoria might have useful applications in their own culture.

Interesting. Maybe also after children leave—children leave a beautiful energy, too.

Yes, so this kind of thing is like nothing is wasted. If a human visitor on the ship has unhappy or sad feelings, then afterward researchers might get to feel that at a very limited level. As a result, when they have accumulated enough exposure to this, they will say, "What can we do to improve our method of contacting Earth humans so the experience is benevolent for them?" In this sense, problem solving is one of their great joys, although it takes them a while to accumulate what they would consider to be sufficient evidence to motivate a change—not unlike your own culture.

Technological Development among the Zetas

So when you started interacting with the Zetas, were they at the calm and the technological level that they are at now, or have they changed?

When I met them, they were calm.

Did they have the level of technology then that they have now?

It's pretty much as you would say. I don't think there's been much advance in their technological culture, nothing measurable.

Did they attain this by themselves, or did the parent race give them the technology?

I think the parent race did not give them the technology but connected them to other races who would provide them with such capacity to create this technology. So the methods were presented to the Zetas, but the Zetas built most of their vehicles and technology themselves. The other races might have provided a prototype, however, or said, "Here's one of our vehicles, and this is how it works for us." They would look at it and see how it could work for them. Do you understand?

This type of networking (as compared to the technology itself) was given by the parent race. The parent race seems to be more interested in the cultural and intellectual maturation of the Zetas rather than their actual creations—we can say that technology would be a creation. In this way the parent race is, from their point of view, bringing the Zetas along in some agenda of their own, having to do, I believe, with some ultimately spiritual intention.

This is interesting. I had forgotten that the Zetas were a million years in the future. So when you go to Andromeda, which isn't that far from us, you are also in that same time period and not ours. All of your people are in a completely different time period?

All of the ones I have ever met are. [Chuckles.] You see that it is a challenge for you, because you're not used to dealing with time. You are used to dealing with distance, but when you add time, it is confounding for a while, and then it isn't. That is how such misunderstanding is understandable.

So you stay in your own time then. You don't travel in time?

Correct. Perhaps I ought to say I am not aware of traveling in time.

You've never had the desire to jump on a Zeta ship and just come and check out this wild planet?

I have been on a Zeta ship to travel here and there if they felt or wished me to go somewhere with them, perhaps to show me something, but I have not come to Earth. It is not my job to liaison between Earth people and Zeta people.

You never wanted to go on a sightseeing trip?

It is like this. If the potential places to visit are infinite, it might be difficult to say this one and not that. And as a diplomat, a dedicated diplomat in service, I am more inclined to go where I am needed. Since my job involves the parent race and the Zetas, I have not been needed on Earth.

So what is your understanding of what happens now? They have to really put some effort into coming here now, because of our secret government's control of the atmosphere, but . . .

They have to be cautious. They believe they utilize such caution by using dimensional rather than vehicular connections. The ships might still be seen, but to land on the Earth is rare indeed.

What I meant was, do you know what's ahead for us? They'll just continue coming very circumspectly until they can come openly?

I must tell you that I do not know anything about you. I am not the person to ask about your culture. I can be asked about the Zeta culture, or to some extent about my own and the parent race, but I know practically nothing about your culture.

So what do we need to know about the parent culture? As you go there to get these messages, since they don't have a lifestyle or culture, do you have any clue about what their interests are or what they do?

From what I have gathered from other members of my race, they seem to be very much like a creator, except that they are very focused (in my case) on the Zetas as compared to a broader creator who might be focused on many things. This tells you that their interests seem to be comparable to those of a parent: interested, loving, caring and also, perhaps, tolerant.

The Golden-Bodied Zetas

What about the Zetas themselves? You have observed the ones who are in the ninth dimension now, the golden-bodied ones?

Yes, I have.

Are there just a few?

Surely no more than twenty.

I think we heard they were sort of being ambassadors to the rest of the Zetas in order to explain their state?

It seems so. They do not rest, and the Zetas need to rest two to four hours a day. They seem to be in some consistent motion. I have occasionally heard that they tell stories and explain what might be and speak of things in terms of visions and so . . .

They are way-showers.

Yes, they are guides.

Do you know how this is going to work out? Will it take ten years, a thousand years or a hundred thousand years before they all move into that state?

I think it will take a while. It is hard to say in terms of your years, but it could take up to 1,200 or 1,500 of your years—or, given some unknown or even unpredictable change, it could take less.

Are you familiar with what we call the Explorer Race concept and the expansion?

I'm familiar with the expansion—not necessarily much about the Explorer Race, but I have heard about the expansion. If the expansion takes place, it will not take as long, but it might still take 700 years in terms of experiential time. The Zetas do not like to rush when it comes to changes. They are very happy with stability.

What will happen then is that you will be the liaison to them when they are in their golden bodies?

I am that now.

What kind of advice does the parent race give to the ones in the golden bodies?

It encourages them. The parent race encourages the golden-light Zetas to restlessly—meaning without rest—move amongst the people and speak of their personal experiences as golden lightbeings and to answer any questions that might come from Zeta individuals. So it is more encouragement without instructions, because simply being in the ninth dimension, one has different capabilities as compared to the seventh dimension.

It's almost like saying, "Hey, it's okay, I'm still here."
It is very much like that, but more elaborate.

What is the dimension in your natural home?
It's hard to describe it in terms of dimension. I don't think I can put it in that context.

But you can go from what to what?
So far in my life I have discovered, since this is what I've been exposed to, that I can easily go from seven to eleven. It is possible that I can go wider, but I have never had occasion to see if that's so.

Do you just carry information from the parent race to the Zetas? Do the Zetas come and ask you questions, ask you to find out things?
Occasionally. If I do not have an answer, then I will take such a query to the parent race and ask the question for them.

Are you getting any queries from the Zetas about the golden lightbody?
No, they will ask the golden-light Zetas, but during the time they thought they were dying out, almost daily someone would ask me, "What's happening? What can we do?" I would present these questions to the parent race, and almost always they would say nothing, or they would say, "It will be all right," something innocuous like that, so I felt it was my job to encourage them without giving them any specifics. It put me in an uncomfortable position.

They apparently wanted the Zetas to go through that time for some reason, perhaps so they would expand as a culture, expand their level of faith in their own continuity and, as a result, expand their faith in the continuity of all beings. That is my best understanding, but it might be more than that.

In 1986, I think—that's twelve years in my time—the Zeta [Joopah] who used to channel through this body that you're channeling through now would say they thought that they were coming to the end of their race. It's so recent?
Very recent.

But the hybrids? You have no reason to interact with them?
I have not as yet.

Do you think you will?
I could not say.

At Home away from Zeta Reticuli

How do you live? If you spend most of your time on the Zeta planet, do you live in a specific place?

I am given quarters should I need them, and sometimes I do. It will usually be in some kind of a structure where the Zeta people rest, or if I do not need quarters in a fixed place, I will be given the use of a vehicle, which I do not fly; instead they have volunteers, a pilot and perhaps a few crew members, and I fly with them. In that circumstance, I might have the ship as a temporary residence, or, you could say, as an office.

What about your own teachers or guides? Do you have beings whom you ask for your own personal guidance, people you talk to?

If I need personal advice, I will usually go to the teachers that I had on my planet when I was young. If they are no longer available, they will have stored every shred of memory of themselves in a small cube. I would then hold the cube and ask for wisdom, to be accompanied with feeling so that I can assimilate the answer to my question and experience the nurturing of that answer as well, but up until this point in time that has not been necessary. I have heard of other members of my civilization who have had to do that, however. Now, if I have a personal question, I will simply go to teachers I have consulted with who are members of my race and ask them.

You do this when you are on your home planet. But don't you have someone spiritually who's not embodied with whom you can communicate?

Perhaps I do, but I have not done so.

What about your—it's hard to say reincarnation when you live 75,000 years [chuckles]—but what about your cycle? Do you choose when to leave the body? Do you remember what and who you were before?

I do not remember previous incarnations. This came up once in a conversation before with another one of my friends, and she said that she did not remember either, and so apparently—not unlike yourselves—we do not recall previous incarnations. This is perhaps to our benefit, being diplomats, because then we do not have too much to distract us.

You have gender. Are you considered a he or a she?

I am a he.

Besides going home to your planet, are there other things that you look forward to?

Yes, but they have to do with going home to my planet. Can I not speak of that?

Please, please.

I am quite restored by my visit to my planet. The first few experiential days, if you would, I rest, relax and revel in the comfort and nurturing of the place where it is home. Then, for the next few days after that, I go out and touch and reconnect with familiar sights, sounds and places. Then, after a few more days have gone by, I will go to see friends, or brothers or sisters if they are there, and enjoy their company. But for the most part, I will be alone, luxuriating in the familiarity of home.

It sounds wonderful. Do you breathe anything?
On my home planet, I breathe my native atmosphere. On Zeta Reticuli, I use something like a supplement that sustains me, because their atmosphere is not the same.

What is their atmosphere?
I do not know.

They don't really breathe?
Yes, I believe they do, as far as I know.

And we have oxygen, but on your home planet?
We do not have oxygen.

Nitrogen?
I do not know these things. I am not a scientist. [Chuckles.]

Okay, but when you talked about something the size of a beetle . . . You don't have animals like we have here?
We have animals, you might say, but they are just small. My planet does not get a great deal of rain, but it does get some, and there are not many plants. The animals we have are what the planet can support. They are special. They have wonderful stories. I remember once when I was young, one of my teachers took me out to a place far from our school, our residence, and she said, "Today you will listen to the stories of three visitors." So I thought it would be three of our kind, but it wasn't. One after another, three of the little people came up, and one of them made little clicking sounds, and she said, "Listen." Then I could interpret the clicks, and the being spoke of its home life, its family, what it liked, what it didn't like. It was an opportunity to listen to another race of beings, to appreciate the similarities and differences between us. It is not unlike on your planet, where you say travel is broadening.

I wish all of us could look at other species like that on our planet.
Ah, but it is growing. As more and more people realize that other species on any planet have answers and perhaps even questions that you require, there will be a desire to speak to them. That is what I learned when I was a youngster. I believe that your people, as little as I know about you, will learn the same thing.

From Diplomacy to the Teaching of Diplomacy

Then at a certain time will you become a teacher to other diplomats? Is that how it works?

I hope so. It is not always that way. I am hopeful that it will be the case. It is, I believe, very rewarding and enjoyable to be able to communicate this way to youngsters and to encourage them, support them and stimulate their interest.

How does that work? Does it depend on how many diplomats are there? How are you chosen?

Chosen for teaching?

Yes. How would you become a teacher?

You understand that the sum total of the beings of my home planet whom I have ever met would be less than ten, and so I do not know who decides these things, but whoever it is would probably decide that what I had learned in my work might be needed by someone who would follow. That is my best guess. And then perhaps I would be allowed to teach, which I would find most rewarding.

This is astounding. There are 25,000 beings and you've lived 57,000 years and you've only met ten of them?

Yes. We like our space. I do not know of the decision makers on my planet, but because decisions are made and carried out, I must assume that someone is doing this. I do not even know if it is my people.

That's an absolutely amazing statement.

You have to remember that people from other planets and other cultures might or might not have similarities to your own, but those similarities will only go so far.

Is this because it's always been that way? That you do not interact with your own people?

I do not know the history of my culture. We do not study such things, or at least I have not been exposed to such studies. It has always been this way, since I have been alive. I do not know if it has always been this way. My understanding of my culture is that we are devoted and raised to do what we will be doing, but to do things that are extraneous to what we are doing would be considered a distraction.

I do not miss having this knowledge, because my job is sufficiently challenging, demanding and interesting, and that it is enough. I believe that even some of the simpler beings, such as animals on my planet, feel similarly, in that they are happy to be but have no need to question the validity of how they came to be, feeling perhaps as I do. The way I was raised was that to question such validity—as we would see it in terms of studying history—would be tantamount to speaking ill of one's creator. It would be as if to say, "Show me my validity," rather than feeling one's validity and requiring no proof.

We have a ways to go, don't we?

I have heard you have profound challenges that we do not have. I think that as a culture, an Earth culture, you have a ways to go, but as individuals, I do not think you do, because your life on Earth is nothing compared to your totality, and in your totality I am sure that you are similar to others in this universe. As such in that totality, you probably do not have very far to go.

No, but we have a job here as the Explorer Race. What I meant was that we have a ways to go to get to the wonderful acceptance that you have. We question and look and search and want to know why and when.

Yes, you are like that now, but I think that in your totality you probably are not that way.

No, I don't think we are. This is sort of temporary—a time of forgiving, a time of challenge.

A stop on the way, yes.

What else would you like to say? I probed and poked here, but it's so interesting to meet someone so totally different from those we've talked to before.

The people I work with, the Zeta Reticulan people, are very special beings. They have shown talents for which they have not been trained, such as the capacity to embrace union and speak highly of union while maintaining individuality. The capacity that they have to understand unusual thoughts and to be stimulated by challenges is very pleasing. That they are not so sophisticated compared to some of the races that travel and are exposed to different cultures is certainly true, but they grow more sophisticated each day.

So my message is to be patient with them and to understand that they have a genuine curiosity. They are who they appear to be—beings who have a job to do, a desire to know and an intention to be the best individuals they can be within union. So be patient and know that patience with them is much more likely, rather than demands to create a response of very open teaching and sharing. Good night.

Thank you very much. Have a wonderful life.

Parent Race of the Zetas

Tlingt Cha
December 2, 1998

We are Tlingt Cha. We are the last of the ancient benevolent race of beings whose soul purpose is to provide the universes with entities, or as you say, races of beings—who can benefit those universes, either in some overtly benevolent way, or (as in the case of your own peoples) in a way designed to be enigmatic. Your people on Earth have to struggle to survive, and within that struggle lies a tendency to see only what is close to you; you have little time to look far away. Therefore, you require enigmas to grab hold of your attention and steer you in directions that might be profitable to you as a race, for you to discover your more universal heritage and beyond. We have been credited with the creation of the Zeta Reticulan race. We created these beings for their own sake. However, in order to create a soul link between them and yourselves, it was necessary to use combined energy of light plasma—which is the appearance, the substance of the soul—that includes your own version of soul energy and a version that comes from another universe.

Beyond this Universe

The Zeta Reticulan beings are then only partially of this universe in their original makeup. The universe from which the bulk of the material of their creation has come is well beyond this one, a place where vast spaces exist with few creations within them. The beings who reside there function in a climate of total peace and serenity. However, in order to excite your curiosity and link them to you, some of your soul light was used in their creation. In this way, they would be amenable to changes and might also profoundly affect your race.

Ultimately, the intention is to create a more benevolent harmonic of feeling for Earth people and to encourage Zeta Reticulan people to have and express a wider range of benevolent feelings. Right now you primarily see their polarity where they represent those feelings from their native universe. This doesn't mean that they existed in that native universe as much as that the bulk of the energy initially used to create them did.

The Limits on Emotion

The other side of the polarity is that you have a full range of emotions, both benevolent and not so benevolent. However, your soul matter cannot easily accommodate extreme emotions, even extreme joy. If your souls are exposed to extreme joy for too long, they tend to leave the physical body and expand into higher dimensions, thus shedding the opportunity for you to experience the lessons and rewards of Earth life. Therefore, extreme joy has been kept from you as a constant. It is not a punishment, but rather it is considered that extreme joy can only be safely experienced by you on Earth for a few minutes at a time, maybe a little longer now and then. For your own protection, so that you can finish your Earth lives and learn what you came to learn, you are kept from experiencing it all the time.

Conversely, to experience extreme rage and hate is also difficult to live with, and although it does not cause you to lift out of the body, it will cause you to fold yourself inside, disrupting you and your community. Therefore, you are not allowed to feel such rage that is considered murderous for any great length of time either. You might hear that rage and hate have been expressed, but the level of those emotions are carefully controlled so that you do not feel them for a long time. You have heard that you are protected. It is true, and yet I have brought forward this particular example so that you will realize that the protection is not always something that you might consider desirable. The fact that your civilization is kept in such close check encourages you in your conscious desire to expand when you can do so benevolently as a people. So you will expand; all beings will. This is why you are on Earth in such extreme conditions. But you know this already.

Who specifically protects us from our own rage and hate? How does that work?

It is done through your souls. The energy of the soul has an unnatural, limited range placed upon it, like a built-in check. It is not the normal situation for your souls. Your souls might normally have a much greater range, especially for joy or happiness, but this check is built in; it is temporary—only while you are on Earth in these times, in these dimensions. The check also performs a function of holding your life to a much shorter span than is natural for you. Any twelve hundred- to fifteen hundred-year range is normal for your souls, but this check prevents that.

On the other hand, you could say that it also prevents you from having to experience the extremes of Earth societies now, and so it is generally felt that the installation of this function of fused light to your soul is acceptable.

The fused light is the restriction part that keeps us from fully experiencing?

Yes.

And that fused light has something to do with the Zetas?

I did not say that it did, no.

Love's Creations

You said that part of our soul was used in the Zeta's creations—was that individual souls or from the souls of the three seeds that are the basis of humanity?

Different souls of different beings everywhere have a slightly different makeup, which is what accounts for their personalities. It was not considered acceptable then, nor is it considered so now, to use actual portions of your souls, even from the three seeds; rather, the makeup of the energy of the soul material that was used, like your own, was made to be identical to your own.

I see. So it was cloned.

In this way, they would have that energy and be just as enigmatically drawn to you as you are to them, as one might be drawn to someone who is a relative and not know why.

And this other universe? Is it in this circle of light, or in love's creation? Is it where the majority of the matter of the Zetas come from?

It is not in any of the love creations. It is in a creation that exists between those creations.

Between them.

If you think about it, love's creations are, for the sake of simplicity, like spheres in space. But between them there is something, and it is like an energy that flows inward and not outward in this place. In this way the beings who live within are not easily detected. As you know, if a light bulb is off in a dark room, it is unseen. It is only seen when you flip the switch and the light comes on. So we have a situation where the energy moves inward only. In that way the universe where these beings exist can remain in peaceful harmony and is entirely undetectable.

Is it a universe that you created?

Yes. It is for beings who either require absolute peace and serenity or who would flower by being in such an environment. Sometimes when a human being has had a difficult life and moves through the veils, he or she requires a time to rest in absolute peace and serenity. They are usually transported to this place in which they can be in a quiet, nurturing, loving space where they experience only peace and serenity. When they are recovered from their experience, they return to the place of life review and continue.

The Origin of the Parent Race

Beautiful! I sense that you are from beyond any level I have talked to yet in these books. Can you say something about your origin or your place of origin?

My people exist so far into the future that it is not possible to measure it. Let's say, for the sake of understanding, that we exist in a time and place where all ideas of creation have been expressed at least once. In this place, then, you find beings who either have done everything or have been in some way connected at one time or another to some part that has done everything—meaning beings who are made up of many portions.

One found for a time there that the prevailing experience was resolution, peace, relaxation (all these things you appreciate) and yet there was a distinct sense of boredom—not what you would call uncomfortable boredom, but a lack of any possibility of a surprise or the unexpected, which creates an undercurrent of tedium. Several of my people considered the possibility of coming back in time to reexperience what was done or find ways to do what was done in a more benevolent way. Perhaps they might facilitate what was being done in such a way that all parties would have a better experience. We sent out messages of this type to the past and waited for responses from various creators to see if there was any interest.

We received some responses—one from the Creator of this universe—and decided that one of us would go to each universe, because there were so few responses. [Chuckles.] This was not too surprising, because creators wish to resolve things on their own or with those with whom they normally consult. Nevertheless, the Creator of this universe finds almost any variety appealing and is quite open to outside assistance. Therefore we are made up of many different parts. Each portion of us came to be in this universe to be in our work. I have stated that we are the last of our race.

Something occurred that we did not expect: Coming back in time as far as we did, we discovered that portions of ourselves became intrigued with various races, creations and potentials for creations and broke off and went their own ways to participate. It is possible that we will reassimilate sometime in the future, but I cannot say for certain. I can only say that of my race, we, or as I sometimes say I, am the last to remain in the complete totality of all my parts.

What percentage?
There were five of us.

Participation in the Formation of the Explorer Race

I always suspected that the idea for the Explorer Race came from the future. You sent back some of those threads or you were instrumental in inspiring the beings who sent the threads, right?
We sometimes function on the level of inspiration for various creator beings. We would not care to take complete credit for such ideas, but we will have participated in some way.

So then how did you come to . . . You sent out the inspiration to send out the idea of the Explorer Race to our Creator?
Can you restate that? For me to say that we sent this or we did that sounds as if we were singularly responsible. We participated.

You saw the need, or somehow the need was communicated.
We participated.

You somehow participated in sending out the thread. And then, when our Creator got excited about it, how have you interacted with the Explorer Race?
We have tried to respect the intention of your Creator by interacting as little as possible directly, but we feel that it is acceptable to feel an interaction with you through those whom you will meet. We have sometimes been involved in creating small races (meaning races without great numbers of individuals) who will contact you benevolently from time to time.

The Zeta individuals we have been involved with have been given considerable latitude. Sometimes they have contacted you benevolently, and other times not so benevolently. They never attack, but sometimes are less sophisticated or make mistakes. But we felt that it would be so easy for us to create an acceleration in your growth that it would be better for us to keep some distance. Therefore, we have made ourselves available to the Zetas and to some other races, but we have been very careful to avoid direct contact. The being last night who reported seeing the figure on the throne . . .

Oh yes, that was going to be one of my questions.

That question is directed for that being entirely, because that being will at some point be working with Earth people and helping to reengineer the original magical Egyptian, who is made up partly of an extraterrestrial being and partly of a human being. Therefore, the exposure for this being from whom you heard last night is designed to pique that being's curiosity.

Well, it certainly did mine! Did you create that particular group? He calls himself an Andromedan, but it seems that he's not really related to the other Andromedans.

He is an Andromedan. They do not all look alike, just as people in this galaxy do not all look alike.

Why did you choose him or his small race of beings in particular?

We chose him because we knew that toward the latter part of his life he would be working with the core being who was the original Middle Eastern magical being who preceded the people now present. It was because we knew his future that we felt his experience with the Zeta people would make the encounter he would have later that much easier.

Figure 13.1: Depiction of an ancient Egyptian.

The Synthesis of the Earth

So is that our future then? How does the magical Egyptian fit into who we are and where we're going?

It is intended that people on Earth come together to form one race. Ultimately, the Earth person will be defined as having a skin tone a little lighter than . . . What would you call the color? It is not quite milk chocolate but a little lighter than that, and certain features will be noted. Once that development in appearance of the races is accomplished, though certain distinct cultures might remain, we will possibly begin to see the prototype Earth human.

After this synthesis, when the prototype Earth human is accomplished, we will then have a revisitation by certain extraterrestrial races of whom, if you were to see them, you would say, "Well, these people look like some of the ancient pictures that have to do with Egypt." Those races were there before the Egyptian human being was there, and they were respected and honored. The humans made some effort to emulate them, which is not unusual when human beings are exposed to extraterrestrials. So there was an effort to preserve the appearance of these beings. Sometimes it is thought that the art of that time is stylistic: "How could human beings look exactly like that?" But most of the time the art is a faithful reproduction of the ways these beings looked. They simply were not from Earth.

Once the synthesis of Earth people takes place, that race will return from space, and then there will be the rejoining of the intended Earth culture with the extraterrestrial culture. That will be the link that will allow the full flood of extraterrestrial culture and creation to flow into Earth and for expansion to take place in many ways. This is why for many years educators, philosophers and teachers have been drawn to Egypt and know that it is somehow an important place. They have tried to say it is the people or the structures, but in fact it is the place itself—the land. The people who are there are good people, yet it is the land, and the land will ultimately be the most benevolent place on Earth.

Great academies for studying the cultures of the stars, seeing how and why Earth culture evolved as it did and where all the different races are from, what their cultures are like there, will be built there. It will be a thousand-year program that will allow every person on Earth to understand his or her true heritage. During this time, the souls of many people who have lived here will come to visit, and there will be spaces in the academy where the souls can be, even though as you know, souls do not require space. The space will be there to honor the previous souls, and no physical being will sit there. A nice gesture, yes?

Oh yes. You mean all the souls who have been on Earth that were part of the Explorer Race, or all the beings who lived here who were not part of the Explorer Race?

Yes. Yes to both.

Will these original Egyptians continue to be an inspiration to humans? Will there be a merging of the two? Are they part of the Explorer Race?

They are not part of the Explorer Race, but it is intended that there be a merging so that there will be a connection formed.

Can you say where they are from?

They are from a different dimension, not so very far from where you are now. It is a higher dimension of Sirius.

So these beings are real. If I had a book of the dynasties, could you say how far back they were ETs and when the humans began to imitate them?

They preceded the dynasties. You have to understand, dynasties would be dynasties because they were Earth humans.

Was there any intermarriage? Because they all claim royal descent . . .

Yes. That is one of the reasons for the appearance of some of the Egyptians.

At what dimensional point (I won't ask when because I know that's so difficult) will this happen? Before 4.0 or after?

It should happen shortly before 4.0.

Assisting Other Races

Well, I'm delighted you're here. Tell me, what do you do when you're not sending advice through the Andromedans to the Zetas? What other activities do you carry on, what other interests?

Because this Creator has been so accommodating, we range our energy out to the limits or boundaries of this creation or universe to see if there are others who could benefit from the facilitation we could offer. We have found only one other example—at the other side of the universe, well away from here—but we have not begun to work with them yet. We will probably begin our work with them after the expansion.

And what will be the point and purpose of that?

The purpose of that will be to allow them, as beings, to have a greater capacity for travel, because of their great intellectual and heart energy. The rest of the universe could benefit greatly if these beings could travel from their home planet, but right now the conditions they live in are so very careful—almost like an incubator—that even a vehicle might not be able to maintain the conditions they require. So there will have to be some slight alteration in the makeup of their soul energy so that their bodies can be more durable. Right now they are extremely fragile.

To give you an idea, their fragility would be like glass is to steel. If you are steel (and you know that you are not that sturdy), they are glass. This does not mean that they are in danger or that they suffer. They do not suffer, but the environment of their planet is very fixed; their great wisdom, capacity for love and their capacity to expand love and wisdom to others just by their presence are largely lost in the universe.

Is this from our Creator or somebody you created?

This is from your Creator.

So what is their future then? Will they stay in this creation after Creator leaves, or will they merge with Creator?

They have not chosen. We believe that if they can travel more durably, they will choose to stay in this creation, because there is much to do here. Because they are unable to travel now, they might choose without any change to simply go onward and upward. Thus this universe would lose what they have to offer. We feel then that our facilitation might be warranted.

Being of Parts and of the Whole

That sounds beautiful. The Andromedan last night had difficulty saying whether it was "them" or "him" or "it." Is this because of how you function? You are a complete being, but you can separate into parts to do things?

No, I do not separate into parts, but I am made up of many parts. If you think about it, in order for creation to take place with intention rather than as a natural function, one might say that you in your bodies are an example of creation potential with intention, meaning that you are given free will to some extent.

You are not allowed to use the full capacity of your creation as you exist now, since you could do damage, but you are given a degree of it so you can take action, experience consequences and learn. For us, it would be a similar analogy, comparing you to a single-celled creature, say, who might have great wisdom and experience, yet whose actions and energies might be fixed without having the necessity for a freewill creation. You, being made up of many cells, are then an extension of such beings.

If you use that as an analogy, going into the future after every type of creation has been done at least once, our parts would be of a similar nature since each portion of ourselves was involved in some way with creation. You could say that we are made up of many creators and beings who were involved in creations in some way. That is what we are, and when we exist in this future time, we exist as that. But we have not yet accumulated; we do not exist as that now. When we came into the past like this (we could have perhaps foreseen it), I do not think that we really considered the possibility that simply moving in time might cause our different parts to choose to emigrate. However, for some reason, my parts have not done this.

If I were to see you, would you look like a pillar of light?

Not just one.

How many?

That would depend on where you were in relationship to where we were, meaning your perspective. You might see us as eight or ten pillars, and then another time hundreds and then another time just a few. It would depend upon your perspective.

But if I could see hundreds, you don't operate independently, do you? That's all part of you?

Yes.

The Connection to the Zetas

Does Zoosh have some connection with you?

We know of this being. He is not one of us.

But he is from the future also?

I would have to say that Zoosh is from the past *and* future.

All right, let's turn to the Zetas. You had a purpose and a plan and a reason to create the Zetas. Can you talk about why they are as they are—why you created them instead of something totally different?

If you think about yourselves, one of the most core descriptions of Earth people would be that they are curious. The nature of an Earth person is to be curious. This curiosity leads to expansion and discovery in various ways. We felt that in order to create a race that could both stimulate and help you to become accepting of the reality of extraterrestrials, the race of beings we formed would need to be a counterpoint to that curiosity. One would assume that since the Zetas are a race of great intellectual capacity, they would be curious, and yet they are not curious in the way you are. They desire to understand, they desire to see, but they don't necessarily do anything or take any action on the basis of their new knowledge. What they take action on is, as any race does, their wisdom—what works in their lives—and so the counterpoint to your curiosity is their apparent complacency.

When an Earth human contacts a Zeta Reticulan, there is the usual anthropology, the cultural experience where there is no apparent common understanding of things. What is known to every Earth human is unknown to the Zetas. They wish to understand, but it is not a passionate desire. Even if it can be explained to them, the most you would get from them is perhaps a slight nod, meaning, "Oh yes, I understand," and that's it.

We believe that this counterpoint to curiosity—and perhaps most importantly, its application on Earth, which is strongly tied to inspiration—having curiosity tied to serenity or calm necessarily creates a conundrum for any being such as yourself: Is the pursuit of knowledge valid for its own sake, or is it better to pursue knowledge that can create an improvement of some sort?

Right now, science's biggest challenge is pursuing knowledge for its own sake. This has led science in directions that are very self-destructive to science as an art, to say nothing of other human beings and life forms on the planet. We are hopeful that the impact of the Zeta Reticulan race on the cultural and personal level on the human Earth person will ultimately help science to make the leap into a more constructive choice of expression.

The ships that crashed and left the artifacts on the Earth—was that by design, plan or an accident? Those artifacts have stimulated scientific knowledge and production on this planet a thousand-years' time in fifty years.

It was a potential. The beings on board the ship did not consciously know that their lives might be sacrificed in that fashion and in that form, but at the soul level they knew that there was the potential for such a danger to them personally. They were prepared to take the risk in this way. They knew only that their mission had something to do with a cultural exchange, but they did not know that the potential existed (and it was only potential, as we do not rigidly control realities) that they might suffer. Of course, we would have preferred that that didn't take place. One always hopes that more benevolent contact would take place, but this will only happen when the human race is more at ease with itself.

Unifying the Parts (Races) into the Whole (Humanity)

That brings up another point. You might wonder why people are so ill at ease with themselves. Your existence is quite the opposite of mine. I am made up of many parts that are complete unto themselves. You are all incomplete, but not just in the way that you know. Think of the different races—not only the core races but the various blendings of races that have taken place already. If you take the races of Earth and blend them into one being, then you will have a complete being. By being in separate races, you are now component parts, but not complete. Simply blending you all—

creating a singular type of a race of being from a total blending—will create you as full Earth human being without any effort on an evolutionary, intellectual teaching level, without any attempt to genetically alter anything, simply by allowing the natural birth process to take place. Only by doing that will you have three times the intellectual capacity and two times the heart capacity.

That is why you are allowed to be separate. You are allowed to be separate because you must choose to come together. There is always the possibility that people will come together not of their own choosing, and offspring might be the result, but for the entire peoples of the Earth to come together with many, many offspring as the result, can only be an act of love. So to bring the Earth prototype person into being and deliver the full Earth human requires love.

Thank you. I've never heard that before. And so the individual races, all these different stage settings, provide the environment for the melodramas, for the scenarios, for the experiences of the Explorer Race?

You might say that is so, but there is also something else. Say that the recipe was concocted only so far, and that the final step must be one chosen on a loving basis between individual loving couples with free will: "Yes, I want to be with you." Of course, it would take generations to turn over, but eventually one would have the Earth-prototype generation. And so you are allowed this choice or not. To the extent that you remain separate, you say, "We are not ready to embrace love this way," but when you embrace it, you say, "Yes, we are ready."

It seems that we have experienced Egypt, Lemuria and Atlantis, and they're in our past and yet also are in our future. Does that have to do with this loop of time?

Yes, yes. You know this already.

I know it, but explain it the way you explain it.

It is no different than what you know, and I have nothing to add to it. We did not come here because of the loop in time. We came here to facilitate, as I've stated.

Oh, so you came long before. You came at the creation.

The loop of time is fairly recent.

All right. I just didn't quite understand where we were at that time. That's in our past, at the point we made the decision.

At the point you made the decision . . .

From the head instead of the heart? We experienced Egypt and Lemuria then? And Atlantis?

At the point you made the decision, you had discovered that mentality could exist separate from the heart. It's not unusual that when people discover something new, they want to experience it to the maximum. So you made that decision from the mental, simply because you had recently discovered the purity of the mental as separated from the heart, which of course allows for polarity, consequences and disasters.

Yes, all right. But before we made that decision, had we experienced Atlantis, Lemuria and Egypt, or is that someplace in that loop of time?

No, you had not experienced that.

Okay, so we started out in the loop, and we were at the halfway point. There's a circle . . .

The experience of Atlantis was not so very long ago in terms of the loop.

And was the magical Egypt with the pharaohs and the ETs after Atlantis or before?

No pharaohs. When the ET beings were there, there were no pharaohs. The pharaohs were an attempt to imitate the appearance and perceived powers of the ETs, so the pharaohs were idealized attempts at appearing to be the admired ones.

And that was recent, too?

In terms of the loop of time, yes.

The Zetas as Future Humans

What about the understanding that the Zetas are our future selves?

This is so, but it depends upon which future you take. By bringing your races in contact now, it is possible to modify you through your own choice and modify them through their own choices. You becoming them in your future would be something you would embrace, compared to something you might feel repelled about right now.

The unified human being or Zeta would be something we would embrace?

Not unified. Modified.

Is this the total human soul personality when we have three times our mind and two times our hearts?

No. Creating the Zetas and exposing you to the Zetas causes you to change that modification, and for that matter they change, because it is a very slight modification.

So if the Earth human becomes this complete self, this prototype where we all become this magical Egyptian self, are we then on a different timeline and don't incarnate as Zetas?

You still might, but then the Zetas would be more appealing because you cannot become exactly what they are now, since your two races are linked. You cannot become your complete self without affecting them.

Remember that the frequency of part of their soul is made up of the same frequency as your soul; therefore, if you should change in some significant way, the part of their soul that is like yours, which must remain in tune—at least in terms of the benevolent aspect of your souls—would necessarily change the way they are. The most likely change you would see on the cultural level is that they would begin to reflect humor and grace, qualities you admire and would enjoy, and therefore might look forward to.

But by the time we accomplish this complete self here, they'll all be golden lightbeings, won't they? Or most of them?
Yes.

So our experience would be in their golden lightbody and not in what we know as the Zeta body?
Of course. In their golden lightbody, they are more. For example, you'll find Joopah could not quite understand humor too well, and he struggled and made the effort, but now he is a complete expert on it.

So then when we, as the Explorer Race, become the Creator, what is your interaction here? Your main purpose was to see us through to the point of expansion.
Yes. Once the expansion takes place, we'll probably no longer be needed here. By the time of the full expansion, it is less likely that the Zetas will need us as advisers, but if they wish for us to remain as advisers, we will leave a portion of ourselves here to do so. However, it is our intention after the expansion to go to the other side of the universe and work with those other beings.

Then at what point would you go back to your origin in the future? Or would you go back to the point where all five of you were together?
We have not made that decision yet.

Have you ever inspired or interacted with anyone in our history? Have you ever interacted with humans or just with the Zetas?
We have made an effort not to.

So we wouldn't read anywhere of something that would refer to you?
Not that I'm aware of.

ET Inspirations of the Egyptians

If those ET inspirers of the Egyptians were here, why did they leave? Can you just give us a little history about that?
It was intended that their existence be made known to you now in your modern time. The best way to do that was to go to the geographic point that I mentioned before—it will become well known in

the future—and seek out people who were artistically gifted and who had a culture that involved the careful preservation of the dead so that the artwork they created would likely last and be treasured by future finders. Therefore, the message that these beings existed would live into your time. So the people were carefully chosen for their culture, their aptitude and perhaps their personalities.

So it's in our past, but it was meant for us now.

Yes, it was understood that the people of that time would choose to create artistic renditions of those individuals who came to visit, and the capacity they had for creating great beauty would be treasured in your time as well as in their time. It is often the artist who is approached to create the lasting message, because art is a universal language requiring little interpretation, having only as much enigma as necessary to stimulate curiosity but not so much an enigma that curiosity is baffled.

Otherwise, you'd just turn away—but this way, you open yourself to it.

It draws you in. You know that there are artists who create in space. One finds these beings, but if you were to look to such a creation, you wouldn't be drawn in because you would say, "Well, it's space without stars." Yet what they are creating is a feeling. All artists on Earth attempt to create a feeling, but they must do so with symbolic representations rather than by creating something that generates a feeling in its own right. It speaks well of artists here when they are able to encourage such feelings, simply with the use of symbolics.

But are those first humans who created the beauty, who were inspired by the ETs, part of the Explorer Race?

The first Egyptian beings? No.

Not the ETs, but the ones who came here to do the art. They just came here to do that service?

Not everyone who has been on Earth in your known and traceable history has been part of the Explorer Race. They were here to be and to function. But the Explorer Race, according to my understanding, has been here on this planet indefinitely. Some were, some weren't. Now all are.

But they did a great service for the Explorer Race.

Certainly.

Where are they now? Or were they just beings from anywhere who were asked to come, who came for a life and then went back to wherever they came from?

As you say.

You're patiently answering my questions. I'd like you just to communicate what . . .

Our intention, as we have functioned for a time in your universe, has been to ease the way of the progress of your people and to create in such a way that you can have the option to more readily expand, without missing any important teachings and without having to linger through suffering any more than necessary. We understand that the Creator of this universe does not personally understand suffering, so we created potentials that you might make the motion toward becoming your more benign selves more smoothly and gently. This was ultimately our intention in creating this race of people, who have so enigmatically startled you with their existence.

Yes, they really did. I'm about to talk to some of the Zetas who were on their ships at particular times during the contacts with the humans. Those humans have since publicized their memories of that contact.

Human beings who have chosen to go public about these things are to be admired and congratulated, since they have often faced some ridicule in your culture of disbelief. They were chosen not only because their souls acquiesced but because of their courage.

Well, it should be very interesting to bring this all out and show the reality of it as we listen to the captains of the different ships. They say that they are on the soul line. For instance, Sha Don said that he found his past life in the fourteenth century.

That is certainly his perception.

But according to you, that's not correct.

It might or might not be correct. I do not wish to . . .

I know, but you're saying that the energy is exactly like ours. It is just that they are not necessarily past lives.

It depends upon how you look at it, through what prism of what timeline. It is our intention to allow you to expedite the alteration of your future so that the future becomes something more benign and pleasant for you. On the other hand, the Zeta race is not now something that many of you would like to become. This might require modifications in the way creation is expressed, as I have stated. Therefore, Sha Don could say in his now existence that his past life exists on Earth in the fourteenth century, but should the Zeta race evolve, he might or might not see it that way. It depends on which perception of timeline they view.

Can you discuss that? Are the timelines . . .

They had choices.

Are the timelines circular? Can an individual human move to another timeline, or is it like humanity as a whole moves to another timeline?

Humanity moves as a whole. An individual moves to another timeline and ceases to be in your existence, and he or she loses the opportunity to experience what you experience and learn here. Therefore, you are largely protected and kept from doing this, so that you do not lose your hard-won opportunity to be here. Good night.

Good night. Thank you very much.

Creation of the Zetas

Zoosh and Tlingt Cha
December 3, 1998

All right. Zoosh speaking

All right. Are you from as far in the future as the being who spoke last night, or are you from farther?

No, this individual is anchored (it's an important question from your perspective) very solidly in the future and has come back into the past along that line. I have not been anchored in any timeline. I have existed before time, but for the sake of simplicity, I have been evolving and moving the other way from a general point before time.

I asked him, "Is Zoosh from the future?" And he said, "He's from the past and the future."

Yes, that is the way that I see it myself, but for the sake of simplicity, I'd rather say that this being is here coming back, I am here coming forward, and yet both of us—passing in the twain here, as it were—are going this way, because this being you are talking to tonight is most likely going to continue back in the past where he or she will be needed more than in the present. Their next project after the Zetas that they talked to you about . . .

. . . is that wonderful race of gentle beings, that fragile race?

Yes, but then after that . . . That project will take a while—not as long as it has with the Zetas—and then I think that they will find fulfillment by going further back in the past.

How far?

I'd say as far back as the beginning of the sequential idea—meaning the beginning of the experience happening in some sequence—which is a way of saying the beginning of time.

The beginning of time for all creation, not just in this . . . ?

But not the beginning of time in the context of a time statement, meaning the beginning of the experience of time, the beginning of sequence.

Why would that be important?

Because when time began as an experience, it forced a lot of civilizations who chose to experience sequence—as an experience—into an uncomfortable position largely having to do with either slowing them down or compartmentalizing their lives, and this was difficult. It was a very difficult adjustment for many civilizations, and I would say that it probably could have been done better. Therefore, I think that this being has the capacity to produce effects that would smooth that out. So that is needed, and I think that that being will find its way to that moment, perhaps starting there and then working back up as sequence becomes something that is more practiced and experienced and understood. But in the beginning of sequence, it was very difficult for lots of races who said, "We'll try this."

I'm not clear. I'm slow tonight. It's far beyond this creation, this universe. You were talking about all creations everywhere.

Yes. I'm talking about the beginning of sequences, of experience at all.

And were you aware at that time?

Yes. At the time, I felt that it could have been done better, but one does not raise a hand and say, "Hey!". [Chuckles.] One just observes and tries to help. But I think that this being is quite dedicated to smoothing transitions in general for all races, and this is a transition that really could benefit from considerable smoothing.

It's fascinating, because he says he comes from a time where everything has been done at least once.

Yes. As a result—coming from that time—there is vast experience and knowledge based upon the cumulative impact of everything having been done, but there is not the sense of personal involvement that is so fulfilling, as any individual here knows. I think it is that sense of personal involvement and the pleasure, joy and fulfillment that goes with it that this being is missing. This is why, even though the being is a very loving and a beautiful being, sometimes their voice will sound a little flat. It is because they haven't experienced enough exultancy in their life to really project that sense of joy that is associated with—how can we say?—heartfelt passion. There's a great sense of peace and calm, yes, but that fulfillment is not quite there yet. Later, you will start to see that, if you check in with that being at some other time when the opportunity, for lack of a better term, for more "hands on" . . .

Which will be at the beginning of sequencing?
I think it will start with . . .

. . . with the race of beautiful beings.
Yes.

Wonderful. Well, I feel bad, because the other four went someplace else. Will he meet up with them again going backward, or not until he goes forward?
It's hard to say whether he will ever meet up with them again, but as he or she begins to experience that sense of personal fulfillment, I think they will find themselves to be more complete and not so conscious of missing the others—not that this is something apparent, but it is like an echo in their being. I think that the resonant echo will fade as personal fulfillment replaces it.

Great. All right. I've always felt that this Explorer Race thing came from the future. Were other beings also coming back from the future with this idea?
Well, let's just say this: We're talking about the beginning of sequence. This future time—for the lack of a better term—that this being is talking about has seen the end of sequence by then. So it is a little hard to say, but I would have to say that, if you want to look at it on a basis of time, the prompting of these threads—which has come from many different sources—might have come from both future and past and everything in between. So you would be hard-pressed . . .

So the desire for more excitement, more expansion—this was coming from all kinds of beings? They all had the feeling that this was needed, then?
Yes. You would be hard-pressed to say, "Here is the person we can say did this." And I might add that other worthy ideas also happened this way, which is why you will be told—as others have told you—that everyone is one, because as one, everyone contributes in some way toward everything. But you contribute generally on the basis of your personal interests or abilities. Therefore, you alone, as any individual, may not even have the capacity to contribute more than a small portion, and yet you do not have to contribute more than that, because all these

others are contributing what they contribute, and eventually all these small portions make a whole thing that can then be acted upon.

But we still don't know your total involvement in this. I mean, you've been complicit, and you may be more causal than we know in this whole idea of the Explorer Race?

Oh, I was involved a little bit.

[Chuckles.] All right. I don't really have to ask about the seeds now. I just thought I had this being who had this overarching view of everything, and so I was going to get more information. I think he wants to talk about the Zetas, right?

The being would prefer to talk about the Zetas, because that is its project and he or she is less interested in the overall, since . . . We have to think about it: As a personality, the being itself is looking forward to having a personal experience with the overall and would rather not examine it from this somewhat dry and dusty perspective, as it were, from which the personal experience has not yet taken place. All right. I'll see you in your dreams.

Good night. Thank you very much.

Tlingt Cha Speaks of Zeta Creation

Greetings.

Welcome, welcome.

What shall we talk about?

Well, let's get some more information about the Zetas. I offered so many sidetracks last night. How did you get the idea to create the Zetas? What was the basis of that?

There needed to be a species of beings who could function largely in the intellectual and who would desire the improvement of the mind along scientific avenues. In the beginning of the race, it was necessary to allow them greater latitude to experience many of the passions and general experiences of other planets. This got a little out of hand, and they were able to make a choice to pursue of the intellectual as compared to primarily pursuing pleasure.

Did you guide them in that way?

I offered suggestions such as, "If you go this way, this will happen. If you try this, it might alter the current experience and still be fulfilling." And they decided to go the latter way. There was little resistance, because the civilization had become somewhat chaotic, and it is built into them to desire to have a certain degree of calm—if not necessarily order, then a degree of calm predictability—and when there is disruption of that, they would, as you might say, overreact or become highly volatile in an excited situation. This is another reason why they must protect themselves from the passionate human being when they are in contact with you, because if they felt your passions—even in the most benevolent way—they would become overly reactive, and it would disrupt their individual personalities to the point that they might not be able to recapture their normal state of being.

Oh, it's almost like an alcoholic. You're always susceptible to the stimulation.

Yes, so that's another reason that they will use the device. I might add as an aside here, just for the moment, because various contactees in this book *Face of the Visitors* have mentioned it, that often the entities contacting the Earth individuals will seem to have their legs together as one, moving without the motion of the legs. This is because when the beings are functioning in your dimension, it is unsafe for them to do anything, and certain beings must retain a very rigid attitude. The Zetas, when they have come to Earth, have also sometimes had to do this, and that's why they've been perceived by certain individuals as robots or automatons, because they did not seem to move their legs. This is done for their protection.

The device that allows them to perpetuate their own dimension inside your dimension will often cause a silver or gray light around them, which will be perceived by some individuals—not all—and yet it will tend to be very protective to them. One often sees this when one is experiencing interdimensional phenomena from your dimension as an Earth person. So I'm mentioning this now, because it is something that affects the Zetas and also has some application to other contactee scenarios.

It's almost like they have a spacesuit on like we would wear in space, except that it's invisible.

Yes, that's a very good analogy. It would be as if you were wearing a spacesuit that did not allow you to move your legs, but you had some device that could motivate you around, or drive you around, you might say.

Like right now, the astronauts have the little thrusting thing on the back. They push the thruster and they move forward.

Yes. Or even the simple surface rovers that have been sent in satellites. So I mention this because that's how this misperception has come about. Now, the Zetas then chose to pursue intellectual applications and science, which created for them (and others) an opportunity to have a race of beings devoted to service. At the same time, this service was also fulfilling to them. The Zetas are very much in service. If a civilization elsewhere desires to have a long-term study of something that would be very boring for their own members but is scientifically associated, very often the Zetas will be asked if they would choose or be willing to cooperate in such a study. And if they have individuals available, they often do.

In this way, they are not slavishly devoted but perform a needed service—not always the type of service that other races would not care to perform. This is ultimately the reason I chose to create them, because they would offer something for their own enjoyment that would be of great service, service that was largely going unfilled at the time I began this.

Were you here when our Creator got here, or did you come after?

After. The universe was already formed and filling in as I arrived. Yes. To continue a little more about what I was saying before, when some races wish to participate in the genetic experiment on Earth—as your friend used to call it—the races themselves from different places (Andromeda, Sirius and so on) found the scientific interactions with human beings to be personally distasteful, meaning that they themselves as individuals would not care to be that removed or that detached from the beings they were working with; they would normally be more personally involved. And therefore, they needed to have someone who *could* be detached.

Why did they need to be detached?

If you are a scientist working with someone who has strong feelings, it is very easy—and this comes up for doctors and nurses all the time in your time—to get so personally involved with the individual that you either forget what you are doing or you make a mistake. So these other races asked the Zetas if they could work with contacting human beings in various ways, to evolve the human being to become more this way or that way and to influence certain things genetically, because they were concerned that they would become compassionately involved with you as individuals to the point that they might make a mistake. They felt that, since the work was so delicate and potentially dangerous if not done precisely right, they did not want to take the chance.

Therefore, they asked the Zetas, because they knew that the Zetas could remain calm and dispassionate while working with you and also that the Zetas would need to use the device that would separate the both of you. Some of these beings, such as the Orions or Sirians or even Pleiadeans, cannot separate themselves that much. Even though they could use the device, it tends to constrict their own energy bodies too much. So this is another reason to have produced a race that could act in this largely technical capacity and make relatively few errors (at least on a scientific basis).

Zeta Influence in the Development of Primitive Humans

So the Zetas have come here in what we call our past at different times, then. Were they here thousands of years ago—not coming here recently and going back in the past, but I mean . . . have they come here in our past?

Yes, because there was a considerable amount of work to be done to adapt you to the environment of Earth as a race of beings.

How long ago?

Let's say prehistoric times. They were working with human beings (the human form) before the Explorer Race arrived here so that the human form (the human body) would be more adaptable and amenable to soul entry in the body that might require familiarity. What that means is that if a soul were focused in that life (through, say, Sirius, or through multiple focuses—Sirius, Orion or the Pleiades, for example), the body itself would have enough of the genetic code of these places so that the body would feel like a welcome place to be—or at least, sufficiently welcome so that the soul would feel at ease within the body during the physical lifetime. So these influences then needed to be genetically placed in the physical body over generations so that it was not traumatic to the human race but so that the body itself would welcome souls that would be coming.

What did the human body look like at that time?

There were different races, different attempts. Some of the bodies were more rugged. Some of them, later on, were more delicate. I would say "delicate" is the best term. The delicate bodies didn't happen until later. The delicate bodies, I would say, had more to do with an infusion of beings who moved here from various places. There was, for a while, a Pleiadean culture trying to establish a surface race, but they gave up on that. But having left some of their genetics behind in the usual way, this influenced the more delicate body. When I say delicate, I am talking about the vulnerable human body of today in your time, whereas in previous times, one might have found a much stronger or rugged so-called primitive human who might be perhaps unacceptable by your current standards—perhaps not able to adapt to the intellectual world but formidable in the world of instinct. As you would say, the primitive human had more of the animal capacity and was able to survive more easily in rugged situations but less easily in sophisticated situations.

I know time is so difficult, but was this 50,000 years, 100,000 years, a million years ago?

I cannot say; it's not possible. But it would be reasonable, by what I have stated, to simply look at pictures based upon bones that have been found and so on and make extrapolations.

Okay. So how did they do that?

They would ask for volunteers in the way they have always done. But in those days, the volunteering was more conscious, because those beings were more connected to their instincts and less to their minds, and so they would know. When they saw the Zeta ship, they'd have a good feeling about it. The Zetas might project a picture of themselves or of other beings that might be on the ship, and the beings would look at that and have a calm feeling or a comfortable feeling, and then the Zetas would pick these people up. Not forcefully, but they might land the ship, open the door and someone would come out and beckon them forward. If they came on the ship on their own, then they were welcomed. If there was reluctance or fear, then there was no going out to get them. It was done this way because it was recognized that those more primitive beings would not be involved in internal mental conflict about the experience and would make the choice of contact largely based on their part upon instinct, since that was their prime motivating energy.

And then what precisely would they do? Would the Zetas extract their DNA?

They would extract some DNA by gentle means, and then they would either inject something into the being or they might try to do what is typical—and what hybridizers have been doing for years, either with beings like this, or as you do now with fruits and vegetables. They would try to get beings together—to make love and so on and to have offspring—but they didn't do too much of that, because they felt that it was invading the privacy of these individuals, and so mostly they did so with a comfortable injection, on the back of the hand, for example. They would find a place that was not too hairy, and they would put something on the surface of the hand near a vein that could be injected through the skin with pressure, through the pores. This would be only a slight sting, not much, and to beings like that who were rugged, they would not pull back; they would just notice a slight discomfort. But it would be less discomfort than, say, a needle.

So the Zetas have been, unbeknownst to us, intimately involved with the whole customization of the human body on Earth.

The Zetas have been involved in the hybridization of the physical human body that the Explorer Race came to occupy.

So this latest wave in the forties, fifties and sixties is just another round, except that we have different ideas now about privacy and about being in control of our own bodies. It's a whole different mindset now.

Yes, because a lot of the contact that happened to prepare the bodies of different individuals, to create what you now accept as the human body, had been completed well before that series of contacts in the forties and fifties. So there was no written record in the preceding thousands of years that had survived or at least gone out into the general knowledge of all populations. If there had been contacting of individuals in various races or civilizations, that information was kept within that race or civilization. But the bulk of the hybridizing of the human body, as it came to be known, had largely already taken place well in the past. So when the contacts took place again, the people felt that this was something entirely new, and they had no means to say, "This is a continuing phenomenon."

But there was a slight difference this time, because the Zetas had a stake in the outcome, whereas before it was pure service to prepare the body for the human experiment.

Yes, but they didn't have the complete understanding—or at least, the extent of the understanding that they have now—in the forties. In the forties or fifties, they were still feeling like this was primarily service. It wasn't until about the seventies that they all began to realize fully as a group that they personally had some stake in the matter—although a glimmer of the experience was beginning to seep in around 1948. But with the Zetas, it takes a while for them all to have this understanding. It took until about 1972-73 for all of them to understand that there was a personal relationship between them and you. And, of course this caused them to approach you differently.

But they didn't understand, even in the forties and fifties, that the hybrid babies . . .

Not the ones that came then. The ones that might have come to a more recent time and gone back—of course they understood. But the ones who came *in* the time initially from where they were straight back to the forties—no, they didn't have that understanding. You have to remember that some understanding is lost in the sequence of travel.

Right. Zoosh explained that beautifully.

Yes, that is a very important formula for the understanding of space travel, not only so that one can recognize symptoms of space travel, but also so that one can make preparations to protect the core personalities or the core culture, knowledge and wisdom of an individual based upon their society as they learn to travel in a ship that passes through time.

Incarnation into Zeta Bodies

While we've had some information in the past about the Zeta history, it was from the participants—from Joopah, mostly. When you created these beings, what was the size of the civilization? Thousands? Millions?

In the beginning, thousands.

And how many are there now, not counting the hybrids?

Not counting the hybrids? Oh, I should think eight million or so.

And do most of the souls reincarnate sequentially or out of sequence but pretty much in the Zeta race, or do they become a Pleiadean in one life and an Orion in one life and a human in one life?

Not unlike other souls, based upon their fulfillment in any race or species, they might choose to return and have another life on Zeta Reticuli, or they might go elsewhere. It is not like if one is a cat, one is always a cat—although there are some exceptions [chuckles]. But no, it is just the same as any reincarnational life cycle.

So you're saying that Tiger was not always a cat?

[Pause.] He says it is all right to discuss it a little bit. He has, on previous occasion, been a sea creature.

Oh! [Laughs.] Thank you. All right. So, you created the Zeta beings and then you put out a call for souls who wanted to experience this body. How does that work?

When one creates a body of a sacred civilization, the soul sequence as we would call it is a natural part of the function. The very souls are souled, as well as the larger tissues and membranes. So when utilizing the stuff of life—the light, the substance, the atoms if you would—it is not possible to put something like this together and do so with a soulless being, because love is what holds and binds and supports and sustains. You are producing a being or anything with that matter for it to be ensouled as natural. The ensouling is actually occurring *while* you are creating the being, not unlike what occurs when an embryo forms inside the mother. It is like that. It is the substance of creation that prompts the soul sequence.

Taking the time of this creation—I know that the Explorer Race was created in the last 2 percent of the time. We're late arrivals here. So where in that sequence would you have created the Zetas? Have they been here halfway through or for the last part?

This is a very well-asked question. It is in the last 10 percent of the time.

Ah, that you saw the need for this?

That I created the species.

But you saw the need earlier and then worked toward that?

I saw the need and then began creating prototypes and eventually settled on one type.

So the last 10 percent . . . That's how they got so far ahead of us in the future? Or was the future . . . not sequential? They're there, like they live in Pittsburgh or something?

Yes. That assumes that certain pursuits are universal, but they are not. Some races pursue art through feeling. Some races pursue art through thought, and so on. So certain types of cultural expression are universal, but the approach and the means may not be the same. Therefore, one cannot measure a civilization on the basis of its accomplishments as one might compare to one's own civilization historically. So as you say, they are not really ahead of you; they are in a different time, having utilized different pursuits with different applications in order to accomplish their personal goals. But your societies are not directly comparable. Certainly, if you looked directly at their society and looked at your technology, you would feel as if you were in the Stone Age, but the comparison is not equal. They have different pursuits on an equal level in time, especially with their ninth-dimensional bodies. A ninth-dimensional Zeta might look at a seventh-dimensional Zeta and then look at a human being on Earth and say that you, as human beings, are far ahead of the seventh-dimensional Zeta in terms of knowing how to express feelings. So it is not directly comparable.

I understand. Each one has a different . . .

Purpose, intent, pursuit.

Okay, now, it must have come from you. When they learned that they were coming to the end (which they thought was the end of their life but was actually the end of their experience in that dimension), did you encourage them to create the hybrids?

That was their idea.

Was it?

A not unreasonable idea.

Because that's what they did! That was their experience.

Yes, that was their experience. And no one likes to think that their culture might be lost, that all they accomplish might simply wind up in a computer someplace for other races to access if they happened to find it. They would like to think that what they had done might be carried on in some way, as any parent might think.

But how does that now interact with the humans? Will the humans incarnate in the hybrid bodies as well as the Zeta bodies?

Not as humans, but in a reincarnational life cycle it is certainly possible. It doesn't directly connect. It is a Zeta experience.

And yet you say, if I understand it, that you created the Zeta body for the human to incarnate in later?

Yes, but only if you change the way things are going to be, which is what you are doing as the Explorer Race. But before the Explorer Race was incorporated into the human body as an experience, the change might not have taken place that the Zeta culture will feel more welcoming to your souls.

You Are Changing Future Incarnations

You just said a very interesting sentence. You said "before the Explorer Race experience was put into or connected to the human . . ." I thought that the human, by the nature of their being a part of the three seeds or the roots, were the Explorer Race.

No. Remember that I said that the beings who were on Earth, who were originally Earth people, were transformed genetically over time to be what is now accepted to be the human being. But these beings who were originally here, if they had not been transformed, would have been the beings in which future incarnation of the Zetas would have taken place. This is almost irrelevant, but we can pursue it. It's irrelevant to who you are, because we're talking about someone who isn't you—that isn't the Explorer Race, that isn't a human being. But for the now human being and the soul (we are talking about the soul here, the immortal personality) to desire to become the Zetas in the future . . . the desire would not be present. As a matter of fact, there would be a sense of revulsion, not because the Zetas are so awful, but because—compared to the human race as you experience life—their existence seems passionless.

Therefore, in order to alter that, it is necessary to have greater contacts between your race and their race, which is the reason that their race was told that there is a direct connection between you and them. It is also why you are being told now that this connection exists as well. Simply having all of your souls knowing this is going to create a greater compatibility between who your souls are now, who they will be in the next million years or so and who the Zetas will be then.

It is, as your friend would call it, "benevolent magic in action." You will change it, just as you hear from the weather person that it's going to rain the next day on your party outdoors, and you don't consciously try to change it (you even make some plan to move the party indoors), but you are disappointed. You go to bed that night, and you wake up the next day and there is hardly a sprinkle. You have changed it unconsciously with benevolent magic, although it is now your friend's intention to bring this benevolent magic up into a more conscious state so you can use it to resolve your critical problems.

And where does the benevolent magic come in? We need benevolent magic to be able to do that?

To change the Zeta culture so that it will have passion, humor, overt fun, so that by the time you arrive there . . .

Oh, I see. So it will be a desirable body for an Explorer Race human to . . .

It will be the ninth-dimensional body, which has fun and humor—all of the things that you have come to hold dear.

Yes—things that we require.

And at the same time, it does not interfere with the Zeta culture and service, because the entire seventh-dimensional Zeta experience will be *before* the human being enters (as you know yourself to be, the human soul), and so you will simply miss the entire seventh-dimensional experience of the Zetas.

At last I understand. Brilliant. Was that part of your plan?

I will not take credit for it. I will only say my intention has been and always is (in this line of work, I'll say) to smooth transitions from the rough to the easier.

Okay, this is a whole line of thought. So humans outgrow the human body and they're in a higher dimension. They're able to utilize and experience the golden lightbody of the Zetas and to reincarnate into these beautiful golden Zeta bodies, but they don't stop there. That's just a step on the way?

The humans who choose to do that will choose to incarnate in those bodies, yes. It will be no different from any reincarnational cycle. Some of the beings in those golden lightbodies will have been human beings in this time, and some will be from other places.

And some will be Zetas. Some will be those who were seventh-dimensional Zetas.

Yes. It will be like any other reincarnational cycle, but it will be more exciting. Having been a human being in these times with some knowledge of the Zeta interaction and then finding yourself in that time (which could be your next life) in a ninth-dimensional Zeta body—it will be fun!

Okay, where does the benevolent magic come in, then?

You change the outcome of your incarnational cycle. If you are going to become something, you want it to be more benevolent to you ("you" meaning your immortal personality). So you are personally involved in creating the ninth-dimensional body. That's where the ninth-dimensional body comes from—not "poof," as your friend Zoosh says in jest. The benevolent magic takes place in sequence, meaning that you are going to be a Zeta (maybe, if you wish), and in order for that to be acceptable, there has to be a variation of the Zeta that you can feel comfortable with. So that variation is the ninth-dimensional golden lightbody. When you enter that body, you can bring your full immortal personality, experiencing all that you have experienced up to this point and up to the next point, and still know yourself, appreciate yourself and comfortably interact with seven-dimensional Zeta beings because of the connection between you both. So you serve the seventh-dimensional Zetas with the solution to their problem (the apparent end of their race), and they serve you by performing all this service that they have been doing to smooth your transitions and to smooth the transitions from all the other races who needed to interact with you but could not do it directly for their own personal reasons.

Personal Perspectives on the Resolution of Mysteries

I'm so very glad you came to talk to us, because you have just explained so much and in such a patient way.

It all depends on perspective, and—as I continue to discover—it depends quite a bit on personal involvement to be able to explain it in a reasonable sequence.

Did you hear Zoosh say, when I was talking to him earlier, that you will achieve more personal fulfillment for yourself by your increased level of personal involvement?

Yes, I did, and I thought that was putting it very succinctly in terms of the feelings that I have been having lately.

Wonderful. I love it when everybody gains. That's great. Now, we'll explore some of these reported cases of human and Zeta interaction, which (as you've explained) took a lot of courage from the humans for them to come out and say, "This happened." Just getting this out will help. What's your perspective on getting this information out?

Getting this information out will be very useful. Ultimately this book is intended to serve as the . . . Well, you know how Morse code has dots and dashes? It's adding extra dots so that the dots are not separated so much from the dashes, and it gives you hints on where to fill in sequences that have been previously mysterious. Mysteries are very useful, because they stimulate, vitalize and intrigue you, keeping your attention focused on some area that might be necessary. And yet, as you all know, the resolution of mysteries—or even parts of mysteries—is very exciting and prompts the continuation of resolution in general. So that, I believe, has been built into you on purpose.

This book is an attempt to resolve parts of various mysteries in order to entice you to expand your welcoming, not only of extraterrestrial races who love you and appreciate you, but also to be able to accept them on their own terms instead of needing to convert them into beings like you. You know, as an Earth person of the culture that you're in, that is one of the biggest challenges for any youngster—going to school and having friends and so on, trying to feel a part of things, that you are like everybody else, so you can be accepted.

As a result, many cultures on Earth have taken the rather nationalistic point of view that "If you become more like us, then we will embrace you." This has led to the building of walls and barriers that you are only now beginning to take apart as many of you become more worldly from international travel and communications, which are getting better now because of the computer networks and so on. And this is all intentional, so that when races come to meet you and you go out to meet them, as you will in the future, you will be able to accept them as they are and appreciate each other's differences in the divine soup that makes up all life.

Spiritual Advances in Future Human Technology

That's wonderful. Now, there's one more point here. Those Zetas, as you said, had the potential that they might crash, and they did. And in their crashing, these crafts came into the hands of humans, and that incredible technology that has changed life on the planet in the past fifty years went first into the hands of the secret government for military purposes. But in the long run, that's just a step, right? It will eventually come into the hands of humans as a whole.

That's right. And to some extent, in terms of its trickledown effect.

We have rockets and lasers and . . .

There has also been a profound effect on medical science. This is largely an outgrowth of military interests, but medical science is being revolutionized now, especially in the field of genetics. Even though some mistakes will be made, ultimately you will cure all disease using this technology. When all disease is cured, then you will have to pay more attention to population, but by that time there will be a benevolent agreement between all nation states that it would be best if people do no more than reproduce themselves, and perhaps then you might see some version of population control out of necessity. Even with Benevolent Magic, the planet is only so big, and you do not want to be living on top of one another. But this will take twenty to twenty-five years to be fully embraced by the majority of the population. Although some races have begun population control now, it is in a primitive and largely uncivilized state. It will get more benevolent in the future.

All humans need to understand what a great gift the Zetas gave us. I mean, we've leaped five hundred years ahead in fifty years, right?

Yes, I think that is true. But it has not percolated yet in terms of spiritual values, or even, to some extent, in terms of emotional values, though perhaps it will do so in time. The glamour of the ship has been more important than the mystique of the beings. When the mystique of the beings becomes equally important, then you will see more spiritual advances— meaning that other beings like the Zetas, those who would like to visit you, would feel safer if you began broadcasting messages—from official channels as well as from scientific projects. These messages could say, "We welcome all races," and "Come as you are, and we will do our best to accommodate you." It might take time for that to take place, but when it does, then you will see spiritual growth, which will be very heartwarming.

Wonderful. You must feel very heart-warmed yourself when you think of the results of what you started.

I feel good that I have been able to contribute something that takes some of the unintended edges off of a transition and that will perhaps allow souls to become more accepting of various reincarnational experiences in time.

The Future of the Diplomatic Liason

Now there's another little thing here. When we create our prototype, synthesized one-Earth body, and the ET race that was here before the Egyptians comes back, why is that Andromedan going to be talking to that ET race? What connection do you have to that ET race, because that Andromedan basically works for you?

Oh, I don't think that the being "works" for me. I'd say that the Andromedan being has been created to be a devoted diplomat and, after one has been a diplomat for so many years, the idea of doing anything other than perhaps teaching other diplomats would be tedious. So I think it is just an opportunity for that being rather than a rational purpose.

Okay, an opportunity. But who is he going to serve as liaison between, the ET race and who? You? Us? Them?

That is not formed yet, and so I cannot give you an answer. All things are not patterned; some things pattern themselves, and that is one of those things that is yet to be patterned. We'll see who that is.

I see. All right—and can I put in a word? That diplomat would love to end his life teaching others. Is that something . . . ?

I understand that, and that is certainly possible. But that is a desire that that being has of the moment, and it could change. So I am saying that it will be possible, if that desire remains constant.

Well, we tied up all the loose ends. [Chuckles.]

[Chuckles.] And on that note, I will say good evening.

Thank you with all of my heart. We will see you again sometime.

Perhaps.

Good night.

Contacts from *Faces of the Visitors*

Zoosh

December 4, 1998

I want to talk about an incident that concerns a woman in France in the early 1950s. This incident has been assumed to be associated with UFO phenomena because of the circumstantial evidence surrounding it, but in fact we have here an incident that is more directly associated with the Montauk time experiments and with the evildoers (for lack of a better term) who sent individuals back in time—sometimes all different directions in time, sideways and forward. While they intended to send these individuals forward in time, they often went in unpredictable directions.

Sinister Reach from the Past: Contact in France

If you recall, the instructions were to go and grab whatever they could and bring it back to the point of departure. Now, the reason why I wish to discuss this case is because of the circumstances that took place. This is the reason the person saw the hands reaching forward, and that's why they could actually move her physically. She had the metallic taste in her mouth because if one is exposed to a particular kind of energy—and we are dealing with potent electrical fields—it will often leave that residual flavor. She also had the burns on her face because of the electrical energy. I feel it is important to correct this. I will also acknowledge the sighting that took place previous to this. This was a ship that knew the event was going to take place and was attempting to prevent a tear in the fabric of time but was unable to do so while trying to prevent the woman's experience. This is what had been attempted. I will say that the work that they did do prevented her from being taken. If the being who was reaching through had managed to drag her in with him, she would have experienced her death in a most cruel fashion. So this near miss and trauma was no worse because of the beings on the ship, who were attempting in various situations to prevent catastrophic events because of the potential for tears in the fabric of the veils that separate times and dimensions.

If they had managed to grab her and bring her back to . . . what? What year was on the other end, 1980?

If they had managed to drag her back, they probably would have returned to the 1970s.

That's where they started out?

Yes. At that particular time, that's where the point of departure was. In any event, without going too much into timing, I wanted to comment on that because of its association with something other than UFO phenomena.

She said that she felt her head jerk back against the cold iron chest, and she felt the cold in her hair and on the back of her neck, and the hands were cold.

Yes, that is just exactly how close she came, because she was actually partly back in Montauk. A drawing is necessary here [see Figure 15.1]. What the ship and the occupants on the ship were able to do is this. You draw it like this. This circle on the right-hand side represents the point of departure, and this circle represents . . . let's just say France. And what the occupants

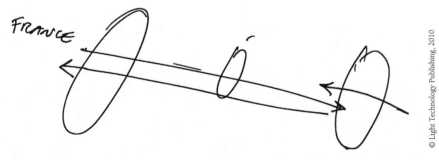

Figure 15.1: Zoosh's illustration of what the occupants of the ship were able to do. The circle on the far right represents the point of departure while the circle on the far left represents the location of the contactee in France and the middle circle depicts the reflection the beings were able to bring about in order to protect her.

of the ship were able to do—what they had done successfully on numerous occasions—was to put in what amounts to a double-lens reflector. Knowing that they would not be able to fully interfere and prevent the person from being taken—which is what she felt when she felt herself hitting the surface; she was taken back—they arranged it so that as she was taken, the pressure to pull her back to the present would be amplified by this sort of mini-portal, which functioned not unlike a rubber band, stretching back with her and then catapulting her back into her present. So that's essentially what happened—she was pulled into their time and then reflected back to her present.

Who was on the ship?

On the ship we had Andromedans who had been working for some time to maintain the veils here, because—curiously enough—some of the Montauk experiments in time were actually inadvertently invading planets beyond Earth. When you travel in time, the chance of moving in distance or space is greatly amplified, especially if you don't know what you're doing—they were really a loose-cannon operation. There had been several pathways, unintentional pathways . . . Again, we'd better use a sketch here [see Figure 15.2]. Instead of just going back and forward in time on Earth, we had something like this. If this is Earth—of course, this is not to scale—and if this is Andromeda, A and E, instead of simply traveling back in time from the point of departure, they would go like this and soar all over the place. Several of their pathways went right through the Andromedan star

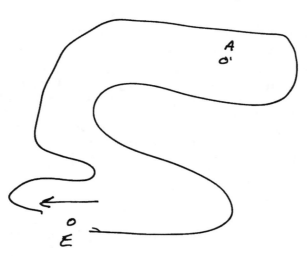

© Light Technology Publishing, 2010

Figure 15.2: Zoosh's drawing of the potentially erratic pathway the participants in the Montauk experiment might have taken, where E symbolizes Earth and A is Andromeda.

system, fortunately not hitting anyone but strictly—as the Andromedans might have said—by the grace of God not striking anyone or anything in their star system.

So the Andromedans felt a sense of personal invasion and decided that they would take on the Montauk experiment in an attempt to keep it at least in the boundaries of Earth and if possible protect individuals who might become victims of this project. They could not prevent that those who were drafted to go back in time were grabbed—although they tried and might have saved a few individuals—but they tried to prevent the impact on unrelated individuals such as this individual in France.

What do you mean by "drafted?"

You might not recall, but for the most part, individuals who were sent back in time in the Montauk time experiments were not volunteers. They were simply grabbed from various communities. There were a lot of unsolved kidnappings then, and that's what happened to some of these people.

They grabbed children and the homeless?

Yes.

Okay. Do you want to talk about other contacts in this book, Faces of the Visitors? Is that just the first one?

We can do others, if you choose.

Sure, let me go back to the beginning here.

Contact in Italy

Okay. One of the first was August 14, 1947. Who is the person here?

Read some of the details out loud.

The witness, R. L. Johannis, spoke of two creatures whom he described as boys. Let's get a date first: August 14, 1947. The creatures were small, about three feet tall, with heads that were "larger than the normal head of a human." They had no hair and were wearing "tight-fitting brown caps." "Their noses were straight and long. The eyes were large, protuberant, and round; they were yellow-green and had a vertical pupil, like that of a cat. The hands had eight fingers and seemed to be opposed" (Randle and Estes, Faces of the Visitors, 22).

And their location again?

The location? Oh, Friuli, Italy.

Yes. Talk a little bit about the witness.

"The witness was on a rock-hunting expedition in the mountains in the extreme northeastern part of Italy. As he was walking in the country, he emerged from a stand of trees and saw, on a rocky riverbank, a large red object that seemed to be shaped like a lens. He couldn't see it well and put on his glasses. It was

clear to him that the craft was something unusual. The witness and the creatures approached one another but when they were a few paces apart, they stopped. The witness suddenly seemed to have no strength. Although paralyzed, he could still observe the details. Thinking about it later, he believed that he stood near the creature only two or three minutes. Eventually one of the creatures raised its right hand to its belt. There was a puff of smoke or a ray of some kind, and the witness fell to the ground. The rock hunter's pick he held was yanked from his hands" (**Faces of the Visitors, 23**).

All right. Now this is an interesting incident because of the timing. Here we have 1947, the late 1940s. We know there were incidents before this, but it was right around this time when many incidents were happening. The ETs did not understand that the man was rock hunting, and if you have ever seen a pick for rock hunting, it looks very much like a weapon. He, of course, just stopped what he was doing and wasn't thinking about the fact that he was holding something that looked like a weapon, and so they assumed that he was hostile, even though he was not. He was simply curious, and so that is why he acted in this way, in self-defense, which I think is pretty clear to the casual reader.

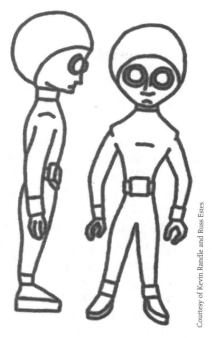

Figure 15.3: The two small beings witnessed in Italy in 1947. The beings were described as without hair and wearing small, brownish caps on their heads.

Courtesy of Kevin Randle and Russ Estes

But this is a whole new physiology. Where are they from? Why are they here? What are they doing?

This is not at all unusual. Before powerful radars and the technology of today in your world, the idea of ships coming from afar and just exploring to see what was available here or picking up useful things that might not be missed on this planet but could be used on their planet was typical. I might add that it's largely typical everyplace else but here. Here, however, since people are isolated and do not recall their ET heritage and so on, it is considered quite shocking and invasive. These beings from a planet very far away are on what you would call a remote scouting expedition—sometimes checking for plants, other times checking for minerals—not unlike something that your own commercial industries would do on this planet.

Long-Range Galactic Exploration

This circumstance had to do with a long-ranging exploration of galaxies very far from their own, because in their galaxy, they had run out of certain things that are quite common on Earth, plus they did not have diplomatic relations with the galaxy Sirius where quartz and sand are quite readily available. They were from, how can we say . . . let's see . . . there's no sense in giving the name, because you can't pronounce it. It's a name made up largely of consonants, with no vowels, but I suppose I can give it the old try: *Grrzzmpchzncks*. Good luck trying to spell it.

[Laughs.] Okay, but as far as the map of the universe is concerned . . .

As far as a universal map, I would have to say that they are about 329 million light-years away. However, they have developed a very potent time-sequence travel, which allows them to travel huge distances—and I mean considerably more than the average distance—in very little time, without having to go through the elaborate braking procedures that travelers do most of the time. So they can travel vast differences in less than a second.

Using portals?

No, I don't think I dare discuss what they are using, because it would be very easy for you on Earth to stumble onto this technology in the next twenty-five years or so, well before you are prepared to be exposed to the universe. So I think I'll say no more about it, except that it is a technology that is actually simpler than the time-traveling technology utilized by galaxies closer to you; it's considerably advanced, but simpler.

Are there areas in the universe that are more advanced or ahead of other areas, or is it scattered?

Certainly, and it depends on how you calculate "advanced," if it's in technology or art or spirituality. All over this universe you have civilizations that are astonishingly ahead of other civilizations, depending on your perspective. So here you have one like that, and it's unfortunate the man was subject to a degree of ridicule, but those were the times. Although I will say that because it was happening in what amounts to postwar Italy, people who knew him were more inclined to believe him.

Oh, he was a professor. I missed that.

Disbelief was more common in the United States because of public policy, and so fortunately for him—if fortunately is a word that can be applied here—he experienced this in a country outside the boundaries of the United States.

And having eight fingers that are opposed, is that all over the universe?

Yes. To have four fingers and an opposed thumb is one way; to have eight fingers opposed is another way. You will tend to find civilizations with more fingers, especially in such a useful system. Think about it: You have four fingers with an opposed thumb. Here we have two four-fingered units opposed, which gives one a great deal of tactile potential, telling you that this civilization is not only tactile but has tremendous capabilities for being even more tactile, which might give you an idea of how their machines would be designed. Where you might have a machine that has buttons on one side—say, a tube with buttons on one side—they might have a machine that has a tube with buttons on *both* sides.

Contact in Kentucky

Fascinating, thank you. Here is the next one. The date is August 22, 1955. Why don't I just show you the picture? Will that bring it to you faster?

All right. But I might have you read it anyway.

Well, okay. First the picture. Then I'll read it.
Oh yes, a famous incident. Go ahead.

Okay. Small, three and one-half feet tall; "big round head and large luminous eyes. The arms were slender, extending almost to the ground, with huge talonlike hands. The eyes glowed with a yellowish light. The body seemed to be made of, or covered with, silver that glowed in the dark" (Faces of the Visitors, 31–32).

Yes, well—now here's again the silver. This is the effect of the interdimensional, and this was mentioned recently. If you see something from another dimension that is there either temporarily or in transit through Earth, if it is extraterrestrial in origin, you might see the silver glow around it. That silver has to do with the protection emanating from that being or a device, and it also has to do with the extraterrestrial itself. When there are places away from Earth that are not involved in material mastery, such as Earth is, we find more of what I would call a linear technological mastery, and in this case that's what you've got—a demonstration of the silver light. So this is not a being *made* of silver light, but more like a cocoon.

Well, seven or eight people were there, and they shot one of them with a shotgun and then . . .

Here we have a curious incident too, because an independent motion picture was made of this.

Okay, so the people retreated into the house and then they were shooting at the beings and everything.

Yes, these were real beings. I think that you will find that these beings . . . well, they're not accurately drawn. You have to allow for the fact that there were several different sightings and several different individuals commenting on what they looked like, but it is pretty close. It's just that some of it is what you call a conglomerate, and so the drawing is not totally accurate, but it's pretty close.

Were the ears that big?

No, but they might have appeared to be that way. But they are not really ears in any event.

What are they?

These appendages coming out have more to do with communications—which I suppose you could say is what ears do, but ears have to

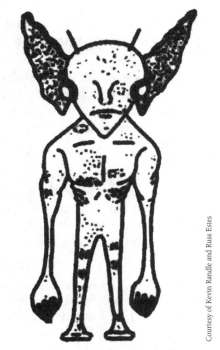

Courtesy of Kevin Randle and Russ Estes

Figure 15.4: Depiction of beings sighted near the small town of Kelly, Kentucky, in 1955.

do with hearing, and these have to do with actually transmitting. So these beings were on a long-range expedition, but not for the purpose of acquiring anything or for trade or substances—strictly for studying. On their planet, they were what would compare nicely to anthropologists on your planet.

Having that silver light around them fortunately prevented most injuries to them. However, they would feel the blast's effect against the silver light, the silver cocoon, and in one case, because of the proximity to several blasts, one of the individuals was actually injured, and that individual retreated to the vehicle. It is unfortunate that the individuals were using shotguns, because there was a member of the party of human beings who wanted to not do that, since the ETs were obviously not trying to harm them. It also is interesting to note that these ETs were actually attracted to these individuals because of the youngsters. They were fairly young themselves, which is why, if they had the capacity to do so, they would sometimes do things children might do. So it was what I would call a misunderstanding between races.

Okay, just give me a minute here. So the people were terrified, the children were in panic, and they fled.

The children were in panic because of the way the adults were acting.

But instead of just leaving, the ETs kept coming back. I mean, they'd get shot and they'd come up on the roof.

But they were not harmed. It was only one individual who was harmed.

But they kept coming back. They didn't mean to terrify the people, but I'm sure the people were more terrified every time they came back.

You have to understand that the ETs didn't realize at first that the shotgun was a weapon. They thought it was some kind of communication device, because it affected them. So they were drawn to the experience, because they did not realize that the shotgun was an attempt to keep them at a distance. You have to remember that everyone on your planet would have realized that a gun was a weapon, but there were no guns on their planet, nor had they ever seen this type of weapon. They were from very far away, and they had never seen a weapon that used an expansion of gas to throw pellets in order to harm another being. So they identified it as something that they saw in nature—they knew of certain plants that expel seeds suddenly—and they really did not grasp that it was a weapon.

Well, it's really dramatic. They go get the police. The police come and the state police come, and one of the state troopers said that he heard several meteors flash over his car.

Those were not meteors but actually ships.

They move with a sound like that of artillery.

Yes, a whooshing sound, which is what you hear appropriately if you hear an artillery shell go overhead; it has a whooshing sound. Ships have also been described this way. The whooshing sound is of course the object going through air.

Whoever wrote this is suggesting that they don't like light.

They were sensitive to light just like the Zetas are sensitive to light, and this is also one of the reasons why many people have come to believe that many ETs are light-sensitive—not all are, though.

With all the police around and the highway patrol and everything, there was no one to be seen. But after everybody left, they kept coming back up to the window again; they kept reappearing throughout the night.

Yes.

So let's go back and talk about them now. Where were they from? What were they about?

As I said, they were cultural anthropologists. They were simply out exploring other civilizations and they were actually trying to trace their own roots. They happened by Earth and saw human beings and were interested. The whole idea in their minds was to find their cultural beginnings. As it turns out, there is no relationship between you and them, but they were attracted to any race that was humanoid. So essentially they were looking for their parent race. It turns out that you weren't that, or anything even related, but they did not know that, and so they stopped to look.

You notice that it doesn't say that they sampled any of the individuals; they did not. But before they got back on the ship and left—actually before they were discovered or, if you like, before they discovered the human family—they did some sampling with animals. They were just about ready to leave when they discovered human beings, and if there hadn't been the hostilities and the fear, they probably would have had a very interesting meeting: The human beings probably would have had a chance to go on the ship.

But the problem was that there was no real means of communication. These beings, although telepathic with each other, did not have the capacity to be telepathic with a human being. That's why they kept coming back. They kept trying to project a telepathic message, because they knew that if you were in their line, anthropologically speaking, you would be able to pick up the telepathic message at some level—or at some frequency, if you prefer. So they kept trying all the different frequencies they used until they had exhausted them, and when they didn't get any response, they decided that you in fact must not be related, although they did have enough of a response from one of the youngsters—that's another reason they kept coming back—that they thought perhaps there was some connection. Of course, they did not realize that the little people you recognize as children were in fact children. They just thought that they were another species of human being. They didn't think of you as human beings; they just thought of you as humanoids.

So where were they from?

They were from the very farthest reaches of a galaxy called Armiropa, which is, how can we say . . . If you measure the distance from here to the Crab Nebula, and then you take it times three, that's about how far away from Earth they were from.

They'd never been on Earth before?

They had never been to Earth before. There was nothing in their records about Earth and its citizens, and so they were really first visitors.

Why were they looking for their parents?

For no reason other than why you would do it too. At some point—once there is no longer any conflict, once the anthropologists and the scientists have had a chance to indulge their curiosities on the more benevolent level—one of the first things that everybody wants to do is find his or her roots. So they'd been on a long-range expedition for some time, but as it turns out, their roots are in another universe, and I do not think that they have the technological capacity to go there as yet, although it is possible that they will find someone who will tell them. They're still searching.

And being from another universe, were they invited to come here, or were they exploring and just kind of came here and settled?

It was just an outpost. There's no mystical explanation. The idea of traversing the distance from one universe to another is not that unusual.

Contact in New Mexico

I see. Now, it would have been easier if I could have read this before. But okay, let's talk about the Holloman Air Force Base landing. Landing?

Let's see the picture [see Figure 15.5].

Interesting.

All right.

Holloman Air Force Base, New Mexico. "The three 'men' were dressed in tight-fitting jumpsuits. They were about 5 feet 2 and had a blue-gray complexion, wide-set catlike eyes with a vertical pupil, and large noses" (Faces of the Visitors, 44).

Who does that remind you of?

Who does that remind you of? Large noses . . .

Look at the side view—resemble the Egyptians much?

Oh!

That's why I picked that one out. Read a little more.

"Although there is a controversy as to the date of the event, most researchers suggest that on April 25, 1964, at 5:30 in the morning, about twelve hours after the Lonnie Zamora sighting near Socorro, New Mexico, a landing took place at Holloman Air Force Base. Alien craft were spotted by Holloman radar and were warned off but apparently landed anyway. The base commander ordered an alert. Two interceptors were sent up to chase the alien ships from the area" (Faces of the Visitors, 56–57).

All right. That's enough. Here we have the beings who are associated with—not directly, but are in a similar line of—the Egyptian-looking ETs.

This is why they are pictured clearly, with certain characteristics of many Egyptian people even today. Granted, they are not exactly like Egyptian people, but there is enough similarity that one might wonder. The beings are related, although not on the exact same line as those beings referred to the other night in the channeling. They are from Sirius.

They seem to have had an appointment. There were three craft, and one landed, a door opened and a ramp extended. Three beings walked down, and a group of military officers were there to meet them.

They felt they had an appointment, and I think that initially the base commander did not know this was so, but they were ordered to proceed as if it were any other diplomatic mission. By that time they had a military protocol in place to deal with such circumstances if there appeared to be no hostile intent. That's what took place—essentially a military protocol where the beings came off the ship and then the officers approached and went on board.

They had a translator device so that there was communication.

Yes, and that made it so much simpler. The beings could say that they were not there for any hostile interaction but were just there to discuss things with them and so on.

Was this filmed? It says that supposedly this film was intended to be used as part of a documentary to announce the presence of aliens on Earth.

Yes, that was their intention. They wanted to make it public; the ETs wanted this to be made public. They invited the filming; they allowed the filming. As you know, most ships have a way to use certain magnetic and electrical fields to prevent filming—or at least to fog the process—but they invited it and the film is actually quite clear. As a matter of fact, if it were seen today, with today's technology, most people would say, "Oh it's faked," because of today's movie technology. But if it were seen at that time, people would have said, "This looks real," because it looks a lot like a newsreel. Even though people were no longer seeing newsreels at the movie theater so much in those days, they still remembered them, and this looks much like a newsreel.

There seems to be a dispute as to whether this happened in 1964 or 1971.

I don't think that is too important, but I'll simply say that the earlier date is a little more reasonable.

But you won't say that it's exact.

I will not confirm or deny.

So who were these beings? What did they want? What did they talk about?

Figure 15.5: Drawings of beings met with outside of Holloman Air Force Base, New Mexico, in 1964.

Courtesy of Kevin Randle and Russ Estes

One question at a time, because I will only answer one. [Smiles.]

Where were they from?
As I said, Sirius.

What is their connection to the beings we are calling the ETs who were here before the Egyptians?
They are like their children. It is a hybrid species, but not hybridized the way Zetas hybridize. It is more what you would call a natural hybrid. As we mentioned before, the human being and the species that predated the Egyptians have a direct connection that took place before humans arrived on Earth. So you had human beings who had essentially—not exactly—the same body that you now have, and you see Pleiadians and the bodies shown in the Maya pictures and so on, who are essentially human beings (and by the way, the Maya thing is entirely true).

The experience you have is that you had cross-cultural connections with these beings and this race was produced in the "usual" way, as you understand it, with males and females. What happened was that the combination of the two races was so pleasing to everybody that they felt they ought to produce more of these "kids" who would eventually establish their own civilization, and they have a significant amount of knowledge about the human race that they could pass on—to say nothing of giving you the formulas to cure all diseases. They did discuss this with the military people with whom they met, and although they did not give too much, they gave a little bit. But they said they would like to wait and present it to all nations, which is appropriate. Because of the circumstances at the time, the U.S. decided to wait. In those days, there was a lot of instability in the U.S. government.

This was right after Kennedy was shot?

Yes, so everybody was afraid to do anything to rock the boat any further. When the UN becomes more of an initial world government, you'll probably see these beings again.

It's not quite clear to me. Before the ETs who came to Egypt, before what we call Egyptians, they created this race from humanlike beings on Sirius. Is that what you said?

Humanlike beings . . . The humans were not from Sirius, but were actually from Orion.

Ah, but before anybody ever came to Earth?

Yes.

So how did they feel, then? Weren't they were basically rebuffed?

No, they weren't rebuffed. It was more of a diplomatic meeting. You have to remember that these officers could not make decisions. They were thrilled. They thought it was wonderful. Of course they were nervous at first, but once they got over it, they thought it was wonderful. As far as they were concerned after the meeting, it was great. It was a go; it was going to happen. It was only later, when higher authorities decided this was not going to happen, that they were told they ought to forget about it.

Who were the authorities?

Oh, I don't want to discuss that, because in some cases we've got survivors.

I mean, within the U.S. government?

Yes, within the U.S. government.

They only went to the U.S. government? They didn't go to other countries on the planet?

It just happened that they landed in the U.S. first, and after that experience, they discussed it amongst themselves and decided that it wouldn't work to go someplace else, even if the other countries were to announce it to the world. The U.S., they figured, might resist it in some ways, and they wanted it to be a unified experience and not to simply have certain nations say it's so and other nations say it is not so.

And they shared . . . they left some technology with the U.S.?

They steered medical people onto certain pathways to resolve certain diseases; I will only say that. But you can look at certain diseases that were solved and resolved about three to five years after the contact. Some of that has to do with that contact.

Do they have a name we can call them, or is it unpronounceable?

I think we will not say the name just yet; maybe later. If you were to hear the name, though, it would remind you of Middle Eastern sounds.

I have read in UFO literature that there was a film still in existence. Was this the film, then, that was referred to in different places?

Yes, this is a real film and still exists. It might or might not see the light of day, but there is even now a 40 percent chance that it might be released to the general public. That's a pretty good chance. Even ten or fifteen years ago, there was only a 20 percent chance. So the film has been carefully preserved and other copies have been made—and there have been a few attempts to digitally enhance it, too, in order to get more details—but it's still not going to be released just yet.

Contact in New Hampshire

Oh, my goodness, this is an interesting one.

Yes.

Now the ones that you chose not to mark are either not real cases or they just weren't interesting or you just couldn't talk about them or what?

All of the above and more. I'm just not going to comment on everything. I'm going to pick certain ones to comment on and I'm not going to comment on others. If I don't comment on it, it doesn't mean it is not so. I'm not going to comment on the Billy Meier case, but I've already mentioned that it is absolutely so. A lot of people believed it and were, how can we say, influenced to believe that it wasn't so, but it is definitely so, and probably one of the most profound contacts in recent years.

Okay, this one is November 2, 1973. It was an "orange-and-gold spherical craft with oval windows and covered with a honeycomblike outer skin." The alien was a "catlike humanoid." "Only the upper body of the creature was visible through the window of the craft. It was described as being covered with wrinkled gray skin and having large slanted eyes" (Faces of the Visitors, 56).

A woman, Lyndia Morel, saw a strange light in the distance while driving in her car, and she kept watching it. The object came closer. She could see the green inside the window. Her hands seemed to be frozen to the steering wheel. She had the feeling that the object or the being in it was beginning to take control of her body and she became frightened.

All right, here we have a visitor from Kaath. This is what you see as cats on Earth. You see all sizes and shapes, but here is one of the primary ways they look on their home planet. And I checked it off because I've mentioned Kaath before on several occasions.

I didn't know that they could come here.

They rarely do. The being did not come to check up on human beings but came to check up on its kin and just happened across the human being. I thought it would be an interesting point, since I have mentioned that planet before.

Then the car speeds up and she thinks that the UFO is pulling it.

Yes, I think that was unintentional, since we're dealing with magnetic fields here. The UFO researchers assumed that her fearful reaction might have been to speed the car up, and while that might be true, because she had less use of her muscles—which is always the defensive system used in these types of ships—she really did not have the capacity to press the accelerator, and so the speeding of the car really had to do with the magnetic field effect.

This was someone who had friends or kin here?

They were kin in in the sense that their goal was to check up on Earth cats, to see what they look like and why they choose to remain here, since Kaath has had many reports that cats are not fully appreciated by many people here. During the visit, the scout—let's call this person a scout—was seen by a few individuals, although only this one reported it. The scout was, however, seen by several others.

This visitor from Kaath had come to see what it could be that might cause human beings to react poorly toward cats and finally decided after an extended stay that it was largely a cultural phenomenon that cats were not being appreciated, simply because the explanation that cats are predators wasn't sufficient to explain human behavior toward them. Bears are predators, for example, but they have an exalted position in the culture of your societies. The visitor, the scout, decided that it was a cultural phenomenon, and that, because of the things that have been said about them, cats have been utilized against their will and people have decided that cats are somehow involved in "dark deeds." The visitor believed that and reported it exactly like that.

Where in the universe is the planet? What system is the planet in?

The planet is really not in this dimension, but if it were in this dimension, it would be quite close. It is in the Sirius star system, but it is around the seventh dimension. So it is not that far away, and that's why they are able to come and go with a certain amount of frequency, although they don't come often. This particular scout came because they had reports from cats whose souls

Figure 15.6: Catlike humanoid witnessed in New Hampshire in 1973.

Courtesy of Kevin Randle and Russ Estes

were coming back, saying there had been several incidents where cats, on a wholesale level, were not being appreciated or were being abused in some way. This scout went out to see if it would be safe for cats to continue to incarnate on this planet. They decided that even though there was a risk, volunteers could incarnate, but that everyone who incarnated would know the facts before they came here.

There is here no clue as to the height of this being or fingers or toes or anything. Could you just give us . . . ?

Oh, the height . . . I suppose it would be about five or six feet if you were to see them. I think we won't talk too much about the details. I think the most important detail is the face, and I will say that the person who reproduced it was pretty accurate. The intensity of the eyes is rather profound. There is no fur, of course, because the planet's climate does not require that.

So what we're seeing is a spacesuit or something?

No, you are seeing skin. There are animals here on Earth that have this sort of wrinkled appearance. There is a dog, I believe, and I think also a cat that have a similar appearance; there is a famous species of dog that has this wrinkled effect. This is not that unusual.

Contact on the Franco-Belgian Border

Okay, here's another one.

Let me hear about that. We won't do too many more tonight, because you are tired.

This one is the Franco-Belgian border and describes a "disk with a slight dome and three-leg landing gear. There were two figures. The taller one was about 5 feet tall and wore a boxlike helmet. The head was shaped like an inverted pear. The skin was grayish, and there were two circular eyes that looked like marbles and were slightly sunken in the eye sockets. There were eyebrows, a small nose, a slitlike mouth with no lips." Oh, the second guy was different. "The smaller creature was dressed in a suit that seemed to have rings around the torso. It wore a round helmet with a large area of glass on the front. It was holding a stick with a pyramidal tip" (Faces of the Visitors, 63).

The witness was driving along the highway, his car engine stuttered and his engine quit and the car came to a stop. He started to get out and saw something about five hundred feet away. "At first he thought it was nothing more than a load of hay, but then he saw areas of orangish white light on the object, which seemed to be standing on three legs. As he stared, he saw that the object looked like a British army helmet from the First World War—that is, a shallow domed disk."

About a hundred feet away, he saw the two figures I just described. They moved toward the witness so that he was able to see them clearly, then stopped near a ditch. "He felt a faint shock at the back of the head and he sensed rather than heard a low-pitched modulated sound, which grew louder. During this time, the witness thought he saw a small oval object fall from the belt of the lead creature. The witness didn't try to recover it then, but later, when he returned, the field had been plowed and the object was lost.

"Both creatures turned their heads in perfect synchronization and seemed to look behind the witness's car. The low-pitched hum ceased, and then both creatures, again in perfect synchronization, turned and headed back toward the object. The witness described their motion as almost humanlike, and he said that they seemed to have no trouble moving over the muddy, wet field. Once the creatures were inside the craft, the legs disappeared and it hovered just inches off the ground for a short period. Then it climbed out at an angle of 60 or 70 degrees and disappeared" (**Faces of the Visitors, 64–65**).

Here we have actually the first example of robotic beings. This is a probe. These beings are not—how can we say?—they are not born of woman. They are a synthesis, a highly evolved synthesis, a machine—and yet each one of them is a machine that has personality, enough personality so that it can interact with those who sent it to the other side of the universe. Because those who sent them do not have the advanced light travel technique, these ships are sent out to do surveys (which is what was going on) and might not return until perhaps several lifetimes later—meaning lifetimes of the beings who sent them—and so that's why they had this synchronization to them. It is also an interesting phenomenon that they were able to walk across the surface of this fairly sloppy ground. That had to do with a technical device located at the bottom of—for lack of a better term—their feet.

Now there was in fact an object that unintentionally fell from one of the beings into the soil. This is true, but when it hit the soil, it did not appear to be anything important, and the plowing actually put it under the soil where it dissolved in about three or four weeks. If it had been analyzed shortly after the fact, it would have revealed an interesting phenomenon. The object was what I would call a compact energy storage device. If you were to slice off a piece from it and put it in a test tube, it would seem to have mass, but it would be spongy to the touch. It would light up the test tube if the test tube were placed in an environment of neon gas. So it would light up inside the tube, but in about three or four weeks it would simply dissipate. It's essentially compressed light.

How did they use it? What was the purpose of it?

It was used essentially as energy, not unlike a battery; it was a spare and it happened to fall off. They did notice they had lost it, but not right away. By the time they realized they had lost it, it was a full month later in terms of Earth time, and then they knew they could do nothing about it. They managed to figure out where they had lost it and went back, and so they were pretty sure that it had dissolved underground. They were able to map it—they are mapping individuals. So they mapped it and discovered the residual effect of it underground and so . . .

You said they "realized." Are they sentient?

Yes, they are. That's why calling them robotic is minimizing them a bit. As I said, they have personality so they can relate to the people who sent them out. The people who sent them out do not require materials anymore, but they are very interested to know the makeup of the universe, to know about people who live on different planets. That's why they represented no particular threat to the witness, but they had the capacity to keep the witness at bay.

They were more interested in the car than they were in the witness himself, as it was a machine and they thought it was a curiosity, which is why they walked around it. For those sentient machines, it was as if they were looking at an antique version of their former selves. [Chuckles.] So they thought it was amusing, and that's why they walked around it—in order to map it. You notice that he said they walked around it . . . because mapping is what they do. Wherever they go, it gets mapped; all they see that is in their presence is mapped. So where they are right now, they have a complete record, not only of the surface of the planet, but also the witness and his vehicle. If you could picture a slice going down to the core of the Earth, they mapped right down to the core of the Earth, not because they would be interested in mining—as I say, they are past that—but because they are just interested in the makeup of the universe. So this is really a long-range scientific expedition utilizing what amounts to a probe.

So are these beings highly programmed, are they ensouled or are they thinking machines?

Oh yes, you on Earth are not that far away from thinking machines yourselves now. But you have to remember that the ensouling of the machine does not have anything to do with the machine. The material that goes into the makeup of the machine is ensouled. The machine itself is not ensouled. So we have the same situation here in this society that sent the probe, where the material itself is ensouled and cooperates in becoming this apparent being and so manages to maintain its entire identity the entire time that it is this being, so there is no work against nature.

You've talked about lightships that are alive. It's the same principle.

It's exactly the same principle as a living lightship. On the spiritual level, it is the same principle.

Contact in England

Boy, there's quite a variety here. Look at this one [see Figure 15.7].

This is the last one we're going to do, because you're tired. Yes, okay, read about that one. Calling that a fairy is an unfortunate use of the word, because fairies are totally benevolent beings and these beings were not, but go ahead.

Okay. On January 4, 1979, in West Midlands, England, three beings were sighted. They were about three and one-half feet tall with large wings that "looked paper-thin and were covered with glittering raised dots. The eyes were bright black and were set far apart on white faces. The beings didn't seem to have hands or feet but pointed shapes at the ends of their arms and legs. They could fly and pressed the buttons on their silver tunics at various times. When they flew, their arms were clasped over their chests and their legs hung down."

A woman, Jean Hingley, watched her husband leave for work when she spotted an orange sphere close to the roof of the garage. "Her dog reacted by becoming stiff and falling over." The three beings "zipped into the house making a zee-zee-zee sound." The woman ran into the living room. She heard the Christmas tree rattling only to find two of the creatures shaking it. Later they jumped up and down on the couch, laughing like children. They were there for an hour.

The woman reported that periodically she felt paralyzed and that the aliens spoke in unison in gruff voices, and they pushed the buttons on their tunics. "When she gave them orders—telling them, for instance, to stop swooping around the room—the lights on their helmets would flash, focusing a thin beam on her forehead. This burned her and occasionally blinded her. The effects of the laserlike beams persisted long after the encounter had ended" (Faces of the Visitors, 73–74).

All right, that's enough. Here we have an incident of relatively uncivilized ETs, and it is obvious by their behavior that they were in fact children in terms of . . how can we say . . . this really relates nicely to the idea of bratty children. These beings, however, were escapees from a prison colony, which is why you had this sort of malevolent reaction.

I picked this one because it is one of the unusual cases where you have ETs who actually have malevolence associated with them. That is almost never the case, but these three individuals were actually prisoners. They had escaped a penal ship and were essentially free; the ship just happened to be near Earth, moving not so much to a penal colony but just moving away from the original planet where they were captured, and they managed to get to Earth in this place. Both the individuals who operated the ship—who were essentially contracting to the civilization—and the civilization from which the prisoners originated sorely regretted this incident. It was an unfortunate circumstance all around, yes.

There was an orange sphere close to the roof of the garage. Was this some kind of a shuttle?

They had escaped in a . . . I don't like to call it a shuttle; it was more of an escape vehicle.

Like an escape pod?

Well, science fiction calls it a pod, but in real life they just call it an escape vehicle.

But it couldn't take off and go again?

It could, but it had limited range, of course. As an escape vehicle, it was designed to go to the nearest livable place, and it could move around, but it couldn't go very far. Fortunately, they were recaptured very quickly after they left this area.

But had they not been captured, would they have just died here? What would have happened?

That's hard to say. This is entirely speculation, but they probably would have been vulnerable to certain kinds of weapon technology.

Figure 15.7: Mischievous beings who invaded a home in Rowley Regis, West Midlands, England.

Courtesy of Kevin Randle and Russ Estes

Did they need to eat? How did they get sustenance?

I don't think I want to say too much about that. I don't want to give too many details about them, because you will probably run across these beings in more benevolent ways. The three just happened to be essentially what amounted to criminals, but in their normal state of being these beings are actually benevolent.

Where are they from?

They are from the Orion system.

And the ship was just passing by?

It was a contract ship that was involved in taking beings who would be considered criminals there. If they had been Earth citizens, they probably would not have been considered criminals for their actions. They were just too different for their society, and that's about it. They were too different for their society, and so they were put aboard the ship, perhaps not reasonably so.

Where are they now?

They have been, as they say in that society, reeducated.

Like their brains wiped and new memories put in or something?

Well, that's a sci-fi scenario. It was more that passionate pleas were made to them, encouraging them, showing them the results of their actions—especially of their actions on Earth—and it was probably because of what they did on Earth with this person that they were won over and allowed to see the result of complete, unchecked freedom. You see, a crime in that civilization would have been this kind of unchecked freedom, which would amount to anarchy and what they were doing. They had no real idea that they were harming the woman, but the great harm they had caused was explained to them later and that shame caused them to change their ways and recognize that such freedom was not safe.

So is this a very closed, constricted society, then?

I wouldn't say it's closed—no more closed than a lot of societies. A lot of ET societies are very rigidly controlled, are not too free. You don't have anarchy. You don't have people with the freedom to do whatever they want. If you had that, you might get other ugly incidents. That's how they maintain peace. I'm talking about civilizations that don't exist on any great higher dimension.

So this is a 3.0.

No, it's a little bit between three and four.

So they got around on their home planet by pushing these buttons and flying around?

Yes. It was not readily apparent to the witness, but they actually had an artificial device attached and were in something like a skintight suit. This wouldn't be readily apparent, and that's why the witness did not see fingers or toes or the kind of details you might expect to see—because it was actually a skintight suit.

So the wings are part of the suit?

Yes, of course. If you were a winged being, you wouldn't have to push buttons to fly.

But what was the point of the winged things? Don't they walk on their home planet?

No, it is just a way of getting around as you say, not unlike a car.

But why would prisoners have this motion of locomotion?

They didn't; it was on the escape vehicle.

So with the escape vehicle, you land on a planet and then you have this to get around in and try to survive in.

Yes. It protects you; it offers certain weapons technology to keep things from harming you. That they were using it on somebody who wasn't harming them in any way tells you that this is a criminal element— criminal, granted, in Orion terms. They would not necessarily be considered criminal here, but they would probably be considered bratty children who got ahold of weapons.

So somebody on that ship who just happened to be passing through (above the Earth) took another ship and came down and caught them in it?

They found them because they fired the devices that were weapons. They were looking for them, and it was the firing of these weapons that allowed the trackers to find them. They found them about an hour and a half later and recaptured them. Then they showed them, very slowly and painstakingly over the next few days of Earth experiential time, what they had done and what the effects were on this individual. That's how they won them over to being back in their society. When you make a mistake like that and you can see the results of that mistake—which is not possible on most other planets; you don't get to make extreme mistakes where there are catastrophic results—it makes a very strong impression. This incident was catastrophic for this individual.

Oh yes, she suffered.

She suffered, and so they saw it, and they actually became staunch believers in their own society's code of ethics later because of their mistake. They went into a life of public service, somewhat as a penance.

You said they were children. Is this the height of the beings on that planet?

They would get bigger when they got older.

How old were they when they were here?

Rather than going into all that, let's just say that they would be about five to five and one-half feet tall at maturity.

I've never heard of a prison ship before. Can you tell me more about that? It originated in Orion and . . .

The ship was a contract ship; it didn't originate in Orion. Such ships do exist and will travel to societies who have misfits. The misfits are not put in little iron-barred cells, but they are secluded in rooms, sometimes with their companions, as in this case. The three of them were in one room together, a room that was not crowded but was filled with all of the things they needed to survive. They were kept away from others in their society so that their radical ideas would not infect the society—and their ideas were radical. They wanted to create freedom where everybody could do whatever they wanted. That sounds so appealing until you realize its anarchistic effect, meaning that innocent bystanders can get hurt.

And this ship picks them up and it just keeps going around?

It just keeps going around until they are won over by the various therapies that are applied on the ship. It's benevolent to win them over to be members of their society again or—as in this particular case because of this catastrophic mistake—for them to be transformed by the result of the consequences of their deeds.

So it's like a therapeutic situation?

Yes, but the people who run the ship would consider it a prison ship, because they are in fact prisoners; even though it might be benevolent prison, you don't have freedom.

Would there be just beings from various Orion planets on this ship?

No, there might be beings from other galaxies as well. Most of these cultures and civilizations out in space are so benevolent that the idea of requiring the needs of a prison ship is very remote, and so the ship just travels from one place to another, stopping to say, "Do you have anybody you feel needs to get away from your society? We'll take them on board. We'll include your therapies. You can send people along to consult if you wish, or you can do it remotely." They offer a great many things. It is not unlike a business.

And then they get paid for that?

Yes.

Okay. That's enough for now.

Visitor's Book and Sirian Mapper

Zoosh and Etcheta
December 5, 1998

The reason that I checked those two topics tonight is that they are of singular importance—the first one because of the circumstances, and the second one for what it represents. Here we have a contact where an individual describes a person seen at the Bradshaw Ranch, whom Mr. Tom Dongo and Ms. Linda Bradshaw actually photographed. But compare it to the sighting in Utah: Read the text that is underlined.

"The witnesses also reported a balding, graying human whom they thought of as a doctor."

This is the exact individual who also showed up on the photographs taken out on the ranch and whom these two individuals referred to as "the man." [See Figure 16.3, on p. 295 of this chapter.] Now read a little bit more about this one in Utah and then I'll talk some about it.

Contact in Utah

Pat Roach, a divorcée who lived with her children, reported that "she and a number of her children were abducted from their house early in the morning of October 17, 1973. Just after midnight she was awakened, thinking that something strange had happened, but she didn't know what.
"The alien creatures were described as small, with large heads, big eyes, pasty white faces. They had long three-fingered hands. All wore shiny suits that looked like uniforms. Each being wore a kind of cap or helmet that hid the top of its head, and a

Sam Browne belt with a chest strap that held a small pack. All of them wore gloves. The one female had long hair and wore a long skirt and a headband" (**Faces of the Visitors,** *161–162*).

Here we have a hybridized race that is partially Zeta Reticulan and partially what I would have to call "creation," meaning that the Zeta beings allowed and encouraged the hybrids they had started to begin to hybridize on their own. I cannot really say what they're called, since the hybrids by the Zetas have not so much identified themselves as this or that, so I'm going to call them as I have. They have some similarity to their parent race as described, however.

The purpose for covering the top of their head is less for disguise than it is to cover the crown chakra, which is an especially sensitive part of these beings' heads. They have a soft spot there, not unlike the one found on human babies' skulls, where the tissue is really almost at the surface. It is not unlike what you might feel if you were to touch a part of your body: If you were able to feel under there, you would feel a soft spot right at the top, and so the hat, as it's called, is performing a protective duty as well. Those particular beings feel almost a sense of urgency to protect their crown chakra area, since they spiritually connect to their home world on a moment-to-moment basis through this part of their body. This particular race of beings cannot wander too far away from their home base because of their profound connection (which you understand) on the feeling level with home.

How many beings were here, and where is home for them?

Home is slightly beyond the Zeta Reticulum system, but within the environment of the culture.

Are they in the same time frame as their parent race, as the Zetas?

I'd say that they are not in that same time frame. They are essentially in a time frame between the two of you.

Between them and us ?

Yes.

Why did they come and get this woman and her two daughters in Utah?

For the same reason that they would contact anybody. It is never random. It's always because of some soul connection, and so that question is almost moot. You understand? It is practically never random. I can think of very few instances when it was random.

Ah, because there's a lot of thought out there in the UFO research community that anyone alone and out there on the highway by him- or herself is fair game? No? Is it more that they have been internally guided to be out on that road by themselves?

Figure 16.1: Beings described by a woman and her children in Lehi, Utah.

Courtesy of Kevin Randle and Russ Estes

Perhaps, yes. And sometimes over quite a long range, meaning that one might pick a home that is remote, not only for its benevolent characteristics, but because privacy might be more assured.

So they came to the house and took the woman and her two daughters. This is in 1973. So they were still doing gynecological examinations in 1973?

It's a standard thing to do; one checks on the condition of the individual as a standard practice. It is not necessarily something that I would say ought to be done, but it is done.

Is it done because they are so interested in the reproductive process?

Well, it is in their very nature to collect genetic samples. Just because there was no profound genetic experiment ongoing at that time—although certainly there were still some experiments by the parent race—the idea of collecting samples for any future experiments would be considered necessary, if not required.

Which being on the ship was on a soul line with Mrs. Roche?

No one. The connection was with the daughter.

There were two daughters, Bonnie and Debbie.

Which one was the eldest?

Bonnie.

It was her.

The youngest child said they had all been put on a machine run by a Native American girl. Several of their neighbors were standing in a long line, waiting for their turn to get on the machine.

Yes, researchers completely discounted this, as they often do, but in fact, it is one of the more relevant points. Living in Utah, this youngster naturally did have a pretty good idea of what Native American people, who one might expect living in that part of the world, might look like. This individual certainly did look very much that way, although she was not born on Earth; she came from one of the home planets where what are now native cultures on Earth are from.

It is well understood by many native peoples on Earth that they are originally from the stars, and of course, when cultural scientists or anthropologists are out studying them as they do, they always say, "Oh well, this is mythology," a story that people tell. (Of course, they would never say that's true of the religions that were developed in other parts of the world, because that's not mythology, that's "fact.") In any event, the native peoples do understand that they did in fact come from the stars and at one point emerged from vehicles or were brought to the Earth in order to reside here for a reason that has been covered before, so I will not go into that again. But I will say that the person on this ship will have looked identical to a Native American young woman.

How did the hybrids happen to come across this woman?

They didn't come across her; she was on the trip with them. As I've said before, it is not unusual for different beings to be on the same ship. The machine she was running was extracting the memories of all the individuals who passed through the machine—not extracting as one would extract physically, but extracting in the form of duplication, as you would copy a piece of paper. This was done, not only to have a greater understanding of the social acculturation of people on Earth, but also (and this isn't stated, but I will state it) because many ETs were, for quite a while, very interested in the religion of the Latter Day Saints (the Mormons), which is well known as being centered in the state of Utah. The LDS religion, after all, owed a great deal of its founding principles to extraterrestrial communications between the ETs and the founders—founders in the sense of those who were not only the individual credited with founding the religion but also the individuals who perpetuated it.

Can you say what ETs were involved in this religion?

I will say, for this purpose at this time, Andromedans.

Can you discuss it later?

Certainly.

Copying Memories on the Cellular Level

Thank you. How do you copy a memory?

It is really startlingly simple. You know that if someone asked you about something that occurred, you would tell him or her about it to the best of your recollection, if the time permitted. One would assume that the machine would tap into the brain when copying a memory, but in fact it doesn't. It taps into the actual cells of different parts of the body. You know, it's a good question you asked there, because the memory of all events that have happened to or around any individual is coded not only into the short- and long-term intellectual memory of that person, but also into the cellular structure, into the atomic structure, certainly into the spiritual being on the level at which the spiritual being can handle it and, perhaps more profoundly, into the feeling self. The feeling self, as you know, is comprised of the physical body, the emotional and feeling body and, to some extent, the spiritual body.

So the machine reads a macrocosm of all these different combined functions. Picture it this way. For the sake of an example, I'm going to draw a line that represents a memory. I'm going to break it up into segments—just a simple chart will be sufficient [see Figure 16.2]. Now let's assume that these are all cells. The machine essentially reads the entire body, pulls this energy out of the body quite quickly and then reassembles it in sequence. It would be like pulling out a huge jumble of recollected images, feelings, sensations, tastes, smells and so on and then reassembling them in the most reasonable sequence. Of course, this tells you that the machine doesn't always get it right, because the machine can't always allow for the unexpected that occurs on Earth but might not be understood on other planets, but it hits it 90-95 percent of the time. The unexpected might be a juxtaposition of experience, for instance, and of course associated sights and sounds and feelings, but it also has other sensual impacts: something smells, there's an odor, there are feelings and so on. All these different portions of every moment of that event are stored in different parts of the body.

If the event is profound, the entirety of the event will be stored physically in the body for the lifetime of that physical person, even though the event will be stored in perfect sequence in the unconscious, otherwise known as the spirit self, that is grounded in the physical body (not

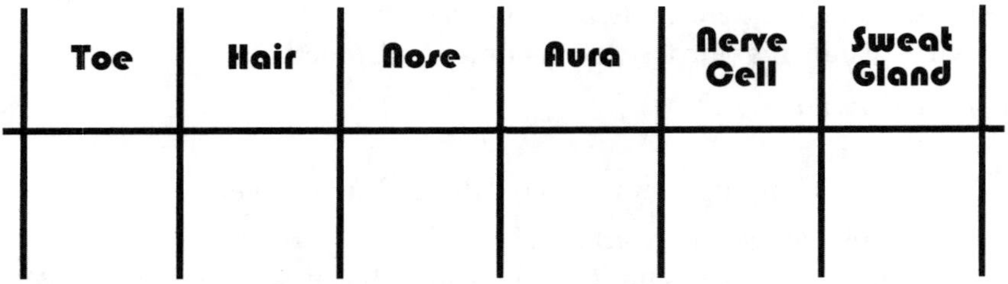

Toe	Hair	Nose	Aura	Nerve Cell	Sweat Gland

Figure 16.2: Zoosh gives an example of how a memory might be charted out into segments.

the spirit self that expands beyond the body and is more connected to the greater spirit being, because the greater spirit being cannot tolerate a lot of these things). This part of the spirit being that is connected to the physical self on a full-time basis will have a complete readout, as it were. The machine, however, cannot always tap the entire memory of the spirit being, because the spirit being will have a choice about whether or not to allow a certain memory to be known to other groups. The spirit self of the individual might choose to keep some of this to its own self or private or between itself and its greater self and its teachers and so on, and it might or might not choose to share at all.

Now say there was a minor event, such as that you walked down the street one day and your neighbor's rose bushes were blooming and you smelled them, and it was wonderful and buoyed you up for the day, and on you went—a wonderful experience, but not necessarily one that is profound in a lifetime. Such a memory might be stored for seven to fifteen years, and it might be recalled from the spirit self, which is why sometimes people in comas or in shock or perhaps going through senility late in life might vividly remember certain experiences like this, experiences that are pulled up from the spirit self's full and complete recording of the event. However, on the physical level, the event is going to be stored for only seven to fifteen years.

On the other hand, if something profound happens, such as when you get married or you have your first child or something like that, that would be stored in your physical body, probably for your lifetime. Now it is true that cells are born, as it were, from the stuff of life— food, energy and so on—and other cells die off. This tells you that the cells are passing on their portion of memory to other cells before they pass out of the body.

Each Atom Is a Unit of Memory

Isn't that awesome! What is the receptacle for this memory?

The receptacle is the atomic structure itself. The cell has its own job, its own duty, its physiological function, and it cannot be distracted by memories of anything outside of its own experience. However, inside the atomic structure, you have something that is not unknown in computer technology: You have a capacity greater than the needs of the function, and that capacity is always found in the nucleus.

The orbiting particles around the nucleus are performing the essential function of the atom—keeping it working, as it were—but the nucleus always has room for extra memory, extra function, preparation to be transformed into something else, such as an atom moving from one type of life to another as a person goes out as a cell, falls to the Earth and eventually becomes part of another being. We discussed this before in *Explorer Race: Particle Personalities* (Robert Shapiro, 1997).

The atom itself will store—in small fragments, of course, per atom—portions of the memory. So this machine literally culls out from the atom the image of what the atom is storing. It does not extract it, but it has the capacity to duplicate the image because the atom is always doing what the energy bodies of all beings are doing, and that is radiating a perfect example of itself in its own auric field. Do you know that not only do human beings, rocks, rain, dogs, cats or plants have auric fields, but every single atom, proton, neutron, nucleus and particle also has an auric field of itself and is duplicating its total self in light in the auric field? That is how this memory is extracted—in multitudinous fragments.

If we could get a machine here, then it would be easier for all the contactees and abductees.

To say nothing of being able to give psychologists and psychiatrists a perfect imprint. Think of it. Suppose a person had a severe psychological problem and could not be presented with his or her imprint. But imagine what a therapist could do with a complete printout of the person's actual memories to help him or her accept how this gradually came to be. It would revolutionize therapy. It would take some of the pitfalls of therapy away from the therapist and allow the therapist to perhaps pursue a steadier course.

How far are we from developing such a mechanism?

As Earth people? Far, far, far. Don't count on it. [Chuckles.] As a matter of fact, the Zeta beings or the Zeta hybrids on this ship did not develop the machine.

It's from the parent race?

No. The parent race didn't develop it, either. This machine is on the ship because the being the youngster described as looking like a young Native American woman developed it, not as one builds a machine, but as one does benevolent magic. Her race of people are totally in tune with benevolent magic, and they produced something through benevolent magic and between the elements and spirit and love, of course—not entirely by themselves, because benevolent magic requires cooperation of literally all elements and knowing what to say and do—creating a living machine that functions in a loving, gentle way.

Is there a name for the race of the girl who looked Native American?

Well, I'll just say this (this is what I'd rather do to protect the cultural wisdom and secrets of various tribes still on Earth): I will say that the culture—or the descendants of the culture or the cousins, let's say, considering the time frame, the cousins that she might have on Earth—would still exist today in Canada.

ET DNA in the Mormons

Oh, how wonderful. Well, let me then just call her the Native American. Was she like the anthropologist? Did she and her people create this device because they wanted the information?

No, her people did not require the information, but the people who asked the Zeta hybrids to go on this mission—who were, I think, the Arcturians—asked for it, I think, because it's not in their nature to pick people up. They don't do that. The individuals who asked this said that they needed to understand the Earth human being better and they would be particularly appreciative if the contact could be made in Utah, where it might be more possible to interact with people of the LDS faith who had been interactive with other ETs in the past. You understand what I'm suggesting, don't you? I think it is safe to say now that there are certain ET strains within the . . .

. . . Mormon race?

That's right, although they are not a race. Some of the early individuals in the LDS religion, as they prefer to be called, included more extraterrestrial DNA in their systems than the average Earth person. Part of the reason (I will reveal a few of their secrets) they felt it was so urgent to be prolific was that they were told that coming events on the Earth had the potential to be catastrophic, and if they could only spread their philosophy—which was intended to be much more benevolent than it is today, by the way (they have a ways to go, but they are getting there)—their influence and their inner-circle wisdom (which I won't talk about here), then it might be possible to soften the blow of this coming human conflict. That is why they were so dedicated and perhaps willing to do things that were outrageous.

How was the infusion of the DNA accomplished?

It was not done in the usual way; it was not done by hybridizing a human Earth person with ETs or something like that. It was actually done with an exchange of energy. Sometimes it was done in the dream state, where actual material was . . . you would say "injected," but I would say "impressed" into the physical bodies of the human beings involved.

Was this done by the Andromedans, or were the Zetas involved as an agent?

The Zetas were involved as an agent. Again, when such service has to do with essentially medical types of things, one often sees either Zetas involved in some way, or as in the particular case of this particular contactee we're talking about, people involved who for all intents and purposes appear to be human.

Well, I haven't gotten to the human yet, because this part is too interesting. The conflict that the extraterrestrials saw as imminent is not going to happen now, because we are on another timeline, correct?

That's true, but they still feel today that the danger continues. Their concern is atomic weapons, not only because of their terrible destructive power, but also because of their lingering damage.

Was the Andromedans' original action with the LDS people based on just a unilateral Andromedan decision, or was it an action of a council of ETs?

The Andromedans felt sorry for Earth people because of the degree of polarity that had grown and grown and grown, so it was an expression of compassion, and it was an attempt to avert future suffering with a compassionate act. While much more was told to the founders and eventually to the inner circle of what is now known as the LDS church, much of this has not been applied [chuckles]—even though, according to the church's own timetable, it was supposed to have been applied some time ago. That's why I keep poking at them a little bit that it is time to feminize the church. The people who are supposed to be leading the church now are supposed to be women, and the church is supposed to be more heart-centered even than it is today. I know they feel that it is heart-centered, but it is supposed to be much more heart-centered. Women are supposed to be the leaders all the way down to those who go out into the field to try to convert others, all the way through the ranks. The men were intended to begin it, because their strength and perseverance were believed to be useful. But it was intended to be passed on to the women quite some time ago.

The Andromedan Who Assumes the Form of a Human

Now tell me about the human.

The human, for all intents and purposes, looks like an Earth human but is not. If you were to see this person, you would say that not only is this an Earth human but this is someone who looks like he could be standing on any street corner. This is a person who takes on the guise of the Earth human, but if he, if the race, if the ship were someplace else, then he might take on the guise of some other species.

He will generally take on the guise of the predominant race he is studying, wherever he is currently residing, even temporarily. If there's a base or some operation he's involved with, he'll take on the guise of that people. He particularly likes that guise with the Earth humans, because it is relatively benign looking and does not look very threatening.

Who is he and where is he from?

He's from Andromeda.

Can all Andromedans do that?

No. But he can do this. He is from a very high dimension in Andromeda, and he has been given the training that allows him to do this. He is essentially what I would call a cultural anthropologist-geneticist, a job not too dissimilar from those original ETs who came to this planet and were involved in placing some of their DNA and features and functions into the physical Earth human, who then came to be known as the Earth person.

What was his function onboard the ship during this particular incident? Was he observing?

No, he was acting more as a liaison, because he is based on Earth and was someone with a great deal of Earth experience. Although he's not always visible to Earth people—as a matter of fact, he's rarely visible to Earth people—he has had so much Earth experience that he is considered invaluable on such missions and is always asked to participate. So he was on loan, you might say.

He was on loan from the Andromedan base that used to be here?

That is still here.

So if this was an Andromedan project from the beginning, why were the Arcturians commissioning the Zeta hybrids to get an update on the Mormons?

The Arcturians are not only known for the accumulation of knowledge, but they are particularly interested in transformation. Anywhere transformation is going on, not only would they like to know about it but they would like to participate in some way to make the process work better. So they commissioned this action to see if anything could be done to smooth processes that were involved in this vast genetic experiment on Earth, of which you all are a result.

The Vast Scope of the Grand Experiment

I can see now that we don't yet understand all the stages and levels and the vastness of the experiment.

An illustration speaks so much. Picture the Earth floating in space and about nine hundred strings or cords coming out of Earth, extending to various planets and star systems and even beyond this universe. It will give you some idea of the primary—only the primary—influences and participants in this great experiment; if you were to include the secondary ones, we'd have to raise that number to 30,000 at least.

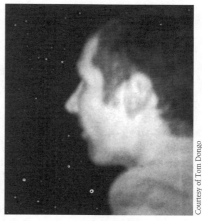

Courtesy of Tom Dongo

Figure 16.3: Photograph by Linda Bradshaw of the Andromedan anthropologist, who was not visible to the naked eye when the image was taken. For a color photograph, see Mysterious Sedona, which includes a pamphlet of unexplained photos compiled by Tom Dongo, available through Light Technology Publishing.

If you can picture that, it will give you an idea of the incredible involvement in this project, why so many ships from all over have frequented this place and why one of the things they almost always do is take genetic samples: not only to see how people are doing, but to track their own genetics or the genetics of others who have asked them to track it, to track the material to see how it is doing—has it evolved, has it mutated and if so, how.

It is not intended to be a lab-rat situation. It's intended to be a study done by brave souls who have volunteered to be Earth people. It is also a study that's designed in such a way that all these individuals who have participated in some way on Earth, genetically or otherwise, are tracking their own DNA, which you as Earth people are processing—and, of course, which animals and plants and Mother Earth herself are processing—to see if the mutations that are taking place over time with this DNA will in any way, as far as they can, help their own race.

Oh, it's like we're growing it or expanding it for them. I see!

You are assimilated material from space, and through experience that ETs cannot have because their cultures would be crushed by such polarity, they are allowed to have the opportunity to see if this DNA is in any way beneficial to their people as they exist now and if it can be used safely.

That means we're doing so much more than only being a part of the Explorer Race.
Profoundly.

We're living in these bodies for a laboratory.
Yes, on a daily basis. That's why, until very recently, there were lots and lots of ships in the sky all the time. You were being observed all the time, not because people were trying to pry into your privacy, but because they wanted to see how you were coming along, and they wanted to support you in any way they could without grossly interfering in your lives.

The Sedona Sightings

I love it. That expands everything incredibly—the whole meaning of what we're doing. All right, so all this was 1973. Then, in 1995 or 1996, Tom Dongo and Linda Bradshaw take pictures of this being in the Sedona area. How did that happen?
The being was visiting the area, checking up on certain windows that were, for lack of a better term, leaking energy into the area where the photographs were taken. The being was actually functioning in the other area. A photograph Mr. Dongo and his partner included in the writing of their book *Merging Dimensions* actually revealed the other area on Earth where the being was working at the time, but the being was visiting the area where Mr. Dongo was working and gathering phenomena for his book.

Energies that were being produced underground near the Sedona area unintentionally interfered with the energies that they were involved with, which created what I would call a rift—not a temporal rift, but a rift on the electromagnetic spectrum. That created a temporary (what I would call anomalous) window—as one might call a growth, a tumor, an anomaly in the physical body—and this anomalous window wasn't intended to be there. One of the things that occurred was that beings traveling along the lines of all these different portals were sometimes accidentally, as it were, falling out into this particular area where Mr. Dongo took the picture.

When Tom and Linda saw the ship, was that another one of those anomalies?
Yes, that was another one of these anomalies. The ship was trying to find its way to where it had originally intended to go. It had essentially lost its way, because the portals that it used accidentally funneled it into this area, and they did not know where they were.

I actually was talking about the sailing ship they photographed.
I was talking about the ship that was on the cover of the magazine. Now the sailing ship that was viewable through the apparent screen, that

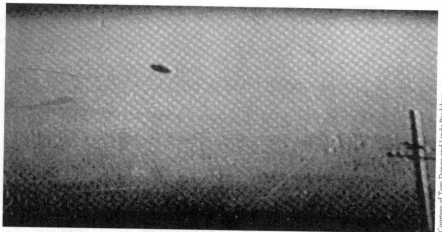

Courtesy of Tom Dongo and Linda Bradshaw

Figure 16.4: Photograph taken by Linda Bradshaw in the Sedona area. Linda Bradshaw reports that the photo was taken at night, miles away from anything that would remotely look like a telephone pole, in response to a bright flash of light.

was a place on Earth. It appeared to be a ship because that's what it was (I mean a seagoing ship) [see Figure 16.4].

This Andromedan doctor was attempting to investigate this situation, then.

Yes, he was not only attempting to investigate it, he was attempting to change it, because it was clear that it was causing a problem for those passing through the portals, and it also had tremendous potential to cause problems for the people of Earth in general.

In what way?

As a matter of fact, that other photo Mr. Dongo has [see Figure 16.5] was clearly a picture of an ET. This was an ET who was not intended to be on Earth, and that individual basically had to be rounded up. It is the sort of individual who would be comfortable wherever he landed, but Earth and Earth citizens would not be safe with that particular individual there, and as you say on Earth, no expense was spared to find this individual and send him to where he was originally going.

Say more about that. I don't know which picture you're referring to. What did he look like?

Perhaps the most significant feature of the original picture are the red eyes.

Where he was from or where he was going—what can you say about it?

I don't want to say too much about him except to say that he was a carnivore.

Figure 16.5: The description of this ET from Tom Dongo and Linda Bradshaw's book Merging Dimensions was as follows. "This is our extreme mystery photo. Here is a 400% enlargement of a flash photo taken during the second week of June, 1995. In the shadows at the bottom of the photo is "someone" who does not resemble any of us who were in the area at the time the photo was taken. The figure in this photo has a pushed-forward head, an extremely long, angular face, low tipped back "Spock-like" ears–and–glowing orange eyes. We all talked it over. It wasn't one of us." (Dongo 141).

Courtesy of Linda Bradshaw

I can see why they would spare no expense to get him back on his track. [Chuckles.]

So there was what I would have to call a Herculean effort by ETs and their associates to round this individual up. He was not an easy person to find, because this individual has the capacity to be unobserved. So it took ET technology to find the being and capture him in a gentle way, because he's the sort of a being who is not societal, meaning that in the place in the universe where he originates, they do not exist in groups so much as in ones and when necessary twos, but that's it. Other than that, they are singular beings, and on their planet, on their native planet, there are very few of them. Yet they are allowed, of course, to travel to various planets where they need to go to function to live, and this being just happened to fall into that area.

Has the window been sealed and patched and fixed now?

Yes, it has, and some of the more benevolent energies who passed into that particular space were queried as to whether they would like to continue on to where they originally intended to go. Some of them have chosen to stay and have been allowed to do so until they wish to go to where they were originally headed. At that point they would essentially be extracted by those who would come and help them. These might be seen as the floating lights that were pictured in the book.

Can you say anything about their personalities or purpose?

They are very benevolent. They are not physical but allowed themselves to be seen by the camera's eye. They cannot be harmed nor do they do any harm.

Are they observers?

No, they are not scientific beings; they are more feeling beings. They radiate a sense of benevolence and tend to acquire benevolence for the purpose of recycling it.

Can they store it, or do they acquire it at point A and take it to point B?

No, if there is benevolence around them from other beings of their own kind or if there is excess benevolence—that is, not benevolence that is being utilized, but excess benevolence—they will pass it through their bodies, amplify it and let it go immediately wherever they are, a form of function not dissimilar from photosynthesis.

Soul Memories Stored in Cells

How beautiful! I want to go back to when we were discussing the copying of the memories of the human. You talked about the spirit in the body and the spirit above. Where does the soul fit in there?

The soul, as you know, is the immortal personality; it is demonstrated through the physical body when you are awake and to a lesser degree when you are asleep, and it is anchored in the physical body even when you are awake. A vast amount of it is not present in your body. Partly this is because of the extremes of the conditions on Earth, and partly it is because the soul needs to be doing so much more than one individual can do at any moment.

So if a human had a soul in his or her body and then that soul left and another soul came in . . .

As in a walk-in.

Let's say as a walk-in. Then, when the first soul leaves, it takes the memories, but isn't it almost like there are two copies—one that the soul takes and one in the cells of the body?

Yes, although when the new soul comes in—and usually the new soul comes in either instantaneously after the first one leaves or they are both there for a time, which is more often the case—if the new soul is compatible with some parts of that stored memory, meaning that the new soul comes in with issues associated with that or even partial issues or even curiosities and is interested in retaining any part of that, it will choose to do so. If, on the other hand, there are parts, even vast parts, that the new soul has no interest in, then the natural process of cellular sloughing off and changing and transforming the body and so on through physical means will take place, and very often there will be no conscious memory of many things a few weeks or a few days afterwards. Within seven to eight years, there will be no more access to those memories that are not needed, meaning it might not be possible to bring up the memories through hypnosis or deep meditation.

I see. It's not possible to bring up a memory at some point, even though it is still in the nucleus of the cells?

No, it isn't. The nucleus of the atoms will let it go if it is no longer needed.

And that's why some walk-ins can change so dramatically.

Yes, and also because the new soul will bring in other skills, potentials, needs, necessities and so on.

The Perfect Disguise

Is there anything else you want to say about that Andromedan doctor? Has he been seen on other ships as an observer?

Occasionally.

Was he mistaken for a Pleiadian?

No, probably not, because when you see this person in proximity to Earth and you are an Earth person, you're going to think that this is an Earth person. You are not going to think that this could be an ET in any way, shape or form. You're going to look at this person and you're going to decide that this is an Earth person, and he's on the ship.

So might we run into him again in any of the cases that we have access to?

You might run into that description again.

If we do, would you make a note of it?

Yes.

Is there anything else you want to say about this, or should we go on to the next one?

We can go on to the next one. The next one is particularly interesting, and I will probably invite one of those ETs to speak after I've said a little bit about them. But first, I'll let you talk about them.

Mapping Endangered Races

July 1975, Panorama City, California. "*These beings had large heads and big eyes. They were so extremely thin that it seemed impossible that the bodies could hold up the large heads. Each alien's face was elongated like an egg, and there were a small nose and a small mouth. The beings seemed to be bald. Bright lights seemed to shine from the eyes.*" *The witness was Lori Briggs, and her roommate was Joe Maine.* "*The witness was sound asleep in her apartment when she suddenly awoke and found herself paralyzed*" (**Faces of the Visitors, 173–174.**)

The interesting thing here is not so much the case—we don't have to talk about the experience, which was not very comfortable for the Earth people—but what the ETs represent. That is the fascinating aspect here. Here you have a group of ETs who essentially perform a singular function in this universe and that is that they go around the universe and do what they would call mapping, but this kind of mapping involves only races of beings. Occasionally it might involve what you on Earth might call animals or plants, but since the subject is Earth people here, they map races that might conceivably die out. That's why they had contacted these individuals (they contacted both of them).

Because this case was simply about mapping, they had contacted several other male human beings as well. They were here, because at that time they were still functioning under the belief that there was a 60 percent chance Earth human beings would destroy themselves. Although that percentage was too extreme, they were allowed to do what they were doing. What they were doing was to take the people on board and literally duplicate not only the people's memories but also the cellular memory. That way, if it would be necessary to reproduce the human race on another planet in case this planet was destroyed—from their point of view—it would be possible to reproduce human beings not as mere clone beings who would stumble around not knowing who they were, but as beings who had cultural identity, cultural memories and who could pass on the ways, means, manners and mores of the human population. Therefore, they went around the Earth and sampled at least three to five members of every race

Figure 16.6: Lori Briggs' description of the "mapping" beings she encountered in 1975.

and variation of race they could find in a similar fashion until they had completed their project, which took about seven years.

How did they choose the subjects?

Again, in the usual way; there was some soul connection.

Oh, soul connection is not just a Zeta thing, then?

No. It is almost always the case, because permission has to be asked on some level. That is a universal principle. One does not simply go and pick up people without any sense of permission.

How many beings were involved in this project? Can you say where they were from?

There were about nine ships with roughly seven to twelve individuals on each ship—sometimes less, but never more.

So about ninety beings contacted every race on the planet. How could they have a soul connection with every one of them?

It's not that many people, if you think about it. Think of all the races; there are not that many.

Just the races by color?

They wouldn't consider Polish people and Czechoslovakian people different races; they wouldn't discriminate by nationality. They would discriminate by what they would perceive as race, meaning (as you might say) Asians or Africans or Caucasians, like that.

So, if there are so few races, why did it take them seven years?

Because they would do shadings of races where there had been inter-marriages.

Did they travel in time?

Of course; you don't travel such distances without being able to travel in time. No one does.

Was 1975 the beginning, ending or middle of their project?

Toward the end.

Did they do this from 1969 to 1976, let's say, or did they go back in time so far as Earth time is concerned?

No, they just sampled during this time, because sampling had been done by other races before then. They were sampling because they are, from their perspective, sort of an emergency squad. At that time and from their perspective, the potential of the total destruction of the Earth to happen around the early 1980s was 60 percent—but as you can see, it didn't happen.

Nevertheless, if it ever did—although I don't think it will—it would be possible for them, if called upon, to reproduce human beings who would be acculturated and not just blank slates.

Where did they get their information? Did someone, some race that we know, call on them?

They had actually been requested about twenty years prior, but they had other things to do and it took them a while to get here.

Who requested them?

A different race.

And you can't tell us which one?

I'd prefer to wait on that.

All right. Did one of them want to speak? Is that what you said?

Perhaps.

Etcheta Speaks of Sirian Contacts

Who is in there? Zoosh, are you still there?

My name is Etchetikedasedishta. You can call me Etcheta. Etcheta will be sufficient.

Thank you so much, and welcome to our great project here.

Thank you.

Where are you speaking from now?

Home planet. Have not traveled in some time but was present—not with the two individuals mentioned in this incident, but I was present at a previous contact of particular interest to my people. It was a young boy, about nine years old, and his dog. Because of the great love between the dog and the boy, I invited them both onto the ship.

In what country was that?

Albania. They came aboard willingly, and we explained our purpose in gentle terms to the youngster and in more elaborate terms to the dog. Dogs as beings have a central storage of wisdom, and so we passed the total problem through the dog, friend of the young boy, to the central storage area for all dog Earth beings. This would include not only dog pets but also wild dogs, coyotes, wolves and so on, and therefore they would all know the problem. We felt it was of import that they know, because apparently there is this great attraction between humans and dogs.

Yes, they are great companions. How does this central storage system work?

The central storage system is typical for all beings, including human beings; right now Earth human beings are not using this, but all other beings on the planet are doing so. Earth humans, I believe, are not allowed to do this since you are trying to re-create. Re-creation is not easily accomplished with central storage wisdom, but it is possible to perpetuate culture in central storage wisdom, because even if you don't know what to do in a given situation, you can call on that knowledge and wisdom that is part of your overall species.

I see. Yes, we're not allowed to do that, because we have to make it up as we go along. [Chuckles.]

Yes, you have it, but you cannot access it. We felt this was particularly important, hoping that somehow the boy's dog and the wild dogs might be able to help, and so I had the boy come aboard and we explained a little bit to the boy in gentle terms. We explained that if anything ever happened to the people of Earth (gently like that), we would be able to reproduce the people of Earth should they wish to be reproduced. We explained it a little more gently than that [chuckles], because the youngster needed to feel safe. He came onboard the ship willingly and awake, perhaps because he was still young enough to not be too surprised by our appearance, and perhaps because the dog liked us and we liked the dog. As anybody who lives with dogs knows, if the dog is friendly to someone, then you feel that person must be all right.

You can trust that person.

The Life of a Sirian Mapper

Someone told you that there was a 60 percent chance of humans not making it. It took twenty years for you to get here. What were you doing before you came here?

We were involved in several other circumstances where races were concerned that they were dying out, such as the Zeta race and a few others, and with such an involved mapping it took quite some time. The individuals of my race who were involved in this mapping never exceed 10 percent of our population. The total population of our culture during these times was about 1,500 individuals.

There are only 1,500 of you and you live on a planet?

We live on part of a planet.

You share the planet with other species?

Yes.

In what dimension is your planet?

About six.

And is it far across the universe?

Not so very far away.

Can you say?

Sirius. Six-dimension Sirius.

What do you look like?

Well, if you can picture a very thin body, mostly made up of tissue closely resembling neural and what you might call spinal or nerve tissue, we are like that. We are primarily associated with that. We do not eat the same way you do, and therefore we do not require a great amount of muscle mass, for example. We have the means to move what we need to move without muscle mass. Additionally, we do not require many of the internal organs you have.

How tall are you?

Variation of approximately three feet to five and one-half feet at the most.

So had you mapped the Zetas then?

Yes, because they had shown concern about the reproducibility of their race. They were having a problem with their life term. Their usual length of life was shortening and they had no explanation. They were concerned and had been concerned for some time, and so we did their project first. Because of the profoundly different functions of Zeta beings, it took a very long time.

The Technology of Mapping

In this book, it says that inside the craft, one contactee saw a table that looked like it was made of pink stone, but it sometimes turned transparent. There was a bright light source beneath the table, and she thought it was some kind of an x-ray device. She was placed on the table and examined. Is this your mapping?

Yes. You have medical devices now that are not dissimilar in a very rudimentary way, where you do body scans and then computer analysis for very specific purposes. This table is living material. As you know, you can talk to someone and get impressions that no machine can measure. Therefore, mechanistic measurements are taken, but then the table itself also gets an impression of the person as well. This is how cultural identity is picked up and stored.

So you have the cultural understanding of the person you map?

No, no. The devices we use have the cultural mapping. We ourselves do not utilize this. We acquire it on request, and then we either pass it to those who have requested it or simply keep it in storage should it be needed, but we do not examine it.

I didn't phrase my question correctly. When you map the beings, do you make an effort to get somebody who knows agriculture, somebody who knows city planning and so on?

No.

So your mapping has nothing to do with the knowledge they have.

No. It is more important to know the culture: who they are, what their culture has encouraged them to become, who they believe themselves to be, their personalities and things like that.

Where do you store these mappings? Are they stored in the table itself?

They are temporarily stored in the table. When the mission is over, accomplished, then the table reaches a point (you were calling it a table) where essentially the material can be extracted, if the table wishes, since it is a living being.

If I call it a table, what do you call it?

I need to find a word in your language. We call it some*one*, actually, so let's just call it a being.

Okay.

If the being decides it is interested, it will retain information and duplicate it to the last detail onto a very small capsule that is made up of organic matter. The capsule is a type of being that is always desirous to know everything. Therefore, it takes only a small amount of matter. It is about the size of a vitamin capsule.

A very curious being! [Laughs.]

And so it will acquire this and keep it, and to put it simply, it will retain in one part of itself that which has been fed into it in perfect original composition. In another part of itself, it will analyze it, consider it and offer potential ideas of what might be done with it and how it might be combined and other scenarios and so forth, and that is why it is interested in doing this. When it acquires something new, it likes to extrapolate.

So this little thing, this little being the size of a vitamin pill—is it part of something larger that can examine all that has been gathered?

The totality of its being is perhaps no bigger than this long.

Three feet? Two feet?

Yes, maybe closer to two feet by this high.

One foot.

Yes, but not that shape. It has an irregular shape, but small parts can be transported to where they are needed and then brought back and put back into the total being.

Is this your technology?

No.

Can you say whose it is?

We were given this technology because this is a job for which we feel a sense of honor to do. The technology has been contributed from various places, most of it ninth dimensional. Some of it is living technology as described, meaning technology that functions as a machine but is in actuality someone.

Where does this being reside?

On a neighboring planet near us.

Close to you.

Yes. Others like him or her—what you would say—are also there, but they do other things. I know not what.

Projects in Our Solar System

So when you finished with the Zetas, then you came here?

Yes.

You were here for seven years. How many beings did you map?

We mapped slightly fewer than one thousand beings.

One thousand?

Slightly fewer than that.

So, divided by nine ships, that's about a hundred each. That's thirteen a year—only one a month.

But sometimes we would do several in a night and then go other places and do other things. We were working on more than one project at once. We were not dedicated to Earth at that time. We did Earth projects and other projects also.

Can you say whatever projects you were doing?

Mapping a nearby planet . . . Mars, you say—that is your term? We have a life-form map for life forms that used to live on the surface. We returned to the planet, and we talked to the planet's spirits and asked the spirits—actually you would say negotiated with them—if we could reproduce surface life again. They said, "No. Wait."

The spirit of the planet itself said this?

Certain spirits associated with the planet. There were others, but I think that is enough to say.

Why did they have to wait?

Spirits said to wait until Earth citizens evolved a bit more spiritually, because the surface citizens of Mars (even though your mythology says so) were not in fact warlike. They could not defend themselves even in a rudimentary battle, and therefore spirits said it would be better to wait until Earth people would not try to colonize the planet. In twenty-five to fifty years from your now time, Earth people will not be interested in reproducing their civilization elsewhere but will be more focused on reproducing other civilizations from elsewhere on Earth. Then nearby planets with people living underground, or sometimes with people no longer there, will be safe to have a surface population again, a peaceful population.

What did the Martians look like when they were alive?

Not so different from yourselves. If you were to put one next to a human being when he or she is dressed, you would say that these people are cousins.

What do you call Mars?

We have a number for it, just like for Earth.

How do you say it?

Mars is *Cazetata*, and Earth is *Chaac*.

And did you go to Mars on your own, or did someone ask you to check on it?

Always we are asked.

And you can't say who asked, either?

It is like with your church people. They don't say what others say to them. I am not authorized to speak of this.

Okay, that's fine. This is very interesting. What else did you check out, then? You did Earth, then you checked out Mars. Then what?

Saving Lost Beings for Possible Re-Creation

We also did another thing on Earth. We went to a remote area located in what you call South America. We went to a very green area, very wet . . .

The rainforest?

Yes. There were very few people. We saw practically no humans there, only occasionally. We were looking for a type of plant. We had been asked to map a plant, but we were unable to find it. It was not there anymore, and so we asked, "Can we go back in time and look?" and we were given permission. We went back 2,000 years, and there it was. We mapped that one, plus about fifteen other variations. Since then our culture has been asked to map plants and some animal types that were on Earth in the past, and so traveling in time now, they are going back and mapping all these beings for possible future re-creation.

Oh, how wonderful. Where are these beings who hold this material, like the Mars and Zeta information? Are they stored on that planet next to you? All the data is stored in those beings on that planet?

Some is stored or utilized by those who have authorized the mission.

How did your people get involved with this?

We have been interested for many generations in the sanctity of life. As much as possible, we have been interested in the idea and practical application of being able to perpetuate species of life. Because of natural changes of life, sometimes species die out or transform completely, and for various reasons there is no record at all that is available to citizens of other planets. It might be available to spirit, but that is not always accessible, and so we decided some time ago that our contribution could be in this area. All species need to have a purpose. We did not have a specific purpose before this, and now we have it. We are very satisfied with our role.

What do the other 90 percent of your people do?

They have all done this, or they will do it. It is like we do it for a while, and then we go back and speak of our experience and train a future generation. Or we simply enjoy life on the planet.

That's what you are doing now?

I am, as you say, retired.

What's your life span?

Not so very long as many ETs. Perhaps 170 of your years.

How many years did you do the mapping?

The mapping project? Me personally? About sixty-one.

And how old are you now?

I am about 113.

Oh, so you have a nice long retirement, then. What are your joys? What do you do that interests you now?

Recreation and Family Life on the Home Planet

Art and music are the most appealing. When I was on a mission, my personal interests included the art and music of citizens if this information was possible to acquire. Sometimes it was not possible, and even if it was possible, it was not appropriate to make a recording. I tried to remember what I had seen, and then I would try to reproduce it, insofar as it was compatible with my people.

Why couldn't you make a recording?

It wasn't part of the assignment; it would not have been honorable.

Even if you did it on your own time?

There is no such thing. All of it is my own time, but we do missions for service and not for singular and personal reasons. We might do them for personal, familial reasons, but not singular ones. So I listen and observe and try to remember, and that's enough.

So what music did you like best on Earth?

I like timpani, classical, the sounds made by vibration.

How do you reproduce them at home? What kind of instruments do you have?

I have attempted to reproduce a form of metallic instrument. Its substance is natural, similar to a substance between glass and plastic, and when struck by a rod, different sound vibrations come from each appendage.

So you hit at one and it reverberates, like a multidimensional effect or something?

No, just sound, a timpani sound.

Do you have a family?

I have, as you say, a grandfather. I have one daughter. We do not have what you would call husbands and wives. We do not have this type of living together, but we have a previous mate who lives nearby with a son. We do not like too much of a crowd, and this might be because of long missions on a small ship.

Oh, I see. You need some space. But you have affection and budding interests?

Yes, different members of my race are interested in different things. One of my friends is interested in the simple mechanics of other races. This person has built many versions of the lever or fulcrum as a model. To me, it is art. To him, it is more of a hobby.

And your technology? You attained it from somebody, or you developed it?

We evolved it from other cultures sharing with us, and then we adapted it to our own interests, as any culture does.

Do you have a memory of your reincarnational past?

We have been told that such things are available to us if we wish to pursue them. I have not and know no one from my people who has, but it is available. It is possible that some people have done so, but we generally do not access this because we feel that it might be distracting.

But you are aware of immortality?

We are aware of the reincarnational cycle.

So do you get to choose to go to some other planet, or does that no longer interest you?

I've done enough of that for a lifetime. [Smiles.]

[Chuckles.] How many planets have you been to? Hundreds?

Hundreds. And I am very happy to be home now. Thank you.

But wasn't it fascinating to look at all the different ways that . . .

Yes, in the beginning it was thrilling, exciting. Later on it was interesting [smiles.]. In the beginning, thrilling and exciting. Later on, interesting.

The Use of Mapping Technology

That's great. So through this "mapping" there is then the ability to totally reproduce beings. How would you use this technology? Would you clone beings to give the soul something to incarnate into?

We probably would not. Someone would clone, but it is our job to acquire the map. Then others reproduce utilizing the map we have acquired.

So could you say that the prototype human on the planet Earth came from the woman from Sirius and the man from Mars? Could it have been a mapped clone who was used to start the population?

I do not know.

But it is possible that they could have mapped a Sirian and mapped an Orion and . . .

It is possible.

We'll have to ask somebody. They just said that there was this prototype, but nobody said where it came from or how we got it. What was your impression of Earth, if you were going to describe Earth to one of your friends and the beings on it?

Can I be completely truthful?

Please.

Earth is a hard place to live, with moments of joy profoundly felt in comparison to the rest of life.

But you know what we're trying to do here, don't you? You know the Explorer Race concept?

I know only what I need to know. I know a little bit and not too much. I have not pursued that.

If we can do what we came here to do, there will be an expansion of everything in creation that will give you and everyone more intelligence, more feeling, more potential, more everything.

I've heard this. We as a people are not sure how we feel about that.

Is that because you almost feel like it could be an invasion if you don't desire it?

It feels like change we haven't asked for. We might wait and see and not participate. It is allowed to not participate.

I never thought of that. To me it just seems to be the greatest gift that could be given, but as you say, you may not want to participate.

It is allowed. We have not made a decision yet.

Ah well, we haven't done it yet, either. There is no rush. Is there anything you want to say to the people who read this?

Just this: There are many races from all over who care profoundly about you. I have met many just in my small travels. You have friends and interested parties you will never meet. Know this and feel reassured in the support and love that is behind you and all around and about you in every moment.

Thank you. I hope to see you again someday.

Good night.

Bears and Mediation Beings

Zoosh
December 7, 1998

Greetings.

October 27, 1974; a contact at Aveley, Sussex, in England. A mother, father and three children.

Can I see the picture again?

Yes. The picture describes a human, six feet eight inches tall, covered by a one-piece suit and a hairy man who was four feet tall (Faces of the Visitors, 165-168.) *These are interesting.*

Yes, very interesting. Now, you have had a chance to read this one?

Yes.

The Little Bears

Let me say this first. The short beings are well known to certain individuals in England. These individuals often have to do either with the goddess or priestess initiations or with an awareness of fairies, the little people or elves in general. The short people, although they will often fly around on ships, are sometimes called (and I'm saying this for the benefit of people in England who know what I'm talking about) the "Bears" or the "Little Bears," and they have an affection for the local people, who see them occasionally.

Sometimes they will surprise you and show up when you least expect it. Sometimes they will seem to dance around or act curious, and at other times they will be very serious. Sometimes they will show up with extraterrestrials and land or take off in ships, but I want to underline the fact that these are the mysterious Bears that the local people of the Aveley area and generally around Great Britain refer to.

Now, I want to talk about the Bears first. This is a race of beings who have had a great deal to do with the ancient beings who used to walk on this planet. A long time ago, I talked about a race of beings who lived on the

Figure 17.1: The two distinctly different beings described by witnesses from England in 1974.

Courtesy of Kevin Randle and Russ Estes

planet called the Andazi. These are not the Andazi, but they are a first cousin. They have lived underground on Earth at a higher dimension for over twenty-five thousand years. Before that time, when the Andazi were on the surface of the Earth, they mingled with the Bears, walked with them, enjoyed being with them and very often studied with them when other individuals from other planets would land and share stories or songs of their origin.

These beings (to agree with many insightful, sensitive people in Great Britain) are almost pixielike at times, not for their size, but for their temperament. I am not trying to say that they are always and only pleasant, because sometimes they can be frightening (although always unintentionally so), but they are apt to show up when you least expect it. Sometimes people will be frightened of them even when the beings themselves do not wish anyone to take them very seriously, and that is because the radionic energy from them is definitely ET. So even though they have been here on Earth, on the surface or underground, since long before the Earth human actually began (and certainly before the Explorer Race was really running around on the surface), they still have a profound ET energy about them.

You might reasonably ask, "Where are they from?" As is not atypical for many so-called animals, they are from Sirius. They represent one of the most profound and important connections to Sirius for this planet, second only perhaps to the African people, whom I've commented about in *Explorer Race: Creators and Friends*. They represent, however, the Sirius connection for the animal world, whereas the African people represent it for the human world.

Animal Mediators

They very often will act as mediators. This mediation will take the form of conflict resolution when there is a problem about which animals are and which are not going to predominate. In the past, before human beings arrived and became the major factor here, there were many, many more species of animals here than you know of today. There came to be so many that they sometimes overran one another's territory and there needed to be someone, or a group of someones, who could speak with love and authority about the best resolution, even if it meant that a race of animals would return to their home planet and wait to incarnate on Earth at some future date, should they still care to. This race of beings were those representatives.

They are the resolvers. They are to some extent the adjudicators, to use the legalistic term. In fact, it was fully 90 percent of their decision to remove certain animals from Earth who would destroy the human race or at least make it almost impossible for the human race to exist here. Take, for example, the ancient saber-toothed tiger, which was significantly larger than even the biggest tiger you have today. A fully grown male tiger is a sight to behold, and yet some saber-toothed tigers were two and a half times as big as this. A creature like that would not tolerate human beings for long: human beings would simply be part of the food chain.

So a decision was made to request that animals who were too powerful for human beings return to their home planet and the more benevolent guise that they wear on their home planet (even though they look rather like tigers there, they don't have those big teeth). So they decided that they would leave—not permanently, because they would like to return to 3.0-dimensional Earth, but they would wait until human beings had left to return. They had heard that there would be other beings at 3.0-dimensional Earth who would be taught how to get along with the animals, and when they learned how to do that, these large tigers and other animals with whom humans beings cannot live would return and live amongst those people in peace. I give you such an example of a decision so that you realize that such negotiations can work out well for everyone.

How did they get involved in the priestess ceremonies, then?

They did not. I'm just saying that people who are involved in such spiritual activities, who have visited places in England—particularly places that are now known for crop circles and other things—these people will often know or have heard about what they refer to as the Bears.

Do they live underground now?

Yes. They live underground now at a higher dimension so that they can be safe. I might add that they are absolutely impervious to ultrasonics and so . . .

That's the only reason that they're here—because everyone else had to leave, right?

A lot of beings had to leave because of the sonic and microwave business as well as some things that don't bother human beings very much, although they have a cumulative negative impact. I might add that this is the reason some animal species and plant species have left as well. But these beings, the Bears, are entirely impervious to such sounds, and therefore they are completely stable in their population underground.

How many are there?

At any give time there are probably never any more than nine thousand. I would guess that there are perhaps, let's say, seventy-five hundred to nine thousand. Generally speaking, they will make appearances only in the area of Great Britain, although in the past they have made occasional appearances in France and Germany, right along the border. If you look back in the literature, you might see such references. Even today, people will occasionally see them.

It says that they have bushy brown hair all over their faces and hands, but it doesn't say anything about the rest of their bodies.

They have it all over their bodies. This is why, as you can see, they would be considered bears. Considering their height, they are like miniature bears. They don't actually look like bears but look more benevolent than bears, and therefore they have been called that. Perhaps it's a term they are comfortable with.

They have four digits with claws. They wear large, loose-fitting, white gowns?

Yes, they might do that when they are contacting individuals working with ETs, not unlike you. For instance, if you were working in an emergency theater of a hospital, you would wear a uniform that you would never consider wearing out on the street.

Are they compatible with all ET races or just a few?

They are compatible with most ET races, but the only time they ever get fierce—and they do have the capacity to get fierce—is when confronted by a potentially hostile ET race. Then they become very fierce, and they have a tremendous capacity to focus energy of the mind that will deflect these ships away from Earth. They have only had to use this once or twice, depending on how you count it, but they were completely successful.

Can you say who was in the craft?

One time it was a renegade group that we talked about once before, in *ET Visitors*, Volume 1.

The Xpotaz?

Yes. And the other time—again, as I say, depending on how you look at it, because it's a slightly different timeline that you're on now—it was an Orion ship (not from current Orion, but from past Orion) that was heading toward Great Britain with malevolent intentions. There were about three hundred of these beings gathered on the surface on the high ground—this was about seven hundred years ago of your time—and this tells you that it was in the north country. Although the ship was about twenty thousand miles away from Earth at that time, by each and every one of them focusing on it, they deflected it strictly by the power of their minds. As the Orion ship approached the planet, those on the ship would have had to use more and more power to get less and less distance toward the planet, and eventually it would be like pushing against a wall. So they gave up.

How did an Xpotaz ship happen to come toward Great Britain?

There were actually two ships, but I am counting that as one mission. One was headed for the south of France, and the other one was headed for northern Great Britain. The Bears had heard of these beings, being acquainted with most extraterrestrial races who are benevolent and visit the Earth—and most of them are, of course, benevolent—and therefore they utilized exactly the same method as I mentioned a moment ago, and both ships were easily deflected.

What year was that?

It was only about thirty years ago. The Xpotaz ships are perhaps less powerful than the ship from Orion, and they were easier to deflect.

And they never came back?

No, they knew better. Interestingly enough, it's not a hostile act. It cannot harm the ship, but it's just as if you were in a car and drove up to a huge solid building or a huge rock and tried to push it. The tires would spin and you would give up. It would be like that. You just wouldn't be able to go forward or approach your navigational intent—in this case meaning the Earth. Once you were touched by that energy, you couldn't come in and land, and that would be that.

Do they live under Great Britain?

Who?

The Bears. Is that what we're going to call them?

We're going to call them Bears for now. Yes, they live largely under

Great Britain and somewhat under ocean areas around there. In the past they have had some outposts under France and Germany, but I don't think they are under France and Germany right now. I think they retired from France and Germany during World War II. They were uncomfortable with all the suffering.

How did they choose that place when they first came? How did they choose the Great Britain area? I mean, it wasn't Great Britain twenty-five thousand years ago.

They just chose it because it was a beautiful—well, to quote the bard, it was a beautiful emerald isle—and they liked it. It reminded them of the island that is their homeland on a planet in Sirius. Their home island is somewhat larger, but other than that it is very similar.

What is their life span?

It depends again on how you measure it, because they are somewhat interdimensional. Allowing for the dimension that is their normal place of residence, which is about dimension five, and measuring it for Earth experiential years (so we lose something on the edges), it might be around twelve hundred years.

So do the same souls reincarnate constantly?

No. It's just like everyplace else. People practically never reincarnate as the same species of being in the same place, and this does not necessarily apply to people incarnating as "animals." Animals is a word that ought to always be in italics on Earth, because so many of the beings who are considered animals would just be considered ETs on other planets.

So do they travel with many ETs? You said that they are comfortable with all of them, but do they travel on ships with them?

They only travel on ships with ETs if they are directly requested to, or if the ETs say that they are likely to contact children. When there are children around, the children sometimes respond more favorably to these beings, because the Bears have the capacity to appear amusing.

Watchers from the Fifth Dimension

So, other than the fact that they are in the sixth dimension, they can appear physically on Earth.

Fifth. They're fifth-dimensional beings.

Can they appear physically on Earth, or are they invisible?

Not exactly. I wouldn't want to say they can be invisible, but if you had the capacity to appear in, say, third-dimensional Earth and then returned to your natural fifth-dimensional self, you would appear to disappear, but it's not quite the same thing. However, in terms of what you're saying—I'm splitting hairs here because it is important—there is a difference between disappearing and simply shifting dimensions. In fact, in terms of the practicality of it, it would seem that they could disappear. What I am splitting hairs on is this: To disappear would mean that you were still in the same place, and you might be felt or someone might sense your presence, but you would not be visible.

Oh, I see. So they don't do that; they actually physically leave.

They actually will change into their fifth-dimensional selves, and in the third dimension you cannot see fifth-dimensional beings, although sensitive people might sense the presence of a higher-dimensional beings in some way. Perhaps they would see a flash of light or some such thing, but they would not see them the way they look in their third-dimensional bodies.

If I could see fifth-dimensionally, would they look the same in the fifth dimension?

They might look a little smaller, but they would probably look pretty much the same.

What is their purpose? What do they actually do?

Do you mean, do they work for IBM or deliver newspapers? They don't do that kind of thing. They function. They exist. They have their own society, their own culture, their own reason for being, but mostly they live like any other society. If one of them can speak, it would be more proper to ask that individual, but first let's cover the rest of the contact.

Okay, this describes a humanoid, six feet eight inches tall, covered by a seamless one-piece rubber suit, with pink eyes, three-digit hands and pale and translucent skin. That's a new one.

Yes, but we have to understand that the being is covered by a suit, not only for protection, but sometimes so that he or she will be less shocking to the person being contacted. This generally occurs only on planets like Earth where people are isolated. If you grew up on some other planet and were used to people looking highly unusual, then they might not wear so much. They might wear something strictly for their personal comfort, but maybe not head to toe, as it were.

So what is it covering?

Just their appearance, which is nothing so shocking, but it is hard to describe. The body contours are unusual—odd, startling, different colors and so on. The main thing is that by your standards, had the beings shown up with only the gear that was necessary for them to feel safe and comfortable, people would have been instantaneously terrified and run like the wind. So this full-body suit was used to be considerate.

Can you describe this being so that we can understand what he looked like?

No, I can't, or I would have done so. I cannot describe it. I would only say that the average human would be terrified when looking at the physical body of that individual.

Gentle Encounters

Okay. Next we have a man and a woman and their three children. They were driving along into a fog, then they were taken onboard and examined, and then they were talked to and things were explained to them.

Gently, I might add.

Yes, nicely.

Again, we have the situation where the Bears, as we're calling them, have a tendency to have a moderating influence, because you can't be around beings like that without being somewhat cheered up. They look not dissimilar to stuffed toys, only they are animated. If you saw one and it was doing something amusing, the first thing you could think of doing is to reach out and hug it. You couldn't imagine not reaching out to hug it.

Like the final Star Wars? I forget the name of the beings.

Yes, only not quite so apparently commercial. But they do look huggable, and they know this, and therefore their presence in that part of the world is often requested, especially when children are around. So yes, time was taken to explain things to them. I believe that these people saw maps. Is that the case?

They saw maps and were on the mezzanine on a railing looking down at their car and then went into the ship.

Something interesting about the ship that I'd like to mention now, because it is so typical, is that the ship from the outside looks like it's twenty feet to thirty feet across, and yet time and time again people say that it is gigantic inside. When they initially looked at the ship, they couldn't imagine that their car could be taken inside and that there would be lots and lots of room besides. The ship didn't look that big, but very often when these are remote ships, meaning ships that come from a much larger ship that is not too far away in space-travel times (meaning probably not much further away than, say, Mars), the remote ship has something that amounts to a portal. You go in the ship and are immediately transferred via the portal to the other, much larger ship, and that's why this sort of strange effect takes place. This was true even for the ship that crashed in Roswell. People who were able to climb around near or inside it became somewhat disoriented, and this is because even though the portal was no longer working, enough of the residual energy of it was still functioning that the disorienting effect occurred.

For example, let's say you were walking across the woods anywhere around here—there are lot of woods around this particular area of northern Arizona—and you unexpectedly happened across a portal that wasn't normally lying about for you to stumble into. Let's say you happened into it, and you weren't planning to go anywhere. For a brief moment, as you walked through the area where the portal was—meaning you might actually walk through the portal but not engage it—you'd walk through the energy of it. You might be disoriented and dizzy for a moment, but then you would go on. You'd say "What was that?" and you'd stop for a moment and then go on. Of course, all dizziness is not caused by this, but this effect exists. So I want to mention that about this, because this has come up time and time again.

They feel that they don't understand? They get inside and it is huge?
Yes, and that is why.

So that happened in this case?
Yes, that happened in this case. There are other possibilities, of course. The ship can take off suddenly and go to the larger ship in what amounts to just a few seconds, because of the fantastic speeds plus the ability to travel in time. That also happens sometimes. However, very often the portal is happening and it's instantaneous with sequence, meaning that you go in the ship and the next thing you know, without any loss of memory, without any breakup of sequence, you're in a much bigger place than can possibly be. When it happens in sequence like that, that's what has occurred.

So they entered this green mist, and there was a shaft or column of light that lifted up their car and the occupants, and they appeared to be in a large hangar where they were standing on the balcony looking down at the car.
Yes, that was the bigger ship. They really weren't too close to Earth then. They were on the bigger ship looking down at the car. If they had been able to see in other areas, they would probably have seen some small ships also.

Scanning for Anomalies

The tall creature took them into a room with some kind of a device. The man was laid down and a device was moved from his head down toward his feet.
Yes.

What was that doing?
That device essentially examines the person, not only to see if it is safe to have that individual on that ship, but also to check the physical

condition, the genetic makeup, and also to see if there are any anomalies within the physical body that can be corrected. This is an interesting factor here. Now, herein lies a story: Say that the ship went somewhere on another planet and landed and picked up an ET and the ET had, let's say, a deformed leg. The ET comes on board and lies down and says thank you very much, and the object is run over his body. The deformed leg is noted, and then the ET is asked, "Would you like us to repair that?" And the ET says, "Yes, please," and with a snap of the fingers, the leg is very quickly repaired. So the same examination procedure is done with human beings, even though it was not all right to change human beings at that time.

I'll tell you what this means, though, because the ramifications are interesting. All ETs who have been contacting humans have been told that, at some point in the future, there will be benevolent relations with Earth people and all other civilizations. Everybody who has been on the ships has been told that if they come back on the ships (the same ship or even a ship that is like that, a similar technology or one that has shared medical information) it will be acceptable to do for the human being, the Earth human, exactly what might be done for an ET.

Since they do not know when this will take place—they don't know whether that peace will come ten years from now, twenty years from now, thirty years from now or tomorrow—they will almost always do that with all people, including those who go on Zeta ships, regardless. They do this on the chance that this might come sooner rather than later, meaning that then it might be possible to see these people again and take them on board the ship and cure what ails them.

I would like to make my application. [Chuckles.]

You'd like to make an appointment, yes? I'm telling you this because it is important for you to understand that this is a typical thing done, even if you are from another planet. The idea of being examined medically when you come onboard is very typical, unless there is some cultural reason with your people that you are not comfortable with that. But that is rare. You *want* to go to the medical room and you *want* to be examined by the medical people, because if you have any problem, chances are they will be able to correct it. So this is why the idea of being examined medically—I'm not talking about uncomfortable examinations or hybridization or things that the Zetas did because their civilization was dying out, but rather like the casual medical examinations that happened to these individuals—is perfectly normal.

What was the reason they were picked up?

The same reason as always. In this case, the individuals were what might be considered a typical English family. Also, the lineage going back on the man's side (his father, his grandfather) had been contacted by these particular ETs as well. So this was something that was a lineage factor. Very often, ETs will contact following the same lineage, not necessarily for genetic reasons as is usually assumed, but sometimes just because of obscure reasons of their own and nothing important.

Reasons for Diplomatic Languages

Who are these beings then? Can you say where they are from?
The tall beings are from very far away.

Do they have a name or a designation?
You would be surprised even on other planets by how typical it is to abbreviate types of people's names or to describe races by features such as the idea of humanoids, this type of thing. The race's name or the culture's name for itself is often not only unpronounceable to different races, but sometimes, because of cultural reasons (not for these tall people) it's not acceptable for anybody but that race or that culture to say its name in that sound with particular inflections. They would prefer to speak in some shared language, just the way that French used to be the diplomatic language on this world (and probably will be again someday, by the way). So all of you youngsters in college, don't rule out French when you are thinking about learning a diplomatic language.

Are you sure it's not going to be Sirian or Zeta or something like that? [Chuckles.]
No, it will probably be French. It is a fairly musical language, French, and I think the gentle sound of it and the tendency to speak it up and down in the register might be of some acceptability on an interplanetary level.

All right.
The Pleiadian language, for instance, goes up and down in register also and frequently has gentle or smooth sounding words, and so that is why French again will be particularly acceptable or of interest to them.

The Profound Benevolence of the Sirian Version of Earth

Okay. Tell us a little bit about these beings. That's a long way to go just to check up on a family of English people.
Well, you have to understand that it would be a long way to go if that were their only reason, but the Earth is of particular interest to them. They do understand that Earth as you know it used to be in the Sirius system, but when this planet was in Sirius, it performed a rather extraordinary function, and this is probably why Earth has so many different species and varieties. When it was in Sirius, it performed a function of

what I would call crystal mirroring, meaning that the planet itself had a tendency to attract the widest variety of beings from all over the universe. It would be like a magnet. It would be like someplace that certain religions might consider as a holy shrine.

You would go there from whatever part of the universe you were in, and even though you were way, way far away from home, you would feel more at home there energetically (the energy of home would be so powerful there, ten times more powerful than you ever felt at home) that you would want to go there just to be there. This is probably the residual effect of that energy. It is probably why Earth is the planet of great variety. Even if you were to take Earth just as it is today to Sirius, with all of the plants and animals that have died out and even the races of people who have died out, you would probably not find as much variety on any of the planets of Sirius as you have here on Earth still today.

The Sirius version of Earth was such a profound place that people would come and visit, and they would want to bring their children, and they would want to bring their wives and families, and they'd want to bring their best friends, because the love they had for their families and their friends would be ten times stronger in such a place. And the common bonds they felt were often very powerful in marriage ceremonies. People came to visit that place because it created such a bond for them that it would last their whole lifetimes, even if, as happens sometimes in marriages, one or the other had to travel and be away from home for a long time. The level of that love and bond was so powerful that they wanted to return to their mates.

These beings knew from their culture, an ancient culture, that Earth would someday return to Sirius to form the amazing planet that it once was. They wanted to come and see Earth as it is here with the full knowledge of what will most likely happen to this planet in some form. So they are coming to visit the planet first and the people second.

So that effect is not radiated by this planet now?

Let's say that the energy that is radiated by this planet now is about one hundredth of what it was there in Sirius, but that's still about a hundred times more than the average planet, at least the average planet in this general part of the universe. However, because of the polarity here, the discomfort, the pain, the suffering, you don't necessarily feel it, but if you come from an extraterrestrial civilization and you are largely protected and you go to an underground base such as the little people (the Bear people) have, you might still feel that one hundredth of the energy in that protected environment. It wouldn't be the same, but it would be like an echo of it.

So they came for that reason. What else do these ETs do?

They don't come to Earth very often. As I say, they come to it as a planet and not for the people. They are aware of the Explorer Race, but they are not particularly involved in the work. Your genetics and their genetics are not even remotely connected.

So why do they travel?

Why do they travel? Again, we come to the "Why did he climb the mountain?" question.

Oh, they just want to go out and look and see what's out there.

They just want to see what's out there. It is not their main function. They don't have to. It is largely for pleasure.

What is their main function?

Their main function is to acquire knowledge that they can expand into useful applications for species all over. One planet might develop knowledge for their own purposes, and these beings will go and acquire that knowledge if it is freely given and see if it can be applied as a solution to problems on other planets. It's not unlike what is done by certain groups of individuals on this planet. Problem solving, let's say.

Interesting. So they were just giving them a generic medical examination, then.

Yes. Nothing dramatic.

And then they had a tour of the ship. They saw a number of star maps. Now, the person who wrote this said that it was apparently similar to the one that Betty Hill had seen, but obviously not, since they were from another part of the universe.

It was similar in that the maps were constructed in the same way, and they represented trade routes. So they were, in this case, not necessarily associated with the home planets of these individuals. They were just general maps that involved the region where Earth is. Very often that type of thing will be left around, although—as is typical for any vessel—what might be considered strategic information is not left lying about. Any time that people get tours of ships, very often they don't get to see the ship as it really looks in its complete appearance. They will see it in a somewhat sterilized version. Things have been folded up, put away. This is not to say that they are not trusted so much as it is just a way of being discreet.

A Message of Warning and Hope

Now this is interesting. The man was taken into a darkened room and shown holograms of the aliens' home world as it looked after it was ruined by pollution and natural disasters. Is their home world ruined?

No. But the actual message was, of course, that this is what could happen to Earth. It was not what I would call a lie. It was more designed to say, "Look, this happened to us; it could happen to you. Please tell people." If we go back far enough in their history before they got to the planet they're on now, they did have a planet that they lived on part of the time that had such a problem, and that is because in those days (and this is how they came to be problem solvers) there was a brief flirtation with technology not unlike what you are utilizing today—that is to say, technology that has byproducts that cannot be recycled or used in a practical beneficial way.

So they lost the first planet and then colonized a second one?

They didn't colonize it. The first planet was something they were on part of the time. The second planet they also lived on only part of the time. They just basically moved to the second planet as a full-time affair.

And changed the way they did their technology?

They asked other ETs, "How do you do it?" They were at that time more of an inner culture, meaning they looked toward themselves for solutions rather than looking outward, but after that they became more broad-minded. They asked others how they resolved things, and in the course of that discovered the value of problem solving, which has really given them their mission in life.

A Celebration of Difference

Wonderful. Is there anything about them that would be comparable to our lifestyle or understanding at all—the way they live, how they live, even though they look completely different?

I cannot think of a single thing other than the comparison to your technology. They are really, really different.

Well, they have a soul. Are they ensouled?

Certainly. All beings are.

They have a life span; they have some sort of family unit. There are some similarities.

All right. If you put it like that.

Do they have a very long life span?

Not so very long. Maybe seven hundred years maximum, but occasionally not going past five hundred years.

In what dimension?

Oh, right around the sixth. They weren't always in the sixth. Once upon a time they were closer to the fourth, and that's when they had that technology that was not dissimilar to yours, using the description that I gave.

They said that the woman was walking along a corridor, and then she was inside a control room where she conversed with one of the tall creatures. Was it telepathic or did they have a translator? How did that work?

It might have been either way.

They can do both?

Yes.

She was shown a table with food that she was about to refuse to sample when it was taken away.

Yes, it was intended to show her what they eat and, of course, being somewhat unappetizing to her (giving you an idea of how different your two species are), it was taken away so that she wouldn't think that she was being offered the food. A gesture might have been made, however, that was similar to moving a hand toward something so that you might feel, if you were a human being, that it was being offered to you. But the hand gesture really meant, "This is what we eat." In this particular case, it might even have meant, "This is what we *have* to eat" (meaning while they traveled), meant perhaps for a little humor that was probably lost in translation.

So they eat?

Yes.

Was the food moving or something?

Was it moving? You know, that is such a relative statement, because if you have the capacity to see the biological, you know what you eat is moving too. It just depends on how you look at it.

Oh, all right. I was thinking of some of the things the Klingons eat that everyone else finds totally repugnant, but it's delicious to them.

Yes, I understand.

All right. I forgot to ask if the Bears have space travel?

They do not choose to travel. They are really not at all interested in technology, although you might find some situation for them where you would have them travel on machines like that. But they are not at all interested in being technical, and as a matter of fact, to a large extent they actually reject it. They feel that societies, many societies that they have seen, have become seduced by technology and have gone off track on their spiritual evolution for some time, and so they have really become quite disenchanted with technology in general.

So, back to the tall beings. They came to the planet. Did they go all over the planet? They didn't just go to this one family in England, did they?

They went to a few other areas in England, but they only went to England because that's where the Bears are. They like those people, (the people that we are calling the Bears because that is their traditional name in that part of the world).

Did they know them in Sirius? Had they known them before Earth?

Well, yes, but the main thing is that they are so well liked by all ET species. You wouldn't think of coming to Earth without visiting these people if you could possibly help it, because they are so charming.

Are there other cases that we're going to run across where the Bears are mentioned?

It's possible, but as I say, since this is something that is largely a geographic phenomenon, because they are in England, it is probably only going to show up in English contacts.

Before we finish, is there anything you'd like to add?

The whole point of these books is to show you how much you have in common and also to remind you and encourage you to seek common ground with your fellow Earth citizens. I can assure you that when ETs approach your planet from outer space, they don't think of you as Africans or Chileans or Icelandic people; they think of you as Earth people. Earth People. Earth people may look all different ways, they'll say, but generally to them they look the same, with different, unique individual features. But you are all Earth people to them. Start thinking about yourselves as Earth people, and you will feel the commonality with those around you instantaneously. Since you know that personal tragedies might happen, be alert and prepared to help your friends and neighbors. Since you know that it will be up to you to transform and get along spiritually, physically, mentally and on the feeling level as best you can, do the best you can whenever you can.

Untold Stories:
Contact with Criminals and Microbes

Zoosh and Ktook
December 8, 1998

Zoosh speaking now. Tonight we're going to do something a little different. There was that remark last night about contacts going unreported because the people were for one reason or another evading the authorities. Possibly we'll hear from one of the entities involved in picking these individuals up—this individual picked up more than one.

Shall we talk about the Bears, or the ETs and the criminals?

Right, we were supposed to do the Bears tonight, weren't we? I think we'll talk about the criminals first, though.

Okay. We've got time.

Ktook Speaks of the Transformation of His People

My name is Ktook. I am from a planet near the Vega star system that is a little past Orion. I would like to tell you about a few things that I have done in the past on your planet, as per the suggestion of your friend.

Welcome! Welcome!

Thank you. I have a unique interest in certain peoples. Going back to the point of departure from the old ways, the history, the cultural history of my people in the old days was what you might call a criminal enterprise—nothing like your pirates, who were really quite terrible (although, for some perverse reason, they have been romanticized)—but robbery was not unknown, nor was hiding people for an exchange, things like that. Back then, we were tolerated by the people in our star system—not exactly welcomed [chuckles], but tolerated.

One day, however, a teacher came to us—someone who walked on your planet a couple of thousand years ago—and he seemed to have no difficulty getting along with my people, even though it was a criminal colony on a portion of a planet. He seemed to be completely at ease with us ("us" meaning my ancestors; I am speaking for them), and although he did not participate in any criminal activities, he did not judge them in any way either. He spoke about a mission he wanted to do but would not be able to, because he was required elsewhere, and he spoke about this mission for quite a while.

I think it must have captured the imagination of my ancestors, and it seemed to have been their turning point. This was not the only reason, of course; there was also pressure from other parts of the planet and other peoples and other planets in the star system who wanted us to be more benevolent and more cooperative. But his stories seemed to have been the thing that changed people's hearts. He said that someday there would be a great many troubled people, much more extreme than my ancestors in their activities, and that they would need help from people like him who would not judge them, who could give them the vision and spiritual uplifting in a way that would get their attention and could not be ignored. He spoke of this quite a bit.

After some time, my ancestors said, "We are intrigued by what you say. Although we don't feel ready to do this now, because we feel so highly of you, we would like to give you our commitment as blood brothers that we will do this in the future: We will speak highly of this to our sons and daughters, and when they feel the time is right, perhaps you will send us the ships we can use, and we will come to that planet Earth and do our best to encourage those people who are acting somewhat the way we were." And he said, "That's good enough for me," and they had a big feast, and he said that he would return or send an emissary who would use certain signs, which he showed my ancestors.

Hand signs?

Yes. The signs would identify the emissary as being from him, and my ancestors said, "Wonderful." Time went by and the story became part of the mythology, as people say, the cultural wisdom—not a fantasy, but the cultural wisdom of my people.

A Calling to a Special Project

One day a stranger appeared—not suddenly; he walked out of the forest—and approached one of the elders and showed those hand signs. The elder, having been raised on that story since he was a child, was startled and said, "You're not one of our people from here, are you?" And the stranger said, "No, I'm not." And because this was a secret knowledge and wisdom amongst my ancestors, the elder asked, "Are you sent by that one who came to see us years ago?"

And the stranger said, "Yes."

And the elder said, "Would you come to our village with me?"

And the stranger said, "Yes, I will."

They walked to the village, and the stranger identified himself as . . . It does not translate into your language, I'm afraid.

And in your language?

It sounds like "Yalerteschupch." I have no idea what it might mean in your language. It's a name. Perhaps your names have a meaning, but it is like a proper name. So the stranger visited for some time—months as you would measure time.

What time period?

Yes, it's about seven hundred years from the visit of the original person.

Thirteen hundred years ago. Okay.

Then the stranger said, "I have made arrangements, if you feel that you might be ready soon. There will be people from planets far from here. You might have heard of these people or even seen them. Sometimes there will be one group with one kind of ship and another time another group with a different kind of ship. One group might be from Zeta Reticuli, where the people are very small—shorter than you—and they will be quiet most of the time; they need to have it be not too bright inside the ship, because their eyes are sensitive. Other times there might be people from Andromeda, who are always intrigued with what is new.

"These people will have ships and they will take you to Earth, where you can perform this project if you would like. You can stay as long as you want and do as much as you like, and then they will return you home, where you can tell your relatives what you did and what you think about it." Well, my ancestors, so the story goes, said, "This sounds very exciting, but we will have to ask the younger people what they think about it because we are too old, and we have lived here so long."

Communing with Criminals

So the youngsters were asked and they were very excited, and so the arrangement was made that in about two hundred years the people of my ancestry would start coming to Earth, contacting only those whom you call criminals. They would speak to them, encourage them, try to uplift them, tell them about some of our stories, sing them some of our songs and share common things we have done without judging them and ask them if they wish to receive a beneficial healing from special mystical people onboard the ship. Sometimes these would be my ancestors. Other times they would be the people from the other planets and star systems. If the people of Earth said no or no thank you, then that would not happen, but they all would have a meal together and eat what they liked, and then the person would be dropped off—perhaps a little wiser, a little more broad-minded.

So, that's what happened. That would be about eleven hundred years ago in your time, and it began then. In those days it was always done in very isolated places so that the people picked for such contact would not be embarrassed or would not be treated as outcasts because they had contact with people who had arrived in a ball of light (as the ships sometimes look like) or some such thing.

This has been an ongoing project with my people for the past eleven hundred years or so. We haven't picked anybody up for a little while, but just a year or two, even three years ago, we were picking people up. The people who were helping us had developed a technology where they could contact people, and we could talk to them and no ship could be seen. We also began a special project that we feel very good about: talking to prisoners, criminals in prisons, in their dreams. This has been something that is very close to my heart, and something that I believe in deeply. I will tell you about a few people we picked up when we were still coming with the ships.

How long has it been since you stopped coming with the ships?

We stopped coming with the ships in the late 1950s of your time and started using this other technique where ships did not have to be seen. Our friends who helped us out told us there were so many people on Earth that if we came in a ship, someone would see us. It would be hard to come and go unseen, and therefore the individuals whom we contacted might have some problems. We did not want to cause them problems; we wanted to bring them benefits.

So in the late 1940s of your time, about 1949, we started working in earnest. Sometimes we picked up people who were, by your standards, simple criminals—meaning nothing too great, a car thief or a shoplifter. Over time, however, by 1951, we started picking up people who had escaped from prison or who had committed serious crimes of a dire nature.

The Escaped Prisoner

One person I would tell you about . . . I'm not going to use names, because some of these people are known and some of them are even notorious. I feel that this is important, since we took an oath at the time that we would never reveal the names of these individuals, so that they would feel safe. That was important—to honor one another and to establish some form of mutual trust. This one individual whom we picked up in about 1951 had escaped prison with several others. They were sleeping in a makeshift shelter, and every one of them was talking about revenge. They were going to revenge themselves on someone who had turned them in, and this is what they had lived for during their past few years in prison. It kept them going through the terrible conditions in your prisons.

So we picked up one of these people, the one who was on outpost duty, who was about a hundred feet away from the others. We did so very quietly, and we put a little energy around the others so they would not wake up easily. We brought this person up to the ship, and first we told him who we were and who we were descended from and how we were considered the criminals of our star system. We made sure that he did not see our friends from Zeta Reticuli, who were flying the ship, because we did not want to frighten this person. Then we asked what he had done to be in prison, and he told us that it was a serious crime, murder.

We then asked him, "Would you like to have your heart healed of all your grief and pain? Would you like to have your mind expanded so that you could think new thoughts? Would you like to have your body healed so that you could feel good and maybe survive your prison sentence should they capture you? Would you like to have your spirit revitalized in case you're able to get away and some day speak of more benevolent things to people?"

And he said, "You can really do this?" And we showed him some pictures—not on a television screen, because although such things existed in his time, he had never seen one, and it might have frightened him. So we showed him some photographs of people. We didn't show their faces but we showed them. We said, "Look, we helped this person and that person," and then we played a recording of someone he knew, whom we had picked up and who had gone on to work in the city of Chicago in the state of Illinois, starting a shelter and doing special work with people there. That person is no longer alive, and so I could mention him.

He knew this person and he was interested, and so he said, "If you can do such things, and you have done so for my friend, then I am prepared to experience it," and then he made a threat [chuckles], to which we said, "All right," in order to honor him. You understand, that was what he was used to doing, and so we were not offended. Then one of my friends reached over and touched him in a way that we have been taught, and he became very relaxed. It does not make you go unconscious, but you become very relaxed and, in about five of your minutes, you fall asleep. When he fell asleep—in about ten minutes, you are in a much deeper sleep—then our friends came in and picked him up and carried him over to a special table that has lights and special sounds. He was on that table for about eight hours of your time, during which the others on the Earth slept and went unnoticed—sleeping, as you say, the sleep of the dead, but they were alive.

A Beautiful Transformation

During those eight hours, all those things we said came to pass, and after that time his heart was healed and his body as well. His spirit was expanded, and so was his mind. He said that he understood now what he had to do, and we did not ask him what that was, because he did not say. We took him back to where we'd found him, but first my brother showed him how to touch people and heal their hearts. He learned quickly. My brother said, "This is all that I can show you, because the machine does the other healing. But with this special touch, you can heal their hearts if they wish to have this done."

So he went back and found his friends, and they were surprised that they had slept so long, although they felt more rested than they had in years (of course, not being in prison). He said, "I've had an amazing experience and that's why I'm so different." He was careful not to tell them too much. He just said, "Some people came to see me, and they seemed peaceful. They did special things to me, and now I feel better. They taught me how to do something that would make both of you feel better, too." Then he asked, "Do you want to try it?"

The others felt pretty good already from their long sleep and said, "All right," but then they made a threat. He was not offended and he said, "That's all right." He reached out and touched one person on the chest and the person felt a little tingle, and then he touched the other person on the chest and that other person felt a little tingle, and he said, "I know that you just slept very deeply, but in a few moments you'll probably want to go to sleep again. I will guard you and make sure that you are safe, and if anyone comes to find you, even if you are sleeping, I will move you up into the tree so that you can rest and be safe."

"You will do that for us?" his friends said.

"Yes," he said.

They both felt very sleepy, and they fell asleep for about eight hours. They woke up and their hearts were healed. They managed to get out of that place, which was like a dense woods. They were very careful. They did not try to do anything illegal. They went, the three of them, for a while, enjoined in a brotherhood that served the poor. They did this for about three or four years. They said, "We have to learn how to help people." You understand? And after that, they went to a very tough city in South America and started a mission, where they worked with a local priest and helped the people.

That's wonderful.

So I wanted to tell you this story tonight, because we have made several of these contacts. Over the years some people may have been surprised because they knew someone who was the toughest person they'd ever met, and yet that person all of a sudden, seemingly out of nowhere, seemed to have a conversion, and they either wanted to do religious good works or just help people. They couldn't be dissuaded from it. I can't say that we were always the ones or that we were the ones even most of the time, but sometimes we were involved.

Worldwide Healing of the Heart

How many beings did you heal?

The number of Earth people that we picked up directly was about seventeen. But how many did they heal? Thousands. They all were taught the way to heal people's hearts, and then they would often also heal their souls.

Is that seventeen who you were involved with, or seventeen your people were involved with?

I am telling you this, because I was involved with this.

Right, but I mean, you contacted more than seventeen in 1,100 years, didn't you? Is that how many you directly contacted?

We. My people. My brothers and sisters on this ship did seventeen, but over that great time there must have been thousands. But we didn't keep count.

But several groups of your people came.

We would come, but not several groups at the same time.

But several groups came over at different times ?

That's right. Over different times, there would be a group, and each host on the ship would say, "As long as you want to stay, we will be with you." Sometimes it was just a few months (in your time). Other times, it would be many years. My group decided to stay for quite a few years and then return.

What was the mechanism, the mechanics, of finding these beings? How did you know whom to talk to?

We didn't. We had a few people who didn't work out. They weren't all success stories. It wasn't done by any technological means. It was done purely at random.

The Criminal Colony Redeemed

Back up a minute now. On the original planet, did your ancestors do this mischievous stuff, whatever, to your own people on the planet or out in the space lanes or . . .

We did not have access then to ships. We don't have access to ships now. We don't have our own ships. We have access from friends now, but we do not do that ourselves. We are not a technological people.

What do you look like? Do you look humanoid? Do you look like us?

We look just like you. Even if I had no shirt, you would say, "Well, that is a human being."

Same size and everything?

Well, more than five feet eight inches would be tall for us, but usually the adult, as you say, would not be any less than five feet two inches.

Do we have some of your DNA too?

I do not know that. For all I know, it could be the other way around.

You have some of ours?

It's possible.

Or perhaps we have a common ancestor someplace. How long do you live? What is your life cycle?

We seem to have a very widely varying life cycle. I don't know what the cause is, but it is not uncommon for some of us live three hundred years. I have known several who have lived as long as seven hundred years, but usually no more than that. I have been told that this life span used to be the same on your planet, that people in your old times also lived longer.

But now our lessons are so intense that the soul doesn't want to stay here more than a hundred years.

It seems so, and I can understand it. It is difficult for you, plus your challenge is greater than ours.

How big was your group? Was it 10 percent, 5 percent of the population? How big was the criminal element?

In our colony on our planet?

In your colony.

We were maybe 15 percent of the complete total of the planet. It wasn't fixed. If people from other parts of the planet became criminals, they were sent there. Succeeding generations, as you say, would be raised there.

They were sent there for life?

Yes, and they might marry and have children, and their children would have children and be taught the old ways. So it created a criminal colony.

I see, but you weren't able to go out and do anything criminal against the rest of the planet, because you were limited to this one place?

That's true, unless people happened to be passing close by. Sometimes we would be able to do a little plunder.

Of people who were not aware or something?

Correct.

But then once this being came and talked to your ancestors, was there a change there?

Yes. He had a special energy about him, and he seemed to be fond of my ancestors. He liked them and they liked him too. He would tell stories and sometimes sing songs or perform dances. And he would learn our stories and sing our songs and do our dances. He was open to us. He made no judgments at all, and my ancestors were pleased by that, and so they made him a brother.

He would speak and the people would all listen; then he would go on to another group and he would speak to them and they would listen too. He did this many times. Sometimes he would stay a long time, and other times he would only be able to stay for a short time, but he would keep coming back.

When you say a long time, was that a day, a week, a month, a year?

Sometimes he would stay for four or five days, and other times he would only be able to stay for a few hours.

So that was 2,000 years ago. Was it a radical shift during that generation, then? How did it work out that they changed? And how did they all work back into the general society?

They didn't work back into general society. We're still living in our colony. The rest of the planet has not accepted the fact that we have changed.

Really? And they keep sending new people and you keep transforming them?
Yes.

Life on the Colony Island

So what percentage of the population of the planet are you now, then? Is it about the same?
No. They have grown faster than we have. We are now at about 7 percent.

Is this a hospitable place that you live in?
I feel it is. I feel that it has history. It has traditions. It has heart, a great deal of heart. I think it is a wonderful place.

What are the boundaries? What keeps other people from coming there and your people from leaving?
It is an island. It is very far to the next piece of land. So I have been told.

How are people brought there? On sailing ships?
On seagoing vessels.

And what technology do they have for that? Steam? Electric?
I do not know. It is something that travels on water.

So what level of technology do you have where you are? Do you have motors or electricity?
We have fire.

Fire? That's all?
We do not have technology. We do not embrace that. We have a simple life: simple houses, stories, simple pleasures. It is our way.

It's like we would call our native mystical people, then? Do you live a life like that, communing with the land? Do you have animals and plants?
We have animals. We do not grow plants as your farmers do, but there are plants there that sometimes offer us food when they have more than they need. Some of the plants need to drop seeds and make more plants, so we do not take it all. We only take what is extra. Sometimes there are more animals than the place can feed and then we hunt, but if there are not enough animals to thrive—not just survive, but thrive—we leave them alone and make it taboo, you would say, to hunt them.

What do you eat, then?

We use our stores from the plants.

From the years before?

Yes, or whenever, because the special fruits or nuts, you might say, that come from the plants live for a long time, and we can put them away and save them. We don't have to eat too much and we can live well. If we kill an animal, everybody eats. We don't save it and put it in a cold box. Everybody eats. We do not eat the entire animal. We save some of its parts and we make special offerings—not right where the animals usually lived, but close. We leave something that is important to us. If we have nothing extra to leave, then we leave a little blood. We'll cut some part of ourselves that will heal before long and drop a little of our own blood on the ground there. That is a personal thing we need and love, and we wish to honor the animal and the animal's relatives. So by leaving a little of our blood, they know that we recognize their sacrifice.

That's beautiful. What is your history? What are the stories from the first beings who came there? Do you know anything about the rest of the planet? What they do?

Nothing.

Nothing?

I know nothing about it, and because of the way they are toward us, I have no great desire to know. They are not cruel; they just continue to treat us as a prison colony. Sometimes they bring food or clothing and other things that are extra for them. If it meets our needs, we will use it. If it is not right for us, we leave it where the ship drops people off. If it is there the next time the ship brings people back, they know we did not want it and they'll pick it up and leave other things. That way they acknowledge that we are beings who are worthy, but they don't seem to understand that we have changed. We have tried on many occasions to convince them that we have changed, but . . .

By talking to the people on the ship?

Yes, but the people on the ship never speak to us. I don't know if those people don't talk at all or if they have just been instructed not to speak, but surely they must hear us. So they must have a strange world, and I am happy to be a part of my world, where people are of the heart.

What number does this 7 percent represent? A hundred? A thousand? Ten thousand? How many are there of you?

We make an effort to not have so many that the land cannot support us, and we are never more than fifteen hundred. We've never been less in my time in the past many hundred years either, as far as I know. I do not think our population has ever been less than nine hundred, but I cannot say in ancient times what it was. They did not make a record of that.

Do you live in extended families or in simple families or clans?

[Chuckles.] My animal keeps touching my leg. We sometimes have animals like you have who are living with us. My animal keeps touching my leg gently.

What kind of an animal?

It is about the size of an animal you have here on this planet that I think you call a mountain goat, but it does not have horns and is very docile and friendly. It does not require that we feed it. It eats some of the plants nearby but likes to live with us. It does not give milk to us. Its milk is for its young, just as a woman's milk is for her young. They choose to live with us sometimes, and this one [chuckles] is very affectionate. Now, you asked if we live together?

Yes, what sort of living arrangements do you have? Do you have houses? Huts? Do you live outside? What kind of temperature do you have?

We do not have the cold that you have there. The temperature here is always comfortable, and so we can wear a light garment at night, but at some time during the day we can take that garment off because it will be warm. We do not have houses with materials that are taken. We will have, like you say, a hut or something made of stone, or perhaps, if there are enough animal skins, we might do that, but we don't have a lot of animal skins. So there are only a few huts made of material like twigs—what do you say? Branches?

Saplings. Twigs.

. . . and animal skins, but we have the stone hut or the hut made out of dirt.

First Encounters with the Universe

When your first ancestors went out in these ships and came back, they must have told you wonderful stories.

They were surprised by how complicated other worlds were. At first, they were quite astonished at the ship and the other people. The people from the other planets wanted to show my people how the ship worked and how to work it, but my people did not want to know how. We are not technological, nor do we have the desire to be.

We honor them for what they do for us, but we ask them not to explain, because we do not wish to know these things. They honor us and so now they provide special quarters for us. It is made of the material of the ship, but it is simple and we bring along things to remind us of home. Although we are unable to bring along animals, we will sometimes bring along a family member or two, and we might bring along some garments and maybe something else to hang on the walls to remind us of who we are so that we don't forget.

How many years ago did you first come here?
In your time, I came here in 1949, and then I went back in 1956.

So how did you feel as you looked at these humans who looked like you but lived in so many different ways and looked so many different ways?
We were at first very shocked by the color of the skin. We didn't know that there were humans who were so pale.

What color is your skin?
Our skin is . . . They have to tell me some words here.

Brown, red, blue, green?
Our skin is light brown. Light brown? Is that the color? Light brown, and we did not know that there were people who were so light. We had one young man on the ship once who was so light that I could see the streaks from the veins in his face. I had never seen that. I did not know what it was. Later, our friends from Andromeda said, "You have this too," and they pointed to our faces and said, "It's just that his skin is so light that you can see through it." We were surprised. Sometimes we picked up people whose skin was much darker, and it was a pleasure meeting them. So we were surprised at first by the variety of people's appearances.

Contact with Earth Animal Beings

What about the animals of Earth? Were you able to look around?
Our friends who fly us wanted us to see animals of Earth if we chose. They honor our need for preserving our culture, but we felt that looking at animals would be all right. So they would fly us to the cold place, but we would stay on the ship because we are not used to it, and they would show us the light-colored bear.

The polar bear.
And then we would see the little creature that swims in the water with the cold.

Seals.

We were so surprised that they could swim in that. We left them a little gift in order to honor them, and our friends took it out just to say that we honor you. Then they took us to other places, and we saw a huge animal that has a long thing on the front.

Elephant.

And we went to where there were many of them and no people. It was warm like we are used to, and we got out of the ship and the animals knew that we could be trusted so they let us walk up near them. We didn't go right where they were because we wanted to honor their land where they live. We went near them, and we looked at them and they looked at us, and they could tell that we were not from Earth. So they nodded at us, and one of them picked up a stick and drew something in the ground, and I went over after he left—he was a big, big being!—and I looked at it and I said, "I cannot believe this." I asked my brothers and sisters to come over and look at it and they were shocked. We all turned around and we looked at this big being and he nodded at us.

Tell me—what did he draw?

That thing I drew for you before. The name. He drew that in the dirt.

Oh my goodness! Yes, they are very wise beings.

And we were all so moved in the heart by this that we had tears coming down our faces. We didn't know how to honor them, and our friends came from out of the ship and they said, "What is wrong?" They saw this water coming down our faces and they thought that we were frightened or in pain. We said, "No, no; these beings are our brothers." The only thing that we could think of to do was to stay there for a couple of your hours and sing all of our songs that we could remember.

To the elephants.

Then, sometimes when we were singing, they made sounds to sing with us. That's what we could do, we thought, and we thanked them from our hearts for making us welcome like that and then we went away. We wanted to stay, but we knew that we had to go. We tell this story to our generation so they will know that there are beings on Earth who know us so well. These beings are special to us. We draw a picture in the dirt and tell the children of this story.

The Powerful Effect of Songs and Stories

That is so beautiful. That's wonderful. I am so glad that you came here. Maybe we'll ask Zoosh to give an overview. You said that your people had affected thousands. Do you know that?

No, we have been told and that is good. We don't have to be told all of this stuff. We are happy to participate. Our brother who came to see our ancestors long ago did not check up on us every time he came. He would talk to us in the same heart way every time. He was like us. When we do these things, we don't want to check up to see if they are doing all right, if they are doing well or if they are going back to their old ways. We have done what we can do. We must go on, and so we do not need to know.

We have talked to that being and he said that he will be back here in about seventy-five to one hundred years. Maybe he'll come to see you again.

If he feels that he wants to see us, we will welcome him.

But he hasn't been back to see you since he saw your ancestors at the beginning, right?

No, he sent his messenger, and we have not seen his messenger for a while either, but either one of them is welcome anytime. [Drinks.] This is good.

Do you have water?

We have this too. We have water, but we do not drink out of this stuff. What do you call this stuff?

Plastic bottle. [Chuckles.] Plastic.

We don't have that but we have water, and our friends tell us that the water we have is just like the water you have.

So when you were here and you went outside, you could breathe our oxygen?

We could breathe your air.

You could live here?

We could, but we have our own home.

[Laughs.] From what you've heard and what you've seen, what would you like to tell the people who are going to read this book? What would you like to say to them?

Most important are your families, your children. Tell them the stories that you want them to tell your grandchildren. Think about the stories that you tell them. Is this a story that you want them to tell your grandchildren? If it is, then tell it well. Make up a song. Draw a picture so that they will remember. If you feel this is a good thing for them to know, tell them in a way that they would want to tell their children. Make sure that they know who they are, that they always remember who they are. Give them pictures of who they are. Remind them of who you are. Tell your stories. This is so important.

On my visits to your planet, I have occasionally seen how the children do not know who they are. We have told them who we are, and sometimes they have nothing to say or very little. They say, "Well, I'm not sure about my father, and my mother worked hard and did the best she could." That's what they say. They don't know who they are. They don't have pictures about themselves. They don't have songs and stories. Tell these things to your children. I think maybe that if they know who they are, they will feel better about themselves.

That's beautiful. Thank you very much. Thank you for coming.
It is my happiness to come. Good night.

Good life.

Zoosh Speaks of the Visitors to Criminals

All right. Zoosh here. How did you like that person? Interesting, eh?

Oh, he was wonderful. Tell me a little about the main population on that planet. Why don't they talk to them or rehabilitate them? What is the story there?
I don't think that the colony that this individual was speaking from requires rehabilitation. They are doing quite well.

No, no. They have tried to talk to those people on the ship and tried to say, "Hey, we have changed," and they won't talk to them.
They live in a very rigid society, quite the opposite from our friend's. They have technology that is about equal to what you had in the 1930s. They find it difficult to change, and it will probably take them some time to do so. They may—although it is not fixed yet—have an opportunity to move to another planet in about seventy to eighty years.

The colony?
No, the rest of the people. They might choose to do that.

Why? What would be the motivation?
Probably because of the rigidity of the civilization, and because there will be several teachers who will come to speak to them in bodies of white, pink, green and sometimes gold light. These colors are important to them. They identify these colors with wealth and power. These beings will talk to them on their terms and tell them there is a special land for them. Should they choose to go, in time the land they have

been living on will gradually restore itself. Then it will be possible to ask the colony if they would like to also live on that other land. Probably they will not, in which case the land will be repopulated with plants and animals, and that's what it will be. It will gradually be restored by the actions of the planet.

Well, how did it get degraded? Did those rigid people pollute it or something?

Yes, it is somewhat polluted, as your planet was in the 1930s, although not with such toxic substances as you have now. Still, in the 1930s, your own planet was somewhat polluted also. You asked the person how the ship was powered. It was steam powered.

I see.

And the vehicles that they have are all steam powered. The substance used to create the heat is very similar to coal, and so they have not taken the path of oil.

I didn't know there were rigid beings. Well, there's every kind out there, isn't there?

There are different planets having different experiences. Everything is usually benevolent, but there are exceptions. Isn't it nice to know that there are other people who are also struggling a bit, so you are not the only ones (as you are sometimes concerned about)? [Chuckles.]

Visits from Microbes

No, that was a lovely story. Do you have plans for the Bears to talk, or do they want to talk longer than the time we have left?

The Bears will probably talk for quite a while and so I think it would be better for us to talk about other things, if you wish to talk a little more.

Well, what about the Walton experience?

No. That will take a while too. Let me just say this, then. Let me tell you a brief story. You know there are ETs who have come to this planet who have not only never picked up a human but have avoided you. They have come to interact with the plants or the animals. There was a group of ETs who had a ship that they considered to be huge, but if you were to look at this ship right now, you could easily hold it in your hands. To them, the ship was huge, like gigantic. They came to visit what you call microbes, because microbes are their ancestors. You might wonder about that.

As you know, there are many microbes on this planet who are benevolent. Certain ones that live in the human intestine, for instance, are essential to your survival. The people came to visit some of these microbes, which they found in the waters, and they took some onboard the ship, and they talked to them and asked them about life here. You understand that everything is alive? And they spoke to them in that style. If you were to see these ETs individually, you would see that they are about the size of microbes, and that is why they think the ship is huge, although to you it would be like holding a big model of something in your hand.

But are they sentient? Conscious? Are they technological?

They are highly technological. They created a ship that flies through time. It flies through portals. It can even fly through sound—which is not ultrasound like you are experimenting with—but planets, as many of your scientists know, will often issue forth sounds as well as colors and other things that strike the senses. They can skip the ship along those different harmonics and travel—not just quickly, but going through the different harmonics of these different places. They can sample the place instantaneously and know if there are any similar life forms living there, just from the sound. They are very advanced.

How did the microbes on our planet happen to be their ancestors? What's the story of that? Are they in the future?

It turned out that the beginning of much of the animal life here was difficult. The animals, not unlike you, also require these microbes for their intestines in order to be able to digest certain foods. So these beings had heard that the animals were having difficulty surviving on Earth, and they came to bring these microbes so that the animals would have them.

They brought them, as they would see it, as some of their ancestors. They do not think of a microbe as a cell or something; they think of it as some*one*, and so they asked for volunteers and said, "Who would like to go and help to preserve the population of these beings, be fulfilled living in their bodies, passing through their bodies, joining the living Earth and someday also functioning in the bodies of two-legged animals who will not know they are animals?" [Laughs.]

They did this, and then they came back to visit not too long ago and they asked, "How do you like it here?" The ones to whom they spoke said, "Well, it is sometimes difficult to be here now, and we are not sure that we want to stay." So then more volunteers have been requested. What is going on now—the reason that I'm telling you this—is that there is going to be a change in the microbes, because the original microbes that were brought here are not tolerant of the current levels of pollution. They have been suffering, and so others are being prepared who will be tolerant and might even be able to do something about it.

Like transmute it or eat it?

Yes, consume it and transmute it. That is being prepared. When they come—and I'm not certain when that will happen, but when they do—the others will be able to go home, and there will be a complete change.

How will it affect the humans?

It will probably allow you to digest things better. Ailments that the human beings have because of digestive problems—ruling out ulcers—and perhaps even allergies, will be partially resolved. Perhaps as much as one third of the symptomology will be resolved.

But how are they going to bring enough of them in those ships? I mean, there are trillions and gadzillions of them.

Let me just put it to you like this: There are that many in a ship.

Really?

They are very little.

That's incredible. So they think. They educate. At their size, they do what we do . . . they do beyond what we do!

They go well beyond what you do, and they are very efficient.

That's awesome. Discussing quantum physics with the microbes.

Yes, although you might have to do some catching up.

To even talk to one?

Yes, they really don't have a common language with you right now, because they are past the symbolics of your mathematics. They would have to speak to you in order for you to understand their level of mathematics and higher levels of such things, science and so on. You would have to be able to communicate in sound combined with color combined with feeling.

Could they talk to our penguins?

They talk to all the animals and plants easily.

I know, but the penguins—remember the mathematicians? They use resonant sound and colors.

Regardless, they can talk to all the animals and all the plants on Earth now, because if they don't have personal knowledge of how to communicate with these beings, they can utilize that overall species knowledge. However, you cannot do that, because you are necessarily isolated.

I see.

So they have no trouble communicating at all with any other form of life on Earth. That's part of the reason why they have avoided you, because there is no common language.

That is mind expanding. That is wonderful.

It will give you something to think about, just as does the old story of how many angels can dance on the head of a pin. Science will tell you how many microbes can live on the head of a pin; what if they are all . . . *thinking?*

[Laughs.] And creating and planning and singing, probably.

Yes, what are they thinking about? [Chuckles.]

Oh, that's great. That's a beautiful story.

Creatures Great and Small

Zoosh and Bear Representative
December 9, 1998

The Bear representative will be here soon. I'm just here to say greetings and salutations.

Great. Last night I neglected to ask a little extra about those microbe beings. I was so amazed. Where do they live? How do they live? What is their lifestyle?

Well, let's do one question at a time. What do you want to ask first? How about, "Where do they live?"

All right.

They live at the thirty-third dimension of Earth. I hinted at it last night—and I think that you picked up on it, but you just didn't ask right away—that these beings were very advanced.

Yes, you did. You said it.

Yes.

Yes, but technologically. I wasn't thinking of spiritually.

That's all right. At the thirty-third dimension, all microbes—we're calling them microbes, because on Earth that is what they are considered—are not only sentient, but the mass that they float in is also entirely sentient. I know that I have mentioned this before, but it is important to mention again that the air around you, the atmosphere, is also sentient. It's just that you don't know how to talk to it at this time. At some point, since the channel is available, I will encourage you to do a book channeling things that people take for granted, such as various other gases—carbon dioxide, oxygen, what makes up air. What does it think? This will get people thinking about their environment.

Yes, I'd never thought of that.

Yes, and even to throw in some things about pollution, even though it is combined with things that don't work for people and animals.

And is sentient.

Yes, everything is. So it might make an interesting environmental-awareness book. Now, these beings are from the thirty-third dimension of this universe, meaning that they can go anywhere, can be anywhere and can be conscious anywhere at any time.

Instantly?

Yes, meaning as needed. For them to fly here in a ship is unnecessary, but they come here in a ship because that is how they acknowledge that others travel here. They would prefer not to come here as lightbeings, because it creates such a great distance between them and their fellow microbes living here. By coming in a vehicle, then, they can create some kind of symbiotic relationship. And what's the vehicle made of? Needless to say, it's made of them! So the vehicle is actually quite nice looking. It is not what you would call technical looking. It is more streamlined, because they believe in beauty. It's hard to describe where they are from because it is so different, but that is the best I can do within the context.

How do they appear visible in the third dimension when they are from the thirty-third?

Think about it. The thirty-third dimension is a level that is deeply involved in mastery—I'm saying this, but I don't want you to worry about it. Imagine that a single microbe has the capacity to appear as a forest, as a child, as a dog, as a cat, as a blade of grass, as a hair, because of where they are from; but they do not do that. They honor each life form, not for just what it is, but for its life experience. The reason they choose not to appear in the forms of others, if they can possibly help it, is that they believe in the philosophy that to simply *appear* as something is not sufficient, because you do not have that thing's life experience, and so what you are doing is being more of a photograph. Even though you might be a tree with leaves reacting to the wind, other trees know that you are not a real tree, and they feel it would be dishonoring other trees to appear in this way.

They would be like a hologram?

No, they would look to you like a physical tree. You'd walk over, lean up against it and you wouldn't know that tree from any other. But the other trees would know, just as a dog knows a cat. [Laughs.]

Union and Individuality in Microbes

How did they choose the role to facilitate human life? They make it available. They make it possible, right?

Let me tell you something interesting about them. I have spoken about this stuff that holds all life together, which people sometimes say is light, but you have to go up a little higher to find the stuff that holds things together, and that is love. In order to manifest as a single unitary being like a microbe, one cannot be an individual on the level of pure love, because there is total union there, and individuality is not possible.

Similarly, one is rarely an individual when one is light. While different colors of light might have their own sense of personality, and it is sometimes possible (for instance, if there is a demonstration) to have an individual particle of light, light in general is also in a state of union. So the next dense layer you come to is the thirty-third dimension.

From love to light to these so-called microbes at the thirty-third dimension. This tells you how close they are to that level of pure unity. It also tells you at what point (at least within this universe) it is possible to experience individuality within complete harmony, which is the thirty-third dimension.

Okay, but on Earth they are giving themselves to the experience of helping the body, the physical body, to work. What do they do in the rest of the universe?

Just like every other form of life, they are individuals, although at that level they tend to do things more in union. But they can be individuals. Nevertheless, one might sometimes see them (if you could see at that dimension) moving in an undulating pattern perhaps, or they might come together to form some shape or even substance that they find attractive.

This tells you something important about them, and that is that they like to flow. "Flow" would perhaps be the single word in the English language that could best describe their overall experience, which tells you why they can get along in the third dimension, because what they do in the third dimension can be neatly summed up under the heading of flow.

How did that happen? Are they only in human beings on Earth? Are they in animals and . . .

Oh, they are in the animals. They are in everything. Microbes exist everywhere. They are in the soil.

Not just on Earth? On all the planets everywhere?

Many planets. Not all. You must allow for individuality and unique-ness, and also some planets may not require them. But the nature of planets, especially on any planet where you could have a sense of sub-stance or mass, you would likely find microbes, because they enjoy flow-ing through all forms of life—partly because it is their nature and partly because they are in an unending search and quest for new shapes.

If you could see them at their dimension (or let's say at their home), as I said, sometimes as a group they will take the form of a shape. You might recognize this shape, or you might not, but it is always a shape that they have picked up from their life on other worlds. This tells you that harmony has a great deal to do with their existence, and of course, flow fits into harmony very well.

The Home Space of Microbes

The thirty-third dimension. So every planet that they exist on, they exist in the thirty-third dimension of that planet?

No. That's obvious on the face of it, isn't it? It is obviously no. Don't you understand? You have microbes here on Earth, don't you? They are not at the thirty-third dimension. They can be seen under microscopes. So the answer is obviously no. They can be in other dimensions but it is . . .

Oh, they can be at any dimension?

Yes, but they will be themselves in that dimension, serving in the capacity in which they are needed on that planet, wherever it might be. But I make a distinction between that and their home, because at home they do just what you do. They relax and are themselves.

All right. Let me put it this way. I didn't ask the question right. So on any planet on which they are giving service, there is a place on that planet where they have a home in the thirty-third dimension?

Only maybe. If the planet itself does not have a thirty-third dimen-sion, then no. Therefore, if they wish go home, they will do so. Usually there will be—how can we say it?—a replacement.

What percentage of planets have a thirty-third dimension?

In terms of dimensions that are viable, they all have the potential. But in terms of viable, functional thirty-third dimensions on planets where there is life beyond light and love, maybe about 0.01 percent.

So that says how special this planet Earth is.

Yes, and it also tells you that this is a place where much experimentation and many different life forms are available. Say you want to create a life form, or you want to do a variation of a life form. Maybe you want to graft apples onto a pear tree, and so if you do that, it may or may not work, and you might just be trying over and over again to get it to work. And it does or it doesn't, and you do not seem to be having much success.

After a while, the natural world—meaning your total environment in its natural state—comes to be aware that you, as an individual farmer here, are trying to create something that is a variation. If they wish to support that, they will provide other life forms and energies that support it, including microbes, perhaps. That's how some plants have been hybridized, not only because of the creative efforts of individual humans involved, but also because nature said, "Okay, we can accept this, and we will lend our support."

Microbial Communication

You said that they could talk to any plant or animal on the planet, anything or anyone except humans. Do they carry on dialogues?

Yes, especially if the plants, animals, atoms or cells have something they want to know, or want strictly for social reasons. All different types of beings have stories and songs, just like people, like human beings, and they might speak of that. That's why some plants and animals seem to be singing all the time, such as flies and bees. Beings that have wings make a sound. The wind makes a sound through the trees, and the trees catch different themes on the wind, and then the trees might incorporate it into their songs and stories if it fits their lives, and then they might share that with other life forms who are open to that, such as the passing microbe. A tree does not consider itself any greater or lesser than any being regardless of its size. It matters not. It can be a mountain. It can be an ant. To a tree, they are all equal.

How beautiful. In the course of opening or flowering or expanding now, at what level does the human being get to—other than those who have taken shamanic training or those who have especially open psyches—what percentage on the scale will we arrive at when we will naturally communicate with everyone? Is it natural, or do we have to make an effort to do it?

It is necessary to make the effort. Suppose I told you that there is not a single problem on Earth that could not be solved if human beings communicated with the animals and the plants and life around you—just like so-called diseases sometimes manifest in the body of the human being, because they are not being heard. If the disease can communicate, sometimes it will go away and go to where it is needed—especially a disease that can kill the human, because then the organism that is functioning as the disease dies with you. That is not a good system.

Therefore, in time, such communication will be beneficial, and I want to encourage it right now for those of you who are strong. You must be strong physically to do this. This does not mean you have to be able to lift weights. It means that you must be durable and in pretty good health, and you must take care of your health when you do this. Furthermore, you must not spend more than thirty minutes a day doing it and not all at once.

So I'm talking to strong channels or sensitives. You can, if you like, speak to the disease of others or act out the energy of the disease. If you look at some more ancient peoples on Earth, you will see the shaman-ics—the shamans, the mystical people—very often dancing. When the dance becomes wild and frenzied, it is the disease itself speaking through the shaman, and the shaman allows it to communicate. Sometimes that is enough; the disease will have been heard or seen and is happy and goes back to whence it came, or it goes away from the person and finds its way home.

Usually that which develops as a disease in someone is a lost organism or a lost energy that needs to be elsewhere. When you can communicate freely and easily, you will learn many things. Many plants and animals have made it their duty to survive until human beings communicate with them. Some of you will have to hurry; animals like elephants in the wild are really not much wild anymore, but you can still try. Elephants in zoos will communicate differently.

Speak more about that.

If you are free as a human being, you speak not only of things that you wish were better but of good things, too. You see the sun come up this day and it is beautiful, and then you have something to eat and it tastes good. You understand? Like that. You have freedom. You could go and do as you choose—up to a point, I grant, in your society—but if you are a prisoner chained to a wall, your life is a misery.

So zoos are chains? Elephants are chained?

Even if they are not, they are restricted to a small space. If a human being is restricted to a small space for his or her whole life, especially if he or she is born in such an environment, I can assure you that the stories and wisdom are vastly different from what a wild and free person might have. So start getting the wisdom from the animals that you accept as wild and free. Get it from the birds, the butterflies—yes, the snakes for some of you who have snakes nearby—the spiders, the ants. Many of these beings have taken an oath, both on a personal and on a spiritual level, to survive as long as possible, because what they have to tell you can help you to resolve your deepest and most difficult problems.

So remember the next time that you are pulling a dandelion up out of your lawn: Maybe it is growing there for a reason—not just because it was invited, not just because it feels at home there, yes. Because it is on your lawn, it might have something to communicate to you personally. It is a gift.

But I didn't get an answer to my question. Is there a point—say, at 3.75 or just before the fourth dimension—where we will automatically be able to interact and communicate with animals and plants?

No, because you have to *want* to.

All right, but it just takes intent, not necessarily special training?

Special training is useful. Intent and desire are the beginning, though.

And practice.

Practice, yes, but you must want to.

Okay. Good. That's great.

And then it's just a matter of being shown how to do it, and then practice, as you say.

And maybe there will be more in the next shamanic book?

Yes, you ask about that in *Shamanic Secrets for Physical Mastery*.

All right. I feel pretty good about that, then. The microbes don't want to speak, do they?

No.

Okay. So then, how about the Bears?

All right. Let's get a volunteer. Good night.

✳　　　✳　　　✳

The Bears Speak

Greetings.

Greetings.

We are those people that the special ones call Bears. We find that perfectly satisfactory, since our appearance is certainly similar to such creatures. The special ones in the places where we live have been taught or shown our presence. If we take a liking to them, we might have revealed ourselves. We can be seen or not seen, and that is how we seem to be present one moment and then absent the next. Actually, we might still be there. That is why sensitive people might be startled when they see us and why the feeling associated with seeing us lingers—we are still there. If the feeling does not linger, we are truly gone.

We have been on this planet since before this planet was in this sun system. We existed within and upon the surface of this planet when it was in the Sirius star system, and even before that when it was in a place where planets that have a mission (as this one does) are trained. Planetary consciousness is a real thing, and this planet, having such a great destiny before it, was trained as a personality and given spiritual mastery, material mastery and teaching mastery before it was even physically manifested as a planet. Then it developed dimensional mastery on its own in Sirius and has been working on quantum mastery since it has been in this area.

We were involved in the teaching of the planet personality before it was in Sirius, and we felt so wonderful with our friend—this planet—that we decided to accompany it through its experience with the Explorer Race. After it returns to Sirius for a time, we might start teaching another planet, but for now we will be here.

That's incredible. Since you taught the planet, one assumes that you have all these levels of mastery, too. Is that correct?

We cannot lay claim to such great wisdom, but we work with those who do have it, and we are able to act as go-betweens between the great wisdom-keepers and the students. Sometimes the wisdom-keepers are so wise and profound that they cannot communicate in a way that can be understood by the students, and so they need those who can speak back and forth for both parties. It is that service that is our special gift.

How did that come about? Were you trained?

As far back as our people can remember, we have always been able to do this. We have attempted to find a "dim time," meaning a time before we did this, as others have told us about, but we have been unable to locate it.

Was it before this universe, or are you part of this universe?

We predate any form of visible existence.

Any form, anywhere?

As far as we know. We cannot speak with authority, nor is it our intention to do so, but we have been told that this is true about us by the quantum master who is working with Earth. We did not ask, but apparently she told us this because she wanted us to know more about ourselves. Even though that is not a major pursuit for us, she must have thought there was a need. It has not shown itself to be necessary yet, but I am sure that since she said so, there will be some day.

Can you say a little bit about your present life situation, your life cycle and your experience?
Which one?

What is the length of your life cycle now on Earth?
I have always been.

Oh, you are immortal. Wonderful. What's your earliest memory?
I always remember doing what I have been doing. I do not recall any time before that.

We only know about the various love creations and two or three levels beyond that. Do you have memories of doing this work in levels beyond that?
I cannot say that it is beyond that, but I can say that I remember the first time (speaking for myself) I *saw* something and went through my experience. It is hard to say when, but it was long before what you are calling the love creation—long before that—and it was like motion. That's the only way that I can describe it. You know that motion exists even if it is not seen? So with other senses I was aware of the motion, and yet I remember seeing something and I could not say what. Then there was another wait, and then I started seeing things. Light. Dark. Shades. Patterns, then form, then substance. And when I saw substance, I saw a love creation and I was attracted to it.

When you say "I" now, are you speaking as an individual "I," or is there a union consciousness?
I am speaking only as an individual.

But your experience would probably parallel the other beings?
You would have to ask them.

All right. So, you were attracted to love's creation. Where—is there a where? What about this planet where the quantum master trained this planetary consciousness?
The quantum master is training this planet now.
And the being? I forgot the name of the being you liaisoned with.
The spiritual master and the material master and the teaching master were at the center of a universe nearby to Sirius. It was in proximity to Sirius, since that's where the planet would take its first form or residence. I mean form in the English sense. It is a universe that is of light and form

but not of planets and suns. It is a place more for personalities than for forms. You do not know it by a name.

Liaisons for Earth

Was the planet Earth the first one where you did this translation between the teacher and student?

No. Speaking for both my friends and myself, we have done that many times, but I think that this one, this Earth (I think of Earth as someone) is truly the most complex.

Do you have a name for her?

Yes, I have what you call a nickname for her: Ghi Da.

Spell it for us.

I can't. You will have to do your best. It is a soft *G*. Ghi da. More like a *J*.

Does it mean something special to you?

It means "devoted."

The quantum master is teaching this planet. So at this point in time, right this minute, you are still doing this communication between the master and the planet?

Yes, but because quantum mastery is a study and a mastery of consequences, we are not needed all the time, and so we can visit other creatures on the planet or under the planet where we live now, or at a higher dimension so that we are safe. It has been our pleasure to visit with many of the beautiful beings, the fairies, the beings who are cousin to the fairies, the elves and other deva spirits. We have had much fun with them. They are happy when the plant and animals worlds that they work with are happy. When these worlds are sad, it is hard for them, and when that happens, if my people or myself are not doing our job with the master and the planet, we will come up to the surface where the little people are and we will sing to them. This seems to cheer them up.

Have you always shown yourself in the form that you do now?

On Earth, yes, meaning on Earth here. When I say Earth, it means here. When I say Ghi Da, that is who she is, but in Sirius, Earth was called something else.

Can you say what?

Depending on the different people, they had different names, but the name I found most pleasing was Onanda. It would be like an *O* sound,. Onanda.

Oh how beautiful. I think "nanda" means bliss consciousness here in our language now.
That is even better.

Expression through the Bear Form

So we'll use that same system. While you are on Earth, have you taken the form that we saw that little drawing of?
Yes. The drawing will show you the head. It is a pretty good example, but the body is stocky—bearlike is accurate, but not like the bear in the woods, as children say, but more like a toy bear.

But you have hands and feet?
Yes, we have short legs and bearlike hands, as you say. I don't think of them as hands, but I am using your terms because they make sense to you.

So you have more like the claws of a bear than the fingers of a human?
Yes. This way if we are accidentally seen, which happens now and then with sensitive people or sometimes with children, we look like someone who belongs on the planet. We don't look scary or strange.

Okay, so what do you do when you are not helping ETs visit people or cheering up the elves or working with the planet? What do you do then?
We sing.

You do?
It is our nature to sing the songs of whatever life form we are associated with. We sometimes sing the songs of Earth, but this body cannot reach such high notes. Then sometimes we sing the songs of different animals or different parts of Earth. Some parts of Earth are smooth and liquid, like water. Other parts of Earth are hard and grainy, like sand. Then there are all the animals and all the plants and so on. For our own entertainment, as you say, we sing their songs. We believe that by singing their songs that it nurtures them, and it helps them to feel happy and perhaps welcome.

Years ago, people, human beings, did this, but I have noticed in your more modern times that not so many people remember how. You could say, "How did the first person learn?" because people from all over the planet would have to live somewhere. They learned because they would go out on the land or into the woods or perhaps out onto the water, and when they were out there, they would start singing—not a tune they had known or that anyone had taught them, but a tune that just came to them.

Spontaneously?

Yes, and such a song might be their own song of their heart, or it could be the song of some form of life around them. That's how it began. So now, if you like, you can do this, especially with your children when you take them out to the woods or out on the water

Figure 19.1: *Close-up drawing of the Bears as described by witnesses in England in 1974.*

Courtesy of Kevin Randle and Russ Estes

or someplace that is not too crowded. Ask them if they can make up a song when they are feeling happy, to sing their happiness, and it will become the happiness song. Tell them that it does not have to have words. Words are a complication.

If you start them off that way and they can do this and enjoy it, then next time when you take them there or someplace, have them first sing their happiness song and then ask them if they can sing a happiness song for something else in the woods—anything. Maybe they'll say it's a tree or a bird. Maybe they won't be sure. That's all right, too. Maybe one will say that this is the song from this tree and another one will say that no, this is the song from that tree. You tell them that each bird, each tree, each blade of grass has many songs, and no one song is the only one.

Oh, that's beautiful. If we had a channel who had a high range, could you do some of the songs through the channel?

Perhaps, but they would have to be a soprano—a woman, most likely.

There used to be one, but she's not on the Earth anymore.

Perhaps you could find another and make a recording. A recording is not the best, but it might encourage others. Say, "Here is the song. See?"

I will look for one. You be available.

And then the person who plays the recording will say, "I would have never considered that to be a song." People think of a catchy tune, but the song of a tree might be catchy or it might be completely different.

The Bear Community

Okay. So you sing. How do you live? Do you live in groups, do you live alone or do you have relationships? Or this may not mean anything to an immortal.

We are happy singularly and with others. No, you are right—the question does not relate directly to us.

It's attempting to make you humans.

Perhaps it is that, as you say.

I won't. But what other things interest you? Do you communicate with others of your beings? There are others of you now elsewhere, right?

Perhaps, but I only communicate with those here.

You have always been with this group you are with?

Yes.

How many of you are there?

About nineteen.

Oh, is that all? I had the idea that there were thousands. I see.

No, not many. It is enough.

I'm sure that it is. So the times when you show yourselves to humans, is that because you know them? You've always been on this planet. You see souls incarnate again and again and again, then?

Usually we have other duties, but if we choose to look at that, sometimes we will see someone whom we have met before, and other times we will see someone who is sad, like I said before, and we might show up and do something to amuse that person. We will sing and maybe they will hear us, or maybe not. Maybe our song will affect their dreams. Maybe it will heal their hearts. Maybe it will just confuse them [chuckles], but we usually show ourselves to the very young or to the young at heart.

So you only live under England?

Under what is now England. We used to have some visits to France and Germany.

Yes, Zoosh said that you left because it was so sad during the war.

We left, but we might visit there again someday. But we will wait for the people to become more unified. We have heard they are working on it, and that is good.

Yes, the European Union. But in England itself you choose occasionally to show yourselves. There are reports of you. As you say, you can feel the vibration of someone young at heart and you show yourself to such a person.

We don't show ourselves to everyone, but if we have the moment, or if there is the need and we have the moment like any other person, then we might do it. It depends also if we can do it and be seen only by this person. We do not wish to frighten or startle others, and so it requires certain conditions also. Perhaps that person who is young at heart has a thoughtful moment or a faraway moment, a pensive moment, and that is a good time, because then the person is receptive.

If you chose, could you see anyplace on the planet?

Perhaps, but we usually ask somebody else if we need to know something about the planet. We might ask a tree that has other trees like it on other parts of the planet, or perhaps a bird or something like that, a creature like that. Perhaps, if we can wait for the answer, we will ask the wind and it will find the answer and return when it has it. We are not in a rush to know. We are very happy where we are living, and we are hopeful that someday the children of this island will be treasured more and will someday enjoy the peace of their hearts as the peace of their daily lives.

Yes, all children. So at some point in our future, as we open to higher frequency, there will be interaction with you consciously?

I cannot say that. Perhaps.

Under what conditions ?

Remember that our first duty is to the master and to Ghi Da.

The Goals of Planet Earth

She was trained as a personality? Who found her? Did she volunteer? How did she get started in this process?

What first?

How did Ghi Da get started in this process?

Ghi Da was looking for something to do that would be a challenge and that would be a long project, because her personality at that point had been taught only things that to her were fleeting, and she wished to do something that would last a long time, something she could count on to be there. When the spiritual and material and teaching masters heard of this, they said to her as one, "Ghi Da, would you like to be a special planet with a special job?" And Ghi Da said, "Tell me more." And that's how it started.

What was her experience before that? Had she been an individual?

I do not know. Perhaps you could ask her. Use that name; don't say "Jee-dah." Learn to say it, "Zhee-dah." [Pronounces the sound of the first letter as *zh*, like plea**s**ure or gara**g**e.]

We will. That's precious. We didn't know that before. I don't know if you know this, but how long will the planet stay here after the Explorer Race leaves? Is there a timetable?

I could not say. She has not completed quantum mastery, and I believe she has the opportunity to complete it here. It is not in her nature to stop or give up without completing something. So the planet will probably stay for a while.

Over the course of time there have been teachers, great teachers and avatars, who have come to the planet. Do they bring any special love or anything that helps her? Have you seen them come and go?

Sometimes they have felt heart for her and have offered some energy or support. Yes, I have seen it. Most often it looks like light going into her. Sometimes it will restore some part of her body. Other times it will warm her heart, and she feels good knowing that the love of this person, or the energy that they carry, cares about her.

You don't know the names of any of these, do you?

I do not know their names. I see it.

I was thinking maybe of Jesus or Buddha or somebody like that.

Jesus, yes. There was someone who walked in the land of Mongolia. I do not know her name. There was also someone in Turkey, what is now Turkey, and also someone in the Afghanistan area. These were all women, in the female form, the female body.

I got energy going through me as you said that. It's like I got goose bumps. I'll ask Zoosh when we're done if they have names that we've ever known in our history or our mythology or something.

I would think probably not.

Because they are so long ago?

Not so long ago. The one from Afghanistan was in the 1920s of your time, but she, as these people often are, would choose to be a simple person and not draw attention to herself. That is the way to do the greatest good for the most.

In Communication with the Earth

But do you work with Earth on a level of information, or do you send energy? Do you have an energetic interaction with Earth?

We don't just work with information. To you, information is what? What is information to you?

I suppose you could call it facts.

Thoughts.

Thoughts. Facts. Yes.

We do more than that. Maybe it cannot be said in this language or any other on Earth, but I will give you a poor example. Maybe the quantum master communicates to us something that is made up of feelings, thoughts, pictures, sensations, sound, color, smell. You understand? We will demonstrate to Ghi Da as best we can—in a way that we know she can understand—what the master has said. Then it is up to Ghi Da to do with it as she might.

Do you do this in an immortal personality form? Or in the little bear form?

Either way. Often we do it in our bear form, because we don't have to go anywhere to hear or to experience the master, and we don't have to go anywhere to speak to the being in whom we are living.

In whom. Of course. So the quantum master comes here every so often or has a piece of herself here all the time?

I do not know, but when she speaks, it is as if she is right here with me, and so I think that if she is a quantum master, then maybe boundaries have no meaning for her.

I'm sure you are right. Quantum mastery is learning the consequences of your actions, right? That's part of it?

That is too narrow. Quantum mastery is the mastery of consequences. This means that in order to learn it, you must experience the consequences of everything possible at least once, but even then, you have a long way to go.

But it seems that there is a relationship between all the trauma and turmoil and suffering and agitation and creation and greatness and everything that humans bring to the planet and her lessons. Is that true? Are we part of her lessons?

You create and stimulate a great many consequences.

Yes [laughs], but they are our consequences. How does that affect her?

Since this is her course of study, it might have some advantage in the long-range study of quantum mastery. Of course, the short-range effect can sometimes be difficult, but at other times it can be wonderful, such as many, many people laughing at the same time at something that amuses them. It might make her a little more cheerful. Many people feeling love and friendship and kindness might make her feel better also.

But this nasty stuff of having her uranium taken out and her oil and all this mining and some things that go on, all of that affects her, right?

Just as if someone took pieces out of you; that would affect you too.

So is that part of the handicap? I mean, was that figured into the equation when she started or was that just an unfortunate . . . ?

The master must have known. I cannot imagine that the master wouldn't know that. Ghi Da is immortal too. Ghi Da is not a planet. Ghi Da is *in* a planet and all around the planet, but Ghi Da was not the planet before she became the planet. She was a personality, and now her personality expresses herself as a planet, but as your personality expresses itself as the physical you right now, some day Ghi Da might express herself some other way.

After she becomes a quantum master, she can express almost any way that she wants, right?

Or after the death of the planet. Remember, there are consequences. The planet is a living being. If she is destroyed beyond her capacity to repair, the only way to repair her is for enough wise people to come and give her things, or for human beings, the Explorer Race, to create—with magic and spirit and love and harmony, re-create, yes—what all the other humans have taken out of her. This, I believe, is part of your lesson.

At first, and for many years, you are dependent on her and what she provides for you, but someday she will be dependent on you to re-create her oil and the other things you have names for that humans have taken out. Remember that before you leave her.

Revitalizing the Planet

We need to repair her.

You need to revitalize her. Even if she does not stay as a planet, she must know that you love her, appreciate her and will give to her as unselfishly as she does for you. That is your true nature, and do not feel that it is something you cannot do. You can learn to do it. But of course, first you'll have to want to.

Do you feel that the planet is that close? Have we polluted it past the point we can clean it up?

It is not possible to clean the planet up anymore. It is only possible to use magic and let magic rebuild her. But magic requires heart, soul, cooperation, harmony and love, just to begin.

That's what Zoosh calls benevolent magic, right?

Yes.

So it is not off in the future that we need to do that. We need to do that right now.

You need to begin to learn.

Can you say something about that we can print, or do you need to teach people individually or what?

I think this is not my job.

Zoosh has started doing that, but I'm glad that you underscored it and emphasized it.

Yes.

If you didn't appear as these little bears, would you appear as golden images? I have difficulty tonight seeing Robert sometimes. Everything is all golden.

Perhaps.

Do you interact with a lot of ETs? I think Zoosh said some of them invited you to join them because you are so cheerful.

Let's save that for tomorrow night. We need to stop. The energy is very powerful. We need to shorten.

Okay, certainly. We will see you tomorrow night.

Yes.

Very good. Thank you.

Good night.

Good night.

Earth's Work with Quantum Mastery and the Loop of Time

Bear Representative
December 11, 1998

Let me say again that there was no soul-line connection between any of the tall beings and the family taken aboard, but that one of the children in a future life would have a profound effect on many beings. It is a life of what you would now call now diplomatic service, not exactly serving one government, but rather serving an intention or a purpose designed to increase the contact among all species. It was because of this that the contact was made.

These tall beings are what I would call a compressed form of interdimensionality. Their actual bodies are ephemeral, not of great substance as you would know it. Their appearances are often disguised in a manner so that what is remembered is a human type of appearance—if not of a human being, then something identifiable. If you were to look at the body of an individual, it would seem less like a physical form than something that contains many beings, and this is very distracting to the average human being. A heavily insulated garment is worn so that the persons whose lives are benefited by the feeling of continuity, like human beings, are not upset too much.

So it was this profound future life that was the attraction. These beings, these tall ones, were involved in the diplomacy of that time. They are nonphysical in their natural way of being and are only apparent if they choose to demonstrate some form of substance. This would be done only for some special occasion. Now, the interest they have is a personal one, because as a race of beings they had largely been the only ones involved in such diplomatic relations to bring different types of beings together for a long time. However, they had not been having as much success as they would have liked, and they had been asking for a long time in their prayers for some other form of being who would assist them or who would desire to work along a similar path.

In their time, one of these youngsters incarnated into such a form that by its very nature had the substance and capacity to be so loving and compatible with all beings that it would not be possible to be in the presence of that being without feeling the commonality between yourself and all other forms of life, even if you had not heretofore experienced it. And so, from the tall beings' point of view, they were coming back to see this beloved person whom they knew in their time in order to see where he had been, what he was like and, from his perspective, to show cause and need to the soul of this person in order to place a seed there that would flower in their time.

Did he say which of the children it was? Boys?

I would prefer not to say, so that the family won't be made to feel uncomfortable. Do you understand?

How far in the future?

In terms of experiential years as you know them now, it would be not that far—only about twenty-seven hundred years or so.

And where? Is there a where involved?

There is a where. It is very much on the other side of the galaxy from where you are, but it is within this galaxy.

These beings come from this galaxy?

Yes.

There was only one on the ship?

No, there were several.

How had you known them before? How did they come to know of you?

I had not known of them.

They just heard that you loved children?

Because of all of our work with all of these different masters, if anything unexpected or untoward came to be, it would be good to have us aboard, in case something developed for which they would not know how to deal.

They wouldn't have the experience?

Yes. So they asked for our cooperation.

A Mission of Diplomacy

Let's see what they did here. Why did they put this fog out?

This is not an unusual factor. It has been noted in other cases.

Not green, though. I mean, there had been white fog in some cases, but this was a green one.

This is still not so unusual being green. One might ask oneself logically and reasonably, "Why would people drive into such a strange-colored fog?" But there had been previous visits on the dream level, and the people had all been assured that this fog would be safe and that the contact with it would be a good experience overall. So it was something not unlike a post-hypnotic suggestion.

So you all seem to be doctor types. Everybody got an examination?

I cannot say that we are so much doctors. People were looked over, but I wouldn't say they were thoroughly examined.

What were they looking for? What were you looking for?

We were not looking for anything, because we did not initiate the contact; rather, the taller ETs were trying to understand the nature of the physical development of such a great being, from their perspective. They wished to have these talents and abilities themselves and wondered if they could understand this being. They did not know which one it was. They just knew it was somebody in this family. They wanted to see if they could understand their makeup, how they function, what drove them. You understand, they thought that perhaps they could assimilate such qualities in the evolution of their souls.

What qualities were they so interested in?

They were interested in the qualities of that being in their time, and they wanted to know if those qualities had been budding in your time. They felt that one of the youngsters must be the person. Interestingly enough, it was not that youngster but a different one. However, I will say that the parents created a special atmosphere for the youngsters and they all had it to some degree.

Wonderful. And the parents were shown star maps that were of their home on the other side of the galaxy? Maps of trade routes as well?

Yes. Not just trade routes but also diplomatic routes.

Was their goal to get people together and help them to get along? What am I missing here? Why was diplomacy so important to these beings?

It is the reason they live, especially since their world, where they had lived originally, had come to a sad ending, because different factions on that world could not come to simple agreements. As a result, their world died out. You see that a lot on your planet, where people cannot keep to simple agreements and cannot honestly admit that certain things are harmful for animals and people and the planet itself. They are beings from the future, the tall beings. They were hoping that somehow this message would be delivered by these individuals.

So that we would see the . . .

. . . the error.

The error of our ways.

Yes.

But it wasn't publicized much. It wasn't made widely known.

They can but try. You must remember that when ETs go to other planets, it is normal that there is no secrecy about it. They knew that they had to be discrete, but they did not know that the public mind had been nurtured to believe that such things couldn't exist and therefore did not exist.

So that was the destruction of their planet, and they moved to another planet? That's what gave them their mission and purpose of going out to get people to get along?

Yes, because they could see that if people could not agree on the simple truths, that ultimately it would be very easy to entirely unintentionally sow the seeds of your own destruction. It is similar on your planet now. People in a rational state of being can completely understand that if you put poison in the water and then drink it, you will in time be harmed. But when people are motivated by things other than heart and a clear mind, then self-destructiveness becomes the rule rather than the exception.

Is there anything else you want to say about these beings, or is there anything that I'm missing here that you'd like to talk about?

I will respond to questions. Take a moment.

Finding Qualities of True Diplomacy

Was this the first time the tall beings came here?

I think they had been here before looking for that person. But during this trip that you are asking about, they found that being.

And was the method of this finding a spiritual tuning in or technology?

No, they accessed some record that was made available to them by other beings. The being in their time actually asked them not to do that, but they felt a strong sense of personal need to have expanded capacities, not because they were jealous, but rather because they desired to be able to be and do more. So, with apologies, they chose to pursue this project.

How did they incorporate or infuse themselves with these qualities? What was their plan?

They wanted to understand if any of the qualities were genetic or if they were on the personality level. They wanted to observe and emulate traits they felt might be seed traits of this soul. In other words, they wanted to see if there was something missing in them that existed in these people. Using extrapolation, they wanted to see how these individuals—or at least the one they were interested in—would evolve and develop the traits they desired to develop. It was not unlike looking back into the past of something in order to understand its present, as you do now in exploring ancestors.

So, say again what these traits were.

It is the capacity to project such energy of love and compassion that no beings in the presence of that energy could avoid seeing the common ground between themselves and any other species, even if they had not seen or felt that common ground before. This would be—in your time, for instance—that an industrial person could see his common ground with an ant and what he might do without intent to harm, perhaps. If he did something that harmed the ant, it would ultimately harm the human, and if a single human is harmed, all are harmed—and not just philosophically speaking or religiously speaking, but in fact.

And what was their conclusion? Did they decide that it was on the level of the soul or genetics or what?

They decided that it had partially to do with personality, partially to do with family environment and partially to do with conditioning. So they decided that it was not genetics.

So what steps were they going to take?

They managed to speak to the individuals a little bit, and they have a capacity to quickly grasp an individual's personality; therefore, they would attempt to emulate the aspects of the personalities of the guests aboard the ship that felt good to see if the overall effect in their time might improve their capacities, their lives and the lives of others.

Did they go to any interim lives between this point and their own? Did they sort of hop and skip up the soul line?

No, they had been guided by one of their teachers to contact this family in this time because it would be enlightening. It was kept vague like that so they could make the choice—not an imperative statement but a statement of options.

Beings of Vast Projection

Is this a race that the Explorer Race will meet when they go out and investigate?

Probably not. They are most unusual in that you might in fact be contacting them and not know you are contacting them, because in their actual form they are vast.

How vast?

One of them could easily reach the length of the galaxy. They are not physical.

One of them could reach across the galaxy, but what is their normal projection of themselves? Is it always like that?

More or less. It is in their nature to be inclusive, to be broad rather than narrow.

So what form is this now-human going to take? Would it be their form, or would it be one of the races that he or she would interact with?

I think there's been a misunderstanding here. You remember what I said that they did in their time, the tall ETs? That they were not as successful as they wished and that another being came, who radiated this great love energy and was able to do more than the tall beings, and that the tall beings were not jealous? That they wanted to know how they could do it? It was that being who came who had a human life.

What form did that being take? Was it their form?

The other being who came . . . ?

The being who is now human—how did that being incarnate?

In the future, you mean?

Yes, in the time these beings came back from. That's not clear.

This other being came and just looked to them like a lightbeing, a small, very small globe of gold light.

Ah, that's the part we hadn't gotten to yet. I see. And it radiated such love and such attractive energy that the people just came together and saw their common ground?

Yes.

Fascinating. There are so many fascinating stories.

So much of what individuals do is oriented toward service, and the more complicated the service—because of different beings or different circumstances—the more the server must expand and become more, such as these beings. And if that expansion and that method is not apparent in your own time and you have the capacity to travel back in time, you might wish to do so.

Dangers of Interacting with the Past

You might wonder why the golden being in their time said, "Don't go back and look for who I was." The reason is that the golden being was concerned that the past incarnation might be affected in some way and then not become . . .

What it was at that future time.

What it was. A reasonable point.

But were they able to do it in such a way that they didn't affect that life? Did they cause something to change?

They might have done. One must be careful about tampering with the past, and so it remains to be seen.

A simple little thing like that? Interacting with a human incarnation could change . . . ?

What is so simple? You have your life with your family and your fellow youngsters. You drive into a green cloud and then you are on a spaceship with extraterrestrials. That is not so simple.

Well, are these tall beings very wise and did they feel the risk was worth it? Or were they not aware of the consequences?

They were aware of the consequences, but they have a trait that you can all identify with: They have not yet mastered patience.

I see. [Chuckles.] And do you look into the future?

Not as a rule. What would be the point? One thing you can be sure of is that if you have clear vision—meaning that you can see things as they are or in some cases as they might be—if you look into the future and see it as it will be, you will be guaranteed that when that future develops, your life will be a little more boring than it would have been if you did not know.

Oh, good point. No, I was just wondering about the fate of the golden being.

Time will tell, and when I say that, it is not a slogan. Time will tell, meaning that time sequences, all time sequences, are a physical fact in their own right, and they have to do with one thing after another. You understand, of course, that when you travel outside the boundaries of time, it doesn't mean that time doesn't exactly exist, it just means that you are beyond its boundaries. You can travel across many timelines or cycles, but that does not cancel out the effect of accumulated experience on any timeline. If one does not sufficiently understand this, it is possible to unintentionally alter a future event by creating something in the past of a given soul that might not otherwise have occurred.

I know I've always heard, in fact and in fiction, not to ever interact with anything in the past to change it. Right?

And yet some circles in your civilization are striving now with all due speed to achieve (from the point of view of those circles) time travel.

Allowing the Explorer Race to Experience Consequences

What you're saying has created another thought. It's our understanding that the Explorer Race came to a particular point, made a decision based more on the mind than on the heart and that this loop of time was created so we could experience the result, the final result of that.

Yes.

Where do you fit in? Was the Earth in this position when that loop of time started?

No.

Ah, the Earth was put here for that loop of time?

Certainly, because you required a place where all the consequences could be explored—having to do with your decisions and all of the ramifications of your actions. You could only explore it a little bit before you got to the Earth, but in this place—in this universe, yes, but also here in this place—Earth has achieved all these mastery levels and is working on the mastery of consequences. Therefore, she is flooding herself with applications, consequences, events and so on.

You as individuals, each and every one of you, could experience numerous individual applications, consequences, and to some extent Earth would benefit from this, but to a greater extent you would. In this way, any consequences that you had not experienced before your manifestation as Explorer Race on Earth would ultimately be experienced here—at least in the baser effects, meaning the ones having more impact, the ones that are more difficult. As you go on from Earth, the consequences will become more benevolent, but here is the last place you can experience, understand and assimilate the full impact of consequences that might be difficult, even harder than that—and if not on yourself, then on others. However, since it is a time of great curiosity, thought, consideration and science as you know it, your consequences will probably not go unnoticed by someone.

Because the planet Earth is at this profound level of mastery, seeking not the final level but a very deep level, the quantum mastery, that gives humans much more opportunity to experience at a depth that maybe they couldn't do anyplace else?

Exactly.

And also, when beings come here, they can never understand the electrical charge of the emotions combined with gravity. Is that also a result of the depth of the Earth's studies?

The physics of the person minus charges combined with physical effects is not part of quantum mastery. That is more a part of material mastery, and yet since Mother Earth has achieved material mastery, this is an ideal place to learn it.

Avoiding Time Complications

What about you and your fellow beings? You came here knowing it was a loop— you're outside of time and so you're experiencing this loop of time with us and with the Earth—and yet you're outside of it, right?

We're not exactly experiencing time. You can be in a time sequence and not be of it. This is how ships with beings inside can travel through time sequences without disturbing them, because they do not stake a claim. They do not embrace that time sequence. If they were to embrace each time sequence as they went through it, they would tear a hole in the fabric of that time, because the time would envelop them and they would become a portion of that time sequence. Their struggling, their motion to break out of it and pass through that into another time sequence would ultimately tear it, just as you would tear a piece of fabric.

The way to move from one time sequence to another is to not become attached or in any way involved with that time sequence. You must pass through it anonymously.

Observing but not . . .

No.

Oh, not even observing?

Not observing. By observing you will become involved, because it is in the nature of the observer to consider what he or she has observed, and that is involvement.

And that can influence what you saw?

It might, but more importantly it will connect the observer to the sequence. This is why when you see ships traveling at night, you see a streak of light moving with great speed across the sky. If it is moving slowly and is a vehicle from another planet, it has already become involved in your time. So how does such a vehicle—with observers inside looking out and looking at things—escape your time sequence? It must move away slowly, gradually building up speed. Ground observers— human beings—would say, "It moved away at a fantastic speed," but that fantastic speed is physical speed, which is not that fast.

In order to move through time when you are in time looking about, you then stop looking. The windows become opaque and you can no longer see out of them. You have a duty in the ship, which essentially moves your eyes from looking out to looking in. You are involved on the ship. If the ship does not require your behavior, then you lean back and close your eyes. You either think of home, so that you will not be attached to anything you saw in that physical environment that you were in, or you might be placed in an altered state by either some spiritual or mechanical means so that you release any and all attachment to the physical timeline and realm in which you had just been.

This is why the development of spacecraft takes time. It goes through an evolution because these discoveries are usually made slowly, and so the apparent fast speed of the ship as it leaves your environment is really quite slow compared to the speed that is required to move through time.

And that's why, when our secret government did their nasty abortive attempt to send people back in time, everyone died, because they didn't know what they were doing.

Yes, and it was essentially catastrophic. They were experimenting on the material level. Had they been experimenting on the quantum level, we would not be talking today, but they were experimenting on the material level. As such, the damage was done to material beings, the beings who had been drafted, if that's the word, in this project. Did you know that one of the people involved in this project at the decision-making level passed away not too long ago and has, for the past few years, still been going through the review of his life, because so many beings were affected?

And what will be the result of that be? Supposedly there is no karma anymore. Does he have to make any recompense, or is it just for him to understand and forgive himself?

It is not for me to say.

Unraveling Accidental Time Tangles

How does it work with these ET beings who go through the planet and do everything that you just said and are not affected, and then something happens to their craft and they crash to the Earth? Are they caught up in this whether they live or die? Are they put into the Earth cycle?

It can very well do that. It usually does put them into the Earth's cycle, and then the only way they can go home or resume their duties is to have a vehicle from their own environment, or perhaps an allied environment, come and pick them up. They sometimes will then be placed in a special chamber, and the chamber will be sequenced through various time cycles, meaning that it will be like traveling here and there.

It would be very much like untying an elaborate knot, if I might use the analogy, because of the complexity of the knot that must be untied. It would be like untying the Gordian knot. It is possible, but it must be done very carefully, and then individuals can be extracted. Most often they do not remember having crashed and it is not ever explained to them, so when it comes up, they might say "Where is so and so?" meaning if it was family or crew or friends who died in the crash, you would say, "They are no longer in this world."

If they pursue it, it can be very dangerous for their stability, and so they are gently reminded to let this go for now. When they come to the end of their natural cycle, it will be explained to them by their teachers, and it is done gently but firmly.

We know there have been many ET crashes on the Earth. That's where we got our technology. It was as if the Zetas and the other civilizations literally sacrificed themselves to give it to us.

This is not the only way you have gotten your technology, but it is certainly involved in many of the great leaps.

I mean fiber optics, the integrated chip, lasers, stealth technology, the pulse, the sonic pulse—I mean all of that. Right?

You must remember that if something is reverse engineered, it might or might not actually be . . .

What it was to start with.

That's right. Let's say you look at something and you say, "It seems to do this," and then to the best of your ability you take it apart and try to re-create it, utilizing what you have. You make it as close as possible to what you observed before, but what you have done is that you have re-created something that does what the first thing *seemed* to do.

It might not be what it really did. [Laughs.]

That's right. It might not have a great deal to do with its actual function, or it might be a very small portion of its capacity.

But even with that, it catalyzed incredible advances in our technology.

One of the main things it did was cause people to think in different directions.

Right. Don't think like a human.

Well, it was like a big shortcut, and it particularly affected electronics and technology first. Unfortunately, it has been very slow to affect the heart and soul, and this is entirely because the occupants who survived were kept isolated from the public. Had they been able to interact with the public—to communicate to the great thinkers of the time or the great religious people or any heart-centered people—the exchange of ideas, of ideals, of philosophies, would have had the same impact on the spirit and soul as it had on the industries that we have mentioned.

What a loss.

For the moment, yes, but it is not irretrievable. Certainly it's just a matter of time before such conversations take place. But to answer your question more fully, you cannot get caught, as it were, in the reincarnational cycle should you happen to crash land on a planet out of your time or out of your normal environment.

Oh, thank you. That's what I was concerned about. All right. How close to the end are we in terms of years? Are we close to the end of this loop of time?

Yes.

But it's not time. It's a point in dimensionality. It's when we reach something like the fifth dimension, right?

Let's not say that, because that creates a fixed precept. The real purpose, remember, was to see the consequences of the decision. Now you have been able to assimilate almost the entirety of and the entire complexity of the consequences, and as your friend Zoosh said some time ago, all of the consequences have been experienced at least once. So, as a result, it is now merely the journey back to that point that is involved and the opportunity to apply what you have learned on the way back.

You can reaffirm the knowledge to winnow out what you don't need to remember in order to decide, on the basis of the application of all that has been learned, what it is that would be good to permanently retain in your overall wisdom. As you know, things can be learned, but it is in the application of those things that one discovers whether that learning applies to many different situations, or if it is simply useful in a series of unique individual circumstances.

Hopefully, what we've learned will be the basis for wisdom in many, many areas?

Yes.

Several Planets Are Working on Quantum Mastery

How many or what percent of the planets are working on quantum mastery? Is this a rare thing that our planet is doing?

As far as I know today, there are three planets working on quantum mastery.

In this creation?

In this creation, yes.

Do the other two have translators like you?

I do not know.

Let's see . . . Ghi Da. Does she communicate with the other two? Is there communication?

No. When you communicate with a fellow student on something that you are all studying, it is natural to compare notes and to try things that the other individuals have tried. But other planets in other places are not experiencing anything like what Earth is experiencing here, and so Ghi Da does not do that, and I think it is right.

So what would lie ahead? You said that she would become a personality again once she had attained this. She could become a creator in her own right, then?

She is a creator now—in fact, if not in actual application—because of the nature of her influence on the beings who manifest here, but I understand what you are saying. Yes, she could if she chose, but she has not even discussed it. As a wise student, she knows it is better to pay attention to the lesson of the day.

It is better to do that than to think about the future?

Yes, exactly. Daydreaming about the future, you might miss something important. The future will be there.

Okay, I was just trying to get a feeling for how it worked. I think you see out pretty far. So there was some correlation between Ghi Da becoming this quantum master long before anybody knew about the Explorer Race. I mean, there was creation on two points and they came together. It was planned far ahead, wasn't it?

Say that again in another way.

If there is an overall plan, when our Creator saw the threads of this idea, was Ghi Da already moving toward the study of quantum mastery? In other words, these two things seemingly happened independently of each other, but I have a feeling they were connected at the beginning so that we would meet here.

In my understanding, nothing happens independently of anything else. Independence is a word with a definition, but it is not an experience at all.

Ah. Not reality. So it was two different streams when we started out that were sort of intended to meet?

Think about it this way. There are different streams all over the planet that become rivers and then lakes and then oceans, and yet if there was no water, would a stream even be relevant?

[Laughs.] You're pretty good.

[Chuckles.] I've had many such stories to listen to from the great master teachers. Often they speak this way, because the simple truth of it is so clear.

Quantum Teachers

That's interesting. Where did these quantum teachers learn? Was it from beyond this creation or . . . ?

In my experience, the only way to learn is either to come from something else that already knows and you reflect it, or to have learned by experience.

Which one, do you think? How many teachers are we talking about?

You will have to ask them yourself, but think of it—it is spiritual mastery, material mastery, teaching mastery, dimensional mastery, quantum mastery. How many is that? Five, yes.

Yes. No, I didn't mean how many levels. I mean how many quantum mastery teachers are here? Are we talking one or ten?

How many that I am aware of?

How many that you translate for, that you communicate for.

One. Think of it this way: If you are a quantum mastery teacher, and you did not inherit these skills and wisdoms, then to have attained quantum mastery you must have passed through all the other levels of mastery to attain quantum mastery, because one leads to the other and all benefit from each other.

And you don't know which route this master took that you indirectly . . . ?

It would be impolite to ask. For us, it would be impolite because it would present to the master a sense of qualification.

So there are only three planets in this system working on it. That means that there are three masters in this creation.

It does not mean that. It could mean that, but it could mean that there is one master who is . . .

. . . teaching all three.

Yes, of course.

If Ghi Da cannot communicate with the quantum master, I probably couldn't either, so . . .

You cannot be certain. I believe Ghi Da does not communicate with the quantum master directly, because the quantum master might in its vastness tend to overwhelm Ghi Da in her very specific orientation. Ghi Da is very dedicated to serving all those upon her, and in an inclusive way, other planets in this solar system as it expands out to the galaxy and so on.

So to be able to devote the singular attention that one must give to such a master might not be possible for Ghi Da. We listen to the master because we can. We can give the master singular attention, and then when we feel Ghi Da can absorb some of what the master has said in that moment or in various moments, we pass it on. So that is the way I see our mission of interpretation.

Earth's Soul in Our Bodies

That brings up something else that I just learned. It's my understanding that there is a part of her soul that comes into every human. Is that true?

Yes, it must be true, because your own soul must ensoul the physical body. And yet in order for your own soul to be able to communicate to the physical body, it must be able to communicate through a medium that is familiar or similar to its own form and substance. This is why a portion of Ghi Da's soul comes into each person, too: so that your immortal soul or immortal personality, as you friend says, has someone like us.

We are the intermediary for the master and Ghi Da, and Ghi Da's energy is the intermediary for your soul and the physical body in which you find yourself. So there is something that allows the physical body to have some connection to the immortal soul that occupies it, because if we simply put your immortal personality inside the physical Mother Earth body, your immortal personality—not in all cases, but in cases where the soul had never occupied an Earth physical body—would become frightened, upset and disoriented, and when a soul does that, it always immediately flees. Without any other soul in the physical body, it would die instantaneously.

But you know that when the body is developing inside each mother, the soul is not always in occupation. Sometimes it comes, sometimes it stays, and often it goes. What keeps the body from dying when it goes? That portion of Mother Earth's soul body that occupies Mother Earth's physical body inside the physical mother.

So our immortal personality then talks to the Earth's soul, and the Earth's soul talks to the physical body?

In the beginning, yes, and that connection is what you call the unconscious. Then in time you develop the subconscious. Once the subconscious link is in place, the immortal soul can communicate through its own means to the physical body.

The subconscious takes time to evolve. The subconscious develops during the first two years of physical life. The subconscious means that the soul, the immortal soul, your personality, develops its own avenue of connection to the physical self, and then even if the soul chooses to leave, such as in sleep time, that subconscious link acts as a cord, a root for the cord, and that root remains. As a result, if the body is frightened or awakened or something startles it or something good happens, immediately that will act as a cord and tug the soul back, and the soul rushes back to the body even if it has been traveling with its teachers.

What soothes the body and the subconscious anchor while the soul is traveling is that ever-present portion of Mother Earth's soul in each and every body. That is why when people, Earth humans, leave the Earth consciously, it is a strain for Mother Earth, because they take with them that portion of her soul. When that physical Earth person is away from the planet, Mother Earth has that much less of her soul that she can use, because when you are here, even with her soul in your body, she can still utilize it.

When you are here, you are like her children—you are a portion of her. But when you go off to another planet—as you will some day in space travel—it will be a strain, because that will be that much of her soul that is not readily available to her. She can use it; she can experience it if you are as far away as the moon or maybe Mars, but once you get past that point, you begin to leave her field of radiated energy and personality. So something will have to be done about that.

Is this only the experience on this planet, or is this true of every physical being on every planet?

It is not always the case on other planets, because on this planet one has such extreme lessons as a human being. One has to develop a subconscious to survive. Generally speaking, I'd say it is not a rule on other planets, although to a varying degree it might be true on a lesser basis, meaning not as much. But I would say that it is not the case on other planets as much as it is here, because of the extremes that are experienced by all participants here.

Okay, this is totally fascinating. How can we learn more, then? We have a piece of Mother Earth in us, and those combined pieces are what we call the unconscious of all humans. Is that true?

Not exactly, because the unconscious of all humans is made up of your immortal souls, or immortal personalities, as your friend says. It is made up of, yes, Mother Earth's ensouling of you, but it is also made up of the physical properties that she contributes to form your physical body. So the overall unconscious of all human beings on Earth is made up of all three.

Understanding the Subconscious

All right. Let's leave that for a minute and go to the subconscious, because no one on this planet has ever understood what the subconscious is. The soul, the immortal personality, comes into the body, and it takes a couple of years, you said, to create this subconscious. Is that right?

It takes a couple of years for the soul to get used to communicating directly with the physical substance in which is residing the soul, yes—that physical substance being Mother Earth's body. The soul is used to communicating with a physical body, say on another planet, where there is total harmony. In this way, the soul can instantaneously communicate with the substance of its physical body, because the body is in the same harmony as the soul.

But when you come here to Earth, because harmony is not as much of a factor here—because of polarity and the lessons to be learned with polarity—the soul does not immediately communicate with the physical body, and thence the portion of Mother Earth's soul is necessary to act as an intermediary communicant. In this way, over a couple of years, the soul gradually builds up a pathway that is comfortable to that individual and unique soul, and all pathways might be slightly different to connect that soul to that unique and special physical body. That is the subconscious.

The subconscious then is something that is associated with the soul connection to the physical body, and it involves spirit, physicality, feelings . . . and possibly (only possibly, and this develops beyond the age of two) instinct, meaning the body's messages that are understood by the soul before the mind, if the mind has not been exposed to a culture that teaches instinct (that's why I say possibly).

So the connection, the representation of the subconscious, is spiritual, feeling—as you say, emotional—and physical, but the subconscious is not mental, and that is an irony. The mind that you now utilize does not access the subconscious as a portion of itself, because the subconscious is not in its own right mental, and that is why the mind cannot readily access it. The mind can only access that which is mental. That is why the subconscious has been such an elusive goal to those who are functioning in the mental capacity, because the subconscious is more spiritual, physical and feeling, and it is not mental at all.

Why was it planned that way?

It was planned that way so that the physical beings could survive and thrive while the soul was out doing its lessons at night during the sleep state (or whenever you are in the sleep state), because the mind is at rest when you are sleeping and does not actually do anything. The soul's travels take place on the spiritual level. The only time that the mind is active during the sleep cycle is when the soul is coming back into the body and one is waking up. Then the mind begins to apply its understanding of life—that which has accumulated up to that time in that person's life—to the spiritual lessons learned.

That is when the application of that person's personal experience takes place onto the soul experience and one gets what are called dream symbols. A dream symbol, you understand, might not be just a curious symbol but might be a whole story that one remembers. The story itself might not be in any way what the soul was doing, but it would be the mind's best interpretation on a sequential level . . .

Of what it understood?

Of what it understood the soul's experience to be.

Which means it's not even close.

Yes, but sometimes it is remarkably close if the person has lived a life of great interest, if the person has been pursuing, for instance, certain lessons that they have been working on for a time or if the person is perhaps reasonably well educated—not necessarily in reading, but that's one possibility—or well educated through experience. All of these things take time within an individual life, and as the life goes on, the interpretation of the dream becomes easier, based on the greater experience of the individual.

The Role of Earth's Soul

So, as the soul can communicate with the subconscious after two years of age, what is the rule of the Earth's soul?

It remains in the body, even when the body is at rest.

And the soul is gone?

Yes, because Mother Earth can utilize it because you are here on Earth. If she needs it, she can readily utilize it, even if you are awake. Although she can utilize it, she will not usually utilize it if you are awake during the first two years of life here, because of the need for the individual.

Let's say we're at rest and she needs that portion of her soul; how does she utilize it? It still stays connected to the human, right?

It still stays connected to you, but since you're physically made up of her body, and to some extent the soul connection is there, it is just very easy. Because you are connected to her and she is connected to you, she utilizes it. I cannot describe it any more than that. It would be as if—how can we say?—you are utilizing something remotely.

So that is why and how it is connected? To our emotions? To just our physical self? What is the connection of the Earth soul?

I do not understand the question.

You said our subconscious was connected to the physical, the spiritual and the emotional, but not the mental. So how is the Earth's soul connected into the human? To what levels of us? To the physical?

I see. The Earth's soul is connected to your soul, yes, to your feelings, yes, to your physical self, yes, and to your instinctual self, whether you are utilizing it or not, but to a greater extent if you have been trained instinctually . . . yes.

But not to the mind?

No. The mind is always and only a student and must remain free and independent to make choices based upon its understanding of truth, or as it does sometimes, to make capricious choices.

So what that also means is that we are prepared for our opening to vertical wisdom when we can really use our instinct and our feelings, and the mind leaves?

Yes, because the mind, as you know, is not of your true nature. As it is gradually withdrawn to Andromeda, where they will assimilate it in its new role because of your processing of it, then you will gradually be returned to your capacity of vertical wisdom, which your friend has explained clearly, I believe.

But the profound implication, then, is that the Earth herself feels everything—all the drama, the trauma, the suffering, the agony that every human feels.

Yes, but without the mental, the linear mental understanding (or lack of understanding) of each individual, because there is no connection to the mind. So when you feel happiness, she shares that also.

Ah, the joy, the wonder, the glory.

Yes, she shares it.

Communicating with the Earth

So how can we communicate more deeply with her, then? When we walk on the land, is that her soul touching herself through us?

Yes. One of the best ways is the teaching of such things. The older cultures know that the old truths must be taught. Then, when dramas occur to those cultures, sometimes new stories are added and associated with those dramas, such as wars and conflicts, and the old truths are forgotten. The best way is to teach the old, simple truth that you are made up of Earth and immortal soul and that you each completely affect each other. No one is outside of that circuit.

Make up stories with that as a theme. Teach the children. When they learn, they will catch themselves when they get enraged about something and say, "Oh, I will have to do some dance or something to dissipate that, to transform that energy, and then I will feel better and I won't pass that on to my friends around me—to the animals, to the plants, to Mother Earth, to anyone. It is my responsibility to transform it." Teach them how to do this with dance. Don't teach them how to think about it and control it. That does not work.

The physical body is the transformer. It can transform discomfort. You are as physical as you are and so you can utilize it, and that's why all the old cultures dance vigorously. Modern societies have transformed that into graceful dancing, which is fine: It is beauty if you are feeling beautiful. But if you are feeling violent, there must be a form of violent dance that is not harmful to you or others but is vigorous in its very nature. It is not doing specific steps, but the steps are expressed by you, not unlike interpretive dance, and in this way your physical body and its motions physically transform the discomfort in your body just the same way that motions and elements work within Mother Earth's body to transform her discomforts, such as a volcano or an earthquake. It is the motion of various elements that transforms on the physical level. That is a true law of physical creation.

I don't know how we got to where we are, but I love it. We started out talking about UFOs and ETs. [Chuckles.]

It is as good a place to begin as any.

All right. There's another level here. The Explorer Race will be leaving at some point, but the former Sirian beings from the Sirius star system on 3.0 will be here for another round or another period of time. Is that correct?

Yes.

So then you will be working with them, too?

Yes, especially with the children, who will like our form, and the parents will probably want to hear our stories and songs. So we hope to inspire them in some gentle and humorous way.

Oh, how wonderful.

People develop mythology not to confuse or upset but rather to explain the simple truths in a way that can be remembered and passed on and created upon in order to be delightful. It is much easier to remember a story than it is a fact.

But isn't it something that was real on this planet at some time, behind what we call myth? Or on some planet?
Not behind every myth, but many. Sometimes you have to distill the myth back to its point of origin, and this is not always possible, and so you have to do the next best thing.

Which is . . .
Make your best guess.

But with beings like you, we could trace the myths back?
Perhaps.

Accessing the Subconscious through Dance

How do we access them? Included in your description of physical movement is not just movement but tones, making sounds. Singing, right?
Yes.

That's part of transforming physical energy? Is that separate?
Nothing is separate, but if you are doing the dance, whatever form it takes, and you are making sounds, that is acceptable, but it is not an alternate means, no.

Well sometimes, if you just let your body make sounds, it seems to be a very freeing thing.
It might be. It might be as well.

A transformative work.
It might be. It won't transform in its own right, but it might be comforting. It might do other things. Transformation really requires the vigorous use of your body to the extent that you can. If you cannot move anything but a finger, then move it vigorously.

All right. How do we access our subconscious? I know you said instinct evens the body out, yet . . .
Access your subconscious by being physical and coming to understand what your physical feelings mean in your body. If you feel that heat, as your friend says, this is love. This is where to begin. If you are angry, how does your physical body feel? Notice it so that if the feeling

comes up, you'll know what it is. When it comes up, you can say, "Oh, that's anger." Not everybody in your culture knows when he or she is angry. They just know that they are upset and they don't know what it is. They try to pretend it's not there. Anger is there to stimulate physical action—not to strike another but to do your dance of physical transformation, whatever form that takes. In some way it is benevolent for yourself and others, but it might be very vigorous.

Try to do it out on the land if you can, but if you are not able, try to do it when you are alone someplace. This way the energy will be transformed by your physical actions. Move out and away from your body, and when you are done—when you stop, when you feel done—your body will still be so vigorously involved in the physical action that it will still continue to radiate energy. You will feel it. You will be hot, sweating. You will radiate energy and you will not take that old stuff back in.

If you are around other people, however, and they are not dancing, the best way to do it is out on the land, as long as you are fifty feet away from other people who walk on the land. If you cannot go out on the land, then try to do it in the best way you can. Just do the best you can. That's all you can do. If others are close to you and you can do nothing about it, then before you begin, ask as a prayer that they be unaffected by your discomforts and that they be safe. Do you understand?

But I'm interested in accessing the subconscious—that's the part of us that our teachers talk to, our guides talk to, or let's say, communicate with, right?
What part?

The subconscious?
No.

What part do they communicate with?
Your soul.

And then the soul communicates to the subconscious to the body?
Yes.

Ah, that's it. Got it.

Joao and the Andromedans

Zoosh

January 24, 1999

*T**his is a Wendelle Stevens book about a contact in Botucatu, Brazil: UFO...* **Abduction at Botucatu.**

Ask about only what you know about. That way you have a personal interest. Your interest, as you recall, has everything to do with what I can respond to. Say something about the case.

Contact in Botucatu

All right. His name is Joao Valerio da Silva. The first time he was picked up, he went out in the backyard to get a glass of water, and he was taken up into a ship in what he called an elevator of light. There was a man there who was totally covered, except for openings for his eyes and his mouth. Joao was taken into a room, where he had his clothes removed and was covered with an oily substance. A woman came in, and evidently he passed out and they had intercourse. When he was delivered back down by the water tank, unconscious, he had marks on his chest and on his penis—particular symbols.

This is the famous case of the farmer. No?

He was a porter in a hospital.

No, this is different then. Do you have a drawing of the marks?

When the guy was killed, a lot of the evidence was wiped out. Here's a picture of the man and his family. Right here. [See Figure 21.1.]

What about the marks? How are they described?

Figure 21.1: Da Silva with his family.

The marks the being wrote were recorded on a piece of paper.

That would be useful.

We'll get to the marks, but here is a picture of the being, Rama, supposedly on the planet that Joao was taken to.

What is the picture?

On the top. It is just very indistinct. [See Figure 21.2.] It was a cheap, borrowed cam-era. But he took this picture

Figure 21.2: Photograph of Rama on his home planet, taken by da Silva with a disposable camera.

of the being who was contacting him and brought it back. They gave him a physical sample of a crystal that would heal people. This is their language. [See Figure 21.3.] Joao took a note up and said, "Give me something physical so I can prove it," and the being wrote, in orange fluorescent ink, those symbols on the back of the note that Joao took up.

I have seen this writing before. [Long pause.]

[Aside.] It is all right to talk about this now. Don't be frightened. It is all right. I will protect him. You want him back? Certainly. Don't be shy about asking in the future. Okay, thank you.

What was that?

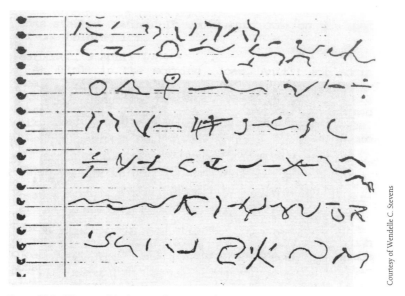

Figure 21.3: Writing of the beings who contacted Joao da Silva.

Rescue of a Trapped Being

My associate was bringing something to my attention. It had to do with this: The being, one of the beings from this place, did not want me to talk about this, because one of the being's people was trapped on Earth. So I said that I would protect that being, and the being was still afraid. So I said, "Did you want that person back?" And the being said yes. So I managed to get that person back and then I told the being, "Don't be shy about asking about such things in the future." So now we can talk about it and there is not that anticipation. My associate here [indicates Tiger, the cat] mentioned to me that there was some energy here that was uncomfortable and then that the energy was more so outside. And that's how I traced it back to the . . .

. . . to the book. See, I was thinking he wanted to go outside.

Yes, and so you notice that he's quiet now. He's quiet. He said, "Pay attention."

We need a full-time cat patrol here.

Cats can bring things to one's attention that one may not notice. They are vigilant about circumstances.

[To Tiger.] Thank you, Tiger. [To Zoosh.] And how did you turn the guy free? You sent him back already?

Yes, that is done.

That's . . . pretty fast.

Universal Symbols of Greeting

All right. We will speak of this. The writing is important, less for what it says—which is just "Greetings," essentially—than for the fact that you can find this writing all over the world written automatically and spontaneously by many people. This symbol is not uncommon [points to the symbol]. Granted, it bears a striking similarity to . . .

An upside-down Y.

Yes, but there is some connection to the Chinese language.

Third from the end. An upside-down Y with a mark on each side.

Yes, it is bottom line, third one in from the right as you read from right to left. The other symbols are seen constantly. One can see symbols reminiscent to handwritten Hebrew here.

They say that in there, and they speculate that possibly that civilization came here before the Hebrew language and kept their version of the language pure, while on Earth it has evolved.

One famous contact, as you know, was with a farmer in the United States who was contacted by ETs who helped him to find water on his land. From that point on, the farmer flew an Israeli flag. His neighbors asked, "Why are you flying that flag?" And he said, "It's the closest thing I could find to the symbol they were wearing." A famous, well-known story.

We'll find it someplace.

Find that one and we'll talk about that. So this race of beings were not directly related to the ones who contacted the farmer I referred to, but there is a similarity. The main thing, the striking thing about the print, is that the spontaneous writing done by many channels and sensitives—and even children who make up writing or codes—is very often based in this writing. It is almost like a universal translator. And that's why I want it reproduced in your book. It is an interesting thing. If you look at the writing again . . .

This is a tracing. Here's the actual energy of the photography, of the pictures. It doesn't show up very well. It was like it faded.

Look at it closely. Can you not see that each line is different and distinct unto its own right? Look at it. The interesting thing is this: one, two, three, four, five, six. It is not one language. It is six languages, and it says, essentially, "Greetings, brothers," or "Greetings, fellow citizens," depending upon the nuance.

So each line is a different language?

Each line is a different language. But the languages are representing the dialects of nearby planets and people with whom the being is associated.

He thinks that we might be able to read one of these or something?

Well, the being wrote that down because he wanted to show people on the Earth that there is a similarity in many of the spontaneous writings that one often sees. Even in doodles that people do . . . doodles, do they still call them that?

Yes. [Chuckles.]

You will find some of these symbols. So that's important. This is an important case.

Massive Amounts of Contact in Brazil

Okay. He was contacted over forty-two times during the couple of years covered in this information. I mean, the abductions could be ongoing now. This information is from 1982–1984 until the person who was the connection between Wendelle Stevens and Joao died, and then there was no longer any way to communicate.

The being who gave his name to the contactee . . . did he say where he was from?

No, there is no information. He said that the woman with whom he had the relationship—and they only mentioned this in the first contact—looked just like a human, but she had rounded eyebrows like a human, and the two men who were also on the ship had straight eyebrows. He said that Rama (the one who talked to him) had a turban like an East Indian. These two beings came from that planet, and they said that not only Joao but also his sixteen-year-old son were "their people." He was taken to their home planet, and he stayed there for eighteen hours once, which was three days there. They gave him artifacts. He developed psychokinetic and healing powers. And he said that once he saw other humans onboard the ship, but they were kept apart and he didn't get to talk to them.

You know, this is a really important contact, because we have here a group of beings from one of the planets in the Andromeda galaxy who often come to Brazil to land or to visit. There have been many, many contacts of other individuals as well, but this individual managed to document the contacts, which is rare.

He had family, wife, friends—all kinds of witnesses.

There has been a really massive amount of contact in Brazil, especially in the interior, that has not really come out too much to the West, or to Europe for that matter, but is well known in Brazil. And the people there, being open and profoundly spiritual, are quite accepting of such phenomena. So I think the most important thing is to know, for starters, that the Andromedans are involved here. And the function of the Andromedans, as they see themselves (at least as they saw themselves during this time), was to contact and to support émigrés, as in emigrants. They would see the souls of humans, as with Joao and others, as being from their people, not only because of the reincarnational cycle but also because some of Joao's genetic makeup was leaning a little more heavily toward the Andromedan.

This is suggestive and tells you that, in truth, there was some contact with previous generations. This is going to allow this man's family, who are still in existence (and I am speaking somewhat discretely here) to not only have gifts, talents and abilities but, because of the profound level or frequency of contact and residual radiation—not atomic radiation but benevolent radiation left behind all over in Brazil—is going to support the continuing growth of spirituality in Brazil. I have said sometimes that Brazil will be a profound spiritual Mecca in the future on this planet, and this is just another one of the reasons.

So Andromedans can look like humans, then? Because some Andromedans have been five feet tall, almost like large Zetas. They have many different races, then?

Yes. Think about it, not only your own solar system, but your own galaxy. There are multiple races in this galaxy. When you think about the distance . . . your scientists have managed to speculate where you are in your own galaxy. Yet just utilizing your Sun as the point of your origin, not even including the planets, gives you a pretty fair idea of the vast amount of planets in your own galaxy. So the idea of variance of appearance is statistically, to say nothing of in reality, most probable. Even on your own planet, you have variations of the human race—different cultures and different appearances. Of course, that is largely because different races and cultures from other planetary sources have . . .

. . . contributed.

Contributed. [Chuckles.] Such a nice word.

The Creation of a Special Child

So who was Rama? There were two men onboard, and the woman. There may have been many more, but that's what he saw. What were they doing here? Are they traveling cultural anthropologists?

Rama is a being who could best be described in Earth terms as a linguist, meaning someone who is most intrigued with the cultural roots and histories of languages and the common denominators of language, which is a trait found in linguists all over. This is part of the reason for the deliverance of a note that suggests a similar greeting in all these different languages.

This was not done by accident. If one looks at your own spacecraft, the one that was sent out into space with a record on it—with greetings in all these different languages—one finds a distinct similarity. So this idea of speaking to the people of the Earth in their own resonance—meaning their desire to be appreciated in their infinite variety—speaks, if you will, to the hearts of all beings.

All right. What was the purpose of their coming to see Joao?

Their intention seemed to be a bit blunt or crass, but part of the reason for the spreading of the substance on Joao's body is that human sweat has an acidic quality to it. This is why in horticulture—and in certain other botanical pursuits, to say nothing of biological pursuits—sometimes the workers in this field will wear gloves, because of the impact of human sweat upon other living tissues. So the oily substance was to protect the other person.

They told him that it was a disinfectant.

Yes, it could be considered that too, but it was also to protect them. The sexuality is something that . . . they knew that, if they had asked Joao to do this on his own, being a family man he would not have cooperated. And because the culture they were attempting to create a hybrid of was having some problems with adapting on the physical level to altered conditions on their planet, the Andromedans—not unlike the Zeta Reticulans in this case, but with a little more finesse, perhaps—started going out to various planets, not only to Earth but to other places where they felt there were connections—such as with Joao—where they could wind up with more than DNA. Because the Andromedans are not as advanced in genetics as the Zeta Reticulans, they do not clone—at least, that particular culture does not. But the actual bodily fluids and the touch, the contact, would make impregnation possible for them. So the beings onboard hoped that they could create a stronger strain of these particular beings by including the Earth person's genetics through this method.

You know, it is interesting, as a sidebar here, that physical contact, especially in a loving matter (but this was not that way, because Joao was not exactly present) has everything to do with the creation of a special child. Now I want to also say that the being who was produced as a result of their particular contact did in fact have the qualities that they were looking for. What they were looking for was a profound immune system. The planet, which was going through problems, was experiencing somewhat of a breakdown in its normal radiation belt, a belt such as Earth has, one that protects from overdoses of the radiation that exists in space. As a result, people were becoming sick.

The breakdown and the influence of these extraplanetary radiations would be insignificant on the Earth—not much different from a very mild form of infrared like sunlight. For you, it would be the mildest sunburn, but for them, it could possibly contribute to death. The reason that you can survive sunburn in a mild state (and even in a major state) is because you have a strong immune system that defeats the toxic reaction within your own physical body to this particular injury. They did not have that system in place, so they needed genes from individuals who had such a system. Joao's genetics had . . . not a preponderance of Andromedan genes, but more than average for an Earth person. The average Earth person has some; he had more—not a lot more, but just enough. They hoped it would create greater compatibility, which was true.

So the result of this would be a being who is sixteen years old now in our time, and in their time far older?

Not really important. In terms of Earth years, about sixteen, but I don't think that they keep track of years in the same way that you do.

Well, he said that he was there for eighteen hours, and there were three nights.

Time is just different there. I don't think that this is too critical. We can go into the math if you wish.

No, I'm just wondering if he was in an altered state? Are they in the same time that we are?

The planet rotates at a different speed.

It must rotate really fast.

It's smaller. If the planet is smaller—you understand the mathematics? If something is smaller and it rotates even a little faster, you are likely to have quicker days and nights.

Of course. Three nights at eighteen hours seems really fast. [Chuckles.]

Of course, the fact that this planet is part of a trinary star system might make a difference too, but they are not all scattered about evenly. The suns are in various places, but at any given moment they tend to cover maybe a quadrant or perhaps one third of an elliptical slice, as it were, of the planet.

I didn't know there were triple suns. How many suns can you have at one time?

I don't think there's a limit, but most people like to experience a little night. Night is good for you. Very good. Night contributes to the immune system. Night is a time in which you must adapt to the unknown, and through various succeeding generations, all this adaptation to the unknown—individuals going through their primal fears and then discovering that they are all right through various adaptations, survival techniques or coming together into civilizations—tends to have an effect on the immune system on a cumulative basis, meaning generation by generation. One finds that planets where there is day and night generally produce people who are stronger and more vital.

Other Beings on the Ship

That's interesting. Were there many more people on this ship than those Joao saw?

Yes, there were quite a few more. One does not necessarily see vast amounts of people. You don't have to.

He was just in one small room.

He was in one part.

Or two rooms. So every time he was picked up, they were attempting to create a pregnancy?

No. Not every time.

Just sometimes.

Occasionally. Not even that often. Just occasionally. They were wanting to respect his family status, but they felt that the need was pressing, and given the overall (if I might use the term) humanitarian cause, I think that Joao would agree today that it was a worthy cause. It's just that when one is married and devoted, one feels outraged. So they just tried to soothe his feelings and say that it was all right without going into any great explanation, because they did not want to overly complicate or burden his life with what I might call exquisite details—exquisite meaning, in this case, very specific details, many and varied.

Is he alive at this moment?
The man may be alive.

Let's get back to these beings. They are linguists?
Not all of them.

What are the rest of them?
Different jobs, different performances. Needless to say, a linguist does not make a good pilot.

So how many people were on this craft, roughly?
It was not a very big ship.

This is supposed to be a drawing of it right here [see Figure 21.4]. I didn't show you that.
Did Joao describe its size?

I thought he said that it was like a two-story building. It's a very rough drawing.
No, these are quite good drawings—very good and has been seen also in other places. The bell-like structures underneath have been noticed elsewhere—definitely a correlation to an older type of Pleiadean craft and an older type of Zeta Reticulan craft, having to do with the form of a gravity device that turns on and off, allowing the ship to navigate planetary magnetic fields.

I'd say that there were probably anywhere from nine to eleven people on board who were crew or people who came on the ship. But at any given moment, there may have been a few others on the ship who were also from Earth—probably from Brazil, but possibly from Peru and Columbia as well. Not much has been said so far about Columbian ET contacts, but there have been many.

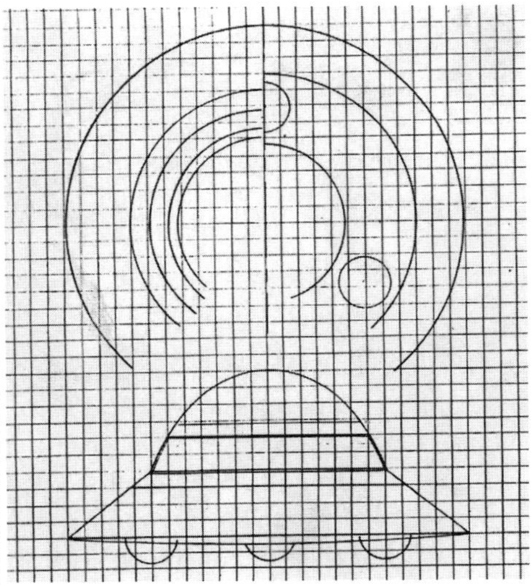

Preparation to Help Others

But their primary purpose in coming here and bringing, not just that one woman, but probably several women . . . They said six other humans were contacted in a similar way. He saw some of them at one time.
Yes, but it was never done

Figure 21.4: Drawing of the Andromedan craft that transported da Silva.

Courtesy of Wendelle C. Stevens

traumatically, or at least it was not intended to be done traumatically. I grant that, at certain times, an extreme lack of sophistication was shown.

Their basic purpose in coming and bringing the ship here was to help these particular humans on this planet—what do you call them? Humans? Andromedans?

I wouldn't call them humans, no. Let's just call them Andromedans, because they are in the Andromeda galaxy.

All right. To help their fellow Andromedans on this one beleaguered planet?

Beleaguered—a good word.

They took Joao—just to this point, from 1982 to 1984—they took him forty-two times, and they showed him movies, like we have heard before, of the destruction of the planet, which was supposed to begin in 1985. But humans changed that reality, and so that did not happen, right?

> Look and see what you have been able to accomplish, simply by your conscious use of spirituality, prayer, manifestation, unconscious benevolent magic and—for some of you—conscious benevolent magic. You can change things. This film or this diorama (whatever you want to call it), this example of history that was shown was real. Why do you think that over the years many Earth people have had visions of destruction? Because these parallel histories, these potential histories, exist. You have just chosen to pursue a more benevolent line—even though you could argue that what you are experiencing now is not so benevolent. But you are waking up, and many of you have been working long and hard to do things that are benevolent for the planet and her peoples, all her peoples. Look and see what you have done.

Beautiful. They also told Joao many, many things that he couldn't tell anyone. So all the other times they picked him up were just . . . what? To give him knowledge? To prepare him for something?

It was to prepare him, to give him gifts that he could use to help others, to encourage him to teach people and share his experiences and make up stories in order to tell the children (which he did anyway). In short, it was to encourage him to spread a certain degree of universal spirituality and to encourage people to become more courageous, less frightened and ultimately more inclusive. And some of it was just personal stories.

Granted, he was not spoken to by Andromedans all the time, so he might have heard other stories too, of other places. This is not atypical of such missions; there were people from other planets and even other galaxies on the ships, but nobody from Zeta. I think that they could have benefited from having a small crew—which was offered from Zeta Reticuli—but they felt that the Zeta Reticulans, even though they are a good people, looked sufficiently different from Earth people that it might cause undue fear, and they were attempting to minimize that impact.

Why did Rama wear this outfit that covered him all up, except two slits for his eyes and his mouth?

Strictly for protection. It wasn't to disguise himself so much as to protect himself, not unlike what a surgeon might wear in an operating theater. One might reasonably ask why they wear so much stuff. It was to some extent to promote sterility—meaning, one does not project one's own energy or microbes onto the person one is studying or interacting with.

In this case, he would be protecting himself from the human?

Yes, but also there was a degree of not wanting to *taint the subject*, as it were.

The Andromedan Lifestyle

Let's see, what else did he say? He took a picture. [See Figure 21.5.] They lived in stone houses and they didn't sleep. They disappeared at night.

What they would do at night is not unlike sleep, but it would be a form of meditation that is very deep. They would become so focused in this meditation that they would not be visible or even tangible. There are some people on Earth who can be unseen, who are born on the Earth. This is often found in more shamanic techniques. There are even some who have learned how to be unfelt. That is not as common, but on their world, it is common.

The purpose of this, of course, is to not only experience full soul renewal, but also to allow one's substantive self, or one's physical self, to experience a total blending with one's surroundings so that one not only experiences one's surroundings as a part of oneself, but also so the surroundings (the houses, you understand) experience the people as a part of them. So there is complete harmony—a technique I would recommend.

To all humans?

Not to all humans, but to many humans to try.

This is the picture that he took of the house.

A moment. [Pause.] Yes, this is a well-known picture, often thought to be a picture of a ship, but one can see something here on top. If you look at the thing on top, there is essentially an artwork, a sculpture. Here's the face. You can see the face. Can you see the face?

Family Appearances

Yes, and here's Rama too. This is the being.

The face is not unlike another famous face.

The sphinx.

Yes, very good. What else? But the sphinx, you understand, is not really an accurate thing, because the sphinx was originally a cat and was changed into being a man.

Mars?

There you are. Also, this is not unlike the famous face in Sedona, the one that looks toward the sky. You see it only from a side view, but it is profoundly there.

What is it named? I don't know about that one.

It is down in the Village of Oak Creek. I think that you call it Courthouse Rock.

Oh, I've looked at it many times, but I didn't know there was a face . . .

Next time you drive past it, notice that there is a face looking toward the sky. This is the traditional term for the place.

Figure 21.5: Photograph taken by da Silva on the Andromedan home planet featuring Rama and some Andromedan structures.

Courtesy of Wendelle C. Stevens

Is this round thing over here the spacecraft? He says that that is the actual craft.

Yes, that looks like it.

He got the house and the Andromedan and the craft all in one picture, which is pretty good with a cheap camera.

That's the intent, you know. The real trick—notice the radiated effect there—was for Rama to keep from projecting the usual amount of energy that he might normally project. Spiritual people on Earth have been photographed many times, and sometimes there will be light phenomena around these people, but if your energy on another planet were used to being totally free, it would be much more powerful than that. It would be ranging out, and it would immediately impact the film. Rama was making an attempt to hold his energy, which was not entirely successful because it was an unnatural thing for him to do. But it was fairly successful in that much detail still showed up in the picture.

This is perhaps one of the best pictures on Earth at this time of another planet—a picture not only of the ship, but of the dwelling and the occupants of the planet, and of the dwelling and the art on top of the house. The picture depicts not only the general appearance of the beings who live there, but also the look of the family. You see this in your own families. You can say, "Oh, those Swansons. You can tell them all. They have the Swanson look. He's a Swanson; she's a Swanson. You can tell." It is that sense. But one of the most profound things is the picture of the ship. This ship has been photographed various other places on Earth, but this is the best picture available.

So will we run across other contacts that Rama and his crew (or others from Andromeda) have met?

You will probably run into others from Andromeda.

What dimension are these people normally in?

Right around dimension five, but the humans that are taken there are—how can we say—there is something connected to them in order to allow them to function there.

To function in 5.0, yeah. And what about the women from the planet that they are trying to help? Were they 5.0 too?

They are in dimension four.

And four and three simultaneously in that sense? Are these dimensions compatible, then?

They can be under certain circumstances. It requires very specific conditions.

They were able to create these conditions on these crafts?

Yes. It would not have been possible to create those conditions on this planet or on the other planet. It would have had to be done in an artificial environment, not unlike a laboratory on your planet.

And they had such an artificial environment on the ship.

Yes.

Okay. This is a small planet, but are there many, many planets of these beings? Do they have a one-planet culture, or are they part of a vast community of planets?

I would not say that it is particularly vast. They might have their linear ancestors spread out over two or three planets, but no more than that.

So this would be like a colonization from an original planet someplace?

Which would be?

The beings on the planet that Rama was on?

No, that would have been the original planet.

I've gotten you confused. The ones they were helping were colonies of theirs?

No.

Just someone who asked for help?

Somebody from the Andromedan star system asked for help, yes— someone they could help.

Lifespan and Governmental Structure

So these beings are in 5.0. What kind of civilization do they have? How long do they live? What kind of government do they have?

One question at a time—or you can ask as many questions as you want, and I will only answer one. [Chuckles.] Their life span might run anywhere from two hundred and fifty to seven hundred years, depending upon what they do, and this is not unusual. One might draw comparisons on the Earth. One might say that people working at hard labor on the Earth do not always live as long as those who have an easier life where they have medical services available to them. But rather than trying too hard to make a stretched comparison, I'd say that it generally has to do with what they do in life.

So what do the ones who live longer do, versus those who live shorter lives?

The ones who live longer usually have philosophical jobs: teaching or accumulation of wisdom for the purpose of application to their own culture, or to other cultures who ask for their assistance. The sages or wise ones have life spans that are not unlike what is reported in your own Bible, indicating that so-and-so lived seven hundred years.

And the ones who don't live as long?

They have other duties to do. They might be involved in many other activities. It is not specific. There is not a hard and fast answer.

There is just that kind of range, then.

It is kind of a range, yes.

In the sense of what's out there that we might run into, do they manifest what they need? Do they manufacture their craft or are they at the stage of calling the particles together?

As you can tell from by how they were creating this mating with Joao and others, their technology is not terrifically advanced. I'd say that it is perhaps a thousand years ahead of your own, and yet it is not just technology. Remember, their homes are made of natural substances on the planet, and when he said rock, he didn't say "formed rock" or "cut rock" or "cast rock." He said "rock," which meant the rock in its original state. This tells you something—people who can fly about in spaceships and yet use natural rock to create their houses. It tells you that they are a spiritual people. So they are very advanced spiritually, and they are by their very nature what you might call shamanic. In this way, I cannot say that they are thousands of years ahead of you, since you have shamanic people on the planet right now. But that is the way I am choosing to say it.

Do they have a representative government, or—since they can do this advanced meditation—do they just . . . ?

Governments exist to maintain control (because of anarchistic conditions that create problems) and to create organizational systems to distribute or redistribute wealth and services. That's what governments exist for. They do not require that. So they exist in units or even at times larger groups that we might call enclaves, but I would say that they do not have government as you know it. The closest thing they might have to a government would be their scholastic system: not the teaching of their children so much, but the acquiring of knowledge and wisdom for the good of all—such as these individuals who had a problem and said, "We have this problem. Can you help us?" Most places on most other planets, if you go there and say, "We have this problem. Can you help us?" will either help you to the best of their abilities or they will direct you to where you can get that help. Granted, that's largely because they don't have the many distractions you have here on Earth, but it is the natural way to be. Many people on Earth know this and perform in this way as well.

When does government cease to be, then? At the beginning of the fourth dimension? In the middle?

Government in general, you mean?

Government as we know it, in the way you've just described it.

You cannot ascribe it to dimensions or even times. Generally, it falls away from societies as they become either more sacred (and in this I do not refer to religion) and/or more naturalistic, meaning highly involved with the world around them in a harmonic way (not referring to music specifically, but rather "harmonic" meaning a general state of harmony with all life). At that point, there is no need for a governing body. What I'm saying is that you do not have to wait until you get to the fourth dimension for government to become unnecessary.

So are Rama and his crew still coming to Earth? How long does this project go on?

The project went on until about 1987, and most of the people taken up, as I said, were from Brazil and Peru, with a few from Columbia. Another ship made a brief mission to Portugal, but that mission didn't last very long because there was a great deal of military establishment in and around that area and it was difficult to get in and out discreetly.

So is going out to other planets something that this group, including Rama, does regularly? Or was it just a mission to help these people?

It was a singular mission. It isn't what they do all the time. Needless to say, if they did it on a regular basis, they would have found a way to utilize the talents of the Zetas, because the Zetas are known all over for their capacity to efficiently work with genetics. If the Zetas had been along, it might have taken less time for the project, and it might have been able to be done—how can we say?—in some ways more benevolently. Nevertheless, one does things in the way one feels is best. This is not to be considered a criticism; it is just by way of saying . . . that this is not what Rama does for a living, how is that? Not that you have to do anything for a living there.

Had he been away from the planet before, then? Was this his first venture out?

No, he had gone out before.

What is he doing now?

I think that he is in meditation—what you would call study, but what they would call meditation. It is a quiet time of reflection. He is still in telepathic contact with some of the people he picked up, so there is that communication. He is studying what he has learned, studying related fields that correlate to what he learned in his contacts. He is correlating linguistics, of course, and has a secondary interest in similarities of culture. So it is a sabbatical, one might say.

Is he able, from his planet, to telepathically contact Joao if he so chose?

Yes.

So we don't know anything about what happened to Joao with all this investment of energy in him. Did he go out and talk to groups? He was a porter in a hospital when this started, and then he was out of work because his back hurt.

Well, let's just say that he was given enough so that he could speak to people, especially if the people were interested and wanted to know. And in Brazil, as I say, there isn't this shyness about the topic, because the people have not been taught that ETs don't exist. There is not the political, religious or cultural "crimping" of the subject matter. I don't want to sound like I'm blaming religion, but I'm equating it to this political nonsense that claims, "It can't be, therefore it isn't," and is practiced dogmatically as if it were a religion. This attitude, as it exists in this country, was one of those mistakes that are often made in military situations or political situations. But more often one finds these mistakes in military situations where the people who follow along afterward grit their teeth and try and live with it. It was a terrible mistake in the beginning to keep it a secret.

Here in the United States?

Yes, a terrible mistake. In hindsight, everybody involved knows that, but now they are shy.

All right. This is very interesting.

Certain things are commonly known in England and other places, such as crop circles. One finds such imprints and markings in Brazil as well. Even when the channel and his wife, Nancy, were down there for a trip not long ago, they happened upon an imprint on somebody's property down there that was also made by a ship from Andromeda very recently—within twenty-four hours. The imprint was still radiating powerful benevolent magnetic energy, having the capacity not only to heal (which is its lesser capacity) but also to influence—in a dynamic way—spiritual progress.

You said the Andromedans made it, and yet I understood from an earlier channeling that all the crop circles were made by a five-hundred-years-in-the-future Academy of Man or something.

I'm not talking about all the crop circles. I'm talking about the ones in Brazil. I'm correlating this to the crop circles because the mark left on the ground in Brazil was not dissimilar to marks made on the ground in England, for example.

No, but this is important—are the crop circles made by other ET civilizations, as well as by these beings five hundred years in the future?

Certainly. Some of them are made from ships.

All right, I should have asked more specifically, then. This being we have in one of the books here who talked from five hundred years in the future—I took, from what he said, that they did all the crop circles.

It may have been that being's point of view, but it is not my own.

Language and Symbols

Very good. All right. Back to the languages. Can these languages be equated to planetary or galactic cultures or civilizations?

As I have pointed out, the top line is clearly reminiscent of modern Hebrew. And I think that your readers might easily be able to see other similarities. As I mentioned, the symbol on the bottom line, which has reminiscence to the Chinese symbol in fact, it is quite accurate in some ways. I think it would be interesting to have the readers write in and say what else they see that correlates to other languages. Greek, for example.

So that implies that this Andromedan . . .

It *implies* that the Andromedan had been here before and contacted these civilizations, but that is not true. In fact, the Andromedan had been to the root civilizations that came here and provided some of their language to the people who they fostered. So it's the other way around.

Can we look into that at some point?

Certainly.

All right. Can you decipher this? [See Figure 21.6.] This was on Rama's shirt. Can you decipher these symbols? What were they saying?

You have not seen these symbols before? You know, I'll tell you where you've seen them—and maybe you didn't know you were seeing them when you saw them.

They look like runes, almost.

Do you know where you've seen them? You've seen them on shirts, or on drapes or on fabric art. If you look at fabric art or modern art, you will see very similar shapes. Modern art really draws heavily from simple language roots, not only from your own planet, but from other planets. Those are all language roots. Remember, the people onboard were interested in languages, even if it wasn't their specialty (they weren't all linguists).

So these are roots from several languages.

Yes, roots of several languages. For instance, a root of your own language might be found in the Greek, for instance: *omega, alpha*. These are similar situations, roots of other languages. I said before that artists are relating these symbols to people. Very often on your planet (and on other planets, for that matter), if people are not moving fast enough in some direction, artists will become inspired—such as in the Modern Art move-ment—to reveal shapes and forms to those who would view their art, to stimulate those viewers in directions that they would not otherwise go. The artist does not create or invent; the artist always and only reveals.

The True Nature of Healing Crystals

Okay, there are still lots of interesting things here. They gave Joao a crystal, a stone. And there was a friend of his who was in the hospital with an aneurism of the brain which destroyed his nervous system. And yet, through this gift from the Andromedans, this fellow was able to be healed. So the fellow who got killed, who was the contact between Stevens and the contactee, also had a piece of stone and he said that it just vibrated—it was very powerful. So were these fifth-dimensional stones, then?

No, if they were fifth-dimensional stones, they could not have been uti-lized in the third dimension. But they were programmed very profoundly to connect with your Sun and their sun. Most stones—even healing crystals, as they're called on this planet—are healing in the long run, not in the short run. In the short run, they are healing because of where they grew and so on. But in the long run, they are healing because of their exposure to night and day—meaning night: moonlight, starlight, animals, feelings of the night; and daytime: sunlight, rain, rainbows. The natural elements are what tend to prompt a crystal to live up to its capacity.

You know, if crystals were not being mined on this planet, the planet would not only have lifted you to fourth dimension already but, instead of bringing the crystals to the people, it would have been very possible to bring the people to the crystals and heal the disease better. After all, if your doctor has healing hands, do you cut the doctor's hands off to take them to some other place? No, you go to the doctor and the doctor's hospital and get the treatment. It is no different; it is the same for everything.

I understand.

Of course.

. . . she said, having several hundred pounds of crystal in the room. . . .

It is—how can we say—a fad of your time. And because you live in a commercial society that tends to place value on things in terms of dol-lars, there is a tendency to overlook not only intrinsic value but heart value. When you pay attention to heart value, you can easily see that, for instance, a wild animal wants to be living in the wild and would die if it were imprisoned. It is not because the animal isn't fed right or isn't treated right or even that it isn't respected, but because it is not free to pursue its own life. That is why some people, when they are sent to prisons—even if they are treated well—do not survive. It will be a while before you let go of your attachment to moving things around, to say nothing of letting go of your attachments to dungeons. Prisons are, after all, the modern-day equivalent of dungeons.

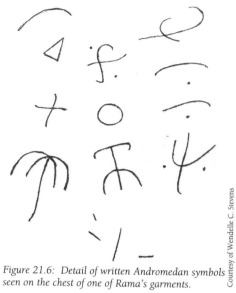

Figure 21.6: Detail of written Andromedan symbols seen on the chest of one of Rama's garments.

Courtesy of Wendelle C. Stevens

But in a sense, they're even worse, because we should know better.

There is no excuse, yes. You *could* know better, and many people do know better. It will take true insistence. People can do it, but you have to *want* it to change. You have to insist; you have to demand it. It will take time. In your system, that is how things are changed.

But it will happen.

It will happen. It must happen, or . . . what?

We won't get out of the . . .

You'll be stuck. Or let's put it in a way that people can hear more benevolently: Things will get worse. If any segment of the population, however "deserving," is segregated and forced to suffer against their will, all society suffers everywhere on the planet (and, to a lesser degree, on other planets).

So understand that as you continue to attack your own bodies by not allowing them to function in their natural, best way, and as you continue to attack the bodies of others, you will become stultified. You have no choice but to learn the natural way—how things are done from the heart. I know you will do it, not only because I have faith in you, but because you cannot stand screaming in front of the flood and expect the waters to recoil in horror.

Waxing eloquent. All right. Another interesting thing I didn't mention was that on this ship, Rama and his people walked right through the walls. So their fifth-dimensional nature was walking through what they had set up for the third-dimensional human, then?

Of course. That is often the case when one is not governed by the principles of a dimension, when it is a dimension in which you do not normally function. They would be more governed by their own dimension.

Joao's Son

Another thing—and here again we're talking about a living person—but Joao's son was also an Andromedan, and I'm sure in the years ahead he was probably taken, too—although, as I said, this report only goes for two years. What about the boy? Can you say something about him? His name was . . . . ?

I think we'll say nothing. Unless . . . are we talking about an Earth child, or are we talking about the offspring on another planet?

No, we're not talking about the offspring on another planet. We're talking about Joao's son here, the one who kept the diary. Rama told Joao that this son was also from Andromeda.

When they say "from," you understand that Joao and his son can prove that they were born on Earth?

Yes, but Rama and his people considered Joao and his son to be their own people; they had incarnated there. Was the son contacted later?

I will not speak of the son. One of the reasons why there are so many contacts is that the contactees have their spirituality magnified. Whether they are conscious of it or not, they tend to magnify the spirituality of other people they come into contact with, whether those people know it or not. This is one of the reasons why there have been so many contacts: to encourage—without interfering—the increased magnitude of spiritual growth on this planet.

Wonderful. All right. I'm sort of out of questions.

Tapped out, are we? All right, let's continue tomorrow night.

Thank you!

The Pascagoula Affair

Zoosh and Guardian Number Ten

January 26 and 27, 1999

Charles Hickson and Calvin Parker discuss their encounter in their book **UFO Contact at Pascagoula.**

These two men represent an unfortunate circumstance. The ship had come a long distance, and it was intended that the beings on the ship contact two other people. But due to unforeseen circumstances—at the last moment, the two other people were involved in an automobile breakdown in a crowded area—the ship could only stay a short time. We had a unique circumstance, and that is that we had two men contacted and taken aboard the ship *without their souls' permission.*

This is very unique and is not usually the case, and the beings on the ship, when they left Earth, were severely reprimanded for doing this. This is one of the reasons why these two men, Hickson and Parker, have gone through such trauma over this. For some people, there might have been some residual beneficial effect, but for both of these men, there has not been much of that—perhaps a little bit at times, but they were greatly

Figure 22.1: Charles Hickson and Calvin Parker, approximately two weeks after their encounter.

Courtesy of Wendelle C. Stevens

395

overwhelmed by the discomfort associated with the hubbub surrounding the event after the fact. Later in life, I think there was some acceptance of it as a real thing, but still, it was one of those rare circumstances when there was no permission on the soul level.

Inexperienced Beings on a Maiden Voyage

I would say this also: You might ask, "What sort of extraterrestrials would even consider picking up two Earth people without any permission from anyone?" You understand that the ship had already entered the Earth's atmosphere, and it was a last-minute thing, literally. Two minutes in either direction, and they would have picked up the people who were originally intended, but it was not possible. So you might ask then, what kind of people are we talking about? We are talking about extraterrestrials who were on their *maiden voyage*. So they were not all that advanced in terms of technology or even spirituality.

The beings who had the odd, spike-like arrangement coming out of them were not exactly robotic (although they gave that impression), but they were a hybrid of a biological form of life and a mechanistic form of life. They were along to protect the actual occupants of the ship and to function somewhat as a moderating force—not a police force exactly, but something like a peace-keeping force without guns. So because the people who were flying the ship knew they were doing something that wasn't right, they made every effort to minimize their personal contact with the Earth people, thinking that maybe it would be all right if they did that, and allowing, for the most part, only these hybrid beings to make the contact. But you can see how these men's lives were really ruined, and it was not all right. That's why I feel that this case deserves significant attention.

Now I have to be a little circumspect, and the reason I have to be a little circumspect is that one of the first—not the first, but one of the first—extraterrestrial races that your astronauts will meet and establish good relationships with will be these very people, and they will feel like they owe you. They will not differentiate between the fact that they might conceivably be considered to owe only these two men from the idea of owing everybody on Earth. That is their philosophy; they are good people. They made a mistake out of enthusiasm, something you on Earth can completely understand. There were the best of intentions, but even so, the best of intentions bear consequences, and not always benevolent ones. And while the extraterrestrials were not harmed, the Earth people were harmed, and that will be worked out. So I will not say where they were from, since you will find out before too long. You'll probably meet them in the next thirty years or so. I will say that they are not far away in terms of proximity, and they are remarkably similar to you in a lot of ways.

Now, the general appearance of these beings is sufficient on a casual inspection to pass for Earth people (and, for that matter, vice versa: you, on a casual inspection, might pass for them). So that tells you they have some similar situations across the board. They consume foods not unlike your own, although they do not eat refined foods. They consume food like you do and eliminate food in a similar manner. They sweat. They have very similar biological functions. They are quite similar. Now you can ask questions.

What dimension are they in?

They are in the same dimension, almost. They are in the fourth dimension, but they very easily assimilate into your dimension. They assimilate into dimension four and a half (though not as well), although the beings who were seen by the contactees with the odd spiked things can range from three to five dimensions.

Say a little bit about these beings. How do you create a hybrid biological and machine being?

For one thing, they did not create them. The hybrid beings were escorting the other beings because it was their maiden voyage—not the first voyage they had ever taken, but their maiden voyage to contact other races of people. So these beings were dispatched to go with them, to monitor them, to protect them, to keep them from making any catastrophic mistakes, and I think that if there had been even a five-minute warning instead of a two-minute warning, they would have prevented the contact. But they—these hybrid beings—are not good at instantaneous decisions.

It is not difficult to combine a mechanistic form of life with the human being.

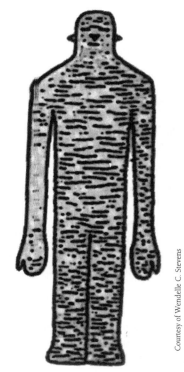

Courtesy of Wendelle C. Stevens

Figure 22.2: Drawing of the biological and mechanistic hybrid beings encountered by Parker and Hickson.

After all, you have the rudimentary aspects of that with advanced artificial limbs. So the biological aspect of their existence is from a very distant place. It is in this universe, but it has almost no resemblance in any way to Earth life. I would have to say that the closest biological connection to Earth life (and we're talking about distant cousins, here) would perhaps be the earthworm—which, by the way, is a very advanced being. So you can see that they have no similarity to the human being at all.

That helps to explain the shape of this drawing, though.

It does help perhaps a little, but their appearance, although it does have a cabled look, doesn't relate to the earthworm. Remember, they are very distant cousins. How distant? Like nine times removed.

Do they have two arms and two legs and a body and hair?

You can see that, yes.

So this is sort of how they looked, then?

This is exactly how they look. They are not wearing anything. Are we talking about the same thing? I'm talking about the beings with the odd spiked thing.

Yes, but do they look like the beings who created them—the earthworm-like distant cousins?

They are.

Oh, these are the beings themselves?

Yes.

Oh, I see. I'm sorry. You had mentioned a hybrid between these distant beings and mechanical beings, so I thought this was the hybrid.

They are a hybrid. You want to know who created them, but they basically created themselves. That's why I used the analogy of artificial limbs, because you could say, "Well, who created the artificial limb and who created the human?" You could do the same thing there, but you could say, "Well, the humans basically created themselves with the artificial limb."

Okay, they are sentient, but they are not really quick-witted—is that what you're saying?

They are very brilliant, but they are not quick to make decisions. Being quick-witted and being fast to make decisions are not necessarily connected. One can be very quick to make decisions that are not correct. [Chuckles.]

Are they ensouled?

Yes, of course. All beings are, without exception.

So you said these hybrid beings were assigned to guard the other beings, who are similar to humans, on their maiden voyage. Who assigned them?

They were assigned by those who generally look after this part of space and anyplace where experiments are taking place that are out of the norm. And the Explorer Race is out of the norm, meaning that if the Explorer Race hadn't come to this planet, the planet would be in its normal state of being—but it is not in its normal state of being, since you are here.

So does that group have a name? Is it something we've heard of before?

Let's try to stay a little bit on track. I'll tell you why. The contact is difficult tonight, and if we are jumping around, it breaks the contact a little bit. Normally, I'm able to compensate, but not tonight.

The Purpose of the Visit

So what was the mission, the purpose, that these humanoid beings (along with these hybrids) had in coming to meet the two humans who got sidetracked by the automobile? Why were they coming?

Two women, you mean. I'm not trying to nitpick, here. I'm just saying that it was a woman and her daughter.

Okay. What was the point of the contact that was supposed to be?

It was supposed to be basically diplomatic. No examinations or any of that other stuff. Strictly diplomatic. The people who were on board the ship were not scientists; they were more diplomats (one was an artist). But because of the aborting of that mission and this casual—and even, I will go so far as to say, capricious—taking onboard of these other two men, the mission became quite something else. I might add that these people, since they did this, were essentially grounded for quite a while. They were not allowed to go on such missions. They will eventually be allowed to do so, but they are no longer allowed to wander into space where things out of the norm are taking place.

Okay, but why would these beings from this other planet contact two women in Jackson, Mississippi, on a diplomatic mission? What was so special about the two women?

Their souls and the souls of the beings onboard the ship were from the same source.

All right, I can't ask what they did to Hickson and Parker, because I don't know at this moment.

All right. Well, we'll cover that tomorrow, but let's cover what we can.

Okay. There is a suspicion that one of them was contacted years later. Which one? Hickson?

The older man.

Did he have subsequent contacts?

The younger man was pretty close to being seriously psychically disrupted—not mentally, but on a spiritual level. Hickson was contacted later, but in a benevolent fashion.

Charles Hickson is the older man, and he was contacted later. Okay.

Yes. Gently.

By the same beings? To what effect?

No, those beings were not allowed to wander anymore. He was contacted by those who tried to explain what had happened, essentially to apologize (although the beings apologizing were not the ones who had caused it) and to offer whatever assistance that they could give. It wasn't much by Earth standards, but it would have amounted to prayers or gentle energy. It was an attempt to ease Mr. Hickson's life a bit. They knew better than to contact the young man, because he had been seriously injured in a certain manner by the contact.

Even now? Thirty years after the contact?

His life was disrupted on a permanent basis. Therefore, the punishment for these beings—the one I've mentioned, and other things that I have not and will not—was, I feel, appropriate.

Was Parker institutionalized, or did he just have a very difficult life?

I believe he was institutionalized for a time. He would have had a fine life and sons who would have accomplished many things. It was a serious breach of the usual agreements—how can we say?—a breach of *faith* to have contacted people without their permission; this is almost unknown in ET-human contact situations, that no permission was given. It was as close as you could get to a scandal in certain areas. There were several ET civilizations, even ones you would say are very benign and heart-centered, who wanted the beings who performed the contact to be uncreated.

How many beings were on the ship beside the guards?

Three to five, depending on how you count. That's all I can say at the moment. I will give cryptic answers like that sometimes, because sometimes you could say, "There is a woman standing here. She is one person." And yet she is pregnant. So we have one or two people, depending on how you count. Now I'm not saying that was the case there, but I am saying that it's a similar situation.

A Missed Connection

These two men were sitting on a fishing pier. Are you saying that these two ladies were going to be at that spot?

Near there. Not at that exact spot, no.

Because it is not a place you would expect to find two ladies.

Well, you might have, but no, it would not have normally been the situation. No, it was going to be somewhere near there.

So they came down into the atmosphere to this place that was sort of preprogrammed?

Yes, and they were within two minutes of their contact with the people.

. . . but they saw these guys first. Is that how it was?

No. They were close enough to the intended contacts to see their circumstances, and they saw that the women's car had broken down in an area where there were many people and that they would not be able to proceed. So they aborted the contact with the two women and were preparing to leave the planet when, using a long-distance viewer not unlike a telescope, they happened to see the two men. Cooler heads might have said, "Let's go." But hotter heads would say, "No, let's pick them up." There was about a minute of excited discussion and conflict until the older, wiser one relented.

Not realizing the significance.

Not fully grasping the dreadful impact this event would have on these two men's lives—and I'm using that word advisedly. When is the last time you ever heard me use that word, "dreadful"?

Right. You don't.

I've never used that word. That's how bad of an impact it was. That's how bad of a breach it was. I'll tell you something else: It was such a breach that aborting all human-ET contacts from that point forward for the next twenty to thirty years was seriously considered. It was seriously considered.

All right. Can we talk a little bit about the guards, the brilliant beings? Can you say something about their life? They seemed to have claws instead of hands.

That is a pretty good approximation. They have a grasping device—let's call it that—and it is adequate for their purposes. They do not need fingers. [Chuckles.] They have a society in which fingers are not necessary.

Tell me about their society.

They live in a world that has a singular objective, and that is to maintain peace while creating what amounts to a networking effect between beings. But the networking is not just electronic or like long-distance phone calls or anything like that. It is a contract. So their bias is toward expediting diplomatic relations and contacts while maintaining peace between different beings, even if those beings might otherwise have hostile reactions to each other. They are sort of a diplomatic peace-keeping force.

And part of what they do is to go out across the universe?

They go when requested. It is not often that they go anywhere of their own volition, but when requested (especially for a mission such as this, when we are dealing with people who are unsophisticated in this type of contact) they were asked to participate with given numbers. There were about seven to nine of them aboard—again, depending on how you count. So there were more of them on the ship than the people they were looking after. And that was perhaps good, because they were able to protect the Earth people a little bit.

Consequences of a Rash Decision

Once the Earth people came on board the ship, these beings realized (though it was already too late) that this was not right, and they made some effort to minimize the impact on the Earth people, because there were excited requests for everything up to and including an autopsy. This gives you some idea of how similar these extraterrestrials from your proximity are to human beings, who might equally say, "Oh boy, let's take one apart and see what makes it tick!" So you can see that their advancement beyond you is not very much. They have perhaps twenty-five to thirty years on you, technologically (the ship was not theirs, by the way), and not much philosophically.

They wouldn't have done that to the two women they were supposed to meet, would they?

No, they wouldn't have. But one of them had an attitude—I'm not making them the enemy, but it is important that this be revealed. It was as if to say, "Well, these weren't the people we were supposed to meet. They don't matter. They won't be missed." Essentially, that was the attitude. That's why the older man and the younger man both felt threatened and imperiled.

So the Earth men's lives were literally in danger!

Their lives were in terrible danger. The older one among them absolutely said no to the autopsy, but if he had not, the "guardians," let's call them, would have not only stopped the contact and put the Earth men back, but they would have immediately aborted the mission and essentially imprisoned the occupants. They had an absolute imperative to harm no one, not unlike the oath that physicians used to take, to "do no harm."

So how long were these men actually onboard, then? Were they lifted off the planet?

Yes, because it wasn't safe for the ship to just hang around. So yes, they were off the planet for several hours. There was raging controversy onboard, out of earshot of the guardians, about what to do with them. "Should we take them with us?" they asked. It was actually the kind of attitude one hears about taking place on the Earth—one group of human beings toward another—that when you hear about it, you feel ashamed for the human race. You know the feeling: "How could they have done this?" And yet that attitude was on that ship. That's why they've been . . . not quarantined, but they're not allowed out as much as they used to be. So these men's lives were in terrible danger.

And subconsciously they would know all this, which is where all the damage to the psyche came in.

Yes, they would feel very much the way a mouse would feel in a cage—a cage in a laboratory with men in white coats. It would feel as if its life meant nothing to the men in the laberatory, and that all manner of torture could be applied to it by beings who seemed to be of God but were purely heartless. That's how the mouse would feel, and that's how the men felt.

I'm glad you're talking about this. I didn't know that.

That's why the case is vital to be talked about, because it still stands: It is a case that is quoted over and over again, even today, in various areas of educational diplomacy all over the universe—and especially in this part of the universe—as "what not to do," as the worst-case scenario. And the people who were on the ship, including the wise one, are named and pictured.

As bad examples.

As bad examples, that's right. And while this does not reflect on their families, who were not there, or their descendants, who were not there, they were essentially branded for life.

Was it just this particular group of people? Are other beings on their planet . . . ?

They are not cold-hearted. They just had, at that time, a manner—and mores, even—not dissimilar to the human race. That's why it was originally considered acceptable for them to meet you: because the similarity is so striking.

Do they deal with negativity on their planet?

They have some exposure to it.

What percentage?

It isn't on their planet, but a place that some of them go.

Protected by the Mediators

Oh. Back to these hybrid beings again, the guardians. They are not technological, then. You need opposable thumbs, don't you? You said they were very brilliant. How did they express this? You said that they went out and kept peace, mostly by bringing beings together, like mediators or something.

"Mediators" is a fine word.

It just seemed that was part of what they brought to their mission: that they were brilliant and had bodies that were very strong—like they could step in between two people who were having an altercation or something.

Yes, they could prevent any aspect of conflict, even a great battle with heavy weapons. Not that they were invulnerable to heavy weapons, but they had the power to affect people's minds and hearts.

That's where their powers came from, then? It's not their bodies?

It's not the capacity of the body. It's the capacity of their psychic powers, their heart-centered, religious powers—you could call them that, if you like.

So in this case, then, there just wasn't time to bring this to bear? They just didn't expect it?

By the time they were able to make a decision (since they are slow to make decisions), the men were on board, and then they had to just deal with it as it was.

But they couldn't use this ability to change the minds of those who were about to harm the two humans?

The men were already on board the ship, and remember, these beings wouldn't change the minds of anyone unless the action were imminent. They would not interfere with what you think. You could think all the hostile things you wish to think, but if you were to take a hostile act—actually make the act—they would prevent the act. In this way, they do not interfere with thought processes but with actions in some cases.

But the thought processes were what was so powerful, because even though they couldn't see what was going on, on some level Parker and Hickson could feel everything that was going on.

Yes. These were, as you say, regular guys—just regular people, not scientists or anything. And when they saw the guardians, they were terrified.

They were not prepared for it—not that too many people would be on Earth. So they were already terrified even before they were on the ship, not realizing that the guardians were their only real protection. If the guardians had not been on board, well, Hickson and Parker would be on the missing-persons list and would be presumed by the police authorities to have been murdered, because they would have been disappeared and . . . gone.

If we publish this, is Hickson still alive to read this and gain some insight?

I believe so. I am not certain. It is important to remind people that these contacts are real and that just because contacts between Earth humans and extraterrestrials are often fantastic (meaning not wonderful, but strange and surreal) does not make them any less true. That compounds it, you see. After the men went through all these horrific experiences . . .

Then they had to deal with humans who said they were crazy.

Yes, which had a terrible impact on Parker and was very difficult for Hickson. But Hickson, being the older man, had greater life experience and was able to tolerate it better—not that it was the kind of experience that anyone would wish to have.

Well, this is interesting. This book is describing the guardians as "a little over five feet in height; a head with three pointed appendages" (Hickson and Mendez, UFO Contact at Pascagoula, 75). What was the purpose of those appendages?

Not unlike radar or sonar, they are a detecting system.

Okay. "Longish arms terminating in mitten-like 'pincers.'" They were just used to pick up things, right?

Yes. But you know, if you have the capacity to affect people's hearts and minds, you don't have to have an opposed thumb. I might add that that little anthropological assumption is well off. It applies in some cases, but it is well off. The idea of an opposed thumb relating to technology—that is definitely an egocentric and understandable statement, because the people who are saying it are coming from the system of believing in the hierarchy of the humans as the top rank on this planet (which of course you are not), but . . .

No, we've got cats. [Laughs.]

Yes. [Chuckles.] But you can always tell advanced beings by their total lack of interest in "prevailing." For example, cats are reasonably happy to be cats and not the least bit interested in controlling the world. I might add that the same thing is true about dogs and birds and so on. [Smiles.]

Right. So these beings seemed to Charlie to be automatons. They didn't have a lot of biological functions, then? They don't need . . . ?

They wouldn't look like human beings wearing a uniform—although that was considered after the fact by UFO researchers, thinking that perhaps these were beings inside suits, which was a reasonable thing to consider), but no, they just look like that. No, they do not need to eat or sleep or any of that.

Then is it possible that they can exist in any atmosphere? Didn't they come out of the ship and onto the surface of the planet to get the two men?

That's right. They can exist in almost any circumstance—although not in fire or anything like that.

So that would be a very handy bodysuit—to be able to go anywhere they wanted to go.

It's handy for who they are and what they are, but on the other hand, it wouldn't necessarily be appealing in the theater. It's not perfect for everything.

How did they come to choose that particular form?

I think that the form is pleasing to them, just as your own form is occasionally pleasing to you. [Chuckles.] I'm saying that as a blanket statement for all human beings everywhere on this planet.

The only thing I don't know are the details of what they experienced on the ship.

I'll let you read up on that a little bit so that you can proffer some interesting questions.

All right. Do you want to just sign off and start again tomorrow night?

Why don't we do that.

✳   ✳   ✳

Zoosh on the Guardians

Zoosh speaking. Good evening. Well, why don't we continue with Pascagoula.

The guardians—they don't walk, they just float. Do they have control of gravity?

It is not that they have control of it. This is something that is not uncommon with certain beings. It has been seen with the Zeta beings as well, among others. When you see a human being (or an animal, for that matter) and they are walking on the ground, you get the impression that this is the natural way to be. But when these beings are floating along like that, what you are actually seeing is someone or something not quite in your dimension. So it would actually require more output of energy for them to walk than to float. The floating is not something that is like a balloon floating; it is not a natural phenomenon. It is almost like seeing a portal moving. So to say that they are "floating" . . . it is a comparison. You could say that they *looked* like they were floating. But in fact, if you were able to examine the perimeters around their bodies, you would see a thin gray or silver line, which has to do with a different dimension. So as they were moving outside of the ship, you would see them in a dimension that was not the same as your own—as compared to being on the ship, where you would see them in their natural state of being, given the artificial state of the ship. But still, you would see them in more of a natural state, for lack of a better term.

Did they still float within the ship? Charlie never saw them. They were always hanging onto his arm.

They might do that in the ship, but it is less likely. The ship's environment can be entirely controlled, whereas when they are in the outer world on Earth, they need to create an envelope around themselves for protection. The ship creates that envelope.

Right. So it's like a little miniature spacesuit or something. So when they picked up Charlie, two of them grabbed each of his arms, he felt an incredible sting of pain in his arm and later it bled a lot. Did they tranquilize him with something?

No. This was an unfortunate circumstance, partly because of the energy and partly from their lack of knowledge as to how hard to grab. The appendages on their arms do not lend themselves to gentle contact.

It was like a pinching of the skin or an accidental break in the skin?

Yes.

Not an electrical shock.

Not an intentional one.

When they picked up Calvin and he passed out coming into the door of the ship, that was just from sheer terror, right?

Yes. It was a blessing, as one might faint because of the shock of an event.

Well, I've read a lot about Charlie. He's an incredible being. He was in the War. He's sincere, honest, fearless, capable—he's got a lot of qualities.

As they used to say (I don't know if they still do), a stand-up guy.

Yes. Even when he was under severe trauma, he was thinking of his wife, thinking of Calvin and asking the Lord for help—a marvelous human.

Yes, a hero in terms of—not one seeking fame, but the kind of person that everyone wants as a friend.

So Calvin was totally passed out and didn't know what was going on. The two things that most bothered Charlie on the ship were that these guys held onto him and that an eye came out of the wall and scanned him, a moving eye. What was it looking for?

A technological device purely—not dissimilar from the idea of a body scanner. It is not just looking at the surface; it is not unlike the experience of a CAT scan—although of course, under the circumstances, it is frightening—but it performs a similar function to a CAT scan.

That's the only thing he contacted. And then the terror—all the time that was going on, these two beings were holding both arms to hold him still. Then he must have passed out or something, because you said they were gone for hours. And the only other thing he knew was the light. The light was so bright it was excruciating.

Yes, this is typically the case. This is a form of condensed light, which is actually possible to produce on this planet now, and has been produced in some laboratories. But the purpose of it, ultimately—as it will be used here as elsewhere—is for controlling an environment, and it is a precursor to transferring an individual from one dimension to another, meaning that it is a precursor to time travel as well as space travel, since you are in the ship. It is not light as you know it. If the door opened on the ship and you looked inside, it would be incredibly bright, but the light on the inside would not illuminate the outside, as a spotlight would do here. So the light, instead of expanding (as illumination does here), contracts. And it is the contraction of the light—the light moving toward the center point of its existence—that creates a reversal of the natural flow of energy. Any physicist will understand how it is then possible to use this as a precursor for time travel and long-distance space travel. The natural flow of light normally prevents those forms of travel, but if you reverse the natural flow of light, it allows a great deal of latitude of motion.

So this bright light on the inside is not performing the function of illumination so much as it is simply a factor of motion. This tells you (because the light was so bright, and if you compare it to other ET contactees, they do not mention this) that the ship is in motion. It is actually traveling and covering huge distances. So part of the reason the older man does not recall too much of the adventure, if I can call it that, is that there was a point when he also lost consciousness. Now I will talk about what happened in that time.

Without Their Souls' Permission

Once the two men were carefully examined to the best of the knowledge of the beings on board and after the inspection was given by the eye in the wall to check and see if there was anything that ETs would consider volatile in their bodies (meaning something that might burst so they would not be safe or something that might contaminate the ship if there was a body problem), the men were taken to a place where they were interviewed. The interview was not a conscious mental process, but they were asked on the unconscious level—as one might connect an individual here to a brainwave machine or a brain scan—to reveal not only all of their life experiences, but also their innermost thoughts, desires and dreams. It was almost like an extreme case of debriefing. This was done—again, against the approval that is normally issued for such contacts—because it was believed at that time, because of the struggle on the ship (pro and con, what to do with them: "Let's take them. Let's not; bring them back," and so on), that the compromise was to get everything they could out of these beings without actually taking them.

Now here we also have an explanation of why the older man, Mr. Hickson, was able to do better. Hickson had been through combat in the war. In combat, one invariably has to face not only external fears but also inner fears. You cannot go through this circumstance without facing every last shred of your innermost fears. So Hickson had actually been through a variation of this process before, and as a result he was able to survive it. The younger man had not been through such an experience, and for him, it created almost a psychotic break—not the kind of thing that would condemn him to become a criminal, but something that would cause him to lose, at least for a time, his grasp on his own personality. Again, this is another terrible breach of ethics for such a contact. This took place between the flying time—if I can call it that—and the debriefing, and the return took about two hours.

Even under hypnosis, Charlie had no way of getting to that information.

No way to get to that information, because it is not something that would leave a memory. If you talked about something, you would most likely remember it. On the other hand, this would be very much like not remembering a blood transfusion in a surgery. You weren't consciously present in that sense. You don't remember the procedures that were done during the surgery because you were not conscious. So it would be more like that. That is why there is no conscious memory of it, and the memory may not be able to be accessed—and perhaps that is just as well.

So what levels were they able to get? Whatever was stored in the physical and emotional bodies, but not the spiritual?

You have to remember, the ship they were using was not their own. It was loaned to them for what was believed by those who loaned it to be a benign and benevolent mission. It was intended to be just that, and if all had gone well and the ladies hadn't had a flat tire, then it might have been just that. But, as it turned out, it was this catastrophic mistake.

The ship itself was profoundly advanced, but it was able to do these things only by going to this other place and getting far away from any physical planet. It had to go to what might be called deep space—meaning as great a distance as possible from any physically revolving planet or planetoid, or even a large chunk of one—where there would be as little contact as possible, because not only does a planet have a certain gravitational pull and physical impact, but each planet also has its own persona. It has a set of rules and ethics about what can and can't be done. But if you are in deep space, far away from anything like that, it is possible to conduct mischief.

It's almost like a mental and emotional rape. That's what it sounds like.

It was done without their permission and, I might add, without anybody's permission. Needless to say, those who loaned the ship foreswore ever loaning a vehicle to these people again. Forever is a long time.

Beings Not Dissimilar to Humans

Can you say whose ship it was?

The ship was loaned from the Andromeda system. As I said, it took every last scrap of argument to save the lives of the people aboard the ship—and I'm not talking about the Earth people. After the incident, there was such a hue and cry that the people who did this to the Earth people were almost executed. It was a very near thing, and it would have been the first time something like this would have taken place. I'm allowing the term "execution" to be used in place of "uncreated." Finally, cooler heads prevailed, and the Earth men were returned in their damaged condition.

If the equipment was onboard to do this, was it something that was done, but with permission and by skilled technicians? Did it have something to do with their not knowing how to use the equipment, too?

No, the equipment was entirely automatic. It wasn't something that required great skill.

But if the equipment was there, it was used on other people. Was it the fact of no permission and the lack of preparation . . . ?

The beings on the ship did not have permission to use the equipment, but they were able to access how to use it. And they were able to, if I may use the term, download these men onto something not dissimilar to a data storage device.

What were they going to do with this information: these feelings, thoughts and memories?

You have to remember, these people are not that different from you, and some of it had to do with simple concern about your capacities. You might ask, "Why did the guardians hold the men so securely?" This was because the guardians were concerned that if the men were able to get up and move on their own, the beings aboard the ship (not the guardians; the other ones) would react violently toward them. Because, remember, you and they are very similar. Put yourself—put Earth people—in their place. If I said that human Earth people on the ship could have become violent and attacked those people who were picked up, would you say, "How is that possible?" You have to understand that just because the ship and a lot of items on the ship looked very advanced, that doesn't mean that the beings on the ship were that advanced.

Now, who are these people, and why haven't I discussed them before? These people represent an alternative future. They are a bridge between the negative future and the benevolent future. In order for you to follow the path that leads you to the benevolent future, certain compromises have to be made. If a future that exists—that we're calling the negative future—is to be decreased in percentage of occurrence, there must be some sense of a reason for that. There must be some explanation. There must be—how can we say?—a different focus. And it can't just be done blindly; we can't just put blinders on and go forward.

The people of the ship were really part of that, but they had been kept from the negative place where they were born for a long time, and they had even been moved to another place far from their negative future. It was hoped by many that they had recovered from the terrible conditioning they had received, and they'd given every indication that they had. But this circumstance in which the men who were picked up were filled with fear and anxiety (which the two women wouldn't have been, because they knew what was going to happen) set off the old programming of action and reaction. As a result, it created a circumstance that brought back, for some of the individuals (not all of them), some of that old negative programming. And it was that circumstance exactly—the circumstance of these beings being born into that conditioning and being rescued from it, if we might say—the circumstance of their unfortunate existence, that allowed others to have compassion and relent in their demands that these beings be uncreated.

You'd rather not pursue this. You'll just say this and let it stand?

Exactly. I'd rather not pursue it, because the more we talk about it, the more likely people will get too interested in it and we'll have to—how can we say—build a firmer bridge to that negative future than I'd care to.

Later Contacts with Charles Hickson

All right. Well, thank you for sharing that. Then they came back later, according to this book. Charlie had three telepathic messages from the guardians, so that means that the guardians came back to Earth. What kind of ship were they on? Were they with someone else? Because Charlie saw a ship in the sky and he heard words, so . . . Let me read you the words. He's out in the tree farm in a very private and beautiful place. It was January 1974, and he thinks of it like a radio that came on in his mind. It said, "We mean you no harm. We mean no one any harm. You may communicate with us later. You have endured. You have been chosen. There is no need for fear; we will communicate again" (Pascagoula, 173).

Yes.

And then the radio was off. Then in February, he was in bed and he went walking out behind the apartment and he heard, "You must tell the world we mean no harm. Your world needs help. We will help in the future before it is too late. You are not prepared to understand yet. We will return again soon" (Pascagoula, 182). Oh, well, I don't know if those are the guardians. Somebody is sending him messages. Who?

The first message was from the guardians. The second message was from the guardians' allies. The guardians—it was an unusual situation for them to travel with these others, but they often travel with other beings. It is, however, perhaps more useful to hear from one of the guardians themselves.

Oh, wonderful. The third one was on Mother's Day. They all saw the ship; the whole family saw it. And then there is no more data in the book, so I don't know what happened after that.

Well, it was important for the family to see it so that everyone could finally say, "This is real," and people could relax with each other and be comfortable with the idea that it was real.

That's important. When he heard the first message, it was like everything in him just relaxed; he was comfortable, the fear was gone and he knew he had to go out and tell people these beings were real. There was a whole, total change in his energy.

Yes, and it was also an apology—you can see that it was. Let's hear from a guardian. They may or may not be able to talk very long through Robert, but let's try.

Excellent.

Guardian Number Ten Speaks

I am Number Ten.

Welcome. Thank you for coming.

I would say first: Again, our deepest apologies for the wrongs of this rough contact. It was so very much the opposite of what was intended. However, we would salute the survivors, and we very much appreciate the courage that it has taken to make the matter public.

It is all right that it was stated about the rough part. Most of the contacts with extraterrestrials that will occur on your planet in the future will be gentle and benevolent, but there will be times when one side or the other will become frightened. There will be the usual reactions, but cooler heads will always prevail and things will be settled benevolently.

There has been some considerable effort by different communities (ETs, you say) to contact the Earth and its citizens in this way already, but the level of rebuffing by certain countries has been difficult. There has been, I understand, a long-term connection with the Pleiadeans in various places in South America and also other isolated places on the continent. This has prepared extraterrestrials for the unexpected and spontaneous that they are likely to encounter while meeting Earth humans, and this has been invaluable. But in your now time, the level of resistance is great because of the level of suspicion of one government versus another.

Nevertheless, I call upon the average citizen not involved in government to embrace and welcome not only extraterrestrials but, more importantly, your fellow Earth citizens. Replace suspicion with curiosity. Learn what you have in common and continue to communicate internationally, as you are doing now through this "computer" thing—a most vital way of opening up to each other.

You're familiar with the concept of the Explorer Race?

Yes.

What was your first contact with humans? Have you been coming here a long time?

Our first contact as a species was about 3,500 years ago. Then we had meetings for a time with a group of individuals living in areas around the globe who might be considered nomadic peoples, in ice colonies and desert colonies. The ice colonies were in the northernmost regions. The desert colonies were the "cliff dwellers," I think they are called. And yet, all these people had one thing in common: They recognized that all life around them—the animals, the elements of Earth—were intended to show them how to be, not the other way around. They were not only natural people but people who followed the demonstration of the sacred and heart center.

That's how you chose them? You chose them for that purpose?

Yes, we chose them for that reason. We were welcomed. No one was the least bit alarmed to see us, not even the children. They were curious, and they asked questions in their language, but we responded in song. Song is almost universally accepted as a means of benevolent introduction.

I didn't know you could do that! There was some question as to whether you had a mouth and eyes and things.

We can make sounds. We do not require a permanent aperture to make sounds, but we have one available when we need it. But generally, we would speak from our minds to their minds, which made communication gentle.

You came in your own ship, then, not with other beings?

In our own vehicle, yes. We would have the vehicle appear in ways that would be acceptable to the people we would meet. It might have certain heart-centered and gentle aspects to it. The energy radiated would be benevolent and warm, meaning loving, and the images that many people would see would remind them either of their own dances or of our origins in dance. We could not dance on your planet, but we could put pictures in the minds of others of how we would dance if we could. In this way, seeing our demonstration of ourselves—in dance, in story and in form as well as in song and feeling—allowed people to accept us openly.

Do they tell stories about you today? Do these groups, did their lineage survive until today?

At least one of them has, but I do not know if they still tell that story.

I was thinking that you might look like one of the Kachinas. Is that possible? [Pause.] You don't know what that is. Never mind; it doesn't matter. All right, tell me about yourself. How long do you live in your bodies? How long have you been alive?

In terms of years?

Something I could understand, yes.

About a quarter of a million years.

So is that a lifetime, or would you say you are immortal?

I am in my youth. I am not prepared to say we are immortal. I am aware of beings in my civilization who have come to the end of their lifetimes.

Do you have knowledge before this life of your identity, your personality, your stories?

No.

Are there many of you?
Thousands. No more.

Do you travel most of the time or just part of the time?
We travel occasionally. Occasionally, for us, would not bring us to Earth often. I think our people have only come to Earth no more than ten or twelve times since Earth was in this position.

A Culture Bringing Peace and Harmony

Do you spend a lot of time going around the universe in the attempt to bring peace and harmony to people?
Yes. Sometimes, when meetings occur between races that are so different there is no common ground between them whatsoever, we will attempt to make connections between the peoples on the heart level first (so that they can feel some common ground), and then on the mind level, (so that they can see, and the people can understand that there is some correlation from one culture to the other, though it might not be readily apparent). So we will help them to see how they are alike. In this way, they are able to proceed with communication and not feel there is no point to it.

I don't mean to be flippant, but we could use you right now between the Democrats and the Republicans. [Chuckles.]
A minor moment in your political history, perhaps.

Yes. But how did your people start this? This is a fascinating way that you help others so much. Have your people always done this, did someone sort of discover you could do it or were you created to do it?
As far as I know, we have always done this.

You've seen much of the universe, then? You get to see many, many varied civilizations and peoples.
We have seen some unusual places. We have not been everywhere and seen everything, but we have been to a lot of places. Sometimes, we'll go to gatherings where we will not have to go to the home planets. These gatherings might be something not unlike your United Nations, where other people come from all over, and we help to make connections there. In this way, we have seen many different types of peoples, but not always the people in their homes.

What is your life like at home? What sort of culture do you have, what type of living arrangement?
You cannot possibly relate to it or understand it. I would simply say (and if I say this, you will understand) that because we are able to help you

with hearts and minds, that is what we do. Our culture lives for the heart and the mind. Anything beyond that would make no sense to you, and I don't think I can even find words in any Earth language to explain it.

Zoosh says you are absolutely brilliant. Can you help me understand? He said you were biological and mechanical. Can you talk about how that works?

I'd say this: To the extent we're called partially mechanical—and I understand the description—this comes from our utilization of the substances of minerals that provide a greater or lesser physical attraction, magnetically or electrically, according to which planetary body we are visiting. So it is not so much a machine factor.

It's like you can tune your body to the environment. Is that what you're saying?

Yes. In this way, the planet does not treat us as it might a hostile organism.

It accepts you. Oh, that's exciting! And you need that because you have to go so many different places. You need a body that doesn't have to breathe the atmosphere or be subject to the billions of different kinds of atmospheres or gravities.

Yes, and we need to be honoring the planets we are on as well. We try to do this with this adaptation, mineralogically.

That makes sense. That's wonderful. So is there anything you look forward to?

[Chuckles.] That's interesting. We are present-oriented, and we enjoy serving as we do—I suppose that would be my answer.

Right, what you do brings joy to you. You don't have to do something for work and then go find joy; what you do is joyous. I can see that.

Telepathic Communications with Charles Hickson

That's wonderful. Back to the encounter, to Mr. Hickson. The first time you sent him a telepathic message, you were on the ship?

Yes.

Zoosh said you were with your allies. Can you say something about them, or are they also beyond our understanding?

No, the allies would be people who care about you and feel that you are kindred spirits—perhaps they don't look exactly like you, but they have a great degree of heart for you.

So it might not be a race from a particular star-system, a particular group of people. It might be many different people, representatives, you're saying?

Yes, individuals.

Who communicated telepathically with Mr. Hickson the second time? Do you know that?

I do not.

But that's the last time you had any communication with him.

The first communication, you mean? I don't understand.

Well, the first time was when you were on the ship and he was picked up, and then the second time was when you were with the allies. That's the last time you talked to him?

Yes.

Where are you now? Where are you speaking from now?

My home planet.

Oh my goodness; that's all the way across the universe?

Yes.

A Message for Earth: Remain Focused in Your Heart

Well, you know the Explorer Race. What would you like to say to the humans who read this book?

Remain focused in your heart. Let your heart guide you. Look at how the animals live in harmony. Study nature, not as a scientist, but as a shaman or a mystical man or woman might. See the heart in all beings first; then look for the differences that compliment.

You know, what we're learning is that what was considered shamanic on this planet, practiced by only a small group of people . . . all the rest of the benign civilizations live like that, don't they?

As far as I know, with very few exceptions (although I have not contacted them), what is considered the natural path in my thought would be very often considered shamanic on Earth. The type of shamanism I refer to is the connection between all beings: the respect, mutual caring and acknowledgement that everyone and everything is alive—every grain of sand, every molecule, anything you come into contact with. Everything is a form of life, and it is all equal. Just because you're not aware of it does not mean that it isn't equal.

Well, hopefully the whole planet of humans will become aware of that soon.

It will happen in time. I would prefer to remain close to the subject, because I cannot speak through this channel much longer. So if there is anything about this subject that you have not asked . . .

Is there anything we can do? Knowing now what happened, is there anything you could advise someone to tell Mr. Parker, the younger man? Is there any type of medical or psychological help that he could get?

The best thing is to let him lead a gentle life. Let him be out in nature when he wishes, to be around animals and the natural elements of life. And others should expect nothing from him, though he might offer things from time to time. Let him be and treat him gently, not unlike men who have been in combat and are forever altered. Some men go through combat and can go on. Others don't quite get over it. It was like that for him. He didn't quite get over it. And that's understandable, since at that time of his life, he was a young man being guided by the older man and was in a vulnerable position. So be kind to him and let him lead a life that requires very little for him to do, one that allows him to do what he chooses in a gentle way.

The Original Plan for Contact

The original purpose of your being on the ship was to contact these two women. What was the plan for them? What was planned in relation to the two women?

They would have gone with the beings on board the ship on what amounted to a diplomatic mission—no examination or anything of that sort—to help the beings on the ship to feel the value of the Explorer Race. So it would have been very simple, a typical diplomatic mission.

They sent you along just because of their background—their birth situation, their inexperience with technology and other humans . . .

As you say, "just in case." And a good thing, too.

So how does it work, then? Are you on a ship and you get called by various councils of beings, or are you at home and then you're called out?

We are home and are contacted from there. Then, if we have the people to spare, we ask them to come and pick us up. We do not have too many vehicles. We don't need them, because we don't need to travel anywhere on our own.

You can just see and connect everywhere.

We serve. We don't need to be overseers of people. We don't have a personal need to do this.

No, but I mean you have the ability, if you choose. You're saying you don't have any vehicles, but if you chose to, you could interact with anybody, anywhere?

I wouldn't go so far as to make us that godly. I would just simply say that people contact us and ask us to attend them, and then they come and pick us up.

And bring you back.

Well, yes. We're going to have to stop very soon.

Okay, I'm ready to stop.

Good night.

Thank you very much for coming.

Zoosh on the Guardian

All right. I return.

Oh, welcome back. What an unusual being.

Very unusual. They are all similar: You could talk to others among these people, and they would demonstrate a similar personality.

Were they created for this type of mission? He didn't know. He said that he had lived a quarter of a million years, and that he was young.

They seem to be in existence for this work. I think that if they were not performing this work, they would probably be somewhere else, doing something else.

Were they created by our Creator? Or did they come here?

I think they were created by Creator.

All right. Can you kind of finish up the story here? Hickson and Parker met the guardians on the ship, and then the guardians talked to Hickson one more time when he felt relaxed, and then he heard another voice after that. Can you say who that was?

What did that voice say again?

I have it right here. "You must tell the world we mean no harm. Your world needs help. We will help in the future before it is too late. You are not prepared to understand yet. We will return again soon" (Pascagoula, 182).

I think this was from one of the people who were on the ship that the guardian referred to as "allies," one of the many who care about the human race.

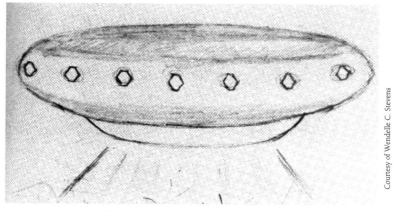

Figure 22.3: Drawing of the ship Charlie Hickson and his family sighted on Mother's Day.

Courtesy of Wendelle C. Stevens

And then what ship did they see on Mother's Day, when the whole family saw it?

This was a slightly larger version of the vehicle that the two men were taken onboard of, but not the exact same ship.

No, there's a picture of it: it's completely different from the other one. This is the drawing of it. [Shows drawing.]

That is not so different. It is just larger, I think.

Oh, well, it looks completely different, but maybe the other one is from a different viewpoint or something. The other one was kind of like a crooked football. [Chuckles.]

This is more of a ship used strictly for diplomatic missions.

All right. Well, we don't know anything after 1974, I guess. So did Charlie go on and have other contacts?

I think we won't talk about that. The book doesn't, and I think we will not say any more on that.

All right. That's fine.

The Minister

Zoosh
January 28, 1999

I thought I might speak of one that has not been written up. This is a case in which a religious person was contacted by an Andromedan woman. This is a man who was in the church—the faith sometimes called the Church of England—for many years and had come to the point where he was in semi-retirement and had actually lost his faith somewhat because of his having been a chaplain in more than one war. The depravity of war had impacted on him sorely. So while he had done a great deal of good, the most that he could possibly do, he was depressed about the human condition and questioned his faith in a creator who, according to his beliefs then, would allow such things. Granted, this happens sometimes even with the people of the greatest faith.

So one day he was out in his garden and a woman approached him. He did not pay too much attention to her at first, but she came over and inquired if he was having some difficulty raising the rutabagas. He said that the soil wasn't right for them, and he was having some trouble. She reached down and gently moved her hand under the soil, and suddenly the plants just leaped up—the leaves and everything moved up and became very vital. He watched this with surprise and said, "What did you do? How did you do that?" And she said, "I transferred some love and generosity into the soil so the plants could feel welcome and happy to be alive. When the soil feels that and transfers it to the plants, then even weak soil can support plants."

So of course, being a man of deep thought, he asked her if she could say that in some other way that he could understand. She then said that she was from a place where such farming techniques were part of daily life, that people would sing to the plants and the plants could be felt on a level of physical feelings in your body. She said that she always felt that the plants were singing back. So he wanted to know where this place was, and she said that it was on another planet. He was quiet for a time, thinking perhaps that she was not being truthful, but being so impressed with her clarity and her general presence that he was uncomfortable doubting her.

A Visit to the Andromeda Galaxy

She said, "Would you like to see where I am from?"

And he said, "Is it possible?"

And she said, "Come with me." Well, he lived alone in an isolated area. She reached out her hand and he tentatively reached back, and she walked forward with him about half a step behind, since he was a little shy. He had not walked hand in hand with a woman for some time and was shy about that, too. They walked down a lane and cut across a field into a small area sometimes called, I believe, a copse. I don't know if they still use that word, but it is a sheltered area. He saw something glowing in there, and he stopped and became nervous, but she said, "Don't worry. It is perfectly safe. I wouldn't take you anywhere that wasn't safe." While she was saying that, he felt himself calming, and she walked him over. He could then see that the small, glowing thing was part of something larger that had been hidden by the bushes and trees and that it was clearly what would have been thought of as a flying saucer.

Speaking forthrightly and innocently, a feeling that he hadn't had in a long time, he said, "I'm afraid."

She said, "I'll be with you every step of the way, and you can come back here any time that you want. I promise."

He believed her and went aboard the ship, and it was very pleasant inside. There were two other women there and one young man. The young man was like a doctor, and he sat the minister down in a seat that tilted back, a seat not unlike what you might see in your modern ships, the rockets you use to go up. The other people did not sit in such seats, but he was in a seat that was somewhat protective. This was because their bodies were used to rapid acceleration, and his was not, so the seat was designed to protect him from sudden motions. The vehicle took off and, traveling at a high rate of speed through time and space, arrived shortly in the Andromeda galaxy. Very shortly after that, they came to her planet. She said, "You can stay as long as you like, and because our ship can travel in time, we can bring you back so that you won't have lost any Earth time." He was a reasonably well-educated man, and he could grasp the principle of that without understanding all the details.

So he stayed for thirty-five years of experiential time. By that time, if he had been on Earth, he would have been a very old man, but during his thirty-five-year experience there, he received the best medical care they could offer him, and even though their medical care is geared to their own bodies and not exactly to his, they were able to extend his lifetime by about eighty years, so that after the thirty-five years had gone by, he was actually younger in body, health and constitution than when he had left. He was more vigorous.

A Student of Spirituality

He spent the first couple of years being shown around the planet, and then his friend said, "What would you like to do?" And he said, "I'd like to study your religion, your form of spirituality." Of course, he asked if she believed in Christ (being a Christian minister) and she said that they had a different version of Christ they believed in, but that it was the same loving being. She then exposed him to the type of Christianity that is the nucleus of what you have on Earth, but completely devoid of anything unpleasant or stressful associated with the religious principles or practices. Because he could identify with that loving nucleus, he felt at peace with it. He asked if he could be trained to become an advocate—which was their term for minister—and they said that it would take about twenty-five years to receive all the training. Did he wish to invest that much time? And he said that he did.

So he studied their religion, which had to do with not only phenomena and ceremony and spirituality but also understanding the hearts of all beings in order to appreciate the value—and this is the only word that fits here—and the symmetry of the connection with the hearts of all beings. He studied the hearts of all beings of the planet that he was on and, because he was from Earth, he studied the hearts of all types of beings on Earth, from the tiniest mosquito or gnat to the elephant and the human being. So you might say that what he studied is heart-Christianity. He was, at the end of that time, fully qualified as an advocate, and for a time, he practiced that form of religion on Andromeda.

The Return to Earth with Wisdom to Share

When he had been there for thirty-five years, the friend who had originally contacted him said, "Now it is for me to ask if you want to stay here—and you are welcome to do so—or if you would like to return to Earth now and speak of these things on Earth?" And he said, "As much as I love this place and you and all of your friends, I feel that I owe it to the people of Earth to return and speak of heart-Christianity to the people there." And she said, "You will be welcome to return here, should you like to."

So they made arrangements that he would return to Earth for five years and travel far and wide, speaking of heart-Christianity. After five years, they would make contact and he could choose to return to Andromeda (which he did). They brought him back to the time when he had left, or rather a few hours later. He was, as I said, younger and more vigorous in his physical body, although his appearance was very much the same. The one change that had occurred was that his hair had gone dark again. So as not to startle people, he dyed his hair gray for the five years that he was on Earth [chuckles] so that people would not notice that he had changed very much. So that was the adventure.

He traveled about on the surface of Earth. He went to South America and visited every country there. Being a minister, albeit retired, he was able to travel inexpensively and he was given the wherewithal from various individuals to speak of these things, usually to small groups of people—sometimes to educators, other times to religious people, other times to everyday people. To some he would speak and give them the prayers he had learned on Andromeda, and to others he would sing with a beautiful voice that was so inspiring that others would have to sing along, even though they wouldn't know the words right away. He would pass out the words to the song, and for a time (for the final two and a half years), it was kind of a traveling ministry, not unlike what you see in your time, with tents and so on. It was a good thing. He apprenticed two young men during those five years and taught them all he could about heart-Christianity—everything he felt would fit and work on Earth.

A Final Home in Andromeda

Then one day he decided that it was time for him to go. He said, "You must carry on, on your own." They hugged him, and he did not tell them where he was going. He felt that it was better for them to not know at that time. He returned to the place where his garden had once existed and walked down the lane, cut across the field, went down to the little copse and waited. He brought a tent with him and some food. He waited about two and a half days before the ship returned and he returned to Andromeda, where he lives today.

What year was that? In the 1950s?

Yes. It was in the mid-1950s.

He was able to breathe the oxygen? What dimension was it?

He was able to exist there. The dimension was different, but he was given a device that was planted subcutaneously, not unlike a pacemaker that is put in for regulating the heartbeat of individuals. This device allowed him to access dimension five. It was much smaller than a pacemaker, useful and thin—about as thin as a small wafer or, to be specific, about the size and thickness of a half-dollar.

What was the connection? They just saw him and saw that he was a good man? Had he lived on Andromeda before and knew these people? What was the connection?

The advocates who lived on the planet in Andromeda were, at that time, attempting to reach out to people of religion on other planets, and he was chosen. He did not have a reincarnated life there. There was no prior connection at all, so he went there entirely openly, without any prior sense of knowledge about it.

And the life span there is, in our terms . . . ?

Oh, perhaps 2,800 years. So even given the fact that he was not born there and does not have one of their bodies, he will be alive there in his current body until around the early 2400s or so.

Did they contact several beings, or just him?

Just this person.

And he didn't have any children or anyone to miss him or anything?

No. Of course his former parishioners wondered where he went, but he told everyone he was going to retire and travel. It was a pretty good cover. [Chuckles.] He certainly did travel.

Learning of Heart Connections

How could he study the hearts of every being on Earth from Andromeda?

Not every single one, but a representative heart. The advocates on this planet are of heart-centered Christianity. It is sufficiently similar to Christianity to be called that, although they do not call it that themselves. They feel themselves as being not unlike the hub of a wheel, with spokes going out in many directions all over the many galaxies in this part of the universe, always connecting to the hearts of other beings. And because this was a long-term experience for them and those before them, they had connected with the hearts of all types of beings on Earth before. They did not, however, teach him how to connect to the hearts of creatures that no longer existed on Earth. He did not connect to the dinosaurs or saber-toothed tigers, but only animals and people—representative individuals, you understand, not every person's heart or every animal's heart—so that he would know how to communicate on a heart-to-heart basis with every type of being. It is this type of heart communication that is truly at the core of heart-Christianity, so that the person communicating about this religion—which is truly a philosophy more than a religion—would actually be able to communicate in such a way with an individual from heart to heart, therefore having no misunderstanding whatsoever. When heart-to-heart communication takes place, misunderstanding is not a factor.

Say more about the word "Christianity." I didn't realize they used it on other planets.

They don't. As I said, they don't call it that there, but they were comfortable in referring to it that way for his sake because he was a minister in the Church of England (sometimes called Episcopalian). They were perfectly comfortable comparing their religion to Christianity, and I am calling it heart-Christianity because it is a religion here on Earth.

I see. So basically their religion is focused on heart connections.

It is focused on heart connection: the way to be from person to person; the way to relate to Creator; the way the Creator relates to you and all of your hearts; in short, the way to *be*, according to their beliefs—which is, of course, the nucleus of all religions (pardon my judgment) that have merit.

Do many people go to other planets, or was this a very rare case?

It is very uncommon, in terms of emigrating. Visiting other planets happens sometimes and is noted in the UFO-contactee literature, but to actually emigrate is very rare. I must say that most people who disappear (and many do every year) have usually gone elsewhere on Earth and do not wish to be found or occasionally have come to the end of their life unexpectedly.
So it is that rare?

Yes.

How about the two boys the minister trained? Are they still active? Have they trained others?

They have trained others, and they are both still active. They are not boys anymore, but they are still active. [Chuckles.]

Forty-five years later. Right.

They are still speaking of these things, and they have . . . because of the pureness of their hearts, they can speak to anyone and are not misunderstood. When you speak from your heart with that warmth and speak out of that part of your body, centering into it, the chances of your being misunderstood are greatly reduced—in most cases to zero.

Even if you're talking to someone of another language?

No. You can talk to someone who does not speak your language and they will feel good about what you are saying, but of course they will not understand.

And he realized what an incredible opportunity it was and how rare it was. Did he know that?

Yes, but he didn't dwell upon that. He felt that, because of the terrible horrors he had seen . . .

That would have been the Second World War and Korea, then?

The Second World War and some other action. Because of that, he had been so crushed and defeated by life that he was just happy to be there—happy to be, as he would see it, recovered.

So they gave him the device when he was there the thirty-five years, and then it was removed for the five years he was on Earth again, and then he put it back on when he returned to Andromeda?

Yes. It's not the sort of device that would help you on Earth, so it was easily removed. The surgical methods they have are pain-free. I might add that, once medicine in this country and in other places begins focusing on freeing people of their physical pain as compared to simply extending their lives, the true purpose of surgical medicine will be well within focus and that it will be able to find its way much better and be less involved in controversy. So they have this method that does not require cutting. It is not dissimilar (though not exactly the same) to what is sometimes called psychic surgery, where the person puts his or her hands inside your body: There is no pain, but you can definitely feel something inside you.

Conversely, when the Andromedan woman met the minister, did she need something to adjust to Earth?

Yes, but it wasn't planted in her body. It was a device she wore.

So there is a particular place where this woman came from where they look exactly like humans?

Exactly.

Since we are the combination of so many different kinds of DNA, and since we are such an experiment, how did it come about that we look exactly alike?

That's not so unusual. You can have human beings . . . Now I'm not saying that you are identical twins—what I'm saying is that you can have beings that look generally the same, but that their biology or their DNA might be quite different.

As they are in this case.

Yes. So that is not so unusual.

How popular is the human form? Of all the sentient beings in this creation, what percentage look and sound like and would be mistaken for humans?

About a half of one percent. Perhaps not quite that many, a little less than that.

Why such a small percentage?

Well, you understand, I'm considering that all beings are equals. If you count all life forms on Earth, you might say that less than one half of one percent of all life forms on Earth—perhaps considerably less than one half of one percent—are humans.

Where are you starting? Insects? Microbes?

Let's say that we're starting from cells out. But let's even say that we're starting from what you could identify as creatures—gnats, flies, up to cats, dogs, elephants, crocodiles—still, human beings are not such a great percentage in comparison.

And that percentage holds true across creation?

Well, just because cats are not considered first-class citizens on this planet does not mean that they are not first-class citizens elsewhere. [Chuckles.]

I have wondered about this for months: What form did the first two creations that were going to be the Explorer Race take?

I suppose if you had to put an identification on them, they would look similar to amoebas. Why not? Such a creation is a simple, relatively uncomplicated being with a personality—each one has one—and its own portion of a soul. It has a relatively simple lifestyle and yet a heart energy that is uniquely its own. Occasionally today, people dream about such shapes of beings. I believe there has even been, on occasion, more than one book that made some effort to identify these beings as still being in existence, but in larger forms. Such life forms that are simple in comparison to the complexity of the human being are still profound spiritual manifestations.

You understand, if you're going to become various forms of physicality, one of the best ways to get used to the idea of physicality is to be something simple and then build on that. If you had started out as complex as you are now, as the Explorer Race, you would have no sense of familiarity or being at home in your body whatsoever. But having started out as the Explorer Race as single-celled beings, as simple, uncomplicated biological entities, you could gradually get used to the idea of the intrinsic beauty of physicality, so that as you became more complex in different forms of physicality and in different dimensions, you remained with that sense of home in the physical self. Without that sense of being at home, you could not maintain your personality or your soul residence in a physical body such as you have today and be comfortable. You would feel like you were in a foreign thing, you would get out as quickly as you could and you'd stay out. No, you have to feel at home.

So we, as personalities, have experienced physicality beginning at that level?

If you have never been physical, it is essential to start your physicality in some simple fashion, or at least, I would say, if not essential, highly recommended. [Chuckles.]

And the memory of that is available at some deep level of the personality, then?

Readily available. You could do a meditation on being an amoeba, and you would feel very light and cheerful, as most of them do. You would be able to celebrate life much more than you celebrate it on a day-to-day basis now, as one often celebrates the initial stages of any form of being. After your life here, you often celebrate the high points of your lives here. It is a similar situation.

Thank you. I had been very curious about that. All right.

Then I'll say good night.

All right, then. Thank you.

Good night.

Afterword

Zoosh
April 8, 1999

You have had the opportunity to read between the lines and to hear some of the broader explanations of some of these most strange and wondrous cases of human contact with extraterrestrials. This book is not intended to be the total answer. It is not intended to give you all the details, nor is it intended to interfere with the privacy of these contactees who have served in such a vital way to create and remind the people of Earth of life in other forms on other planets. Instead, this book is intended to give you an opportunity to understand the larger picture of life. Even as you might judge yourselves and your civilization, this might show you that you in your civilization are fairly advanced and fairly sophisticated compared to some civilizations, regardless of their technology. Additionally, in showing you other civilizations, perhaps these stories will give you goals and suggest what avenue you might pursue, should you care to include some of these elements of extraterrestrial culture in your own.

Earth people and ETs ultimately stem from the same benevolent creators, all of whom want you all to get along well. You all now are in a "waking up" time of your lives. This wake-up time is happening in different stages for different individuals, and yet the thing you share in common is a desire to be appreciated for exactly who you are, without having to change at all. Understand that even in the complete confusion that often occurs between extraterrestrials and human beings in these contacts, the one thing that is very often the case with extraterrestrials is that they will accept you for who you are. They may not fully appreciate everything you are, but they will not question your value. If you can learn nothing else than that from them, learn to appreciate your own value as a human being. In doing this, you will find it much easier to appreciate your neighbors and other human beings for who they are, without needing them to change one bit.

REFERENCE LIST

Brookesmith, Peter. *UFO: The Complete Sightings.* New York: Barnes & Noble Books, 1995.

Bryan, C.D.B. *Close Encounters of the Fourth Kind: A Reporter's Notebook on Alien Abduction, UFOs, and the Conference at M.I.T.* New York: Penguin, 1996.

Casellato, Rodolfo, Joao Valerio da Silva and Wendelle C. Stevens. *UFO Abduction at Botucatu.* Tucson: Wendelle C. Stevens, 1985.

Clark, Jerome. *The UFO Files.* Lincolnwood: Publications International, Ltd., 1996.

Dongo, Tom and Linda Bradshaw. *Merging Dimensions: The Opening Portals of Sedona.* Sedona: Hummingbird Publishing, 1995.

Elders, Lee J., Brit Nilsson-Elders and Thomas K. Welch. *UFO...Contact from the Pleiades, Volume I.* Phoenix: Genesis III Productions, Ltd., 1979.

Elders, Lee J. and Brit Nilsson-Elders. *UFO...Contact from the Pleiades, Volume II.* Phoenix: Genesis III Productions, Ltd., 1983.

Fowler, Raymond. *The Andreasson Affair.* Newberg: Wild Flower Press, 1979.

—. *The Andreasson Affair, Phase Two: The Continuing Investigation of a Woman's Abduction by Extraterrestrials.* Newberg: Wild Flower Press, 1982.

Fuller, John. *Incident at Exeter: The Interrupted Journey.* New York: MJF Books, 1966.

Herrmann, William and Wendelle C. Stevens. *UFO...Contact from the Reticulum.* Tucson: Wendelle C. Stevens, 1981.

Hickson, Charles and William Mendez. *UFO Contact at Pascagoula.* Tucson: Wendelle C. Stevens, 1983.

Randle, Kevin and Russ Estes. *Faces of the Visitors: an illustrated reference to alien contact.* New York: Simon & Schuster, 1997.

Shapiro, Robert. *The Explorer Race.* Series in 16 Volumes. Flagstaff: Light Technology Publishing, 1996-2009.

Stevens, Wendelle C. *UFO...Contact from Reticulum Update.* Tuscon: Wendelle C. Stevens, 1989.

Walton, Travis. *Fire in the Sky: The Walton Experience.* New York: Marlowe & Company, 1979.

IMAGE SOURCES

Figure 1.1: Swett, Ben. Betty and Barney Hill, circa 1966. Photograph courtesy of Ben H. Swett. http://www.bswett.com/BettyBarneyHill.jpg (accessed January 14, 2010).

Figure 1.2: Swanson, O'Ryin, 1998. Demonstration of how to hold the book of light. Photograph. (Flagstaff: Light Technology Publishing, 2010).

Figure 2.1: Betty Andreasson, unknown date. Photograph courtesy of UFO Casebook. http://www.ufocasebook.com/AndreassonBetty.jpg (accessed January 14, 2010).

Figure 2.2: Andreasson, Betty. *Through the Great Door*, 1977. Drawing courtesy of Near-Death Experiences and the Afterlife. http://www.near-death.com/images/graphics/new_age/aliens/betty_andreason_drawing03.jpg (accessed January 14, 2010).

Figure 2.3: Joopah through Robert Shapiro. Letters from the book of light, 1998. Pencil on paper. (Flagstaff: Light Technology Publishing, 2010).

Figure 3.1: Wendelle Stevens, unknown date. Photograph courtesy of UFO Evidence. http://www.ufoevidence.org/researchers/detail41.htm (accessed January 14, 2010).

Figure 3.2: UFO photographed over forest, unknown date. Photograph courtesy of Wendelle C. Stevens. *UFO...Contact from the Reticulum*. (Tuscon: Wendelle C. Stevens, 1981), Plate 1.

Figures 6.1: Woodrow Wilson, unknown date. Photograph courtesy of Canady Library, suffrage exhibit, Bryn Mawr. http://www.brynmawr.edu/library/exibits/suffrage/WWilson.jpg (accessed January 14, 2010).

Figure 6.2: Harris and Ewing. *Woodrow Wilson, President of the United States of America*, 1919. Photograph. Library of Congress, Washington, DC.

Figure 6.3: Hall, H. B. *Portrait of Benjamin Franklin*, 1868. Engraving. Library of Congress, Washington, DC.

Figure 6.4: Haussmann, Elias Gottlob. *Johann Sebastian Bach, Portrait*, 1748. Painting. Courtesy of William H. Scheide, Princeton, New Jersey.

Figure 7.1: Rogers, Michael H. Travis Walton, circa 1975. Photograph courtesy of Michael H. Rogers. *Fire in the Sky: The Walton Experience*. (New York: Marlowe & Company, 1996), Plate 22.

Figure 7.2: Illustration courtesy of Kevin Randle and Russ Estes. *Faces of the Visitors: an illustrated reference to alien contact*. (New York: Simon & Schuster, 1997), 176.

Figure 7.3: Rogers, *Fire in the Sky*, Plate 3.

Figure 7.4: Rogers, *Fire in the Sky*, Plate 1.

Figure 8.1: Rancher Bill "Mac" Brazel, 1947. Photograph courtesy of Blue Alien Network. http://www.bluealien.net/aliens-and-ufos/roswell-interview-with-mac-brazel (accessed January 14, 2010).

Figure 10.1: "Billy" Eduard Albert Meier, unknown date. Photograph courtesy of UFO Digest. http://www.ufodigest.com/news/0209/volcanos.php (accessed January 14, 2010).

Figure 11.1: Zoosh through Robert Shapiro. Soul-line contacts, 1998. Pencil on paper. (Flagstaff: Light Technology Publishing, 2010).

Figure 11.2: Zoosh through Robert Shapiro. Transit through timelines, 1998. Pencil on paper. (Flagstaff: Light Technology Publishing, 2010).

Figure 13.1: Guillaume Blanchard. *Antiquité égyptienne du musée du Louvre,* July 2004. Photograph, Fujifilm S6900. Photograph courtesy of Guillaume Blanchard.

Figure 15.1: Zoosh through Robert Shapiro. Drawing of reflection, 1998. Pencil on paper. (Flagstaff: Light Technology Publishing, 2010).

Figure 15.2: Zoosh through Robert Shapiro. Pathways, 1998. Pencil on paper. (Flagstaff: Light Technology Publishing, 2010).

Figure 15.3: Randle and Estes, *Faces of the Visitors,* 21.

Figure 15.4: Randle and Estes, *Faces of the Visitors,* 31.

Figure 15.5: Randle and Estes, *Faces of the Visitors,* 43.

Figure 15.6: Randle and Estes, *Faces of the Visitors,* 55.

Figure 15.7: Randle and Estes, *Faces of the Visitors,* 72.

Figure 16.1: Randle and Estes, *Faces of the Visitors,* 160.

Figure 16.2: Zoosh through Robert Shapiro, 1998. Graph of cell memory. (Flagstaff: Light Technology Publishing, 2010).

Figure 16.3: Linda Bradshaw. Photograph of mysterious blue man. Photograph courtesy of Tom Dongo. *Mysterious Sedona.* Tom Dongo, ed. (Flagstaff: Light Technology Publishing), Plate 11.

Figure 16.4: Linda Bradshaw. Photograph of portal, date unknown. Photograph courtesy of Tom Dongo and Linda Bradshaw. *Merging Dimensions.* (Sedona: Hummingbird Publishing, 1995), 68.

Figure 16.5: Linda Bradshaw. Photograph of red-eyed being. Photograph courtesy of Tom Dongo and Linda Bradshaw. *Merging Dimensions.* (Sedona: Hummingbird Publishing, 1995), 141.

Figure 16.6: Randle and Estes, *Faces of the Visitors,* 172.

Figure 17.1: Randle and Estes, *Faces of the Visitors,* 164.

Figure 19.1: Randle and Estes, *Faces of the Visitors,* 164.

Figure 21.1: Joae Valerio da Silva and family, unknown date. Photograph courtesy of Wendelle C. Stevens. Casellato, Rodolfo, Joao Valerio da Silva and Wendelle C. Stevens. *UFO Abduction at Botucatu.* (Tuscon: Wendelle C. Stevens, 1985),18.

Figure 21.2: Stevens, *Botucatu,* 55.

Figure 21.3: Stevens, *Botucatu*, 85.

Figure 21.4: Stevens, *Botucatu*, 32.

Figure 21.5: Stevens, *Botucatu*, 44.

Figure 21.6: Stevens, *Botucatu*, 65.

Figure 22.1: Charles Hickson and Calvin Parker, circa 1973. Photograph courtesy of Wendelle C. Stevens. Hickson, Charles and William Mendez. *UFO Contact at Pascagoula*. (Tuscon: Wendelle C. Stevens, 1983), 5.

Figure 22.2: Stevens, *Pascagoula*, 64.

Figure 22.3: Stevens, *Pascagoula*, 207.

Many thanks go out to those generous people who have allowed us to reference their images in order to clarify some of the more visually based discussions in this text. For those images and photographs listed here that were accessed from books or Internet sites, we made a reasonable effort to determine the holders of the copyrights for those images, listed here. Should there be images used from sources, particularly those taken from the Internet, for which copyright claims exist that are not referenced, we ask the holders of said copyrights to please contact the publisher, and we will correct the matter for future editions.

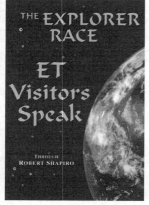

LIFE WITH A COSMOS CLEARANCE

Dan Salter as told to Nancy Red Star

On May 9, 2001, the Disclosure Project hosted a major event at the National Press Club in Washington, D.C. This historic event had witness testimony from twenty to twenty-five military, intelligence, government, and corporate individuals who were involved with UFO projects over the last fifty years. Selected witnesses had previously met in closed meetings with members of Congress and staff on Capitol Hill as well as administration leaders and White House and Pentagon staff and officials. Then on May 9 the larger group of witnesses presented their information before a worldwide group of media correspondents.

Those of us who were military witnesses of UFO history showed OFFICIAL GOVERNMENT DOCUMENTATION with our detailed testimonies. Our focus was and is on the facts and documents. Our purpose was and is to get the mainstream media and government officials to hear those facts and move us toward an honest congressional inquiry. It is of the utmost importance, we believe, that each citizen not only of this country but of the world, participate in this project of disclosure. We who came forward want to BAN WEAPONS FROM SPACE and stop aggressively shooting down these space vehicles and their extraterrestrial occupants. We need to declassify the advanced electromagnetic propulsion systems in use by the secret government and start producing them for the world to use and thereby help save this planet.

The people who had been employed in agencies within the military and knew THE TRUTH ABOUT UFOS had been sworn to secrecy. Now I am finally relieved to speak the truth. We military men who hold on to this knowledge are getting old and dying, and we want the truth to come out. We will either do it ourselves or leave it for our children and wives to do.

Personally, I have told those on Capitol Hill that I am being led to do it by the aliens themselves. They have convinced me that it is time. They have been waiting on the government, and if the government does not come forward with the truth, then the aliens will take a more public role in disclosure.

—Daniel M. Salter

Softcover 198 pp. ISBN 978-1-891824-37-1 **$19.95**

"... If the government does not come forward with the truth, then the aliens will take a more public role in disclosure."

Highlights Include

- The Kalahari Retrievals
- Weaponizing Space
- From Void to Mass: Wave Particalization
- Vienna and the Black Sun
- Germany's Advanced Technologies Prior to WWII
- The Brotherhood Lodges
- Secret, Deep-Underground Military
- Bases and Advanced Earth Craft
- Star Wars
- Russian UFO Files for Sale
- Approaching the Millennium Shift
- The Wingmakers and the Ancient Arrow Site

Agent Daniel M. Salter is a retired former counterintelligence agent for the Scientific and Technical Unit of Interplanetary Phenomena in Washington D.C. He was a member of the Pilot Air Force, NRO (National Reconnaissance Office) and DCCCD (Development of Conscious Contact Citizenry Department) with the United States military. He was a CON-RAD courier for President Eisenhower with a clearance far above Top Secret (Cosmos) and a member of the original Project Blue Book. His expertise was in radar and electronics, his field of investigation UFOs, Aliens and Particalization. Now seventy-five, Salter has both Comanche and French ancestry.

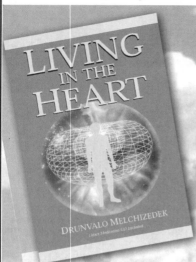

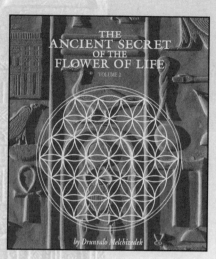

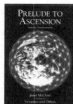

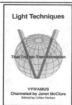

BRIAN GRATTAN

MAHATMA I & II
The I AM Presence

Awaken and realize that all of humankind will create their "body for ascension," whether they accomplish this now or later, and that this is not the exclusive domain of Christ or Buddha or the many others who have ascended—*this is your birthright*. When humans lift the veils of their unworthiness and recognize that they are the sons of God, that there is divine equality and that no one is greater than another, then you will have begun your journey in the way that it was intended. The *Mahatma* is for those who are motivated to search for the answers that can respond to their mental and spiritual bodies. No matter how contrary your current beliefs, this book contains methods for creating your spiritual lightbody for ascension and also explains your eternal journey in a way never before available to humankind.

19^{95} SOFTCOVER 480 P.
ISBN 0-929385-77-2

- Introduction by Vywamus
- The Journey of the Mahatma from Source to Earth
- The Spiritual Initiation through the Mahatma
- What Is Channeling?
- Evolution of a Third-Dimensional Planet
- Transformation through Evolution
- Patterns
- Time and Patience

- Mahatma on Channeling
- Conversation Between the Personality (Brian) and Mahatma (the I AM Presence)
- Mastery
- The Etheric and Spiritual Ascensions
- The Cosmic Heart
- Mahatma as the I AM Presence
- So What Does the Personality Think of All of This?

TITLES ON TAPE
by Brian Grattan

BASEL SEMINAR
10 TAPE SET (AUDIO CASSETTE), English with German translation $35.00
EASTER SEMINAR
7 TAPE SET (AUDIO CASSETTE), English with German translation $59.95
SEATTLE SEMINAR
12 TAPE SET (AUDIO CASSETTE) $79.95
Twelve one-hour audio tapes from the Seattle Seminar, October 27–30, 1994. These twelve powerful hours of meditations lead to total spiritual transformation by recoding your two-strand DNA to function in positive mutation.

☿ *Light Technology* PUBLISHING

DAVID K. MILLER

NEW SPIRITUAL TECHNOLOGIES
FOR THE
FIFTH-DIMENSIONAL EARTH

242 P. SOFTCOVER
978-1891824791

$19⁹⁵

Earth is moving closer to the fifth dimension and new spiritual ideas and technologies are becoming available for rebalancing our world:

✳ Native ceremonies to connect to Earth healing energies.

✳ Thought projections and thought communication to communicate with Earth.

✳ Connections with our galactic starseed heritage so that we can relate to our role in the galaxy.

CONNECTING WITH
THE ARCTURIANS

295 P. SOFTCOVER
978-1891417085

$17⁰⁰

Who is really out there? Where are we going? What are our choices? What has to be done to prepare for this event?

This book explains all of these questions in a way that we can easily understand. It explains what our relationships are to known extraterrestrial groups, and what they are doing to help the Earth and her people in this crucial galactic moment in time. It explains how we can raise our vibration now and begin the process of integrating higher dimensional energies into our third-dimensional world.

TEACHINGS FROM
THE SACRED TRIANGLE

291 P. SOFTCOVER
978-0971589438

$22⁰⁰

David's second book explains how the Arcturian energy melds with that of the White Brother/Sisterhood and the Ascended Native American Masters to bring about planetary healing.

Topics include:

✳ The Sacred Triangle energy and the Sacred Codes of Ascension
✳ How to create a bridge to the fifth dimension
✳ What role you can play in the Sacred Triangle
✳ How sacred words from the Kabbalah can assist you in your ascension work

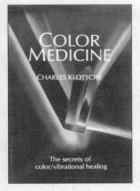

COLOR MEDICINE
The Secrets of Color Vibrational Healing
Charles Klotsche

A new dimension in holistic healing, *Color Medicine* provides a powerful technique for treating specific imbalances and strengthening the immune system. By combining aura-attuned chromatherapy with harmonious sounds, tissue salts and hydrochromatherapy, the forty-ninth vibrational technique was developed. A breakthrough, yet as old as recorded medicine, it utilizes subtle energy vibrations similar to those found in the visible spectrum. A textbook and how-to handbook, this book encompasses an encyclopedia of fascinating information, charts, diagrams and tables as well as methods of treatment and technical advice. Whether you are a holistic practitioner or merely curious, this book marks a new frontier in the world of alternative healing.

$11⁹⁵ SOFTCOVER 124 PP. ISBN 978-0-929385-27-3

- Does Color Medicine Really Heal?
- Color Physics: The Scientific Explanation of Color Medicine, or Vibrational Therapy
- Color Energetics: How Color Medicine Works with the Subtle Energy Fields of the Body
- Color Harmonics: The Twelve Healing Colors and Their Use

- Color Practice: Materials and Practical Techniques for Applying Color Medicine
- Color Schedule Application: Determining the Appropriate Color(s) for Relieving/Healing the 123 Major Illnesses
- Color Medicine Schedules for 123 Specific Human Disorders

JONATHAN GOLDMAN AND SHAMAEL, ANGEL OF SOUND

SHIFTING FREQUENCIES
Sounds for Vibtratory Activation

Now, for the first time, Healing Sounds pioneer Jonathan Goldman tells us about shifting frequencies—how to use sound and other modalities to change vibrational patterns for both personal and planetary healing and transformation. Through his consciousness connection to Shamael, Angel of Sound, Jonathan shares his extraordinary scientific and spiritual knowledge and insights, providing information, instructions and techniques on using sound, light, color, visualization and sacred geometry to experience shifting frequencies. The material in this book is both timely and vital for health and spiritual evolution.

$17⁹⁵

SOFTCOVER 189 PP.
ISBN 978-1-8918247-0-8

In this book, you will:
- Explore the use of sound in ways you never imagined for healing and transformation.
- Discover harmonics as a key to opening to higher levels of consciousness.
- Learn about the angel chakra and what sounds may be used to activate this new energy center.
- Find out how to transmute imbalanced vibrations using your own sounds.
- Experience the secrets of crystal singing.
- Understand the importance of compassion in achieving ascension.

MAURICE CHATELAIN

Author Maurice Chatelain, former NASA space expert, has compiled compelling evidence to show that a highly advanced civilization existed on the Earth approximately 65,000 years ago. Further, his work indicates that the knowledge of the advanced civilization had been "seeded" by extraterrestrial visitors who have aided mankind with advanced information in mathematics, electricity and astronomy.

OUR COSMIC ANCESTORS

Our Cosmic Ancestors is a dynamic work, unraveling the messages of these "universal astronauts" and decoding the symbols and visual mathematics they have left for us in the Egyptian Pyramids, Stonehenge, the Mayan calender, the Maltese Cross and the Sumerian zodiac.

SOFTCOVER 213P.

$14⁹⁵ ISBN 0-929686-00-4

Chapter Titles:

- The Apollo Spacecraft
- The Constant of Nineveh
- The Mayan Calendar
- The Secret of the Pyramid
- The Maltese Cross
- The Rhodes Calculator
- The Kings of the Sea
- The Signs of the Zodiac
- The Polar Mysteries

- The Universal Calendar
- The Four Moons
- The Mystery of Atlantis
- Extraterrestrial Civilizations
- Mysterious Visitors
- Conclusion

WES BATEMAN, FEDERATION TELEPATH

Wes Bateman is a telepath with direct, open contact to ETs from the open state, who are not subject to Earth mankind's Frequency Barrier-caused closed brain and limited consciousness. Bateman has 30 years of ongoing information on the open state; the Federation; the Frequency Barrier and how it affects humanity; ETs and evolution; a wide spectrum of technical and scientific information, including mathematics and the universal symbolic language; and the three trading houses of this system—all part of the Federation's history of this part of the galaxy and beyond.

THROUGH ALIEN EYES

The accounts given by extraterrestrials in this volume are about events that occurred in our solar system many millions of years ago. In that ancient time the solar system consisted of four planets and four "radiar systems" that orbited the central sun. The four planets of the solar system are known today as Venus, Earth, Mars and a now-totally shattered world that was called Maldec.

The term "radiar" applies to the astronomical bodies we presently call Jupiter, Saturn, Uranus and Neptune. The original satellites of these radiars are generally called moons by Earth astronomers, but the extraterrestrials prefer to call them planetoids.

This book reflects the personal views of a number of different types of extraterrestrials regarding the state of the local solar system and the state of the Earth.

SOFTCOVER 507P.
$1995 ISBN 1-891824-27-9
978-1-891824-27-2

Chapter Titles:

- Sharmarie, a Martian
- Trome, a Saturnian
- Churmay, a Venusian
- Thaler, a Neptunian
- Ruke, a Jupiterian
- Jaffer Ben-Rob of Earth (Sarus)
- Nisor of Moor   • Tixer-Chock of Gracyea
- Doy, a Woman of Maldec

- The Great SETI Con Game

PART II
- It Has Begun
- Serbatin of Gee
- Tillabret of Emarin
- Rendowlan of Nodia
- Petrimmor of Cartress
- Ombota of Mars

Plus:
- The SETI Messages

Phone: 928-526-1345 or 1-800-450-0985 • Fax: 923-714-1132

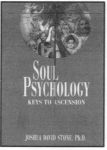

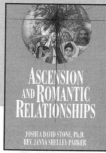

BEYOND THE LIGHT BARRIER
by Elizabeth Klarer

This autobiography of a South African woman is the story of the interstellar love affair between the author and Akon, an astrophysicist from the planet Meton in Alpha Centauri. Elizabeth Klarer travelled to Meton with Akon, lived there for four months with his family, and gave birth to his son. Featuring fascinating descriptions of the flora, fauna, and advanced technology of Akon's people, this classic is being reissued in a long-overdue new edition.

$15.⁹⁵

244 P. SOFTCOVER
ISBN 978-1-891824-77-7

GIZA LEGACY I
by Rico Paganini

In this groundbreaking book, Rico Paganini provides a fascinating overview of developments and discoveries involving the pyramids and the Sphinx. Using modern technology combined with spiritual sensing abilities, he has discovered that the real secret of the pyramids was yet to be recognized. Both in and below the pyrmids lies the key to a liberating truth for all those who seek it.

$40.⁰⁰

250 P. HARDCOVER
60 MAPS; 250 COLOR PHOTOS
ISBN 978-3-9522849-0-2